D1329387

TRACE EVIDENCE

OTHER BOOKS BY BRUCE HENDERSON

And the Sea Will Tell
Fatal North: Murder and Survival on the First North Pole Expedition
Hero Found: The Greatest POW Escape of the Vietnam War
True North: Peary, Cook and the Race to the Pole

TRACE EVIDENCE

THE HUNT FOR THE I-5 SERIAL KILLER

BRUCE HENDERSON

Trace Evidence: The Hunt for the I-5 Serial Killer
Copyright © 1998, 2013 by Bruce Henderson
ISBN-13: 978-0989467513
Published by: BruceHendersonBooks, Menlo Park, CA

www.BruceHendersonBooks.com

To those highly trained men and women of law enforcement
who are entrusted with the profound responsibility of
investigating violent death.

And to the loved ones of murder victims everywhere—
they who, without ever forgetting, somehow find
the strength and courage to go on.

MAY JUSTICE BE SERVED.

CONTENTS

PROLOGUE

It was summertime at the beach.

Palm trees swayed lazily in a steady sea breeze that kept the days balmy and the evenings cool in this San Diego suburb six miles north of the U.S.–Mexico border at Tijuana.

After hanging some clothes out to dry, Esther Underwood, thirty-six, of 447 Casselman Street went in the house to iron. Around 4:30 P.M., she looked out the window and saw that some clothes had apparently blown off the line.

She went outside. Reaching the clothesline, she stood dumbfounded—there were no clothes on the ground, yet garments were definitely missing. The clothespins that had held them in place were still properly spaced on the line.

She looked around the yard but found nothing. Mentally inventorying the clothes still on the line, she realized that her orchid dress was gone, along with two bathing suits. Also, four pairs of nylon stockings.

She hurried into the house and called the police.

AFTER TAKING A report from the lady at 447 Casselman, patrolmen Don Morrison and Doug Gardner were driving past a nearby park on C Street when they were flagged down by a young girl.

Judy Faureck, age nine, reported that while playing in the park about an hour earlier she had noticed a teenage boy on a green bike enter the park. He had caught her attention because he was riding with a cardboard box on his handlebars and a shovel under one arm. The boy had ridden to a gully next to the public rest rooms, where he parked his bike. Carrying the box and shovel, he crossed to the opposite bank and walked a short distance along the fence line. He then dug a hole adjacent to the fence, put the box inside, and covered it with dirt and leaves. The boy, whom the young witness described as being around fourteen or fifteen years old, about 5-foot-4, with short brown hair and wearing a white T-shirt and Levi's, then rode off on his bike.

The officers uncovered the box. Inside, they found the orchid dress and two bathing suits.

The patrolmen contacted a workman they saw cleaning up around the American Legion Hall next to the park. Given the suspect's description, custodian Jack Kearns remembered seeing him that day. Kearns didn't know the boy's name, but he had previously seen the kid in the park with a boy whose family he did know.

The officers went to the address provided by the custodian. They described the suspect and his bike to the man who answered the door. The man said it sounded like his son's friend who lived on Casselman.

AT THE CHULA VISTA Police Department the next day, juvenile officer Leo J. Kelly read the report filed by the two patrolmen.

The boy who lived on Casselman had admitted to burying the box in the park. While the fifteen year old denied to the patrol officers that he had stolen the clothes, the officers arrested him for petty theft and prowling. They transported him to the station house, where they made out a contact report. As was customary with juvenile cases, the boy was returned home and turned over to his parents, who were informed that the case would be referred to the department's Juvenile Office for further investigation. The officers had then returned the items of clothing to their owner.

The incident had been the latest in a series of thefts of women's apparel from clotheslines in the same neighborhood. Any type of crime was such an unusual occurrence in this law-abiding town of seventy thousand residents with a police force that numbered only twenty-three officers that the series of clothesline capers had made the news columns of the ChulaVista *Star*.

Kelly, a U.S. Navy Seabee during the war, was an imposing 6-foot-3 Irishman and father of six children—five of them boys. In his five years on the force there had been just one narcotics bust in town. Homicides and armed robberies were virtually unheard of. As far as juveniles went, it was usually pretty minor stuff. Truancy, some runaways, a few burglaries. One sixteen-year-old boy had been caught stealing pocket change from the school office and was sent to Juvenile Hall. When the boy got out, Kelly tried to get him into the Big Brother program but it didn't happen. When the boy went to see if he still had his drugstore job, he found another kid working in his place. Three days later, the boy hanged himself. Kelly hadn't been able to shake the tragedy. The juvenile officer with five sons of his own would never forget the boy who had needed help and understanding but found few adults with the time or inclination to give it to him.

From his four years' experience working Juvenile, he knew it would be advisable to confront the errant youngster about the stolen clothes as soon as possible.

When Kelly pulled up in front of the residence at 545 Casselman Street, he saw it was one of those small, cookie-cutter stucco houses with slab floors built after the war that sold mostly to returning GIs for something under $10,000 with nothing down. They all had postage-stamp-size lawns, front and back. More than not, each block had at least one flagpole flying Old Glory.

Kelly knocked on the door, and met the father, a recently retired Navy chief working for the post office. He was told the boy's mother was at work. He asked to speak to the fifteen year old—the oldest of three brothers—alone in his bedroom.

The boy sat at the foot of his bed, head hung low. He was a good-looking all-American type, with a thin face and skin freckled from a summer under the sun.

Kelly pulled up the only chair in the room. The juvenile officer had a deep, bass voice that filled a room, even when he spoke softly, as he did now.

"I need to know what's been going on, son."

When no answer was forthcoming, Kelly spoke some more in his fatherly yet firm manner, hoping to draw out this sullen boy who shyly made eye contact but remained mute.

When the boy finally did start to talk, Kelly was not surprised that he stuttered. It fit.

The boy confessed to stealing the clothes.

In fact, he admitted much more. He had been taking women's clothes off clotheslines in his neighborhood for the past year. He couldn't say how many times in all but he estimated he had done it about once or twice a week. He usually ended up burying the clothes in the park or throwing them in trash cans.

"Did you take only women's clothes?" Kelly asked.

"Yes."

"Did you steal anything else?"

"No."

"Did you break into anyone's house?"

"No."

Not only was the boy monotone, but he was so emotionless that he seemed unmoved by his own confession, or even by the fact that a cop was questioning him in the sanctity of his room. That was strange, Kelly thought. Most kids cornered like this would be sweating bullets.

When Kelly stood to go downstairs and talk to the father, the boy went to his closet. He removed a box from the overhead shelf.

In an apparent act of contrition, he solemnly handed it over to the juvenile officer.

LEO KELLY HAD recently received a framed "Good Neighbor Award" from the local Soroptimist Club for his work with juveniles. When he was so honored, Kelly had given a short talk, mentioning that he wanted to get counseling for disturbed kids instead of just shipping them off to Juvenile Hall, but that many families couldn't afford professional services. Afterward, a woman whose husband was a local car dealer came forward.

"Next time you come across a family that doesn't have the money to send their child for counseling," said the well-groomed woman, "I'll pay for the first three visits."

In the boy who lived on Casselman, Kelly had an obvious candidate for help. All the warning signals were there, flashing brightly. By any measure, the boy's family, headed by concerned, hardworking parents, seemed normal. Yet, one of their children obviously had severe problems. When Kelly had suggested counseling for their oldest boy, the parents had voiced concern over the cost.

Kelly contacted the Good Samaritan. She asked him to find out how much it would cost. When Kelly called her back and told her three sessions with a highly recommended San Diego psychiatrist would be $270, the woman came right over to the station house and delivered it in cash.

The boy's parents took him to see the psychiatrist for the three sessions. When Kelly called the doctor to check on the boy's progress, he was coolly informed that such information was confidential. Kelly hoped that the parents would see the value in the treatment and find a way to pick up the ball themselves. He later found out, however, that they didn't.

Kelly remained concerned that something more serious could develop in the future from the type of behavior exhibited by this somber fifteen-year-old boy. Left unchecked, Kelly knew, these disturbing tendencies could escalate. A youthful fantasy that hadn't yet harmed anyone might one day become a frightful reality.

The juvenile officer was haunted, and would be for years to come, by the contents of the box from the boy's closet. On top he had found a pair of scissors, the long-handled kind with an angled cutting edge favored by medical personnel to cut bandages and adhesive tape. The boy's mother, Kelly had learned, was an emergency room nurse at Chula Vista Hospital.

Also inside were the most intimate articles of women's apparel—panties, bras, garter belts, nylons.

They had all been cut up.

CHAPTER ONE

Stephanie Marcia Brown woke with a start before midnight. Something had scared her, but as she lay motionless in the dark, she had no idea what.

A loud, jarring knock on the front door was followed in quick succession by another.

Stephanie was a vivacious soon-to-be twenty year old with many friends, some of whom occasionally kept late hours. She and a roommate her own age shared a two-bedroom duplex, and though the young women often went their separate ways, they understood. That was one benefit of not living at home.

Tonight, however, Stephanie was alone. Her roommate, Patty Burrier, had a new boyfriend and was over at his place more often than not. In truth, Stephanie was a bit envious of all the time Patty was spending with her new boyfriend. Falling in love was much more fun than falling out of love.

Stephanie flipped on the lights and went to the door. When she opened it, no one was there.

That was strange. Who would knock at this hour and run away? Could it have been Randy? Maybe he'd changed his mind at the last minute about waking her? After living together for a few months, they had split up last winter. The emotional scenes so common in the beginning had seemed to run their course, and they got along okay now. Although she had been very hurt by his declaration that he wanted his "freedom," she still cared for him. If they were ever to seriously get back together, she knew it could not be until he had gotten that out of his system.

Stephanie went back to bed.

Her close friends recognized that Stephanie had been moody lately. She was depressed over her fairly barren love life, and disgusted with herself for putting on weight. In the past few months she had added 15 pounds to her driver's license weight of 135 pounds. A statuesque 5-foot-8, she had the height to carry it and turn heads in a bikini. But she felt heavy around the hips and hated the way her clothes fit. She had tried to establish an exercise and diet regimen but her good intentions were too often thwarted. This weekend, for instance, she planned to attend a Mountain Air rock concert at Angel's Camp in the heart of California's gold country with several friends. How could one not overindulge at a time like this?

Stephanie had just drifted off when the phone rang. For the past few weeks she and Patty had been getting late-night obscene calls. If it was the heavy breather, she was prepared to give the lowlife a piece of her mind.

But it was Patty calling from a pay phone. She and her boyfriend, Jim Frazier, had gone out in his roommate's car, Patty explained, and now the car wouldn't start. They couldn't reach his roommate, and Jim, a late-night disc jockey, had to be at work soon. Would Stephanie come out and give them a lift to Jim's place, where Patty could pick up her car?

In spite of the late hour, Stephanie wouldn't have dreamed of turning down such a plea. That was the kind of friend she was. Besides, she had experienced her share of car trouble, and had always been grateful for friends coming to the rescue.

"We're downtown in front of Pine Cove Liquors," Patty explained.

That meant nothing to Stephanie, as she lived and worked on the north side of Sacramento and seldom ventured downtown. So, Patty put Jim on the phone to give directions.

"I get lost in a parking lot," Stephanie warned.

Jim gave her directions, and added reassuringly, "You're only fifteen minutes away."

Stephanie put on shorts, a tank top, slipped into sandals, and grabbed her purse on the way to the door. She wanted to be done with this mercy mission as soon as possible so she could get back to sleep.

It was Monday night and her alarm would be going off early so she could get to her $930-a-month teller job at Sacramento Savings and

Loan by 8:30 A.M. sharp. On the job eight months, she prided herself on never having been late for work. Stephanie enjoyed her job and had big plans for her career. She hoped to promote to loan officer or branch manager one day. Stephanie, who came from a close-knit family with four girls ranging from fifteen to twenty-four years of age, saw no reason why she couldn't one day have it all: a good career, a loving husband, and children, too.

Not the type who feared the dark, Stephanie stepped out the door at 6905 Centennial Way and strode quickly to her six-year-old yellow Dodge Colt hatchback parked in the driveway. The engine started without difficulty, testimony to the efforts of her handy neighbor who had worked on the car a few weeks earlier. With a rebuilt carburetor and new Montgomery Ward tires, Stephanie's little car was in the best shape since she'd bought it—for $500 down and $80 a month—shortly after graduating from high school.

As she backed out, she checked the fuel level—the needle pointed precariously close to E. She'd have to find an all-night gas station that took Visa because after looking in her wallet she realized that she didn't have any cash. This was turning out to be one of those nights.

It had started off quietly enough. After work, she had driven to her parents' home on two acres in rural Loomis, 20 miles northeast of downtown Sacramento. After dinner, she spent the evening doing her laundry and visiting with her parents, Tom and Jo-Allyn, and younger sister, Michaela, fifteen, the only daughter still living at home. Her little sister sometimes needed a sisterly dose of advice or cheering up, which Stephanie was always happy to provide. After calling some friends and chatting for a while, she'd flown out of the house around 9:30 P.M. on the heels of her usual, breezy "I-love-you" farewell to her parents. Arriving at her place a half hour later, she'd put away her clothes, showered, and gone to bed.

Stephanie drove into Elk Horn Union 76 on nearby Diablo Street. She normally pumped her own, and despite the lateness of the hour she pulled up to self-serve, as she was careful with her money. The self-serve pumps were locked, however. The attendant directed her to full-service, where he kindly pumped gas for her and charged the lower price.

It was nearly 1:00 A.M. when she found Patty and Jim in front of the liquor store near the corner of 29th and E streets. Relieved to see her, they hopped in the passenger seat, with Patty on Jim's lap as he gave directions to his apartment several miles away.

Jim apologized for calling Stephanie so late.

When they arrived, they all went inside.

"Okay, guys, how do I get home?" Stephanie asked.

"Look, Patty is going to take me to work in an hour," Jim said. "Why don't you wait and follow us?"

"Yeah," Patty said, "you can follow me home."

Stephanie declined the offer. She was anxious to get back, and didn't want to wait around for an hour.

"I can find my way back," she said. "Just write out directions."

Jim did, directing her to take Interstate 5, which bisects Sacramento down the middle as it traverses the spine of California, mostly through its vast Central Valley. To the south the highway goes all the way to the Mexico border and to the north, Canada.

From Jim's apartment, Stephanie was to take Bingham to Durfee, to Windbridge Road, to Greenhaven, then to Florin Road and the entrance to I-5 northbound, which would take her into Sacramento. He went over the directions with her, telling her which way to turn at each intersection. "Be sure to go north not south on I-5," he reminded her. "It'll say Sacramento."

North was Sacramento and home; south was a desolate stretch of highway—40 miles to the next town.

When Stephanie left, Jim walked with her to her car and made sure she knew which way to head off.

She followed his directions …

Bingham to Durfee—

Durfee to Windbridge—

Windbridge to Greenhaven—

Greenhaven to Florin to the entrance to I-5.

But when Stephanie reached the highway, she drove past the I-5 north ramp—the "Sacramento" portion of the sign was obscured by overgrown brush.

Instead of heading north toward home, she went south.

PATTY BURRIER telephoned the Brown residence the next morning to report that Stephanie's boss had called because she had failed to show up for work.

"Stephanie's missing," Patty said.

"*Missing?*" Jo-Allyn Brown said incredulously. "When did you last see her?"

Patty went into a somewhat confusing explanation about car trouble the night before, and Stephanie getting out of bed to give them a lift.

"What *time* did you last see her?"

"About one o'clock this morning," Patty said. "She was going right home."

After dropping Jim Frazier off at his radio station, Patty had arrived home shortly after 2:00 A.M. Discovering that Stephanie wasn't home, she figured that her roommate had decided on the way back to crash somewhere else—maybe her sister Lisa's, or even Randy's. After the bank had called, Patty checked Stephanie's room again. There was no sign she had ever come home.

"Please, get in your car and drive the route that Stephanie would have taken home," her mother pleaded. "Her car might have broken down. Call me back!"

Jo-Allyn was alone in the house—Tom had already left for work, and Michaela for school. Her knees went weak and she sat down, trembling, at the kitchen table. She knew Stephanie wouldn't miss work without calling in—it was completely unlike her. If she didn't call in, it was only because she hadn't been able to call. At that moment, her worst motherly fear hit her: Stephanie had been kidnapped, drugged, and was tied up in the back of a windowless van on its way to New York or some other faraway place where she would be exploited for her body or photographed for pornography.

Somehow, Jo-Allyn got to the phone on legs she could no longer feel. She called a friend who lived near Lisa to knock on her door—her oldest daughter didn't have a phone—and tell her to get to a phone right away and call home. Then, she telephoned some of Stephanie's friends. Those she was able to reach said they hadn't seen her. She made a point of not staying on the line long, and after the last call, she thought, *Stephanie will be calling any minute.*

When the phone rang, it wasn't Stephanie, but Lisa, who reported that she hadn't seen her sister in days.

Finally, Jo-Allyn called Tom's place of work, the local water district, and asked that a message be sent to him in the field to return home right away. She didn't want to do it, and felt terrible at the thought of worrying him, but she needed him at her side now.

The only reason Stephanie isn't calling, Jo-Allyn repeated to herself, *is because she can't.* There was only one thing left to do: notify the authorities.

As Stephanie resided in an unincorporated area of town, jurisdiction fell to the Sacramento County Sheriff's Department.

When uniformed Deputy Stanley Acevedo knocked on the door of Stephanie's duplex at 11:30 A.M. that morning, he was shown in by an unsmiling Patty. A concerned Jim Frazier was there also. Stephanie's mother, who elected to stay home near the phone, had asked that Patty and Jim be present to speak with authorities since they had been the last to see Stephanie.

By now, Patty was very worried. She had retraced the route Stephanie should have taken home, and found no sign of her roommate or her car.

Jim, who had been so diligent about explaining to Stephanie the best route home and making sure she headed off in the right direction, was also very troubled. He kept replaying the directions over in his mind: Had he written them out correctly? He was certain he had. So, what had gone wrong?

Patty and Jim told the deputy of their car trouble the previous night, and how they had called Stephanie for a ride. They also explained that she was unfamiliar with the area Jim lived in and how he had given her explicit directions home.

"I don't get it," Patty said. "If she had gotten lost or had car trouble, she would have called." Or if Stephanie had stayed at a friend's house, Patty went on, she would have shown up or called by now.

The deputy asked what Stephanie was wearing.

"White shorts and a tank top," Patty said. "Blue, I think. She'd been in bed and just threw some things on to come get us."

Patty found a recent picture of Stephanie and gave it to the deputy. In the snapshot, a smiling Stephanie had tilted her head to one side and thrust her shoulder toward the camera in a coquettish pose. Her mane of wavy blond hair flowed well below her shoulders. Ever since she had been a little girl her dazzling smile was the first thing most people noticed about Stephanie. In person, it was accentuated by her big brown eyes that widened excitedly at the right moment to let you know that her joyful expression was genuine, not forced.

Patty told the deputy that Stephanie had remarked that she didn't have any cash on her. Patty also reported the obscene phone calls, as well as Stephanie's mention of the loud knocking at the door.

Before he left, Deputy Acevedo interviewed Stephanie's mother by phone. To his pointed questions, Jo-Allyn Brown said that her daughter was not overly rebellious or difficult, nor was she on probation or in any trouble with the law. And yes, she was in sound mental condition.

"Anything bothering her?" asked the deputy.

"Not that I know of. She was in good spirits when she was here. She was excited about going to a concert this weekend."

"Do you have your daughter's fingerprints?"

"*What?*"

"A fingerprint card, maybe?"

"No."

"Are dental X-rays available?"

"I guess so," she sighed.

"I have to ask these questions, Mrs. Brown," the deputy explained apologetically.

"I understand. I'm sure her dentist has X-rays. I can give you his number."

"I'll need it."

When Deputy Acevedo returned to the station, he typed up a two-page missing person report that included such details as Stephanie's shoe size (8½ narrow), waist measurement (27 inches), bra size (36D), and vehicle license number (2AEF486).

When the deputy finished, the report was reviewed by his sergeant. Acevedo explained that this case didn't have the feel of a routine missing person. The sergeant agreed that Homicide should be notified right away.

Otherwise, if the report were submitted through channels and left to surface on its own, it could take days to land on a detective's desk.

They also gave Communications a description of the missing woman and her vehicle. A "BOLO" ("be on the lookout for ...") was radioed to all county sheriffs' units as well asCalifornia Highway Patrol cars in the area.

It had been twelve hours since Stephanie Brown had turned south not north onto I-5.

EARLIER that morning, Allen Dakin, fifty, had bicycled toward his favorite fishing hole along a slough of northern California's great freshwater delta, fed by endless tributaries that snaked down far-off mountains.

The supercharged heat that radiates off the ruler-flat Central Valley floor in midsummer was already warming to the task. The land was fertile here south of Sacramento due only to the miracle of irrigation. Days before, the thermometer had soared within a notch or two of a quarter-century-old record for that date of 110 degrees. It would be another scorcher today—the best fishing would be early, the fisherman knew. By midday, he planned to be sitting in his pint-size mobile home with a tall cold one after a fish fry.

Dakin stopped at a flooded irrigation ditch off a seldom-used two-lane road adjacent to a cultivated cornfield. It was his cache for live bait: fat crawdads that bass often hit on. He climbed off his bike, and was working his way down the ditch checking his crawdad traps when he spotted her.

Though the body was floating facedown, he knew it was female by her shape—too, the only thing she had on above the waist was a pink bra. He also knew there was no point in trying to pull her out. She had obviously been there for a while, and was surely dead.

At that point, the middle-aged man panicked. Jumping on his bike, he pedaled away furiously, leaving his fishing rod and tackle on the ground. Not stopping at the nearest farmhouse about a mile away, he passed a dozen more farms as he rode all the way home to call the authorities.

Deputies from the San Joaquin County Sheriff's Department and an emergency crew from the local fire department were the first to respond to the scene at 8:45 A.M. With irrigation water from an adjacent field pouring into the ditch nearby, they used a long gaff to push the body to the opposite bank, where they could better prevent it from drifting downstream.

Two San Joaquin Sheriff's detectives, based in Stockton, some 35 miles south of Sacramento, arrived half an hour later. From the passenger's side of the unmarked car emerged Pete Rosenquist. A trim six-footer, he was handsome in a classic Paul Newman way, with sandy-colored hair and sky-blue eyes. With sixteen years on the force and seven in Homicide, Rosenquist, nearing forty, was the wise veteran. A strong, quiet type, he had a been-there-done-that confidence that didn't come off as cockiness. He was willing to be a team player, but was just as comfortable working alone. This fit the style of San Joaquin's five-member Homicide Bureau, where individual detectives were assigned to murder cases, rather than teams of two partners as in most departments. Whichever detective wasn't tied up in court or was otherwise least busy with "unsolves" would get the "fresh one." If someone needed help with a crime scene or interviewing a difficult witness or making an arrest, he'd ask whichever detective had time to come along.

The driver, David "Vito" Bertocchini—big, barrel-chested, 6-foot-2, under thirty, black hair and matching mustache—was as tough as he looked. On the force six years, he'd been the type of street cop who relished a good bar fight to break up. Now that he was working detectives—he was brand new to Homicide—he missed the action of Patrol. Bertocchini was no fashion plate: he favored nylon windbreakers, polyester pants from Sears or JCPenney, and rarely a tie. Nobody could say, however, that he wasn't impassioned about his work. An old hand like Rosenquist only had to point and get out of the way—the irrepressible Bertocchini would find a way to get the job done, no matter what.

By luck of the draw, this new case had been assigned to Bertocchini. It would be only his second homicide—the first had been the shooting of a drug dealer, still unsolved. Rosenquist was along because he was between court appearances on another case and had offered to help out. These two were opposites, and not just in appearance. Rosenquist could at times be as laconic as Calvin Coolidge, while Bertocchini, with a born salesman's gift of gab, was always on full volume. Yet, in Rosenquist, the sagely Homicide veteran, newcomer Bertocchini would find his mentor.

Before allowing the body to be removed from the water, the two detectives went down the steep bank to take a look. Floating facedown in the water, the shirtless victim's back was exposed. They could see some long twigs and leaves caught under her bra strap. Her back and shoulders were dirty, as were her white shorts. Her legs were not visible in the murky water.

Back at the top, the detectives made a cursory search of the immediate area for any type of evidence. The ditch was surrounded on all sides by tall grass and weeds. There was a makeshift trail of freshly matted-down grass leading down the embankment on the side of the ditch where the body had first been discovered. Midway down the slope the detectives found a woman's leather sandal. A matching one was at the waterline. The shoes were photographed and taken as evidence.

When the detectives gave the word, a bare-chested fire department captain with a rope around his waist went down the embankment and strapped the body into a wire-type gurney used for emergency evacuations. The gurney was then pulled up to the road.

The detectives could now see red abrasions at the front of the dead woman's neck, and a band of purplish discoloration around her neck—the telltale markings of ligature strangulation. Whatever had been used to garrote her was gone.

About then, a paunchy, bespectacled private pathologist on contract with the county arrived. He took the core temperature of the body by making an incision in her back and inserting a probe directly into the liver. It registered 81 degrees. He found varying degrees of rigor mortis in the jaw, the legs, and the upper extremities. He also measured the temperature of the water and the air to assist in calculating the approximate time of death.

Nothing would be official until after the autopsy, of course. But at this point, it was an apparent homicide.

The body carried no identification, and no purse or wallet was found. For now, she was "Jane Doe."

From experience, Rosenquist knew that it was all but impossible to solve a murder when the victim was unidentified. Most investigations, when the killer was unknown, had to start with the victim; her movements in the last hours and days, lifestyle, known associates and enemies, etc. Trying to solve a murder without knowing the identity of the victim was like trying to survey a plot of land with a blank measuring tape. Left to making wild guesses, you had to get real lucky. Like maybe the killer walks into the nearest sheriff's substation and confesses. Or a witness to the abduction comes forward with a description of the suspect or his vehicle. Even better: the killer gets tanked and brags to the wrong person on the next barstool. What a homicide detective hopes for, every hour of every day as he tries to cover as many bases as possible, is for the victim to be identified, so that the real murder investigation can begin in earnest.

After the young woman's body was removed from the scene and on its way to the county morgue in Stockton, Bertocchini and Rosenquist made a wider search of the area on both sides of the ditch, and on the other side of the dirt road. They drove down the narrow lane until it ended within a mile at a deserted farm labor camp. Finding no other evidence, they departed around noontime.

They had a postmortem to attend.

ON THEIR downward trek to the Pacific Ocean, two great white-water rivers, the Sacramento and the American, flow from the Sierra Nevada Mountains into the Sacramento Valley floodplain. At the confluence of these rivers lies the city of Sacramento, the California state capital, settled a century earlier by an influx of farmers, ranchers, gold miners, and railroad laborers.

Today, downtown Sacramento, the center of political power in the nation's largest state, is anchored by a cluster of low-slung skyscrapers, much of their impressive square footage taken up with the day-to-day running of state business. This is home to the state legislature, a sometimes corrupt and often gutless body (to alleviate prison overcrowding six years earlier the legislature cut many sentences in half) with a dismal record for failing to pass meaningful laws, thereby leaving one tough call after another up to the citizens or special interests to pursue via the ballot initiative process.

Notwithstanding Sacramento's nickname, the "City of Trees," so ordained because of old-growth trees that provide street-side canopies of foliage, a more accurate moniker today would be "Los Angeles Jr." Clogged freeways, stifling smog, street gangs, an increase in violent crime, and a seemingly unconquerable homeless problem are among the social ills shared by California's first and fourth largest cities.

Sacramento's surrounding suburban communities—with sun-kissed names like Citrus Heights, Rancho Cordova, Orangevale—sprawl outward in three directions for a thousand square miles, making up greater Sacramento County. The climate, and nearby camping, boating, fishing, hunting, and snow skiing, as well as the close proximity of Reno and San Francisco (both two-hour drives), coupled with a huge employment pool at several once-thriving military bases, have helped to attract a million and a half residents.

At 2:10 P.M. on July 15, 1986, the missing person report generated by Stephanie Brown's mother hit the desk of Sacramento County Sheriff's Sergeant Harry Machen of Homicide at headquarters downtown.

Machen was up to his eyeballs more than usual, as the other three detectives in the Bureau were out on a new double homicide, which meant that everything else came his way. But noting that the report was barely an hour old and had been hand-carried from Patrol up to the third-floor Homicide Bureau, he looked at it right away. In charge of Adult Missing Persons, Machen had set up the reporting procedures, even designing the succinct but detailed forms used department-wide. Six hundred missing persons reports came into theSacramento Sheriff's Department every year, and Machen carried out the majority of the investigations himself. A lot of them involved juvenile runaways, errant spouses, and other individuals who didn't want to be found. Then, there were the others—those who dropped out of sight involuntarily for more ominous reasons.

From what he read, it struck Machen that there were very suspicious circumstances surrounding Stephanie Brown's mysterious disappearance. He called Communications and requested that Deputy Acevedo, still on patrol, be radioed to contact him immediately.

Just shy of 6 feet and powerfully built, Machen was an immaculate dresser who always looked neat and distinguished, no matter how much overtime he'd put in. A seventeen-year veteran of the department, his blondish hair had already been tinged with gray at the temples when he arrived at Homicide three years earlier. Being the only sergeant in Homicide, Machen was officially second in command. In addition to overseeing things when the lieutenant wasn't around, he not only handled missing persons but also worked as many homicide cases as any other detective in the Bureau.

Machen went into an adjoining office: a small, cramped space painted government beige that was dominated by a metal desk of the same color shoved up against the wall and a matching bookcase laden with snappy titles like *Practical Homicide Investigation, Techniques of Crime Scene Investigation*, and *Forensic Pathology*. At the desk, his back to the door, which almost never closed, Lt. Ray Biondi sat in a faded yellow Naugahyde-cushioned chair.

A trim man pushing fifty, Biondi stood several inches over 6 feet. A mop of thick, wavy black hair and full mustache had surprisingly little gray, despite his more than two decades with the department. In every way a cop's cop, Biondi was a no-nonsense manager who had little use for the myopic, bean-counter types that had come to dominate the higher ranks of law enforcement in these days of shrinking municipal budgets. He was skilled at running interference for the detectives who worked for him, so they were left alone to do their jobs, thereby earning their unwavering loyalty. If a detective needed to fly somewhere to further an investigation, Biondi wouldn't hesitate to short-circuit the memo-driven bureaucracy by seeing that the detective was on the next plane, and afterward, fight the often ugly battle to justify the expense to higher-ups. The danger in writing memos asking for something, Biondi had learned long ago, was that someone could say no.

Not given to pulling rank, Biondi considered himself a detective first, and a boss last. He had made it a ritual for he and his crew of detectives to lunch together, an act of social bonding over countless burgers, Philly cheese sandwiches, and bowls of chili that regularly turned into valuable brainstorming sessions about unsolved cases.

Handing Biondi the missing persons report, Machen said succinctly: "Last seen by roommate twelve hours ago. Doesn't figure she took off with a guy."

Biondi read the report through half-moon reading glasses, then flipped them up onto the top of his head and massaged the bridge of his nose between thumb and forefinger.

Few cases received by detectives are as perplexing as missing persons cases. In most other investigations, including homicides, it's generally known at the outset what specific crimes are involved. Not so with missing persons. It's not even certain *any* crime has been committed. For that reason, many law enforcement agencies traditionally wait twenty-four hours before doing any real work on an adult missing person. Statistically, only a small fraction of them end up victims, with most returning home on their own. Missing persons, for these reasons, are not given a high priority by most law enforcement agencies.

Biondi, however, was keenly aware that through the years there had been many unsolved homicides that began as local missing persons cases that had not been investigated at the time, or had been improperly handled during the critical early stages when leads were most fresh. Previously, all missing persons (adult as well as juvenile) had come under the jurisdiction of a separate bureau in the department. One 1980 case, in particular, had led to all adult missing persons cases being transferred to Homicide. Twenty-one-year-old Kathy Neff had left her car at a Sacramento automobile dealer for servicing and disappeared while walking the half mile to her home. Although the case had all the earmarks of a stranger abduction, it had not been worked as a possible homicide. Three weeks later, Neff's body—clad only in socks—was found in an agricultural ditch not far from Interstate 5. She had been sexually assaulted and strangled. It wasn't like Biondi to claim that his detectives could have solved this still-open case had they gone to work on it right after the woman's disappearance. Still, he knew that the investigation would have been handled very differently from the beginning. Veteran homicide detectives would immediately have canvassed the neighborhood where the young woman had disappeared seeking possible witnesses to anything unusual, and they also would have taken alibi statements from anyone in the area who could not be eliminated as a suspect. They did all these things after the body was found, of course, but a cold trail is more difficult to follow. Such foul-ups were why all adult missing persons cases now went to Homicide.

Biondi agreed that Stephanie Brown's disappearance had the feel of a stranger abduction. In fact, the circumstances were so suspect that Biondi added gravely, "I think we're looking for a body," as he handed the missing persons report back to Machen. The young woman, Biondi knew, could at that moment be lying dead somewhere—as yet undiscovered, or if found with no identification, stretched out on a slab at the morgue with a "Jane Doe" tag affixed to a big toe.

Not that Sacramento County Homicide was looking for something to do. The first week of July had opened with two separate murders. Then, the previous night, a thirty-year-old professional hit man from Kansas broke into a suburban Sacramento home—after cutting the phone lines—with the calculated intent of wiping out an entire family. Unhappy that the man of the house had taken up with his former girlfriend, the hit man shot them both as they slept in bed. The man's two sons, ages nineteen and fourteen, were also asleep in the house. The gunman found the older boy's room first, and shot him execution-style. Meanwhile, the younger son had awakened and gone into his father's bedroom. Seeing the carnage, he removed his father's empty .22 caliber handgun and ammunition from a bedside drawer. Returning to his room, he loaded the gun as he stood behind the closed door. When the intruder walked into the room, the steely-nerved youth shot him twice in the head, killing him instantly. The teenager saved not only himself but also the life of his seriously wounded father—his brother and his father's girlfriend died of their wounds. Detectives found in the hit man's car parked nearby 25 pounds of a gelatin explosive packed in a metal box inside a cooler filled with ice and several large-diameter pipe bombs. Apparently, he had planned to do a second job after he finished off the family. This brazen double murder was still being sorted out by all available hands, with detectives busily collecting evidence and conducting interviews.

Biondi believed that a homicide investigation should not move slowly. Witnesses, clues, and even physical evidence are often mobile, elusive, and forgetful. Blood cells are breaking down each moment they wait for laboratory analysis. Fingerprints are smudged, footprints are lost, and memories fade. His habit was to assign every detective available in the opening stages of an investigation so that as little as possible was lost during the crucial early hours. On a fresh homicide, it was not uncommon for detectives to work two or three days and nights straight, fortified by black coffee and occasional catnaps at their desks.

While this meant that virtually everything else had to take a lower priority, Biondi recognized the importance of having Machen follow through on the case of the missing young woman. Given the dire circumstances of her disappearance, it was vital in these early hours to work any leads that could be developed.

Deputy Acevedo phoned Homicide at 2:25 P.M. that afternoon. Machen took notes as the deputy filled in the details: Mom saw daughter the night before. Everything seemed fine. Daughter returned home, went to bed, was awakened around midnight by roommate calling, needing a lift. Roommate and roommate's boyfriend last to see her as she left alone to return home. Drove on unfamiliar streets to get back home. No evidence of family, personal, mental, or physical problems. No history of drug or alcohol abuse. A young woman, who by all accounts led a normal and stable life, had inexplicably stepped off the face of the earth.

"Another thing, Sergeant," Acevedo said.

"What's that?"

After the BOLO went out, the deputy explained, the California Highway Patrol called. "The CHP tagged a yellow vehicle fitting the description around nine o'clock this morning. The plate was close, but didn't exactly match ours."

"Where was it tagged?" Machen asked.

"Hood Franklin and I-5."

Hood Franklin Road was a desolate off-ramp of I-5, Machen knew, 10 or 12 miles south of downtown, but still in Sacramento County.

"She lives in the opposite direction," Machen said. "*North* Sacramento, right?"

"Yeah. She would have had to turn the wrong way onto I-5 to end up there. Easy enough to do in the dark when you don't know the area."

Machen asked if anyone was going to go back to the vehicle to double-check the license plate.

"CHP is dispatching a unit."

Machen asked if Acevedo had a picture of the young woman. The deputy said Patrol must still have it.

Machen thanked the deputy and hung up.

The detective next telephoned Sacramento Savings and Loan, speaking to a branch supervisor named Karen who volunteered that Stephanie was never late to work: "Most of the time, she's early. That's why we were so concerned when she didn't show up or call."

"Do you know of any problems she may have had with any customers?" Machen asked.

"No, there's never been any problems. Stephanie is very popular with our customers."

"What about any personal relationship that may have carried over to her job?"

"Last Friday her ex-boyfriend came over and paid her some money he owed her," Karen recalled. "I was a little concerned, so I kept an eye on them. But that went very well. They seemed to get along fine. His name is Randy, I think."

At 3:25 P.M., Machen received a call from the San Joaquin County Sheriff's Department. A detective who worked Homicide with Vito Bertocchini and Pete Rosenquist was calling around to nearby law enforcement agencies in the hope of finding a name for their unidentified victim.

"We had a fresh female body dump this morning," reported the detective from the neighboring county to the south. "She's a Jane Doe. Dead less than twelve hours. Thought we'd give you a holler to see if you have a recent missing person who might match up."

"Got a description?" Machen asked.

"White female adult, approximately eighteen to twenty years old, 5-foot-8, 150 pounds. Blond over brown. Pierced ears. No scars or tattoos. Pink polish on her toenails, none on her fingernails."

"What was she wearing?" Machen's voice remained level.

"Pink bra. No top. White shorts, blue panties."

"Where was she found?"

"Irrigation ditch on the east side of Correia Road, about half a mile south of Highway 12."

"Near I-5?"

"Three or four miles west."

"You have fingerprints?"

"Not yet. They're still doing the post."

Machen knew the surest way to determine if it was Stephanie Brown would be to contact the department of motor vehicles and get her driver's license thumbprint to compare with prints lifted from the dead woman. Making a positive ID this way was less cruel, too, than asking loved ones to visit the morgue.

"Height, weight, and age fit one of ours," Machen said. "I'll do some checking and get back to you."

Machen immediately called Jo-Allyn Brown at home. Without mentioning that a body had been found, he asked for a detailed description of her missing daughter.

"She has long blond hair, brown eyes. About 5-foot-7, 140 pounds, I guess. She has pierced ears, I think just one hole in each."

"Do you know if she was wearing polish on her toenails or fingernails?"

"No, I'm sorry, I don't. Her fingernails aren't real long, but she's letting them grow out."

"Any scars?"

"No."

If Stephanie's mother suspected anything from the very specific nature of the questions, she didn't let on.

"Anything else you can think of?" Machen asked.

"She got sunburned a while ago and is still peeling in the cleavage area."

Machen asked about the ex-boyfriend. Spouses and former spouses, lovers and ex-lovers are the first potential suspects that must be eliminated in practically every unsolved homicide, as Americans more often kill people they know best than total strangers.

"That's been over for some time," Stephanie's mother replied. "They're just friends now."

No sooner had Machen gotten off the phone than Communications rang with the news that the Highway Patrol had verified that the yellow automobile at the Hood Franklin off-ramp was registered to Stephanie Marcia Brown.

Machen drew a mental map. Hood Franklin was some 15 to 20 miles from where the unidentified body had been found.

Machen told >Biondi, who said he'd make arrangements for a stall at the county crime lab so that the car could be towed in and examined. Machen slipped his jacket on and headed for his car parked out back.

The detective arrived at the off-ramp a few minutes past 4:00 P.M. after a twenty-minute drive south.

Stephanie's two-door 1980 Dodge Colt, California license 2AEF486, was parked on the right-hand side of the off-ramp just off the main highway—about 200 yards before the stop sign at the overpass.

Machen left his coat and tie in his car and rolled up the sleeves of his white shirt. He wore on his belt a holstered handgun and a shiny sergeant's badge. At the trunk of the car, he leaned over and unlatched a plain suitcase. Inside were the tools of the homicide trade, including a flashlight, notebooks, pens, tape recorder, new tape cassettes, magnifying glass, measuring tape, camera and film, and surgical gloves. Popping a new tape in the pocket-sized recorder, he closed the trunk lid and went to work.

Dictating whatever he saw into the recorder, the first thing Machen noticed was the CHP tag on the Dodge Colt's radio antenna, dated that morning a little before 10:00 A.M. Circling the vehicle, he didn't find any body damage other than a slight transfer of dark paint on the left front fender, as if the car had swiped or brushed against something. It looked old.

The car was parked on the asphalt shoulder, evenly spaced between the dirt shoulder and the white line that marked the right-hand side of the roadway. He noted that the driver had had both the time and foresight to pull over safely, out of the flow of any traffic taking that exit.

The driver's side window was down nearly all the way, leaving only about a 1-inch edge of the window showing. Most people did not drive at highway speeds with their window down, particularly at night. It was lowered, Machen thought, as if the driver had rolled it down to speak to someone who was outside.

Neither car door was locked.

Careful not to touch anything before the vehicle could be dusted for prints, Machen peered inside. The keys were not in the ignition. He noted the car's mileage (47,878). The trip odometer showed 31.3 miles.

In the console between the two front seats were several envelopes and a handwritten note: "E Street, right, liquor store, Pinecove Bottle Shop." Some loose papers and a plastic cup were on the passenger floorboard. No wallet or purse was in plain view, nor would they be found anywhere in the vehicle when it was more thoroughly checked.

With a hot wind blowing hard off the open terrain, Machen circled the vehicle again. Widening his search, he looked for footprints and tire tracks in the dirt and any other evidence. Other than several old cigarette butts about 20 yards away and an empty wine bottle that had obviously been out in the elements for a while, he found nothing.

This was desolate country, patchwork green-and-brown farmland as far as the eye could see. No gas stations or pay phones or overhead lights at or near the off-ramp; only a handful of farmhouses on the distant horizon. In the dead of night, something had happened out here in the middle of nowhere that, it now seemed very likely, had ended up costing a young woman her life. But what? And by whom?

At 4:47 P.M., Biondi radioed Machen that the picture of Stephanie Brown had been located and he was dispatching it out to nearby McClellan Air Force Base. It was to be flown down to the scene aboard the department's helicopter, Star One.

"San Joaquin Homicide is en route to your location," Biondi continued. "They want to compare our picture to photos of their victim. But, Harry—they've confirmed their Jane Doe is peeling from a sunburn."

"Understand," Machen said. He was not surprised.

Machen was glad the chopper was coming—he would use it to make a sweep of the entire area and to take some aerial photographs of the scene.

A flatbed tow truck arrived at 5:00 P.M.

"It's all yours," Machen said. "It's going directly to the crime lab to be processed for evidence. Don't touch anything you don't have to."

By then, Machen had taken numerous pictures of the car, and how and where it was parked.

The tow truck driver found that the Colt's emergency brake had been set. He released it. Checking the gearshift, he discovered that the car, which had a manual transmission, was already in neutral. Attaching a chain to the front bumper, the driver worked a power winch to pull the car up onto the bed of the truck.

As the vehicle moved, Machen examined the bottoms of its tires. They appeared relatively clean; not out in dirt or mud recently. Then he checked the ground beneath where the car had been parked. Nothing.

The tow truck left with the Dodge Colt.

When the helicopter set down a few minutes later, kicking up a maelstrom of dust, Machen hopped aboard with his camera. After putting on a headset with microphone—it was impossible to yell over the loud whish-whishing of the rotator blades—he told the two deputies up front where he wanted to go. One of the pilots handed him the picture of Machen's missing person.

They flew the route Machen figured the killer had most probably driven once he had the young woman in his car and under his control. The detective wasn't exactly sure what he was hoping to find—maybe, nearby, some clothing belonging to Stephanie Brown, or even her missing purse along the road.

Encouraging the pilot to fly just as low as possible, Machen kept his nose pressed to the window.

They flew south on I-5 from the Hood Franklin off-ramp to the Highway 12 exit, a distance of 16 miles. Midway, they crossed the Sacramento–San Joaquin county line. They continued west on rural Highway 12 for a few miles, then turned around, as Machen did not know the precise location where the body had been found that morning.

Had he killed her down there, Machen wondered as he looked at the vast fields and interlocking irrigation ditches that lined both sides of Highway 12, *or had he done it somewhere along the way?*

Back at Hood Franklin, Machen found Pete Rosenquist and Vito Bertocchini waiting, along with several Sacramento deputies who had completed a canvass of the area—knocking on the doors of the surrounding farmhouses to find out if residents had seen or heard anything suspicious during the night. No one had.

The San Joaquin detectives pulled out a starkly lit Polaroid shot taken at the morgue two hours earlier before the postmortem had begun. Jane Doe lay naked on her back on a chrome table outfitted with countless drainage holes. Her eyes were shut; her pale lips parted slightly; her hair swept back off her forehead; her complexion clear; her arms at her sides. She was, in truth, a beautiful young woman. Other than the angry dark furrow in the flesh of her neck left by some type of ligature, she might have been sleeping peacefully before awakening to begin a new day.

Machen took out the snapshot of the very alive and smiling Stephanie Brown that her roommate had handed the patrol deputy that morning.

The three detectives looked hard at the side-by-side images, then at one another. Although they would still need a fingerprint comparison for positive identification, there was absolutely no denying it.

Jane Doe had a name now.

CHAPTER TWO

At the postmortem earlier that afternoon on the as yet unidentified body, Vito Bertocchini had found himself in a disagreement with the pathologist before the procedure began.

The detective had simply asked the pathologist to conduct a "rape kit," a routine collection process in cases involving possible sexual assault. The body's orifices are swabbed and the specimens transferred onto glass slides to be examined by microscope at the crime lab.

"We don't need that," the pathologist announced.

Bertocchini looked at Rosenquist. The veteran detective had, an hour before, made a point to tell Bertocchini to be sure and have a rape kit done.

For many years, the only thing that could be determined from blood, saliva, and semen had been an assailant's blood group. As there are only four human blood groups, such information could apply to any one of millions, or even billions, of people. Obviously, this had limited value to detectives hunting for a rapist or killer. Then, in the 1970s, scientists discovered elements in blood and body secretions that made it possible to match a sample to a much smaller number of people. Further advances since then have greatly perfectedDNA analysis, or "genetic fingerprinting." When DNA is extracted from the cells contained in blood and secretions like saliva and semen, it can now be linked to a specific individual. However, there are minimum requirements to conduct DNA work: the dead body needs to be fresh enough to provide biological specimens, and there has to be an adequate sample available for this intricate testing.

"We want to send samples to the crime lab," the low-key Rosenquist matter-of-factly explained to the pathologist, whom the detective knew to be one of the best in the state.

"She was in the water," the pathologist said. "Any semen that was in there has been washed away."

Bertocchini was keenly aware that he was the new kid on the block in Homicide. He hated to start getting a reputation so soon. But dammit, this was his case, and given the circumstances of the crime, a rape kit was called for.

"Humor me," said Bertocchini, his voice now in a don't-fuck-with-me growl that had caused many a street punk to stop in his tracks. He'd had enough already.

The pathologist turned away momentarily, then went over to the foot of the gurney holding a short cotton-tipped swab that wasn't as wide as a pencil. He pried open stiff legs.

"You're not going to get *a thing*," he muttered. "I don't know why you guys even bother."

The pathologist shoved the swab out of sight. Quickly withdrawing it, he told the detectives: "See, you got nothing." Using clean swabs, the pathologist next swabbed her rectum, then her mouth, rubbing the cotton tip of each onto separate slides that would be sent to the crime lab along with the swabs.

Next, he combed out her light brown pubic hair—microscopic examination by the crime lab would determine whether her attacker had shed any of his own hair. The pathologist then made scrapings from beneath her fingernails, which would be studied under a microscope for blood and skin in the event she had scratched her attacker. Finally, he took a sample of hair from her scalp.

Bertocchini would not be surprised when the crime lab reported later that chemical tests indicated the presence of seminal fluid on the vaginal swab and a microscopic examination of that slide detected sperm cells. (No seminal fluid or sperm cells were found on the oral and rectal swabs or slides.) The lab reported that there was not enough semen present to conduct any genetic fingerprinting DNA tests. Bertocchini felt certain that had they been able to obtain a larger sample, they might well have ended up with more conclusive evidence. Of course, until they actually *had* a suspect, these findings meant very little.

Bertocchini and Rosenquist were at the autopsy that day because the postmortem examination is a vital evidentiary link for detectives in the beginning stage of any homicide investigation. Their main concern was recovery of any and all evidence. Exactly how their murder victim died was a key question. The answer could lead them to *why* she had been killed, and the ultimate question: by *whom?*

Experienced homicide investigators have different ways of getting through the macabre ordeal—inhaling the combined odors of formaldehyde and disinfectant and stale death that pervade a morgue; watching a human body be opened up like a ripe watermelon by scalpel, drill, electric saw, and other assorted hand tools; vital organs like the heart, kidneys, lungs, and brain examined, removed, weighed, and dissected. Some old-timers puff on cigars, bathing their smell and taste senses in strong smoke. The trick, most detectives agree, is to remain detached. The body on the table isn't someone they know, and it isn't even the human being it had once been. That person is gone.

For this—only his second autopsy as a homicide detective—Bertocchini kept notes, as it was his case. The distraction was a welcome one. Seeing a dead body was a strong argument to support the existence of a divine savior, he had already concluded. Without the spirit of life, a human body was just a piece of meat.

In his seven years working Homicide, Rosenquist had been present for more than a hundred autopsies. The only ones that got to him anymore were when the victim was a baby or young child. In such cases, the procedure was akin to cleaning a chicken.

During the autopsy of Jane Doe, Bertocchini took down his and Rosenquist's observations, which were later typed up by a clerk and made part of the case journal, known euphemistically as the "Murder Book." The pathologist turned in his own signed coroner's report.

Before the body had been disrobed by a coroner's technician—the clothing would be bagged and labeled and sent to the crime lab—the detectives took another look at the twigs underneath the rear brassiere strap. The longest was about 5 inches, and it was centered under the bra.

This was a big-busted young woman, and the bra was tight. In fact, once her bra was removed, a clear impression was left in her back by the twigs. Even if she had been dragged on her back—the trail of matted-down grass at the crime scene suggested that the body had been dragged to the ditch—it seemed unlikely that these long twigs could get so far under the strap. Besides, they had seen brush with these types of twigs and leaves growing down by the water in the ditch, but none up on top of the embankment. Had the killer placed these twigs under her bra as part of some weird ritual? Or had the bra been snapped together by his fumbling hands in the dark as his victim lay on the ground by the ditch, either dead or otherwise incapacitated, and in so doing did he catch the twigs accidentally inside the strap?

They had also noticed something funny about the way she was wearing her shorts. The waistband was turned *inside*, suggesting to the detectives that someone else had last pulled them up. Had the killer actually taken the time to dress his victim before dumping her body? If so, he had missed one article of clothing: her top. Had he hidden it? If so, why? Or had he taken it?

After the Polaroid shots of Jane Doe were taken, Bertocchini began his report with a detailed description of the victim. "Short blond hair. Brown eyes. One pierced hole in each earlobe. Moderate tan with white bikini-marked areas. On her upper chest her skin is peeling due to a sunburn. No jewelry."

Meanwhile, the pathologist had opened a metal drawer and laid out an assortment of tools on an adjacent chrome table. He slipped on a headset with a small microphone at the mouthpiece, then turned on the tape recorder clipped to his belt.

Looking down at the dead body as if it were a familiar road map, he began. As he worked, he spoke into the recorder with the clinical cadence of someone who had done this hundreds of times before.

"The neck has a discontinuous horizontally oriented 1-inch bandlike abrasion. It is most noticeable in the left anterior neck but also present on the right anterior neck. On the posterior surface of the neck, the abrasion is seen to continue around the left side, where it's quite definite. There's a faint discontinuous extension around the right posterior side. The mark encircles the neck in a discontinuous fashion at the level of the cricothyroid junction."

The detectives had noticed at the scene that the ligature marks around the neck were irregular, which seemed odd. When someone is strangled with a ligature, in most cases the red, ugly band extends uninterrupted all the way around the neck. It had been Rosenquist who ventured that perhaps something had gotten caught between the skin and garrote in those areas where the skin showed no ligature marks.

The pathologist offered no opinion on the matter, and moved on. "There are no fingernail scratch marks or other marks about the neck," he recited. "On the tip of the chin there is a three-quarter-inch mottled abrasion."

Bertocchini leaned in for a closer look. Medical double-talk aside, to the experienced street cop it looked as if the young woman had been slugged squarely on the jaw.

"On the top of the right shoulder at the acromioclavicular joint, there is a 3-inch cluster of three light purple bruises, faint."

She'd been held tightly.

"On the right distal forearm near the ulnar styloid, there is a 1-inch group of horizontal scratch abrasions. Above this, there is a faint 1-inch pink bruise."

These scratches and bruises on her right wrist looked as if she'd been bound.

"On the knees, just above each kneecap, there are brush abrasions measuring an inch and a quarter on the right, 2 inches on the left. Along the left anterior thigh there are faint vertically oriented parallel scratch abrasions. There is also a suggestion of scratch marks oriented vertically on the anterior right thigh. On the medial left thigh, just below midlevel, there is a resolving 1½-inch green-brown bruise with a central area of pallor. Above the right knee on the lower anterior thigh, there is a 1¼-inch pink-brown bruise."

Bertocchini was trying to put some of the scattered pieces of the jigsaw puzzle together. She had been bound, punched, and roughly grabbed. She'd been made to kneel, long and hard enough to leave bruises on her knees, and perhaps forced to lie on the ground face first, as all the scratches and bruises were on the front of her. When her attacker was finished doing all the terrible things he did, he tightened the ligature around her neck—probably from behind—until she could no longer breathe. Her death had not been painless or quick.

"On the knees just below the kneecaps, there are irregular postmortem pressure marks …"

Marks left *after death*. Bertocchini could picture it: The killer had a dead body he wanted to stash so he held her by the legs, under the knees, and dragged her on her back down the steep embankment.

The pathologist removed a fresh blade from a silver packet on the small adjacent table and snapped it onto a scalpel handle. It was time to go internal.

From a point above each breast, he made the traditional opening incision, which met at the sternum and sliced downward to the pubis. The large cut formed a perfect Y. He then carved through the fatty tissue that still held the incision together, not with the delicate, deliberate touch of a surgeon, but with the sure-handedness of a butcher dressing a side of beef.

The rib cage was opened with oversized pruning shears, amid loud snapping and cracking noises. In less than a minute, it was cut free and placed intact at the foot of the gurney. After the autopsy, it would be placed back in the body, which at that point would look more like a hand-carved canoe than a human being. The body would then be sewn up before being released to the family for funeral services.

The pathologist examined the various internal organs, finding them normal and free of any disease. He also cut open the throat and removed the neck organs as a block, then carefully dissected them in layers.

"There are several half-inch to three-quarter-inch glistening purple-black hemorrhages in the strap musculature in the supraclavicular area," he droned on with both precision and detachment. "There is also hemorrhage in the strap musculature over the left lower thyroid area. There are also multiple glistening purple-black hemorrhages in the retro-esophageal area."

When he had finished, the pathologist pulled off his rubber gloves and turned to the sink. "Your cause of death is asphyxia with evidence of ligature strangulation," he told the detectives as he washed. He sounded more conversational now that the tape recorder was off. "I didn't find any gross signs of rape. No tears or bruising in the vagina or anus."

"What's your opinion on the time of death?" Rosenquist wanted to know. That was, he knew, one of the weakest areas of forensic medicine because there are so many variables. The rule of thumb was to figure a drop in the body's normal temperature of about 1.5 degrees Fahrenheit per hour after death. That could vary, however, depending on the surrounding environment. In this case, the body had been partly submerged in water, which could have drawn out the warmth much quicker.

"I'd estimate she died sometime between late last night and early this A.M.," said the pathologist.

That was as close as they would get.

BERTOCCHINI and Rosenquist interviewed Stephanie's roommate at 8:30 P.M. that night at the faded-brown duplex with a postage-stamp front lawn that the two young women shared on Centennial Way.

At the time, the detectives were still waiting on positive identification of the body. They did, however, tell Patty Burrier that Stephanie's car had been found on I-5 south of Sacramento, and also that they had strong reason to believe that her body had been found at another location some distance away.

"We think she got lost," Rosenquist explained, "and was abducted, then murdered."

The color drained from Patty's face.

"I know you've already been interviewed at length about what happened last night," Bertocchini said sympathetically, "but please start from the beginning."

Although she looked shaken and exhausted, Patty recounted the details of the previous evening.

When she was finished, Bertocchini asked if Stephanie was carrying a purse when Patty last saw her.

"I don't remember. But I know she always took it whenever she went out."

Bertocchini asked Patty to describe what Stephanie had been wearing when she had last seen her. It all checked out with what Jane Doe had been wearing, with the exception of the missing top.

"You say it was a blue top," the detective said. "Can you give me some more detail?"

"It's a sleeveless tank top with a flower design on front," she said, pointing to just below her neckline. "With lacy edges."

"Did Stephanie have a current boyfriend?"

"She doesn't have a steady boyfriend," said Patty, who seemed unwilling or unable to talk about her roommate in the past tense. "She used to go with a guy named Randy. I have his phone number if you want."

Bertocchini took the number.

"How long did they date?" he asked.

"About a year and a half. They lived together a few months before Stephanie and I got this place."

"They were still on friendly terms?"

"Oh, yes. They're friendly."

The phone rang and Patty answered it.

"It's for you guys."

Rosenquist went to the phone. After a brief conversation, he hung up and said solemnly, "The prints match."

Bertocchini nodded, and closed his notebook. They would need to notify the parents right away.

"Before we go," Bertocchini said, "I want to ask you something, Patty. What do you think Stephanie would have done if she had been confronted by a stranger or found herself in a dangerous situation?"

Patty's brow furrowed. She seemed to be considering the question very seriously.

"She'd have been real scared, but she definitely would have resisted. I know she wouldn't have been out hitchhiking if her car had broken down. But she might have accepted a ride or help if she felt they were trustworthy. She wanted to think the best of people."

The detectives drove directly to the home of Jo-Allyn and Tom Brown, arriving at 10:30 P.M.

"I'm very sorry to tell you that your daughter's body has been positively identified by her driver's license thumbprint," Bertocchini said somberly.

"You've seen her?" Jo-Allyn asked.

The detective nodded.

"Was she—cut up or—mutilated?"

"No, nothing like that happened," Bertocchini answered softly.

The grief-stricken parents had been braced for the news since two Sacramento County homicide detectives had knocked on their door three hours earlier and begun by saying, "Please sit down." The Browns had seen enough police dramas on television to know what came next.

Lt. Ray Biondi had sent the detectives because he was afraid of a leak to the press—which in every big city monitors police radio frequencies. He hadn't wanted the parents to hear about their daughter's death on the news or from an inquiring reporter.

The Sacramento detectives had earlier told the Browns of finding Stephanie's car deserted on I-5, and of the young woman's body found 15 or 20 miles away that had been "tentatively identified" as Stephanie based on photographs.

For Jo-Allyn Brown, in obvious shock and grasping a wadded tissue now as she spoke to Bertocchini and Rosenquist, the real blow had come that morning.

Ever since Stephanie had been reported missing, her mother instinctively knew that something dreadful had happened. All day, she'd been wondering just how parents of kidnap victims who are never found could endure such an ordeal. *Not knowing* had to be the worst torture imaginable. If Stephanie had been killed, her mother at least wanted an intact body to pray over, say good-bye to, and bury nearby.

Thank God, she's been found, Jo-Allyn thought.

Stephanie could come home now.

TWO AND A half hours later, Rosenquist and Bertocchini stood on the embankment above the irrigation ditch that Stephanie's body had been pulled from that morning. They had come here to check the ambient light at approximately the same time she had been killed the previous night.

A half moon hung sideways in the sky, but otherwise the night was as black as a bottomless pit.

They both understood that this exercise was part of the visceral attachment that a detective inevitably makes to each and every victim.

They wanted to go where Stephanie had gone on her last ride, following the same roads and going past the same terrain. They wanted to be where she had died just twenty-four hours earlier.

They hung around, not wanting to go just yet. Each wanted to stay as close as they could to the crime scene—antennae all the way up and sensors turned on.

One thing that registered with them both was how incredibly isolated this location was, which caused them to ask aloud: How did the killer find it in the dark?

They concluded that he had to have been familiar with I-5 and the surrounding area. On this back road at this time of night—so close and yet so far away from the nonstop traffic of a perpetually busy interstate highway—he'd have had little worry of his evil deeds being interrupted. He must have known that.

As Bertocchini stood listening to about a million frogs croaking contentedly in nearby ditches and ponds, he pondered what must have happened here twenty-four hours earlier. Had she been alive and conscious during the fifteen- or twenty-minute ride here? Yes, he decided, she must have been. Bound and awake, taken away by force … the ride had to have been unbelievably terrifying for her.

Once they had arrived at the side of the ditch, how long had her ordeal gone on? Had her screams filled the night or had she been gagged? Had her attacker killed before, or was it his first time? Had he panicked afterward, or did he stay calm and collected?

Some questions couldn't be answered, but others could, through instinct and deduction. Based on the scene, Bertocchini and Rosenquist both felt they were dealing with a very cool customer, as he had been careful not to leave behind any incriminating evidence. If he'd assaulted and killed her here, as they figured he must have, the killer had shown enormous composure to pick up after himself before departing.

"Pete, why do you think he re-dressed her?"

Rosenquist didn't answer right away. "Maybe he was ashamed," he ventured. "Or maybe he was hoping we wouldn't look for sexual assault. He knows that's a good way for us to find blood type and other incriminating evidence. I'm just guessing here."

Bertocchini found himself thinking about how much he'd like to get his hands on the scumbag who had kidnapped, beaten, abused, and killed a young woman who had so much of her life yet to live. No doubt the killer would prove to be less brave when faced with someone whose hands weren't tied and who could hit back. That was usually the case with creeps. Bertocchini brought himself back quickly from his fantasy of ministering street justice. He was a detective, responsible for collecting evidence and making a case. A good homicide cop had to be tough-minded, he knew, and possess a deeply rooted spirit of detachment. It was his job to stay observant, thoughtful, and within himself, so as to keep an open mind and not overlook a thing.

Two days later, Bertocchini went back to speak to Stephanie's parents. He was looking for as much information about her as he could possibly find—her life, her friends, her patterns. With no suspect or incriminating evidence, it was the best place to start an investigation.

After going down a list of questions, Bertocchini asked if Stephanie normally locked her car doors while driving at night.

"Oh, yes. She was good about that."

"Was it her habit, do you know, of driving with her driver's window down at night?"

"At *night?* No. She kept her windows up."

In examining the impounded vehicle earlier that day, Bertocchini discovered it had a dead battery. The headlights switch was in the "on" position, but not the emergency flasher. Once the battery was jumped, the engine started right up. No doubt the headlights' being on all night accounted for the dead battery. The car had plenty of gas, and appeared to have no mechanical problems. So much for the theory that Stephanie may have had car trouble and was waiting in a disabled vehicle or had walked away for assistance.

Bertocchini had seen the collection of photographs that Sergeant Machen had taken from various angles of Stephanie's car at the Hood Franklin off-ramp. Flipping through the images of the Dodge Colt at the side of the road, Bertocchini had noted that Stephanie had obviously pulled over cautiously and, almost certainly, voluntarily. Having spent many years in Patrol, Bertocchini recognized the manner in which the car was parked at the shoulder, with its driver's window rolled down. It looked like a police stop. He had heard chilling stories of Los Angeles' famous "Red Light Bandit," who decades earlier had pulled young women and couples over at night with a portable red light atop his vehicle in order to abduct and rape his female victims. Had something similar happened out on I-5 that night? Is that why Stephanie had pulled over, left her car in neutral and the lights on? The thought of a dirty cop, or even someone pretending to be a police officer, was among every cop's worst nightmares. Bertocchini had also noted something disturbing about the marks on her right wrist. She'd been bound, anyone could see that, and the bindings were never found. The marks, Bertocchini thought, looked similar to the type left on a suspect's wrist when handcuffs were put on too tight. Of course, anyone could buy handcuffs. As for the possibility of a red-light stop, Bertocchini and Rosenquist had kicked it around without reaching any conclusion. They knew it was just as credible that Stephanie had simply become lost and pulled over to get her bearings or turn around. There were, however, questions: Could she have been surprised in the dark by her abductor? If she had seen a stranger coming out of the dark, would she have lowered her window to speak to him? Without locking her doors? Would she have gotten out of her car to speak to someone, perhaps to get directions?

"Tell me, Mrs. Brown, was Stephanie very trusting of people?" Bertocchini asked.

Jo-Allyn showed a faint, sad smile at the memory. "Oh, yes, very much so. I called her my 'love child.' She could never understand how people could be mean to each other. She was very giving and trusting."

During the course of this interview, Stephanie's mother showed pictures of her daughter.

"She would buy presents for her friends even if she was short of money," her mother reminisced. "She would never turn down a friend in need. I tell myself she was too God-darn perfect for this earth. I know my daughter is in heaven, Detective. She's in a peaceful place where no one will ever hurt her again."

In every picture of Stephanie the detective was shown, her blond hair was quite long—much longer than it had been at the morgue.

"She'd cut her hair?" he asked nonchalantly.

"Oh, no," her mother replied. "She'd worn her hair long since gram-mar school."

A red flag went up for Bertocchini.

"Mrs. Brown, how was Stephanie wearing her hair when you last saw her?"

"In a ponytail. She usually put it up at night."

"I mean—how *long* was it?"

"Mid-back. To her bra line."

Bertocchini wasn't sure how to say this except to the point. "Her hair was short when we found her."

"Short? Then whoever killed her cut it."

It was not open to discussion.

BERTOCCHINI and Rosenquist returned to the morgue the following morning.

Considering the invasive procedures that had been performed the previous day, the body under the sheet looked surprisingly whole. It was to be turned over that day to a private funeral home.

They rolled the corpse over onto its side.

Stephanie's once long, flowing hair was now so short on one side it didn't even cover her ear. Her hair was strangely lopsided: an inch or two long on the left side, and about 5 inches long on the right.

Bertocchini held the ends of a clump of greasy hair.

"It's chopped off."

The hair wasn't shredded as if slashed by a knife but cut cleanly, although it had the definite look of having been hacked off randomly by someone who wasn't going for style.

They interviewed Stephanie's regular hairdresser, who confirmed what Jo-Allyn Brown had said about Stephanie wearing her hair long. The stylist, hired by the family to fix Stephanie's hair for the funeral, had her-self been shocked by the short and ragged condition of her client's hair. In her opinion, the hasty chop job had been done with scissors.

"How do you figure it?" Bertocchini asked the following morning over high-octane coffee at a hole-in-the-wall across the street from the courthouse.

Rosenquist shrugged. "Maybe he wanted some of that nice long hair to take home. I don't know."

Each stayed quiet for a while.

"Those discontinuous marks around her neck, remember?" Bertocchini finally offered. "Her long hair got caught under the ligature as he strangled her. That's why in some places there's no marks."

Rosenquist kept the ball rolling. "Her hair gets tangled in the ligature. He doesn't want to leave the ligature behind. He's afraid of prints. Or maybe—this is a fuckin' pleasant thought—he wants to use it again. So he cuts her hair to free it."

The detectives weren't guessing as much as they were connecting the dots. Bertocchini slowly stirred his black coffee with a spoon just for something to do while he deliberated. "But the guy *brings* the scissors with him. How did he know he was going to need them?"

"Because he'd done it before," Rosenquist said without skipping a beat.

Later that morning, they returned to the morgue and verified that the horizontal band of marks on Stephanie's neck were "discontinuous" on the left side—the same side with the extra-short hair. This made them think, more than ever, that Stephanie's hair had indeed been sheared off after she'd been strangled just to extricate the ligature.

They visited the ditch again the following morning. This time, Bertocchini brought his hip-length wading boots from his garage at home. Only instead of stepping into a fast-moving stream to hook a rainbow trout, he intended to stomp through a muddy ditch looking for something, *anything*, to help catch a killer.

When he was fastened into the big, bulky boots, Bertocchini went out into the waist-high water with a lawn rake. Starting in the area where the body had first been spotted, he began methodically to scrape the bottom. Pulling the rake through mud and silt, he brought up empty beer cans, cigarette wrappers, an oil can, and other assorted litter. They carefully picked through it all.

An hour later, he snagged an article of clothing. Bringing it up to the bank, they unfolded the material and saw it was a blue tank top with lacy edges and a design at the nape of the neck. Before placing the garment in a plastic bag for the crime lab, Bertocchini spotted several strands of hair stuck on it, as if it had been worn during a haircut. He carefully removed the strands of hair and placed them in an envelope.

Also, though it didn't mean much to him at the time, Bertocchini noticed that in several places it appeared that her blouse had been ripped.

Or maybe *cut*.

CHAPTER THREE

"Stephanie was hurt when we broke up," said her ex-boyfriend, Randy Miller, sneaking another look at his watch. "She loved me a lot."

Vito Bertocchini was ready to take this skinny, blond Surfer Joe and hang him upside down by his bony ankles. In the detective's mind, the fact that Stephanie was said to be no longer serious about this God's-gift-to-womanhood jerk spoke well of her.

After fishing Stephanie's blouse out of the ditch that morning, Bertocchini and Pete Rosenquist had set out to conduct alibi interviews and gather as much other information as possible. Her former live-in boyfriend had been at the top of their list. At this point in the investigation, they were as much in the dark as they'd been that night standing above the ditch—with no leads whatsoever pointing to the identity of her killer.

"I gotta tell you I wasn't ready for a serious relationship," Miller went on. "I needed my freedom. She loved me so much, I just knew she'd always be there for me."

But she's not, is she? Bertocchini very much wanted to say to the haughty young man in his early twenties.

Stephanie's mother had put it best in describing the type. Some guys go around looking for the perfect rose, Jo-Allyn Brown had sadly explained, not realizing that all along they had a rare orchid.

"Anything bothering her?" Rosenquist asked.

"She was depressed about her weight," Miller said in the cavalier way thin people are able to talk about someone else's weight problem. "She felt she was getting too heavy. She always wanted to look good for me."

Another furtive glance at his watch.

The bottom line was that Randy Miller had a solid alibi for the night in question. It was too bad, because Bertocchini would have loved to pop this idiot.

"Look, guys, I have a date," Miller finally blurted out. "I gotta get going. Can we finish this another time?"

At that moment, Bertocchini felt a wave of sadness pass over him. Stephanie's body wasn't even in the ground yet and this guy gave his social life a higher priority than the investigation into her murder. She deserved better.

"Sure," Bertocchini said, standing. He suddenly wanted to be upwind as far as possible.

Back at his desk, Bertocchini phoned the south Sacramento field office of the California Highway Patrol, intending to leave a message for the officer who had tagged Stephanie's car at 9:40 A.M. on July 15. As it happened, the officer's shift had just ended and he was in the office, so he soon came on the line.

Bertocchini explained his interest in the abandoned Dodge Colt that the officer had recently tagged at Hood Franklin.

The CHP officer, Joseph Payne, remembered the abandoned vehicle. He explained that his shift started at 5:45 A.M. and that the first time he had driven by the location that morning was when he had tagged the car.

Bertocchini asked whether the officer had noticed if the keys had been in the car.

"They weren't in the ignition."

"What about a purse or wallet?"

"I didn't see one."

"Did you notice if the headlights were on?"

"There were no outside lights on."

By then—five hours or so after Stephanie had been abducted—the battery was no doubt already drained.

"I did notice a map on the ground."

That was something new. "Where?"

"At the rear of the car," said Officer Payne. "It was kinda crumbled up. Made me think that someone must have been lost."

"Did you pick it up?"

"I left it."

No map had been found at the location, but Bertocchini recalled how windy it was out there.

"See anything else?" he asked the patrolman.

"No, nothing. I tagged the vehicle and left."

Bertocchini and Rosenquist went back to the Hood Franklin exit. They meticulously searched both sides of the highway this time, eventually finding a crumbled map about a quarter of a mile away. It was a Mobil road map of California, folded open to the Sacramento area.

On July 19, Bertocchini and Rosenquist were invited guests at Stephanie's big Catholic funeral. It wasn't uncommon for a murderer to show keen interest in a victim's funeral or grave. In one case, a killer had visited the grave site of a victim on the anniversary of her murder and incriminated himself into a recording device hidden by police near the headstone. Now, the two detectives doggedly took down the license numbers of all 123 vehicles present.

Afterward, they hung back in the church, not going forward to visit the open casket as the mourners did following the services. The detectives had already spent their time with Stephanie. It was time now for her family and friends to say good-bye.

A few days later, Jo-Allyn Brown called Bertocchini and asked for directions to the crime scene, explaining that she and her husband wanted to see where their daughter had been found. "We just want to be in the last place she was. Somehow, we think it will help."

"Please don't go by yourselves," cautioned Bertocchini, who could only imagine how difficult the trip would be for the bereaved parents. "If you'll give me a couple of days, I'll take you myself."

That Saturday, he took the Browns where they wanted to go. They drove the route from where Stephanie's car was found on I-5 to the ditch off Highway 12. Her mother commented ominously on what a long ride it was. "I hope she was already unconscious," added Stephanie's father.

Bertocchini hadn't the heart to tell them.

THE WEEK after Stephanie's murder, the detectives were ready to turn over her Dodge Colt to her parents. The entire vehicle had been dusted inside and out for latent fingerprints. Unfortunately, the only ones found belonged to Stephanie.

Rosenquist drove the Colt, with Bertocchini following. At one point, Bertocchini had to stop for gas, but Stephanie's car had plenty.

They had found in the car a credit slip for a Sacramento Union 76 station. It was dated the night of Stephanie's disappearance. The next day, they measured the distance from the gas station to where her car had been found. It was 31.2 miles. The trip odometer on Stephanie's car, when it was found deserted on I-5, had read 31.3. Obviously, she had reset it when she bought gas that night.

During the thirty-minute drive to Loomis, Rosenquist noted that the Colt's temperature and oil pressure were within normal range. As they neared their destination, Rosenquist braked the vehicle hard several times to see if it would stall during an emergency stop, but the engine purred right along.

When they arrived, the detectives asked Jo-Allyn Brown to come outside and take a look at the car. At the crime lab, it had been discovered that the armrest and a metal shield that fit in behind the door handle on the passenger's side were lying on the floorboard.

"Do you know if the armrest might have fallen off or been removed at any point?" Rosenquist asked.

"Not that I'm aware of," said Stephanie's mother. She explained that her daughter had been proud of her little car and always took good care of it.

The broken armrest conjured up another image for the two detectives: Stephanie, who by all accounts would not have gone meekly with her abductor, struggling with someone intent on pulling her from the driver's side of the vehicle, and her desperately reaching in the opposite direction for something to hang on to.

Like the armrest.

LT. RAY BIONDI had a strong intuition that Stephanie Brown had been abducted and murdered by a serial killer. He had no real proof, just a nagging hunch wrought from long experience in such sordid matters.

As commander of Sacramento County's Homicide Bureau for a decade, Biondi had been involved in and directed more than 400 murder investigations. The majority were what cops call "smoking-gun" cases, where there is an abundance of incriminating evidence. In these cases, the killer is usually a "novice" and often someone the victim knew—a spouse, a lover, a relative, a business associate—and is quickly identified. In other cases—known in the homicide trade as "whodunits"—the killer is not so easy to find. Solving these Sherlock Holmes–type cases required skill, dedication, and perseverance on the part of the detectives assigned to them.

Serial killers, who actually enjoy making people suffer and die, represented the biggest challenge of all. And while murder is murder, their victims usually died in the most horrifying ways. Biondi had often found law enforcement to be ineffectual in stopping serial killers, in large part because of a failure either to recognize or accept that a string of seemingly unconnected killings have a common denominator. Instead of focusing on a single killer, investigators tended to scatter in divergent directions. An unsolved murder series has all the confounding aspects of any whodunit with the added urgency of a race against time: until solved the killing would continue.

Serial killers differ from common, garden-variety murderers—they kill not for money or revenge or in the heat of an argument, but randomly, and for far darker reasons known only to themselves. They have no remorse, and can be highly organized. They are hard to catch, difficult to convict, and almost impossible to comprehend. Their crimes may or may not be about sex, but they're almost always about power and control. No one can know when or where they'll hit next, or whom they'll serve up as their next victim.

During his career, Biondi had earned a reputation as one of the country's most respected experts on serial murders. He had helped capture and convict more than his share of serial killers, among them: Richard Chase, the "Vampire Killer," who in less than a month (in 1978) murdered and eviscerated four adults, a youngster, and an infant; Gerald Gallego, a second-generation killer (his father had been executed by the State of Mississippi in 1954), who raped, tortured, and killed at least six teenage girls, three young women, and one young man in California, Nevada, and Oregon (1978–80); Marty Trillo, a gardener who broke into the homes of elderly women in broad daylight and raped and killed several victims (1978–80); and Jon Dunkle, who killed one teenager and two young boys in northern California (1981–85).

Biondi understood how difficult it was to explain fully why a serial killer does what he does (almost all serial killers are, in fact, men). The rational mind views such crimes as senseless and motiveless. They make a kind of sense to the killer, to whom alone the act has meaning. To the rest of us they seem maddeningly arbitrary. Even when a serial killer is apprehended and the case solved, police and the relatives of victims are often left wondering why it happened. Biondi was convinced that a serial killer wasn't made overnight or, for that matter, born to his calling. In some instances, something very negative has happened in the perpetrator's life at a crucial age, then festered inside for a long time until it implodes and starts him killing. No matter what unresolved emotions and unfulfilled fantasies bring him to that moment, after the first time he finds it easier to do again. And he usually keeps getting better and better at killing.

True, in Stephanie Brown, police had just one dead young woman, not two or three. Yet, Biondi had little doubt that she had been a random victim, and her abduction and murder a stranger-on-stranger crime. A random victim of opportunity is usually targeted by someone who kills more than once. For these reasons, Biondi was already very much thinking series rather than one isolated, stand-alone killing.

Stephanie Brown's body had been discovered almost immediately, despite the fact that it had been partially submerged in the deep ditch bordered by heavy undergrowth located off a dead-end dirt road. Logically, she should not have been found for some time, which the killer no doubt counted on. Fate had intervened in the form of the fisherman looking for crawdads. The missing persons report had just been filed and was already being investigated, and also, the jurisdiction with the Jane Doe happened to telephone the law enforcement agency that had the "right" missing person. The match had been made quickly. In Biondi's judgment, they had gotten lucky with this one. Given the killer's modus operandi, Biondi wondered how many of the dozens of unsolved homicides involving young females in the area this guy might be responsible for.

As Stephanie Brown had been a Sacramento County missing person and a San Joaquin County murder victim, either county could have legally assumed jurisdiction in the case. Biondi brought this up when Vito Bertocchini and Pete Rosenquist came to his office.

"I don't want you guys to ever say we were quick to unload a case on you," Biondi said lightheartedly.

Rosenquist shrugged. "You've got the missing persons report, the car, and the abduction. But we've got the body."

Characteristically, Bertocchini spoke with more intensity. "We did the crime scene and the autopsy. This is our case, Ray."

Biondi agreed, even though there was a strong possibility that a serial killer was stalking the roads of *his* jurisdiction. He was impressed with the two San Joaquin detectives; they seemed capable and were taking it very seriously, as working homicide detectives are inclined to do. Biondi could only hope that they would get the support they needed in terms of man-hours and other resources from their bosses. Biondi pledged to assist the San Joaquin detectives in any way possible.

As usual in the beginning stages of a homicide investigation, there were a multitude of facts and pieces of information to sift through; they were looking for pertinent leads while eliminating the worthless ones. It took old-fashioned legwork, and a lot of it.

Take the loud knock at the door of Stephanie's Sacramento home the night she was killed, as reported by her roommate. Had it meant anything? Probably not, detectives had concluded. Door-to-door interviews with neighbors had not resulted in any reports of suspicious persons lurking about. Moreover, if someone had been waiting outside to harm her, he likely would have attacked her when she stepped out the door, alone and in the dark, rather than follow her vehicle around town, striking only after she had become lost on the highway.

There were also the obscene phone calls that Stephanie and her roommate had been receiving for some weeks. The caller was male, and Patty Burrier reported that he knew her name (but apparently not Stephanie's). This wasn't so ominous given that they had a listed phone number in

Patty's name. Also, it was a mighty big jump from obscene caller to kidnapper-rapist-killer. To the detectives, it seemed highly unlikely that these calls, disturbing as they had been for the young women, had any connection to the murder.

Detectives also uncovered a burglary report that had been filed by Stephanie five months earlier. Arriving home shortly after 8:00 P.M., she had heard noises in the back of the house. When she walked into her bedroom, she found that someone had pried open a window. The burglar had fled. Although no property was missing, the television had been unplugged and pulled away from the wall. There was nothing to suggest, however, that this aborted burglary had anything to do with her murder.

Biondi remained convinced that Stephanie's abduction had been carried out by someone unknown to her who happened upon a victim of opportunity. He found Bertocchini and Rosenquist in complete agreement.

Based on the facts of the case and what he had learned about the condition of the crime scene, Biondi speculated that they were looking for a serial killer who was at least in his thirties (most were). He was patient rather than impulsive, and experienced. Biondi assigned the killer these attributes due to the fact that the crime scene had been amazingly devoid of any incriminating evidence. Clearly, he was a hands-on killer (strangulation), as are most serial killers, with New York's "Son of Sam" the notable exception.

Biondi believed that the killer had killed before and was looking to do it again. He was a cool customer, and he knew how to cover his tracks. He had to be a consummate prowler, driving long stretches of road late at night, searching for the right situation and victim. He had found her in Stephanie Brown, who happened to be in the wrong place at the wrong time. Her killer had no doubt developed a taste for all of it—the adventure, the manipulation, the craving to act out his fantasies, and the ultimate power he felt in deciding when someone would die by his hands. Chances were very good he would not stop on his own.

A press bulletin released by the Sacramento County Sheriff's Department urgently requested that residents—particularly individuals who had traveled I-5 on the night Stephanie was abducted—contact either

Sacramento or San Joaquin investigators if they had any information concerning the Brown case. But detectives did not wait for the phone to ring.

In an unusual joint operation by both sheriff departments, with the assistance of the state road department and the California Highway Patrol, a roadblock went up on Interstate 5 at the Hood Franklin off-ramp at midnight on July 29, 1986.

The idea was to stop and talk to motorists on the same day of the week and at approximately the same hour that Stephanie Brown had been abducted two weeks earlier. Had a truck driver or late-night commuter who traveled the route regularly seen anything suspicious that night? Had anyone seen the young woman sitting in or standing next to her car? Or a second vehicle? Or another person? Could their memories be jogged by the right questions?

Interstate 5, it has been written, is "a Mississippi without romance." Cutting a direct swath through the flattest and most vapid portions of the otherwise picturesque Golden State, the highway carries 10 million travelers a year along its 853 miles of California roadway. Yet, it is undeniably the quickest route from one end of the state to the other—from the warm beaches of the south through the vast agricultural heartland to the rainswept north.

Within days of Stephanie Brown's murder, Vito Bertocchini had phoned Biondi with the idea of an I-5 roadblock to conduct a "witness canvass." It was a long shot in terms of coming up with any eyewitnesses, Biondi figured. But he saw it as an opportunity to advertise the case further through the media in the hope that the publicity might generate some new leads in a case that he sensed was in imminent danger of reaching a dead end. The randomness of the terrible crime and the likelihood that Stephanie had been killed by a complete stranger meant there was no link between her and her killer for detectives to uncover, no matter how hard they worked.

The logistics of northern California's second freeway roadblock—the first, some 30 miles northwest of Sacramento, had gone up a decade earlier to find the fugitive killers of two California highway patrolmen—had fallen to Biondi because Hood Franklin was in his county. He had tried to set it up in time for the one-week anniversary of the crime, but the state road department had balked. It would take days to move into the area the equipment and personnel required to pinch off the state's major north-south arterial. The volume of traffic, even at that late hour, would be heavy.

It was clear at midnight on July 29, and cooler than it had been the night Stephanie was killed. A stiff Delta breeze whipped the jackets of the nearly two dozen lawmen who had gathered.

Bertocchini and Pete Rosenquist had shown up with several other San Joaquin detectives. From one of their cars they unloaded a large stainless steel urn filled with hot coffee brewed at their jail. As the road crews were finishing up, the first thing everyone else did, cops being cops, was to grab a cup.

When the roadblock was finally activated, motorists were met with more than a mile of lighted cones and several large trailers with flashing arrows—enough wattage to light a major runway and bring in a 727. Beyond that, flashing red-and-blue police car lights winked angrily astride the broad freeway.

Biondi was there with his crew of detectives. Standing on the hard, asphalt surface of southbound I-5's right lane, he hoped very much that the drivers behind the line of headlights coming their way would obey the lights and temporary "One Lane Ahead," "Merge Right," and "Stop Ahead" signs. Normally, this was no place for anyone without a death wish to be loitering, flashlight and notebook in hand.

Among the first to be stopped were a station wagon from Los Angeles packed with a family headed for an Oregon camping vacation, a semi out of Fresno loaded with tomatoes, and another 18-wheeler sagging with lumber. They kept coming, despite the lateness of the hour, at a clip of two to three vehicles a minute.

"Do you travel this road regularly on Monday nights or Tuesday mornings?" drivers were asked. "Were you driving along here two weeks ago at this time?"

If they answered no, they were motioned on, although not before their license numbers were noted.

If they answered in the affirmative to either question, they were directed to a second area off to the shoulder of the highway where another group of detectives was waiting to question them more carefully.

At one point, the CHP officers up the line began hollering and waving their flashlights.

"Incoming!" someone yelled.

A car containing two elderly ladies had whizzed through the mile of flashing lights and signs without slowing down at all. At the last possible moment, the driver noticed a truck stopped in front of her and slammed on the brakes. The brakes locked up, and the car skidded for the last 200 feet through the slow lane before coming to a stop, sideways, some 10 feet short of the rear of the big rig.

By then, there wasn't a detective in sight. They'd all bailed from their positions, scattering like fallen bowling pins to the road's shoulder. There was a lot of loud grumbling after that about how anyone in their right mind would want to be a highway patrolman.

The roadblock was covered by the television and print press, which had been tipped off earlier in the day with the caution not to release advance notice to the public. In a roadside interview that night, Biondi called the canvass a "valuable exercise that may help to develop more information on a viable suspect."

Unfortunately, that didn't happen.

In all, 296 vehicles were stopped between midnight and 2:00 A.M., when the roadblock was shut down.

The resultant publicity led to dozens of phone calls from local residents over the next several days. No one interviewed by police, however, reported seeing the young woman or her abductor on I-5 that night.

On August 4, not quite a week after the roadblock, Bertocchini and Rosenquist went back to the ditch that they had gotten to know so well. They hoped that another search might turn up more evidence.

The detectives would like to have drained the ditch, but that proved impractical with the continuous irrigation going on until harvest, still two months away. So, they returned with Bertocchini's chest waders and, this time, a pole with a large magnet secured on the end. The water depth was the same as it had been every other visit to the scene: about three feet.

In the area where he'd found Stephanie's tank top, Bertocchini soon pulled up a pair of muddy scissors caught by the magnet. Wiping them off, he could clearly read "Primstyle, chrome plated." They were about 8 inches long overall, with 3-inch cutting blades. They didn't have a spot of rust on them.

Bertocchini felt certain they had found the scissors used by the killer to cut Stephanie's hair and tank top, although it would turn out there was no way to positively match the cut marks on either with the surface of the cutting blades.

When he took the scissors to a sewing and fabric shop, he was told by the proprietor that they were a right-handed model not favored by serious material cutters as they lacked an angled edge. "You'll find these in any variety store," the man added.

The sewing shop owner would be proven wrong, however, as the detective was unable to find a single retailer on the West Coast who carried the brand. He eventually tracked down the manufacturer to the Como region in Italy. With the help of a deputy D.A. friend who visited Lake Como while on vacation, the detective learned that the company, with only a dozen employees, didn't sell many scissors to the U.S. market.

Bertocchini decided to keep the discovery of the scissors hush-hush.

FOR CHARMAINE Sabrah, twenty-six, and her mother, Carmen Anselmi, fifty-two, it was supposed to be a fun night.

Saturday, August 16, 1986, was a rare evening outing for Charmaine—a working, single parent who attended Sacramento City College part-time—since delivering her infant son nine months earlier. Her mother, who had arranged for a sitter at her place, was looking forward to the mother-daughter night out, too. She hoped it would be a needed break for Charmaine.

After making sure that the sitter and baby were doing well together, they left shortly after 7:00 P.M. for Stockton and the Molino Rojo Night Club, where Charmaine's sister's fiancé, Carlos Gonzales, was appearing with his band.

Charmaine drove her two-tone brown 1973 Pontiac Grand Prix, which she had gotten out of the garage the previous week—at a cost of $145 in repairs—after having the car towed in when it had failed to start one morning.

A blue-eyed blonde with medium-length wavy hair, Charmaine had lost the weight she had put on while pregnant, and was back down to 120 pounds—well-proportioned over her 5-foot-3 frame. Dolling herself up for the night on the town, she looked stunning in a black-and-lavender blouse, a dark lavender two-thirds-length skirt, and faux alligator heels.

Shortly after they arrived at the club and found a table near the front, the band began playing. It wasn't more than a few minutes before Charmaine got the first of countless offers to dance. As the beautiful Charmaine twirled and spun across the dance floor under shimmering colored lights, Carmen realized it had been a long time since she'd seen her daughter looking so joyous and alive. Carmen knew she fretted more about Charmaine than her other offspring—no doubt lingering maternal insecurities going back to Charmaine's childhood when she had suffered cardiac difficulties that had necessitated open-heart surgery. She still carried a long scar that started under her shoulder blade and wrapped around her left side.

Life, at times, had not been easy for Charmaine. Her estranged husband had taken their two oldest children, ages two and four, to his native Sudan for a visit the previous year, and never returned. The sorrow and uncertainty of the whole situation had led to a stressful pregnancy. All of it had taken its toll.

Carmen found herself with dance partners her own age, and the festive evening slipped by all too quickly. When the house lights came on, she couldn't believe it was almost 2:00A.M. She had drunk too much, and felt woozy under the glaring lights. It was good that Charmaine was driving—not that driving was an option for Carmen, as she had never learned how. Charmaine had sipped Coke throughout the evening, politely declining all drink offers as she was still breast-feeding.

They were both hungry. As they had already made arrangements for the teenage sitter to spend the night, they decided to indulge themselves and go next door to Arroyo's, an all-night diner, for a snack.

Around 3:00 A.M., they began what should have been a forty-five-minute drive home. They hadn't been on Interstate 5 long before the engine began sputtering.

"This has never happened before," Charmaine said. The car lost power and wouldn't go any faster than 40 miles per hour. They continued on because there was no place to stop on the dark, desolate highway.

Some 20 miles north of Stockton—about halfway home—the engine quit altogether. They coasted over to the right shoulder of the road. Charmaine tried several times to restart the car. The engine would turn over, but not catch. Finally, she flooded it.

There wasn't a gas station, store, or pay phone in sight.

Although both women had heard of the I-5 murder—as had virtually everyone in the Greater Sacramento area who read a newspaper or watched television—neither of them realized that their car had broken down not far from where Stephanie Brown had been abducted from her car a month earlier.

Charmaine turned on the emergency flashers and got out. She opened the hood, but couldn't see a thing in the dark. She knew very little about engines anyway.

Back inside the car, Charmaine turned on the overhead dome light so they wouldn't be in the dark and rolled down the driver's window. Whenever a vehicle whizzed by, she put her arm out the window and waved, hoping to attract a passing Good Samaritan.

After thirty minutes and no luck, she rolled up the window. They discussed trying to reach a residence on foot—they could see a light far off in the distance—but decided to stay put. With Charmaine fighting back tears, they agreed their best option—since Charmaine didn't have auto club towing service—was to wait for a Highway Patrol unit to come along and take them to a phone, where they could call Carlos, who lived in Stockton, for a ride home.

"But you know, Mom, when you really want a cop they're never there," Charmaine bravely joked.

Carmen could see how anxious her daughter was. They had shared their concerns about the car being struck by a passing vehicle. Yet, it seemed safer to remain inside than to stand or walk on the dark roadside. The baby was clearly on Charmaine's mind, too, and she expressed regret for having left him. She had already missed one nursing at his bedtime, and had complained at the restaurant about tenderness in her breasts.

Sleepy and cold, they were startled about thirty minutes later when a pair of headlights shone brightly through the car's rear window. Though they hadn't heard the vehicle approaching, someone had pulled up right behind them. Carmen turned in her seat to see if she could tell whether or not it was a police car. Blinded by the bright lights, she couldn't make out anything.

Charmaine, who had been nestled in the middle of the bench-style front seat next to her mother, slid over to the driver's side and, without hesitation, climbed out.

Carmen was not about to let her daughter go alone. Once she was outside, a brisk wind hit her like a welcome slap in the face. She was glad to see Charmaine cut between the vehicles and approach the other car from the passenger's side. With speeding traffic barreling by only a few steps away, it was the safe thing to do.

Carmen could now see it was not a police car, but a dark sports car of some kind with one person inside. She stayed near the back bumper of their car while Charmaine leaned in the open passenger's window of the other vehicle.

After a few seconds, Charmaine straightened up. "He wants to know if we need any help," she said.

Carmen came up behind her daughter and bent toward the open window. "Yes, we could use a ride to a phone. But I don't know where one is. …"

"I know where there's a phone close by," said the man behind the wheel.

"Okay, then."

As there was only room for one passenger, Carmen said she would go.

"You sure, Mom?" Charmaine asked.

"Yes. I want you to go back to the car and lock yourself in."

They returned to the Pontiac, Carmen to get her purse, which Charmaine handed to her.

"Will you be all right?" Carmen asked.

"Sure. I'll lock the doors."

As she turned away, Carmen was pleased to hear the comforting click of a door lock.

The ride up the highway was uneventful. The man, in his forties or fifties with graying hair and wearing a dingy T-shirt, said very little. When he did speak, such as to mention that he had a business in Sacramento, his voice was so low that Carmen had difficulty hearing him, even sitting so close to him in the cramped two-seater.

Carmen told him about the dance that night, confessing that some members of her family would not have approved because they were "missionary Christians."

The man snickered.

He was familiar with this area, he had assured her, and knew exactly where the nearest pay phone was located. They passed one or two exits before taking an off-ramp. Carmen was not nervous, as the man seemed calm and well-intentioned. As a matter of fact, she felt very lucky that he had stopped for them.

Sure enough, not far off the highway he drove directly to some kind of store with a pay phone out front. Although the store was closed, an overhead light lit the area. He parked alongside and Carmen got out.

She dialed Carlos's number and let it ring at least a dozen times before hanging up. She tried again, in case she had misdialed. There was still no answer. Next, she tried her daughter in Sacramento who was engaged to the band leader. No answer. Her grown son, Bruce, still lived with her at home, but Carmen didn't have a phone. It was too late to call a neighbor to awaken her son, or to phone any of her friends for help. Standing in the phone booth at four o'clock in the morning with a stranger waiting to take her back down the highway, she couldn't think of anyone else to call at this hour. The thought flitted through her mind to phone the Highway Patrol, but she had no idea where she was or how to explain their location. She didn't even know the license number of Charmaine's car. Saying that they were broken down in a brown car "halfway between Stockton and Sacramento" probably wouldn't be enough.

She could see that the man, obscured by shadows inside his darkened car, was still waiting patiently. Suppose he changed his mind and drove away? It was late for him, too, and he probably wanted to get home. If he left her here, how would she get back? She couldn't leave Charmaine *alone* on the interstate.

So, Carmen did the only thing she could think of at that moment: she left the phone booth and hurried back to the sports car. She wanted very much to rejoin her daughter. Together, they would figure something out.

The man started his car without saying anything. Carmen volunteered that she hadn't been able to reach anyone. She asked him to please take her back.

He took the next exit south of where they had broken down, crossed over the overpass, and took a long, lazy circle to merge with northbound traffic. When they came upon Charmaine's car, he pulled up behind it and cut his engine, which he hadn't done the first time.

When Carmen got out, Charmaine was already heading her way. Carmen explained that she hadn't been able to reach Carlos, and didn't know who else to call.

"What are we going to do, Mom?" Charmaine asked.

"I can take you home," offered the man, still sitting behind the wheel. "One at a time. That's all I have room for."

"That's so nice of you," said Carmen, genuinely impressed with the man's helpfulness.

Standing next to the sports car, mother and daughter talked. It was close to 5:00 A.M., and the sun would be up soon. Once home, they could certainly round up Bruce and Carlos to help with the car. They decided to take the nice man up on his offer to get them off the interstate.

"I think you should go first, honey," Carmen said. "I know you're worried about the baby. You need to get back to feed him when he wakes up."

"You'll be okay?"

"Yeah, I'll lock myself in. It'll be light soon. You need to get back."

Charmaine seemed relieved. She grabbed her purse and got into the man's car.

Carmen watched as they pulled away, exchanging brief waves with her daughter.

It was the last time she saw Charmaine.

CHAPTER FOUR

Surrendering to a bone-deep fatigue, Carmen Anselmi settled into the backseat soon after her daughter left, and stretched out as best she could.

About 9:00 A.M., she awoke with a start to the sound of a man's voice.

Turning in the seat, she saw that a black-and-white Highway Patrol car had pulled up close on the right side of the car. The officer had his window down.

With some effort, Carmen rolled down hers.

"Hello," she said groggily.

"Do you need assistance, ma'am?"

"I think someone is coming. At least, I *hope* they are," she said, smiling weakly.

"I can take you to a phone if you'd like," the officer said.

Carmen checked her watch. She was surprised to see that four hours had passed. Probably the man had decided he didn't have time to come back for her. She couldn't blame him.

It was getting so late now, Carmen figured her son would show up sometime soon. But weary of waiting in the car, she accepted the offer, and left a note on the windshield.

The officer drove Carmen to the same pay phone that the man in the sports car had taken her to hours earlier. This time she noticed that it was directly off the Walnut Grove Road exit of I-5. In the daylight, she was also able to see that the store, although not yet open, was a large produce mart.

She called her kindly neighbor, Walter Hicks, who was accustomed to taking messages for the family. Telling him exactly where she was, she asked him to tell her son to pick her up not at Charmaine's car, but at the phone she was calling from. She gave him the number in case her son had already left. If he had left, the neighbor promised, he'd call her back right away. In that event, Carmen would know she'd have to find a way back to the car.

After the CHP left, Carmen waited by herself. She was glad the phone didn't ring. About forty-five minutes later, her son pulled up.

Once she was inside the car, Bruce told his mother how confused he'd been by her message. "What's this about Charmaine's car? And where's Charmaine?"

Carmen went numb.

When they returned home and found that Charmaine had still not shown up—a neighbor lady was watching the baby at Carmen's—she had Bruce take her to Charmaine's apartment. Using a key her daughter had given her some time back, Carmen went inside but could find no sign that her daughter had come home. They went directly to the nearest police station, where Carmen filed a missing persons report.

Given the nature of Charmaine's disappearance and the high probability of foul play, the normal twenty-four-hour waiting period for adult missing persons was not observed. Immediately, a statewide teletype was sent out providing law enforcement agencies with a description of the missing young woman, her attire, the dark sports car she rode off in, and the quiet man behind the wheel who had seemed so helpful.

Based on Carmen's information, the driver was described as a white man in his forties or fifties, about 5-foot-8 to 5–10, between 150 and 180 pounds, gray or graying hair, and clean shaven. When last seen, he was wearing a T-shirt and some kind of dark-colored pants.

Carmen was beside herself for letting her daughter get into the stranger's car. She had been disarmed, Carmen realized, not only by the man's having been so nice but also because he brought her back to the car without trying any funny business. She was haunted by her motherly words of advice to Charmaine: "You should go first, honey.… You need to get back …"

Now home, Carmen broke down soon after her neighbor left. When her infant grandson began fussing, she pulled herself together. Warming the last of the mother's milk Charmaine had expressed the night before, Carmen sat down and fed the baby.

Struggling under a heavy canopy of remorse and helplessness, Carmen willed herself to remain hopeful. She prayed that her daughter would be found alive, somehow, somewhere. *Maybe*, she thought, *the man had dropped Charmaine off in an isolated area and she was at that very moment hiking out to find help.*

As she fed the infant in her arms, Carmen could not possibly know then that she would end up raising this little grandson of hers.

CHARMAINE SABRAH had vanished without a trace in San Joaquin County, three miles south of the Sacramento County line.

The missing persons case was assigned to Vito Bertocchini due to the possibility that it was the work of whoever had abducted and killed Stephanie Brown. Brown's body had been found right away, and Bertocchini had known it was murder from the beginning. Stephanie had been his unidentified murder victim and someone else's missing person. This time, he had a missing person but no body.

Bertocchini considered the similarities in the cases striking. Both young women had disappeared on Interstate 5 within 15 miles of each other during the wee hours of the morning after pulling their cars over to the shoulder of the road. The main difference (and it *was* significant): in Sabrah, there had been an eyewitness. That, the detective thought, had been a very bold move whether or not it was the work of Brown's killer.

At the scene, detectives found the disabled Pontiac still parked at the shoulder. Searching the immediate area, Bertocchini bagged two empty Coors cans and an empty pack of Marlboros, which he gave to a Technical Services deputy to check for latent prints. At the time, Bertocchini didn't know that the man had remained in his own vehicle, so he had the door handles, hood, and trunk of Charmaine's car dusted for prints before it was towed away.

About then, the department's Flex Team, a squad of unassigned patrol officers led by a sergeant, arrived to provide extra manpower. They would carefully search the area, intersecting roadways, and ditches for any sign of the victim, her abductor, his vehicle, and any other possible physical evidence.

Bertocchini headed to Sacramento to meet with Carmen Anselmi. In the middle-aged woman who answered the door and showed him in—she apologized listlessly for still wearing the clothes she'd gone dancing in the night before—he found a distraught mother racked with guilt. It touched a nerve to see Charmaine's infant son nestled in his grandmother's arms. Most everyone who disappears is missed by someone, but this void was particularly heartbreaking.

For the next hour, Carmen recited everything she could remember leading up to her daughter's disappearance. When it came to expanding on her rather skimpy description of the suspect, she offered that he had been "pale-looking," had a "big nose," and spoke in a soft voice.

It wasn't much.

"Do you remember the dome light coming on in his car when the door opened?" Bertocchini asked.

"No, it stayed dark."

Of course, the detective thought.

"Anything else you can remember?"

"He was very quiet and calm. He just drove."

As for the suspect's car, the detective tried to work with Carmen in order to come up with the make of the vehicle. But as a lifelong non-driver, she was so unfamiliar with cars that it proved unproductive. She could only recall its being small, two-door, dark-colored, with a front hood that sloped downward, two bucket seats with "sort of wool-ish" seat covers, and a straight gearshift on the floor. That covered, the detective knew, dozens of models of American and foreign-built cars on the road.

Bertocchini was disappointed. He had hoped that Carmen Anselmi would, under gentle prodding, be able to recollect more details. She had, after all, been inside the man's car and sat practically shoulder-to-shoulder with him during the ride up the highway. But she had admitted to drinking at the nightclub. Alcohol, the darkness of the highway, and the lateness of the hour could all be contributing factors. The detective began to wonder—in the event they ever put a suspect in a lineup—whether their one and only eyewitness would be able to pick out the man who had driven away with Charmaine.

As Bertocchini was ready to leave, Carmen put down the sleeping baby and walked him to the door.

"Detective, something's been bothering me. I'm wondering why—I mean, I was *in* the car with him."

Bertocchini nodded. He knew what was coming.

"Why didn't he take me?" she asked.

"We can't know these things," he said soothingly. "It's really no use speculating."

There—he was relieved he'd found a tactful way to respond. The truth, no doubt, was harsher. The scumbag hadn't wanted Mom. The young, pretty daughter was another story. He'd thrown the old lady back like an undersized trout for a chance at snagging a better catch.

That the suspect had left behind an eyewitness nagged at Bertocchini. Had it been like an uncontrollable feeding frenzy when he came across a young woman he wanted? Had he been willing to overlook some things for a chance to have her? Or was he growing more arrogant, believing no one could stop him?

Carmen, eager to help, agreed to assist in coming up with an artist's composite. A few days later, Bertocchini picked her up and they drove south past Berkeley and Oakland to San Jose, where Carmen had a long session with Officer Tom Macris, a talented composite artist with that city's police department. With Carmen selecting a nose, a forehead, ears, hair, lips, and other facial characteristics from a wide range of generic types, Macris crafted them together. The result was a pen-and-ink sketch of a middle-aged man with eyes set wide apart above an eagle-like nose, long slicked-back hair tucked behind flattened ears, and a lined forehead.

Bertocchini had hundreds of copies of the composite printed up and sent in a special bulletin to police departments up and down the state, alerting detectives and officers from the Oregon to the Mexican border that this "passing motorist" was wanted for questioning in the disappearance of Charmaine Sabrah, who was shown in a recent photograph. Released to the local news media, the likenesses of the suspect and missing woman ran in newspapers and on television. Also, handbills of the composite were widely posted in public places and retail outlets in and around Stockton and Sacramento.

Within the first week, a wave of calls—the majority anonymous—came in from residents reporting that they had seen someone who looked like the composite. These tips resulted in a list of nineteen names, each of whom was contacted in person by detectives. The majority of them were eliminated on the spot, although several were not. Those with a passing likeness to the composite were questioned and had their pictures taken. One man even owned a black two-seater sports car, although it was noted that while he did look a little like the drawing, he was younger and had dark hair with no gray. Another man, the salesman of the month at a local Chevy dealer, was found to be tall, skinny, well tanned, and wearing glasses on a delicate-boned, pinch-nosed Barney Fife face. "This guy must have cheated *someone*," a detective joked to his partner before writing NO WAY next to the salesman's name.

Other calls came in from people claiming to have seen Charmaine. "She was covered in mud and looked dazed and confused," reported the owner of a convenience store in the foothills northeast of Sacramento. She said the young woman was in the company of a Hispanic male—three days after Charmaine's disappearance. "She came in and asked where she was, then walked out. She looked like the missing girl on TV."

More calls came from frightened women reporting suspicious men they had encountered on the road. A twenty-year-old woman told of a fiftyish white male with graying hair pulling up next to her in a red BMW and "checking me out" before he took the next exit. She did not get the license number.

Another young woman traveling with her girlfriend and two small children stated that her car had broken down on I-5 the day before Charmaine disappeared. A "very friendly" man in his fifties, stocky, about 5-foot-9, with gray hair and a thick Irish brogue, had stopped. He volunteered to take someone into the nearest town to a phone, but since he was driving a car with hardly any backseat he said he couldn't take all of them. The women rejected his offer. The man relented and transported the women and children to the nearest town—safely, if a bit cramped.

A twenty-nine-year-old Stockton woman reported having a flat tire on southbound I-5 and calling for assistance on her CB radio. In a few minutes, a would-be savior arrived in a satiny dress and red high heels but looking suspiciously "like a man ... [who] did not walk gracefully in heels, had a deep voice and a protruding Adam's apple." An offer for a ride to a phone was declined.

Bertocchini stayed busy during the first week of the investigation. He interviewed neighbors of Carmen Anselmi's to determine if anyone had seen Charmaine return to her mother's apartment early on the morning of her disappearance, or since. No one had.

He went to Charmaine's apartment with her mother, who indicated that none of her daughter's clothes appeared to be missing. There were no signs of theft or ransacking. Some dirty dishes were in the sink, but there were no signs of a recent meal. The neighbors were interviewed; none had seen Charmaine since her disappearance, or observed anyone else entering or leaving the apartment.

The detective interviewed family members, phoning Charmaine's father, John Byerly, in Arizona and visiting her sister, Angela, at her Sacramento residence. Both confirmed it would be out of character for Charmaine to take off impulsively on an extended trip with a complete stranger. They also dismissed any possibility that Charmaine had flown to Sudan to find her other children.

Bertocchini went to the Stockton nightclub where Charmaine and Carmen had spent their last evening together. Employees remembered both women dancing, but didn't notice anyone eyeing the women from afar or acting suspiciously. When the women left, they had been alone. While two employees—a waitress and security guard—thought the composite of the suspect might be a patron of the club, several other employees, including the longtime bartender, did not remember anyone who looked like that.

At the club, the detective interviewed Carlos Gonzales, the band leader and Carmen's future son-in-law. He didn't recognize the face in the composite, either, and had nothing to offer.

On a Friday evening—six days after Charmaine's disappearance—Bertocchini stopped by the Stockton Holiday Inn, where the local chapter of the Civil Air Patrol was meeting to discuss routine flying exercises scheduled for Saturday morning.

The detective addressed the members, many of whom had already heard about the case. He admitted that investigators were stumped. Pinpointing on a map the exact location on I-5 where Charmaine's car had broken down, he asked if they would undertake an aerial search of northern San Joaquin County and southern Sacramento County the next day, looking for any sign of the dark-colored sports car or the missing woman.

The following morning, two dozen private aircraft lifted off one after the other into a hazy sky from Stockton Municipal Airport, heading for numbered search sectors.

By day's end, the weary pilots and observers had found absolutely nothing to report.

TWO WEEKS later, along about dusk some 30 miles southeast of Sacramento, Marty Mortin, a twenty-two-year-old Hispanic who worked at Lighthouse Marina in Isleton, a sleepy Delta community of a few hundred residents on the north shore of Brannan Island, was bird hunting with his trusty black Lab.

Working his way down a seldom-used shoreline road along the San Joaquin River on the deserted south end of the island, Mortin hadn't even gotten a shot off yet or seen a single bird when his dog froze, head and tail erect.

The Lab bolted seconds later, moving quickly down a dirt levee that dropped to the river. Just before reaching the water, he dove into the heavy brush.

"Amigo!" Mortin hollered to no avail.

It was unlike Amigo to become distracted.

Mortin followed, taking a step or two down the levee. He spotted Amigo on full alert in the thick vegetation 10 feet away.

Mortin brought the powerful pump shotgun to his shoulder and waited. He was too experienced a hunter to fire before he knew what he was shooting at.

Amigo let loose with a confusing combination of whine and deep-throated growl, unlike anything Mortin had heard from the retriever before.

What the hell?

Mortin lowered the gun and took a few tentative steps forward. He saw something on the ground. He stared, incredulous. It was a foot sticking out of the bushes. A human foot.

He took another slow-motion step or two forward, and saw a stiff and discolored hand and arm. The hunter understood at that moment, as a strong stench overtook him, that his dog had tracked a dead body. He immediately pulled the agitated dog by his collar away from the remains.

Back on the road, Mortin slipped a shotgun shell out of his sportsman's vest and placed it on the ground so as to mark the spot.

With Amigo at his side, he sprinted the 100 yards to where his old pickup was parked. Driving the 3 miles up Jackson Slough Road to Isleton as fast as he dared on his lousy shocks, he banged futilely on the locked door of the one-room police station.

Mortin knew a California Highway Patrol officer who lived down the street. He hurried to his place, interrupting the family's late-summer barbecue with the grisly news.

As the CHP officer drove Mortin back to the opposite end of the island, he radioed to his dispatcher to notify the Sacramento County Sheriff's Department, which had jurisdiction in this unincorporated area.

When a sheriff's patrol unit received the call, it happened to be cruising very nearby on Highway 12, which bisected Brannan Island via bridges at either end. The lone deputy was first on the scene.

When the CHP unit pulled up a few minutes later, Mortin left Amigo curled up in the backseat and took both officers down to the body.

It was located about halfway down the levee, which sloped 45 degrees to the river. Just past the body a few feet, the levee dropped off straight to the water.

By the time the corpse was removed from the bushes and zipped into a white plastic body bag for the ride to the coroner's in downtown Sacramento, it was nearly 11:00 P.M.

Even in the darkness, some things had been apparent to investigators under the beams of their flashlights. She looked to be a young white woman. She was nude from the waist up. Her hands were bound behind her back, and the binding was looped around her neck.

She had, no doubt, been strangled.

CHAPTER FIVE

Any question Sacramento County Sheriff's Detective Stan Reed had as to whether the Jane Doe found on Brannan Island might be the young woman motorist missing for three weeks was answered when the veteran homicide investigator showed up at the morgue in the morning.

As Reed entered the lime-green autopsy suite in the basement of the two-story building that housed the county's Forensic Services Center, two technicians in scrubs were removing Jane Doe from the body bag atop a waist-high metal table. Her exposed skin looked more like sunbaked shoe leather than flesh. She had been dead for so long—*months*, not weeks—that the remaining skin had mummified.

Reed was working the case without his usual partner, Detective Bob Bell, which sometimes happened when accumulated caseloads became so heavy; in this way, two detectives could handle twice as many cases.

When Lt. Ray Biondi received a call at home the previous evening regarding the hunter's macabre discovery, the homicide chief knew that Reed, the anchor of the four-man Bureau, was unavailable. Although Reed was officially on call, he was attending his wife's grandfather's hundredth birthday party in Gridley, a one-horse town 60 miles north of Sacramento. It was unusual for Reed to miss a call out, which was why Biondi had granted his most experienced detective the night off. Biondi decided to assign this one to Reed anyway, although another detective would have to be called to handle the crime scene. Biondi suspected that if Reed had had any notion that a new case would come up that night, Stan's wife, Roberta, might well have found herself attending the family celebration alone. Stan Reed was that dedicated to solving murders.

Reed had joined the department seventeen years earlier. He had worked Homicide about half that time, participating in more than 300 homicide investigations. Over the years, his waistline had thickened as surely as his now-graying blondish hair had thinned atop his 6-foot frame. He was a tell-it-like-it-is guy. With Stan Reed, you got no flowers, no mind games, no hidden agendas. Because he was so blunt—whether interviewing witnesses or testifying in court—Biondi knew that Reed could at times come off as cold and uncaring. Nothing was farther from the truth. He was simply all business. He was also dependable, covered all the bases, and *never* gave up on his old cases. Biondi considered Stan Reed to be one of the best homicide detectives he had ever known. To a degree, Biondi considered Reed's ascendancy in Homicide a matter of fate. When Reed joined the department in 1969, at age twenty-five, he was randomly assigned badge 187; in California, "187" is the police code for homicide, as first-degree murder with malice aforethought was a violation of California Penal Code Section 187.

Reed had joined Homicide in 1978. At his first homicide scene, he drew the unenviable job of searching for body parts in garbage cans and Dumpsters in an effort to pick up the trail of Sacramento's fiendish "Vampire Killer." Reed had not complained or made excuses that day, nor since. Whenever the inevitable telephone call came to respond to another scene of unspeakable violence, whether it was three in the morning or during a holiday dinner, he offered no hint of a night's sleep cut short or a personal life intruded upon.

Before showing up at the morgue for the autopsy, Reed had driven south on Interstate 5 for half an hour—beyond where Stephanie Brown's abandoned car had been found and then, a few minutes later, past where Charmaine Sabrah's car had broken down northbound. He turned west onto Highway 12 at its intersection with I-5. Ten miles beyond where Brown's body had been found, he came to where Jane Doe had been discovered. Both locations, he noted, were no more than a mile off Highway 12.

Knowing it had been dark during recovery of the body the previous night, he made a careful check of the area for any evidence, but found none.

Taking it all in at the scene, Reed was in his usual attire of wash-and-wear slacks, button-down shirt sans tie, and an old tan corduroy blazer that his wife usually had to peel off him to have cleaned.

Standing on the narrow, sloped levee that separated the river from the road by only 20 feet, Reed figured that the victim had been killed elsewhere and transported here. It looked like the killer had dumped the body from the road and that it rolled down the embankment before stopping short of the water.

At the autopsy later that morning, the pathologist began by taking a close look at the ligature, which appeared to be an article of clothing. It had been rolled tightly and looped once around the victim's neck, with the remaining portion used to bind her wrists behind her back. The material was knotted twice behind her neck.

Reed recalled that Stephanie Brown had died by ligature strangulation. He added this to the list of similarities between the two cases. But still, he would be careful not to jump to the conclusion that they were the work of the same killer. Not now or any time soon. Stan Reed simply did not operate that way.

Reed was struck by how high the dead woman's hands and wrists were pulled up behind her back by the taut binding. The closer he looked, the more the angle seemed anatomically impossible. He was somewhat surprised when the pathologist reported no broken bones in her arms or wrists.

She had been hogtied so securely that Reed could picture the killer cinching the binding tighter and tighter before finally tying it off. At that point, he could have stood back and watched, as any effort by the victim to try to lessen the strain on her arms would have pulled the loop around her neck that much tighter. She may well have ended up strangling herself.

How quickly death came, no one, not even the pathologist, could say for certain. However long it had been, Reed knew it wasn't quick enough. Her agony was frozen on the death mask: a blackened tongue extended out from her mouth torturously, clasped firmly between her teeth.

The pathologist cut the ligature at two places to remove it. Deep ligature marks were found embedded in the skin at the front of the neck. The filthy, coiled material turned out to be a pink, ribbed tank top. To document how they had fit together, the pathologist meticulously strung the now three separate pieces together with twine.

The victim was wearing designer blue jeans, black suede–type loafers, and gray socks. Checking the pockets and finding nothing, the pathologist slit the jeans up both sides to remove them. Underneath were bikini panties.

The autopsy took less time than usual. The skull contained no brain matter at all, and when the pathologist opened the abdominal cavity he found it swarming with maggots and devoid of any major organs.

Given the delay in discovery of the body and the degree of decomposition, biological specimens such as blood, semen, and saliva could not be recovered. As a result, there would be no rape kit done or lab work to conduct. The only specimens taken from the body were strands of brown hair: head and pubic. These were sealed in an envelope and, along with the victim's clothes, marked with the case number and placed for the time being in a coroner's locker.

In his report, the pathologist described the body as a "well-developed, well-nourished adult white female about nineteen years old, plus or minus two years." She was estimated to have stood about 5-foot-4. The cause of death, he concluded, had been ligature strangulation.

A dentist on contract with the coroner's office showed up at the morgue the next day and charted the victim's teeth and dental work. For identification purposes, he also made impressions of her bite. Later that same day, a Sheriff's Technical Services deputy came to fingerprint the victim. Due to the deteriorating condition of the flesh, he was afraid the usual method of inking each finger and rolling it over a print card wouldn't work. So, he asked a coroner's technician to snip off the fingers at the first joint. Returning to his lab at the sheriff's department with the collection of fingertips, the deputy made plaster casts of each one. From the casts he was able to make readable print impressions.

Twelve days after the autopsy, a Sacramento County criminalist removed the hair samples from the secured locker. Also, because he knew that prosecutors liked having the murder weapon, he took the tank top used to strangle the victim. The remainder of her clothing was left behind in the coroner's locker.

Upstairs, he placed the hair samples and the tank top in freezer storage for safekeeping. Before doing so he wrote on an oversized manila envelope that now held the tank top: "Item 3—Ligature around neck to hands."

The criminalist didn't notice that the tank top, when unfolded, had numerous cuts in it unrelated to the two well-documented slices made by the pathologist in removing the ligature.

Neither had anyone else.

STAN REED considered it a tragic commentary on our times that female body dumps were so common, and that the great majority of unidentified murder victims in America were women.

Each day his Jane Doe remained unidentified, Reed knew the chances of ever solving the case were reduced. It was a rare individual who wasn't missed. More likely, she had been reported as missing by someone, somewhere. The trick was to find that report wherever it might be, and match it to the unidentified remains at the morgue.

Reed checked with Detective Sergeant Harry Machen to see if there were any persons reported missing to their department within the last few months who fit Jane Doe's general description. Finding no likely candidates, he broadened his search to include the extensive files of the Missing Persons Unit of the California Department of Justice (DOJ), which was set up as a statewide clearinghouse to try to match the unidentified dead—through dental charts and fingerprints—with reported missing persons. However, the system for reporting to the DOJ was strictly voluntary, and this posed problems. Many agencies, including Reed's own department, did not always submit their missing persons reports to DOJ in a timely manner. Some agencies never turned them in at all, while others resisted taking the reports in the first place, knowing that a majority of adult missing persons would one day surface on their own. Why spend valuable investigative man-hours when a crime might not have been committed?

Even when a report did get to the DOJ, the odds were against a missing person being matched with an unidentified body. At the time, DOJ had on file the dental charts and fingerprints of approximately 1,400 unidentified dead. Each year, DOJ makes only ten to fifteen matches of unidentified dead with missing persons.

When Reed received the list of missing young women from DOJ, he went down the list looking for individuals who would seem to fit the description of his Jane Doe. Working the phone, a detective's most valuable tool, he learned that a large number of possibles were no longer missing. He crossed them off.

Of those young women still missing—

Cindy Stites, twenty-three, of northern California, was eliminated by comparing her driver's license thumbprint with Jane Doe's prints.

Lisa Beckham, nineteen, of Florida, believed to be on her way to California when she disappeared, was eliminated because it turned out she was several inches too short.

Angelica Lee, nineteen, believed to be California-bound from her native Georgia, was eliminated by fingerprint comparisons.

Two California women in their early thirties—Glenda Ward and Renee June—who seemed too old were looked at nonetheless before being eliminated on fingerprint comparisons.

About then, the Homicide Bureau found itself deluged with a number of new murders. Reed caught the case of Vickie Skanks, an eleven-year-old girl who was sexually assaulted and smothered to death in her family home. He quickly identified a strong suspect but, much to Reed's dismay, he couldn't be charged with murder due to problems with the DNA evidence. While refusing to give up on that investigation, Reed's caseload grew as Sacramento County's murder rate kept climbing that summer and fall.

Still, it wasn't in Reed to forget Jane Doe.

MIDWAY between Stockton and Sacramento on a clear, gusty night one month after Charmaine Sabrah's disappearance, an older sedan traveling the speed limit northbound on Interstate 5 braked to a stop on the shoulder.

It was no coincidence that the driver, a thirty-five-year-old woman, had pulled over very near where Charmaine's Grand Prix had come to a stop.

After turning on the emergency flashers, the woman climbed out of the car and stood at its rear bumper, illuminated by the winking red lights.

Although passersby saw what appeared to be a disabled vehicle with a lone female needing help, there was nothing wrong with the car at all. And, as for the woman, she was far from alone.

San Joaquin County Sheriff's Detective Joyce Holloman was, in fact, live bait placed in a trap to entice a serial killer.

Detectives in four unmarked vehicles were close by—up on the next exit, under the freeway overpass, and on the frontage road. They were in radio contact with each other, and one of the cars monitored Detective Holloman's every utterance via a remote wire she wore under her jacket.

Then there was Vito Bertocchini with a portable radio, hiding none too comfortably in the brambles nearby, within earshot of Holloman. The decoy officer was under strict instructions not to get into anyone's car, and the burly homicide detective was close by to make sure nobody tried to snatch her. As he had promised the nervous Holloman, he would be the "mugger" or the "shooter"—whatever was required to protect her.

When a vehicle stopped, the plan was for Holloman to send the license number out over the wire. If someone stopped who looked like the composite, she would alert the others. Then, she would try to get him to leave—"Thanks for stopping, my husband is on the way." Once he left, the detectives would stop the car down the highway.

It was nearly two hours before the first vehicle, a black-and-silver pickup, pulled up behind the sedan. The man did not resemble the composite, and his offer to render assistance seemed genuine. Holloman got rid of him by saying that help was on the way.

The second vehicle, a Volkswagen with Florida plates, didn't stop until 3:00 A.M. The driver, a college-age male who looked young enough to be the son of the man in the composite, also seemed sincere. So much so that he insisted on raising the hood of the undercover vehicle and tinkering with the engine under the beam of his flashlight. Holloman quickly got behind the wheel, and the car started right away. The young man seemed very pleased with himself.

For Bertocchini, the big rats scurrying about him in the bushes were the worst part of the assignment. They refused to leave him be. "If you hear gunshots," he radioed the other detectives at one point, "it's gonna be me taking out a few of these freaking monsters."

At 3:45 A.M., the operation was shut down. Of an estimated 350 vehicles to pass Detective Holloman in four hours, only the pickup and VW had stopped.

The detectives were back out on I-5 the next night from 11:30 P.M. until 3:30 A.M. Two vehicles, a van and a white Toyota, stopped within the first half hour. A station wagon pulled over the second hour, and two big rigs stopped the final hour. Five would-be Good Samaritans out of 400 vehicles. Once again the license numbers were duly logged, even though no one who stopped looked at all like the composite. At least this night went a little better for Bertocchini: he brought along a big stick to beat back his tormentors.

The next day, Bertocchini was ordered by his supervisor to shut down the decoy detail. He was sorely disappointed, not so much with the lack of success in only two nights but at not being able to continue. He had known, going in, that they would be incredibly lucky to snare a killer in just a night or two. He had hoped they could stay with it for a week or ten days.

He filed a one-page report on the decoy detail. The unsuccessful operation that had tied up six detectives for two nights revealed, Bertocchini knew, just how desperate they were for viable leads.

Bertocchini submitted all the pertinent details of Stephanie Brown's abduction and murder to the FBI's Behavioral Science Unit at Quantico, Virginia, to see what the profilers could come up with in terms of painting a likely picture of the killer.

They responded in writing quickly:
1. The location and condition of victim's vehicle when found was puzzling. This vehicle was found with the light switch in an "on" position, both doors unlocked, and the driver's window down. This indicates to us the victim was pulled over or stopped without evidencing any apprehension or fear.
2. In all probability, the victim was lost, or at least going in the wrong direction when confronted by her assailant, as indicated by the direction of the vehicle.

3. No indication of struggle by the victim could be an indication of her experiencing extreme fear or suffering physical restraint.
4. There is nothing to support the concept of two assailants involved in this crime.
5. The victim died of choking and the body showed no evidence of her attempting to frantically remove the ligature. This supports that she was restrained by some method which limited the movement of her arms and hands.
6. The cutting of the victim's blouse and hair could have been a form of intimidation, control, or degradation.
7. In our opinion, the assailant was familiar with the dump site because of the remote location of same. The method of body disposal suggests that the assailant was without any remorse.
8. Although we are unable to determine the time of the victim's last consensual sexual activity, the amount of sexual activity evidenced does not reflect the presence of two assailants.
9. Some assailants are known to engage in choking during their sexual activities. This choking enhances their sexual stimulation. It is possible that the strangulation suffered by the victim may have been the result of that type of sexual activity.

Was this how it had come down? Reed wondered.

WHEN THE phone rang at home on the afternoon of Sunday, November 9, 1986, criminalist Jim Streeter of the California Department of Justice Crime Laboratory in Sacramento had a feeling it might be work.

DOJ's Sacramento lab served fourteen mostly small, rural counties in northern California that did not have their own crime labs, or criminalists on the payroll. Criminalists—skilled forensic scientists trained in the identification, collection, and preservation of physical evidence—are most often called in to assist in serious criminal cases such as murder, bombings, and arson. They conduct lab tests on the evidence, prepare reports, and testify as expert witnesses.

A criminalist usually has a special area of expertise. In Streeter's case, it was serology. However, Streeter, who had gone to work for DOJ directly out of college thirteen years earlier, had undergone intensive FBI training in processing crime scene evidence and handling serial murder investigations. As a result, he was sent out to a lot of crime scenes—over the years he had worked seven serial killer cases and countless other murders. He much preferred going to the scene to waiting back at the lab.

A criminalist's function at a crime scene varied from collection (or merely helping with the collection) of evidence to the interpretation of physical evidence such as trajectories of bullets, blood splatters, position and location of bodies, drag marks to determine how the victims came to those positions, and what exactly happened to them leading up to their murder.

One reason Streeter preferred being on the scene himself was that evidence collected by others could be innocently contaminated by people who didn't know any better. Also, he would never really know its relationship to the crime scene as a whole. He could be shown photographs, but they were nothing more than a one-dimensional moment in time, usually well after the crime. His own senses of sight, sound, smell, and touch could tell him much more. Had the article of clothing found behind a tree been dropped there or was it thrown? Was the body meant to be found or had there been an attempt at concealment? All of it might mean something when it came to catching a murderer.

Streeter, hearing the voice of a colleague on the phone, knew he'd guessed right.

"Wanna go to Amador County today?"

"What's up?" Streeter asked.

"Human remains found by a deer hunter."

"Sure, I'll go."

In spite of his years on the job, Streeter, in his mid-thirties and with the sinewy build of a marathon runner, remained enthusiastic about his work. The day he burned out was the day key evidence might slip past him—the day cold-blooded murderers might walk because of his mistakes. Sincere to the core, Streeter had promised himself that would never happen.

Amador County, on the western slope of the Sierra Nevada, was in the heart of California's gold country, where forty-niners flocked to stake a claim and strike it rich panning in rivers and digging in mines. And some even did. Today, with a scant 29,000 residents dispersed over 600 square miles ranging in elevation from 200 to 9,000 feet, Amador was still the frontier. Gold Rush hamlets like Buckhorn, Pioneer, Fiddletown, Big Bar, Dry Town, and Sutter Creek might have become forgotten ghost towns elsewhere. But here, they lived on, as did fourth- and fifth-generation descendants of hearty, self-reliant prospectors who refused to give up even after the boom ended well before the turn of the century.

It took Streeter forty-five minutes to reach the Sacramento-Amador line. Continuing another 10 miles through tree-studded rolling hills, he then went south on Highway 124 toward the town of Ione for about five miles before spotting several patrol cars parked on the shoulder next to a fenced field.

Gathering his equipment, including a camera, Streeter clipped an ID badge onto his shirt pocket and climbed over a sagging section in the barbed wire. Not seeing anyone, he zigzagged through scrub oak to the crest of the first hill over pastureland baked brown by the summer's heat. A short distance down the other side of the knoll he came to a group of uniformed deputies at a clearing near the rotting trunk of a huge oak that had been down for some time.

"DOJ," Streeter said to no one in particular.

A deputy pointed to a sizable grease spot on the ground. In the middle of the stain were skeletal remains, including a human skull, that appeared to have no flesh or soft tissue remaining.

As Streeter studied what was clearly a torso, he realized there was something wrong. There were no long bones—no arms or legs.

He saw what appeared to be a black bra around the area of the rib cage. Her dark shirt was open and pulled up. Some type of black material seemed bunched up at her neckline. About 10 feet away he found a pair of panties.

Streeter began to take pictures.

About then, a private pathologist arrived. Some deputies greeted him as "Doc." Balding, potbellied, and sporting a snow-white goatee that looked sharpened at the chin, the sixtyish pathologist returned the greetings with a thick German accent.

Searching the immediate area, Streeter found more remains scattered randomly about—a 12-inch straight bone, a ball joint that might have been an elbow, and an 18-inch straight bone with a ball socket at one end. All these bones were picked clean, too, and several had bite marks. Foraging animals, at some point, had shown more than a passing interest in the find.

Pronouncing the remains as human, the pathologist wanted them moved off the ground. A sheet of corrugated metal was slid under the bones. With a deputy at either end, the remains were taken to a sheriff's pickup parked about 100 yards away.

In the interest of preserving evidence, Streeter would have preferred that the body be carefully bagged and not carted through the field. But he understood the politics of law enforcement: this crime scene belonged to the locals and was not his to run. And when it came to the body, the pathologist was in charge.

Streeter continued to photograph the scene and assist a civilian technician process the evidence. When they finished, he went over to the pickup, where a deputy was videotaping the pathologist's examination.

The remains had been laid out on the open tailgate. Doc, gloveless and puffing on a fat cigar, was measuring various bones. He had already concluded that the body was that of a female in her mid-twenties.

"Now," Doc said, carefully putting the cigar down on the tailgate as if he were in a St. James Place smoke shop, "I'm gonna do a field autopsy." He slipped on a pair of yellow rubber gloves.

"Or maybe a tailgate autopsy," chortled Doc, who, whenever asked how many autopsies he'd performed, claimed to have stopped counting at ten thousand. "No reason to go anywhere when I can get what we need right here. I'm not charging for a regular autopsy, you know. Saving the county *lots* of money."

Streeter was horrified. The pathologist had to be thinking that this was some kind of nothing case that would never go to trial. Otherwise, how could he possibly be so cavalier in his protocol?

"Oh, man, I don't think this is a good idea," Streeter muttered.

The deputy next to him shrugged.

Doc started pulling the brittle remains apart. As he did, various items of clothing—the bra, a skirt, and nylon half-slip—came free. The pathologist vigorously shook out each item like an old washerwoman.

Streeter winced but said nothing.

Reaching a hand inside the skeleton, Doc found a perfectly shaped polished fingernail, which he showed everyone before placing it in an envelope.

A few minutes later, the pathologist turned. "We got strangulation," he said.

Streeter moved in for a better shot and so did the deputy with the video camera.

The black material Streeter had noticed earlier turned out to be wrapped around the victim's neck bones. The pathologist pointed to strands of blond hair no longer attached to the skull that were caught underneath the ligature.

"She was tied," Doc announced.

"Tied *up*?" a deputy asked.

The pathologist nodded, pointing to a black nylon material that encircled both wrist bones.

When he was finished, the pathologist took the skull in his hands and snapped off the upper and lower jaws like a giant Thanksgiving wishbone. In the process, several teeth fell out onto the ground.

Handing the jaws to a shocked deputy, Doc said matter-of-factly, "The odontologist will want these."

Asked how long the victim had been dead, the pathologist speculated that decomposition may have advanced faster than usual. To be completely skeletonized, a body would normally have to be out in the elements for a year or more. In this case, however, due to the extensive "animal activity" and the fact that the remains were in the open on a sunny south slope during a particularly hot summer, the pathologist said the victim could have been dead for anywhere from "three plus months" on.

Streeter left without any evidence. He was told that the clothes and the other items recovered at the scene had to go to the sheriff's office before being delivered to DOJ for analysis.

Streeter didn't wait to get to work on the case, however. When he arrived at DOJ shortly before eight o'clock the next morning, he stopped in to see a colleague, Paul Pane, a criminal identification specialist at the Missing Persons Unit.

Realizing that the key to getting the ball rolling in any murder case was to identify the victim, Streeter told Pane about Amador's Jane Doe in the hope that a missing persons report might be on file with the DOJ that could be matched to the victim. He explained that the pathologist thought she was in her twenties.

"How long she been there?" Pane asked.

"Three months anyway. She was skeletonized, but a pack of hungry critters had really gotten to her."

Pane blinked. "Was she wearing high heels?"

"Yeah." *Lucky guess*, Streeter thought.

"And maybe a purple skirt?"

"What the—"

"Been keeping this one handy," Pane said, snatching a manila folder from the top of a nearby file cabinet. "Knew she'd be found sometime."

Opening the file, Pane started reading.

"The heels were alligator—"

"Right."

"Two-thirds-length skirt was—whoops, *lavender*, not purple."

"Close enough."

Pane read on.

"Sounds good," Street finally said.

"Wish they were all this easy."

As Streeter left, Pane was picking up the telephone to call Amador County authorities. Since it hadn't been possible to fingerprint this particular Jane Doe, Pane knew that positive ID would have to come from dental records.

At noon, the victim's upper and lower jaws were delivered to Pane by an Amador detective. Comparing the teeth with dental charts from the missing persons file, Pane felt there was a match. But wanting an expert's opinion, he made an appointment for that afternoon with Dr. George Gould, a leading odontologist—a specialist in the study of teeth and their surrounding tissue.

Dr. Gould seemed taken aback when handed the two jaw sections. He was more accustomed to working with X rays. But getting to work in his spotless lab, he cleaned the teeth first, then X-rayed them. Comparing that film to two sets of dental X rays taken of the missing person's teeth—ten years ago and seven years ago—Dr. Gould did a careful tooth-by-tooth examination before stating that there was no doubt in his mind that the teeth belonged to the missing person.

Upon leaving the dental offices, Pane and the Amador detective drove directly to the downtown Sacramento address of the next of kin in the missing persons report. Although both of them considered notification the hardest part of their jobs, to delay it would be unconscionable.

At 5:45 P.M. that day, an anguished mother sitting at her kitchen table learned that her daughter's body had been found.

The scattered remains of Charmaine Sabrah had been located, three months after her disappearance, a distance of some 50 miles from where she had gotten into the quiet stranger's car.

As Carmen Anselmi finally heard the news that she had long dreaded, she did not immediately cry. It was as if all her tears had been used up. Instead, she rocked slowly back and forth.

In her arms she cradled Sabri, the bright-eyed, dark-haired baby boy that her daughter wanted so much to get home to the night she died.

CHAPTER SIX

The cackling began a few minutes into the video when the screen showed the potbellied pathologist puffing on his stogy as he leaned over the remains.

Gathered around a conference table at the Amador County Sheriff's Department four days after Charmaine Sabrah's body had been found were Lt. Ray Biondi and Stan Reed from Sacramento, Vito Bertocchini and Pete Rosenquist from San Joaquin, Department of Justice staffers—including criminalist Jim Streeter—and two Amador detectives. They were here to discuss similarities in the three unsolved murder cases in Sacramento, San Joaquin, and Amador counties.

As Doc began to pull apart the remains, Bertocchini let loose with a loud curse, followed by a thunderous: "I've gutted *rabbits* with more care!"

When the pathologist shook out the victim's clothes, Reed practically growled, "So much for trace evidence."

Biondi cringed, too, at the idea of any hairs, fibers, and other microscopic evidence that the killer might have left on the victim's clothes now part of the landscape in western Amador County.

When the tape ended, the Amador detectives were plainly embarrassed by the reaction of their peers. One explained solemnly that Doc was an "old-timer" and the only pathologist available to them that day.

Next time, Biondi mused, *call Dr. Frankenstein.*

No one really held the Amador guys to the fire over the unusual "tailgate autopsy." The general feeling in the room was not one of righteous indignation but rather a collective we'll-work-with-what-we've-got.

As for Streeter, he received validation that what he'd witnessed that day in the field had seemed as peculiar to the others as it had to him. He told himself he couldn't have stopped it. Any effort to do so would only have alienated him from the Amador guys, not a wise move when he was on their turf and, more important, when cooperation between DOJ and Amador might eventually mean the difference between solving the case or not.

The Amador detective went on to explain that ligature strangulation was the cause of Charmaine Sabrah's death, and that she was found with her wrists bound behind her back. He added that her jewelry and purse were never found.

"Could you tell whether her hair had been cut?" Bertocchini wanted to know.

The local detective looked surprised. "We did find some blond hair caught in the ligature but I never heard anyone say it was cut."

Biondi summarized aloud. Sabrah was the third unsolved homicide of a young female in four months within a 60-mile radius that had evidence of bindings, either proven sexual assault or presumed due to the victims' state of undress, ligature strangulation as the cause of death, no ID on the bodies, and transportation of the victims and/or their bodies for some distance.

"I might have been jumping the gun," Biondi added somberly, "but I've been thinking for months, ever since Stephanie Brown, that we had a series working. Now, with Sabrah and—"

"I've seen this scumbag's work," Bertocchini jumped in. "He'll never stop until we nail him."

The rest were noncommittal about any connection—the way good detectives tend to be when they don't have all the facts before them.

Biondi knew the realities of working Homicide. Detectives tended to get comfortable in their own little worlds, assuming that their cases were strictly local. (More times than not they were right.) For that reason as well as their own growing caseloads—why go looking for more work?— they weren't searching for linked murders. But Biondi understood that recognizing the likelihood that these three killings were connected would be the first step to finding a dangerous serial killer, and he had no intention of giving up—not now, not later.

With the exception of Bertocchini, no one endorsed Biondi's idea to form a task force devoted to tracking down this killer, with each agency contributing detectives and other resources. However, everyone agreed to send all their reports on all possible I-5 cases to DOJ, which would copy and disseminate the paperwork to the other agencies. Also, all evidence from the three crime scenes—and any future murders that seemed at all similar—would be submitted to Streeter.

Although Biondi knew this was not the ideal way to investigate a serial killer who crossed over invisible political boundaries about as easily as a flight of blackbirds, he was pleased that all the evidence would be analyzed in one central place.

Nonetheless, Biondi was feeling a dread that manifested itself in a full-body weariness. He understood better than most at the table how unbelievably tough murder series were to unravel, and the incredible amount of legwork that would be required to find and arrest the culprit. Unless they were able at some point to form a multi-agency task force, the work would have to be done by hard-pressed detectives already carrying heavy caseloads.

He knew that Bertocchini had picked up a prison homicide a few weeks after Brown and two new cases since Sabrah's kidnapping. Rosenquist was busy working eight other homicides, several carryovers from previous years.

As for Sacramento County, when Stan Reed had arrived to search the Brannan Island crime scene, it was the thirty-seventh homicide in the sheriff's department jurisdiction that year. That figure did not include twenty-six unsolved cases from previous years that still required attention whenever viable new leads cropped up. It also didn't reflect the Bureau's assisting other agencies with their murder cases (such as Brown and Sabrah) and the man-hours being gobbled up by an ongoing investigation into the Unabomber, who had killed a Sacramento computer store owner the year before (1985) with a powerful homemade bomb.

As for what some detectives were calling the "I-5 series," it wouldn't help detectives that the three known victims had been located in different jurisdictions, and that the two identified victims were nabbed in one jurisdiction and dumped in another. Police agencies were filled with layers of bureaucracy that led to administrative infighting—distractions that could and too often did get in the way of conscientious cops trying to do a job. With the number of jurisdictions involved, Biondi knew that interagency battling,interdepartmental turf wars, bureaucratic red tape, and petty bickering would only increase geometrically.

He could foresee departments (and he did not exclude his own) being unwilling to make the necessary manpower and monetary commitment to form a special task force. Amador County was already making noises that its small detective bureau—three detectives handling every investigation from shoplifting to homicide for 600 square miles—could not become involved in any long-term investigation.

Without strong coordination and cohesiveness, Biondi anticipated that the I-5 series would get chopped into individual cases that might or might not be ardently worked by the appropriate jurisdiction. Even if detectives were given the time to work the cases, collectively their efforts would overlap. For example, information developed by one agency would not always get to another agency that needed it in a timely manner. Such inefficiencies would haunt them from day one.

Biondi was keenly aware that this multi-agency effort to find a heinous serial murderer had all the makings for a cluster fuck, from which only the killer would benefit.

FOUR DAYS later, Jim Streeter received in his Sacramento lab the physical evidence in the Stephanie Brown case. Some of it had previously been analyzed by a small, satellite DOJ lab near Stockton that served San Joaquin County, which did not have its own crime lab.

First turning his attention to the rape kit, he noted that an insufficient amount of semen had been recovered to conduct DNA genetic-fingerprinting testing. Next best would be to run a less conclusive blood-typing test, which was most useful in eliminating a suspect. When it came to fingering someone, these results would only determine how large or small a group of the general population an individual belonged to. In this instance, the field hadn't been narrowed much: Streeter found the donor had any one of several common blood types. Together, they represented 89 percent of the total U.S. population.

Streeter found a single black hair that did not belong to Brown in an envelope containing her pubic combings. Hair evidence, however, would not conclusively prove the identity of an individual. Scientifically, it could only exclude a donor. Insofar as providing incriminating evidence, the most they would ever get from the "foreign" hair would be to be able one day to vouch for its *similarity* to a suspect's.

Streeter looked through a microscope at the several strands of hair found on the decedent's tank top after it had been recovered from the ditch. He found them to be similar to the sample of hair from Brown's head. As the loose strands had no roots, he was able to confirm Bertocchini's suspicions that the victim's hair had been cut. This struck him as odd.

Streeter turned his attention to the victim's blue tank top, which he examined with gloved hands. He kept it inside a plastic bag to preserve any possible trace evidence. Both shoulder straps were cut through just behind the top seam, and the back of the shirt was sliced open from top to bottom or vice versa. He was sure it had been cut, as the thin cotton-material wasn't stretched as if it had been ripped. And the slices were so straight and even that he believed scissors rather than a knife had been used.

Streeter was intrigued by the evidence of cutting. Checking Stephanie Brown's other clothes, however, he found no cuts to her bra, panties, or white shorts.

The next morning, bags containing Charmaine Sabrah's clothing arrived from Amador County. Not long after, a DOJ investigator came into Streeter's lab with the clothing worn by Jane Doe that had been at the Sacramento County morgue since the autopsy.

The criminalist started with Sabrah.

In examining the black-and-lavender short-sleeve blouse he had seen on the remains at the crime scene, Streeter saw that it buttoned down the front. The buttons—which were unbuttoned when the victim was found—were intact and there was no stretching or damage to the button-holes. Both shoulder seams had been cut in the collarbone area. Both side seams were also cut open, and Streeter could see that a strip of the shirt's black lining was missing from each side.

The ligature that had been used to strangle the victim to death turned out to be the missing liner from the sides of the blouse, reinforced with a length of yellow nylon cord knotted in two places.

He next looked at the black pantyhose, which had been cut into pieces, two of which were found wrapped around her wrists.

Both shoulder straps of the bra had been cut. A short section of strap was missing from each side, and had not been found at the crime scene. There was no damage to the metal clip at the back of the bra.

The panties he had found at the Sabrah scene were cut and missing sections, too. Both sides had been cut to the waistband. Missing and not found were a portion of the right front panel and a portion of the left rear panel. But what Streeter found connected to the panties was more peculiar than what he didn't find. A piece of the waistband was wound around a clump of hair.

A microscopic examination would reveal seventy-two strands of hair 1 to 3 inches long that were similar to the victim's head hair. Some of the strands had been cut and others had been pulled out by the root.

The victim's black half-slip had a 9-inch cut in one side seam, running from the hem upward.

Her purple skirt had no cuts.

Streeter speculated that the pantyhose, since it had been used to bind the victim's hands, had come off first. Then, the assailant cut his way through the other layers of clothing; in places, to remove them, but in other instances for less obvious reasons. There was evidence of animal bites on some of the clothes; pockmarked as if made by needle-sharp teeth, they were quite distinctive from the straight-edged cuts.

Turning his attention to the Jane Doe case, Streeter examined the articles of clothing he had received: a pair of blue jeans, bikini panties, and gray socks. The only cuts were up the legs of the blue jeans made by the pathologist in removing them at the autopsy.

Despite other similar factors in the three cases, the unique hair and clothes cuttings found in Brown and Sabrah was not present in Jane Doe.

At that point, Streeter had every reason to believe he'd seen all of Jane Doe's clothing. He did not know about her cut-up tank top that remained in the freezer at the Sacramento County crime lab.

VITO Bertocchini was impassioned, as usual.

An hour away from the first press conference to alert northern California residents to the possibility of a serial killer in their midst, Bertocchini had taken a last-ditch stand against informing the public.

"And Ray," Bertocchini added, "I'm *dead against* giving up the clothes cutting *or* the scissors."

Biondi had liked the burly deputy from San Joaquin the first time he met him. Everything the homicide lieutenant had seen and heard since then had led him to believe that Bertocchini was committed to his cases with a capital C. But dammit, the man was new to Homicide. Biondi, who had traveled this way many times, could see where the trail in the Stephanie Brown and Charmaine Sabrah killings had these past few months gone—from lukewarm to ice cold, as it does in any case that isn't immediately solved. And as for Jane Doe, where to start when they didn't have a clue to her identity?

"We gotta go public with what we know," said Biondi, figuring his *paesano* would just have to learn that he wasn't the only one who carried license to be bullheaded at times.

"But why give up anything?"

Police routinely withheld vital pieces of evidence that only they and the killer knew about. Biondi understood the value in doing so: it could be helpful especially when interrogating a suspect, and also when evaluating tips or leads from informants. Certainly it would be difficult to justify releasing information about specific evidence unless it enhanced rather than weakened the investigation. However, there were times when it was advantageous to release some details of a crime.

"For Christ's sake," Bertocchini groaned, "we could end up with copycats out the kazoo."

Biondi and Bertocchini had boiled over during an otherwise businesslike session at DOJ, Sacramento, with detectives from agencies such as the Alameda County Sheriff's Department, Antioch Police Department, Nevada County Sheriff's Office, and the Sacramento Police Department. The new faces had reported on unsolved cases in their jurisdictions that seemed similar to the I-5 series. The strongest candidates had been presented by a sheriff's homicide detective from Placer County, Sacramento's neighbor to the north: the murders of two young women that fell about a month apart, both found bound and strangled. Placer County had identified a fugitive suspect who was not yet in custody.

As of now, however, everything in the room aside from the two detectives going at each other had become a sideshow. And not one of the armed observers huddled around the table was prepared to leap in the middle.

"Fuck copycats," the normally soft-spoken Biondi let loose. "If we give up cutting, maybe somebody out there *knows* something. Maybe we have an eyewitness we haven't found yet. Maybe somebody will drop a dime and *tell* us something we *don't* know. And Jesus Almighty, right now that's one helluva lot."

For Biondi, this was an old script. For the past year he'd fought unsuccessfully against a similar kind of illogic in the Unabomber investigation. He'd been appalled to learn the previous year that the Sacramento bombing was the eleventh in a series that began in 1978 and which the FBI had kept hush-hush—even after a 1979 incident involving an airborne American Airlines jet that would surely have cost ninety people their lives but for a bomb malfunction. The FBI had kept its dirty little secret for seven long years, during which the bomber perfected his deadly craft. And after the series was forced into the open by the murder of the Sacramento computer store owner, the FBI refused to share important leads with the Sacramento County Sheriff's Department (who had jurisdiction in the local bombing death) or other law enforcement agencies, resisted going to the public with essential information, and failed to honor agreements hammered out during protracted negotiations with locals, who had considerably more experience working homicides (the FBI rarely has jurisdiction in murder cases). Biondi could never figure out why the FBI was so uptight about "tipping off" the bomber. Did they think the bomber didn't already know the details of his own crimes? The FBI not only persisted in keeping the public in the dark, but in the process managed to create an atmosphere of mistrust among Unabomber investigators.*

---

* When the Unabomber suspect was arrested in 1996 after being turned in by his brother, who had read the bomber's long manifesto published in *The New York Times*, Biondi knew how fortuitous it was that copies of the manifesto had been sent directly to the media. There was no doubt in his mind that had the manifesto gone only to the FBI, it would *not* have been made public and the Unabomber might have kept on killing for years. Biondi would always wonder how much sooner the Unabomber suspect might have been turned in—and how many of the sixteen bombings might never have

Having corralled his share of serial killers, Biondi understood there were certain things that should be done in unsolved cases, whether the suspect was a nationwide mail bomber or a homegrown sex killer:

- *Law enforcement's top priority should be to forewarn and protect the public.* This is why we have police, a public service that usually eats up the largest portion of a city or county's tax revenues. When vital information is withheld from the public, residents are unable to take measures to safeguard themselves and their loved ones. In Biondi's opinion, whenever law enforcement conspires to keep the citizenry in the dark, it has shirked one of its main duties.

- *When a suspect's identity is unknown, the only avenue to putting pressure on the killer is through the media.* Authorities need to let the perpetrator know they're onto his actions and that he'll no longer be allowed to operate in a pressure-free environment.

- *Identifying an unknown killer is often accomplished by a public plea for assistance as well as providing the public with information that may turn out to be recognition keys for someone who knows something about the killer.* It makes for a much broader net to have millions of informed and interested people being on the lookout instead of just a dozen or so investigators.

Biondi laid as much of his philosophy on Bertocchini as he thought the fiery-eyed detective could stomach at one sitting.

Utilizing the media in the early stages of an investigation—particularly before a suspect has been identified—had proven invaluable in solving murders time and again. The reason this resource was overlooked by much of law enforcement was because of their mutual distrust, and the unwillingness of cops to open themselves to public inspection.

---

happened, which of the three persons killed (including a second Sacramento man, a timber industry lobbyist, in 1995) might have been spared, how many of the twenty-three people injured could have avoided their suffering—had the FBI only released the letters, documents, photographs, and other information it had so zealously withheld over the years in what turned out to be the most expensive criminal investigation in this nation's history

Biondi had developed some hard-and-fast rules of his own when dealing with the media. Rule #1: Police should know going in that the media doesn't care a hoot about police priorities. Cops need to deftly hook their own priorities to the media's. Rule #2: Avoid raising a red flag by making "no comment" statements to the press, and provide bad news immediately and without excuses. Rule #3: Keep lines of communication open with the press, rather than forcing them to conduct their own investigation, which can result in negative press and derail or damage the investigation.

"Look, Vito"—Biondi took the edge off his voice because, after all, he and Bertocchini were on the same side—"sometimes you have to give up something to get something. Revealing, not concealing, is the name of the game."

"Suppose we give up the clothes cutting but hold back on saying we found the scissors?" Uncharacteristically, Bertocchini had put out the feeler a bit tentatively.

Biondi realized he was about to win one and lose one, which, given the circumstances, sounded like a reasonable compromise. They had both taken a step back.

Earlier that morning, Biondi had been briefed by Jim Streeter regarding the hair and clothes cutting. The criminalist described much of the clothes cutting as "nonfunctional," explaining that it hadn't been necessary in order to undress the victims. He opined that the suspect had cut for other, nefarious reasons.

"As in ritualistic?" Biondi had asked.

"Exactly."

Through the years, Biondi had beheld a virtual kaleidoscope of ritualistic acts carried out by killers of every ilk. Had the two young women been beaten, tortured, burned, mutilated, disemboweled, or beheaded, he wouldn't have blinked. Sadly, he was all too accustomed to such inhumanity by man. But *hair and clothes cutting?* Now that was *really*deviant.

In his more than 400 murder investigations, Biondi had never seen anything like it.

AN HOUR LATER as he stood before eight microphones, several cameras, and three dozen reporters, Lt. Ray Biondi reminded himself not to cross the fine line between raising public awareness and terrifying residents.

To his immediate right was an enlarged map marked with the locations in three neighboring counties where the two identified victims had been abducted and their bodies found, and where Jane Doe had been located.

Biondi cleared his throat. "This joint investigation began when the body of Stephanie Brown, nineteen years old, was found July 15th this year in a drainage ditch."

He turned toward the map and pointed. "Her body was found right here, and her car was about 20 miles away parked here on I-5."

Keeping his delivery calm and precise, Biondi gave the specifics of Charmaine Sabrah and Jane Doe.

The press, of course, had provided earlier coverage to all three cases—giving special attention to Brown, described as "the-girl-next-door type," and Sabrah, the "young single mom trying to get home to her baby." Now, however, they were about to hear a new twist in the cases from Biondi.

"Time factors, geography, cause of death, and other evidence support the theory of a single murderer who lives in one of the three counties or frequently travels through the area. We believe it is the work of a serial killer."

"Among the evidence that supports this," Biondi went on without skipping a beat, "is the fact that all three victims had been disposed of in an isolated, rural area in an attempt to conceal or prolong discovery of their bodies. At least two of the victims were abducted or confronted by their assailant on Interstate 5. Two of them had their hands tied in a similar matter. All were found partially unclothed and were probably sexually molested. Also, clothing on two of the victims had been cut."

"Did you say *cut*?" asked one newspaper reporter without raising his head from his notebook.

"Yes, cut. Probably with scissors."

Biondi explained that these and other similarities in the crimes made it "highly improbable" that the three victims were each killed by someone different. "More likely it is a single killer who may drive around looking for women with car trouble or in some other situation that makes them opportune victims."

He ended by asking the public for assistance, giving a hotline number for people to call should they have any information about the crimes or the victims.

Biondi knew that the media could help turn up the heat on the killer, who, so far, had been abducting, abusing, and strangling women with impunity. Once public acknowledgment had been made as to the presence of a serial killer and what his tactics were for finding his victims, a new army of citizens would be on the lookout. Up to now, the killer had been free to roam the highways, hunt for victims, snatch them in one jurisdiction and dump them in another, and carry out his warped fantasies without having been reported by anyone. Now, the killer would have to be worried. Would someone see him and jot down his license number and call police? And what if he made an unsuccessful attempt to lure a victim? He had to realize it would now be far more likely that he would be promptly reported, and that authorities would receive some nature of useful information.

When Robbie Waters, the elected sheriff of Sacramento County and a former homicide lieutenant, came to the podium, he urged women motorists to keep their cars in good repair and fill the gas tank before taking a long trip. Also, he suggested that women tell a friend the route they planned to take and call a relative or friend when they reached their destination "to let them know you have arrived safely."

In the event of car trouble, the sheriff advised women drivers to turn on their emergency flasher and lock the doors. "Be cautious about accepting help from all strangers. Make an appraisal of each offer for help before stepping out of your vehicle."

Even though the composite of the suspect in the Sabrah case had been widely used previously by the print and TV press, more copies were distributed, along with a description of the suspect's vehicle.

"We hope you'll run the composite again," Biondi said to the reporters after a question-and-answer period. "Somebody out there must have seen this guy."

Biondi knew that going public could crank up a stalled investigation. But as he hit the stairwell for the climb back to his third-floor office, he had a nagging concern about putting the cart before the horse.

If the media did its thing, hundreds of new leads in the I-5 series could be generated. That would be the good news.

The bad: How would homicide detectives already working fifty to sixty hours a week just to keep up with their existing caseloads handle the avalanche?

LT. RAY Biondi received a call two days later from the Placer County detective who had been at the DOJ briefing.

The detective told Biondi that their suspect in the killings of the two young women had been arrested in Carson City, Nevada, the day before. The suspect, David Rundle, had already confessed to the Placer murders.

Had Rundle done Brown, Sabrah, and Jane Doe, too? Biondi wondered. If so, since he'd confessed to two murders, might he be ready to open up on any others?

Rundle had already been brought back from Nevada and was in the Placer County Jail in Auburn, 35 miles northeast of Sacramento on Interstate 80.

Biondi contacted Reed at home, directing his most seasoned detective to hightail it to Auburn. He also called Reed's partner, Bob Bell.

"I'll meet you guys there," Biondi added.

By the time Biondi arrived in Auburn, Reed and Bell were coming out of the interrogation room.

"No go," Reed said.

"What do you mean?"

"He says he didn't do anyone else."

Biondi felt himself deflating like a party balloon losing air fast. Reed and Bell explained they had been careful not to discuss the Placer murders in order to avoid interjecting themselves or their department into that investigation. In telling them about his travels and activities, the suspect had given them nothing about any other murders.

Bob Bell and Stan Reed were opposites in almost every respect. Standing next to each other—Reed in his old corduroy coat and Bell in a snazzy blue blazer complete with pin-striped shirt and fashionable silk tie—the partners looked like Felix and Oscar. While Reed was direct and no-nonsense almost to a fault, Bell had an understated, patient way of dealing with people. The style of the partners sometimes clashed. Whereas Reed wasn't given to wasting time on meaningless theories and could easily lose his patience if he didn't receive complete answers to his very concise questions, Bell could talk to a suspect or witness for hours on end until he got what he needed.

Biondi, who figured that Reed must have taken the lead on this pedal-to-the-metal interrogation, hadn't come this far to turn around and go back without facing Rundle.

"Look," Biondi said, "let's go back in and give it another shot."

Reed shrugged and turned around.

Bell, a button-down type with rimless glasses on a cherubic face that looked like it belonged on an accountant more than a cop, lit up at the prospect.

Rundle was younger than Biondi pictured. Barely able to drink legally, he would have been carded by any legitimate bartender. He was pleasant looking, with a college-boy haircut and neatly trimmed beard. He didn't seem excited, nervous, or remorseful.

"We know what you've done, Rundle," Biondi said evenly, not raising his voice. "Tell us about the others. What happened here in Placer was the end. When did it start?"

Rundle showed a blank expression. "I don't know about any others," he answered in a voice so soft that Biondi had to strain to hear him.

"It really won't do you any good to hold out on us," Bell added in a sorrowful, almost ministerial tone. He had settled in a chair as if he was going to stay awhile. "Why don't you get it off your chest?"

Rundle's baby blues darted from side to side, as if looking for a way out. Finally, with a great sigh, he dropped his head into his arms on the table.

"All right—" His voice cracked.

Was Rundle going to cry? Biondi wondered.

"—I did another one. My first. In May."

"This year?"

"Yeah."

Two months *before* Stephanie Brown.

"Where?" asked Biondi, being careful not to appear surprised.

Rundle raised his head. "Sacramento."

Biondi nodded as if he'd known all along.

Rundle's eyes had remained dry, and his voice was steady again. He'd made a speedy recovery.

"Who?" Biondi asked.

"Filipino, I think. Met her down by the river," Rundle said, as if discussing a prom date.

Filipino?

"Where'd you dump her?"

Right off I-5, came the answer, along the banks of the Sacramento River near the Pioneer Bridge.

I-5 and I-80 met at the Pioneer Bridge over the Sacramento River at the western outskirts of downtown Sacramento—with I-5 heading north and south and I-80 east toward Reno and west into the San Francisco Bay Area. Even though only a couple of miles from the Sacramento County sheriff's downtown headquarters, this location was within city limits. Therefore, it was the jurisdiction of Sacramento's municipal police department.

Biondi didn't recall hearing of a recent murder victim found in that area. Did that mean the young woman's body was still there?

The detectives pumped the suspect for more admissions, but the well had gone dry. Finally, Bell flipped off his cassette tape recorder and they left the room.

Within minutes, Biondi was on the phone to Sacramento Police Homicide. When he was informed that a dead twenty-one-year-old Filipino woman had indeed been found strangled at that location near I-5 six months earlier, Biondi felt like ripping the phone out of the wall.

He well remembered the two stoic, note-taking representatives of Sacramento P.D. at the DOJ meeting forty-eight hours earlier. A homicide detective had arrived with a deputy chief. They listened, and hadn't said word one. Biondi now knew they had sat on a very similar case that they should have presented. Obviously, they'd come to find out what everyone else knew. Shades of dealing with the FBI and other alphabet-soup federal agencies.

"I suggest you take a drive up here," Biondi hissed into the receiver. "We've got a gimme for you."

David Rundle, it turned out, had not killed Stephanie Brown, Charmaine Sabrah, or Jane Doe. (Several years later, after being convicted of and sentenced to death for the two Placer County murders, Rundle copped a plea to murdering the Filipino woman in exchange for life imprisonment without parole on that charge—saving the state, and himself, the ordeal of another death penalty case. Rundle, with several more years of appeals yet to be exhausted, still sits on Death Row.)

Biondi had driven home that night from Placer County in a terrible funk. A young woman had been sexually attacked and strangled to death in the shadow of I-5 a few months earlier, yet those two Sacramento P.D. guys had *said nothing*. He considered it a disheartening example of law enforcement failing to communicate. He didn't blame the detective as much as the deputy chief, who must have been calling the shots. Biondi knew that working detectives generally had no problem sharing information with those from other departments. But when the bosses became involved, it could be a far different story. He'd seen it before and he knew he'd face it again. It existed not only in communications between separate departments, but also behind the walls of virtually every law enforcement agency in America, with the left hand frequently not knowing what the right was doing. At times, bureaucratic politics was to blame; other times, outright incompetency in middle and upper management. In reality, the only people who benefited from such dissension were the bad guys on the street.

An article had probably run in the paper back in May concerning the discovery of the unidentified female murder victim, but Biondi didn't remember reading it. Even if he had, no alarms would have sounded because Stephanie Brown hadn't yet been abducted on I-5. As soon as he began to suspect that a serial killer was active in the area, Biondi had made a point to reach out to other agencies. And now, after weeks and months, that collaborative effort had been nearly torpedoed by bureaucratic small-mindedness.

And people wondered why conscientious cops inevitably burn out?

THREE DAYS after the composite of the I-5 series suspect was rereleased to the media at the press conference—resulting in a flood of new leads called in to authorities—a San Joaquin County Sheriff's Department squad car on routine patrol in east Stockton braked sharply as it approached a busy intersection to avoid a dark sports car that turned left against a red.

Deputy Armando Mayoya activated his flashing lights. When he was sure oncoming traffic had slowed or pulled over, he punched it and made a hard, squealing right through the intersection onto the cross street.

As it was a few minutes before midnight on a Saturday night, Mayoya, a ten-year department veteran, expected soon to be dealing with a tottering DUI.

The dark blue Datsun 280Z had not raced ahead and had obligingly stopped at the curb.

Pulling up behind, Mayoya flipped on a powerful spotlight that illuminated inside the vehicle. The driver was alone in the two-seater.

The deputy jotted down the license number—California 1-*Mary-Boy-Victor*-4-6-6.

It sounded familiar.

Checking a note clipped to his dashboard, Mayoya saw that the plate matched with the one given to him three or four hours earlier by a prostitute who had flagged him down in front of the Capri Motel on what was known as Stockton's "stroll" area.

His informant, Janet Nelson, had been, at nearly thirty years of age, older than most of the working girls hoofing their stuff in spiked heels and short skirts hoping a cruising John would stop and make a date. In her rather accelerated career, however, she'd probably seen as many dicks as an over-the-hill urologist. Mayoya would not be surprised later to learn that many of the girls on the street considered Nelson almost a mother figure. Fittingly, it had been she who decided to stop a cop and possibly save a life.

The story Janet Nelson had told that night was secondhand and Mayoya knew it would never be heard inside a courtroom. Nonetheless, he listened carefully.

Nelson explained she had been sitting with another prostitute, Sheri Zeller, twenty-one, at a fast-food joint earlier in the evening. As they sipped hot coffee and rested their aching feet, they kept their eyes peeled. When a dark 280Z cruised by slowly, Sheri pointed it out, saying the John had previously offered her $1,000 and some new clothes if she'd take a ride with him to Lake Tahoe. Of course, she had refused—no working girl in her right mind would sign up for such a long journey with a stranger. Especially, as Zeller had added, with one that "looked like the picture of the killer in the paper."

Not long after that conversation, Nelson had explained to Mayoya, the same dark 280Z pulled over on the stroll for her. She approached the vehicle, but only close enough to get the license number. Then, she spun around and went back the opposite way. "See, I don't know what he looks like myself," Nelson had told the deputy. "All I know is what Sheri told me."

Mayoya had thanked his informant and kept the license number. He knew that when a composite in such a high-visibility case got media play it could generate lots of citizens' reports—most proved to be a waste of time. But with every uniform in five or six northern California counties looking for the man in the composite, who was he not to take a tip seriously?

Mayoya exited his cruiser with a long black flashlight in one hand, and the other on the cold butt of his .357 Magnum service revolver.

The mix of feelings Mayoya experienced as he approached the lone occupant of the vehicle in the dead of night—not knowing if he was coming upon a serial killer or Joe Citizen who'd had a few too many brews—was something that could not be easily explained in an academy lecture. The sweet familiar adrenaline rush had begun, but for someone with Mayoya's experience there was a definite routineness to it all. Curiosity had a strong pull: Who or what would he find in the car?

Deputy Mayoya intended to write up the driver for blowing the light. Beyond that, being the good beat cop he was, he would play it by ear.

CHAPTER SEVEN

As he had done a hundred times before, Deputy Armando Mayoya stopped short of the driver's door and directed the beam of his flashlight inside the vehicle. He could, in this way, watch the driver without making himself an easy target.

The driver's window was already down.

"Evening, sir. License, please."

Without a word, the driver reached into the back pocket of his jeans and took out a thin wallet. With hands that shook slightly, he removed his license and handed it to the officer.

Placing the license close to the light, Mayoya saw it was issued to a Roger Reece Kibbe, with a street address in Oakley, a small town about 30 miles west of Stockton.

The deputy clipped the license onto his citation book.

"Do you know why I stopped you?"

"Not really," said the driver, craning his neck to look up into the light toward Mayoya.

Mayoya observed that the pupils of the driver's eyes were not dilated; he was clean.

"You made a left against a red light, Mr. Kibbe. I almost hit you."

The driver appeared to nod in agreement.

Mayoya made a slow sweep of the car's interior with his light. On the floor behind the driver's seat he saw something that upped his heart rate considerably.

The deputy silently slipped his gun from its holster, and placed the weapon next to his leg—to decrease his reaction time by a split second or two.

"Sir, I'm going to ask you to get out. Do so slowly and keep your hands where I can see them."

The driver complied.

Mayoya holstered his weapon and frisked the driver. When the deputy was convinced the man was unarmed and posed no immediate threat, he had the driver step back away from the vehicle. The deputy reached inside the car behind the driver's seat and found that the gun butt he'd seen was in fact a pellet gun.

"Why do you have this?" the deputy asked, holding the weapon up.

The man shrugged, apparently happy to say nothing more. But finally, he added: "I put it in and forgot it."

It wasn't against the law to have a pellet gun, but it *was* to brandish a pretend gun as a real one. Realizing he didn't have much to work with, Mayoya asked the driver what he had intended to do with the pellet gun.

"Nothing. I don't want it. You can take it."

"Okay, sir, I will."

Mayoya did not conduct a field sobriety test because it was apparent that the driver had not been drinking. However, the deputy put out the driver's name over the radio for a records check that would pick up any outstanding wants or warrants. This was routine.

Then, he requested that a Technical Services deputy respond to his location for the purpose of taking pictures of the vehicle he had pulled over. This, in other than major injury accidents, was very unusual.

He did so because Roger Kibbe bore a striking resemblance to the suspect in the composite Mayoya had on the front seat of his patrol car. He saw that the driver's age (DOB 5/21/39) fit, as did the other details such as his graying hair, build (5-foot-10), weight (180 pounds), and large nose. Even his car fit the bill.

As he wrote out the citation, Mayoya tried to keep the chatter going. Although Kibbe was not exactly talkative, he answered the deputy's questions. After the pictures were taken—Kibbe seemed not the least interested in why his car was being photographed—Mayoya had him sign the citation.

There was to be a last bit of bad news for Roger Kibbe: the records check had revealed that Kibbe's driver's license had been suspended for failure to appear on a minor fix-it citation (broken tail lamp).

"For that reason," Mayoya said, "I'm confiscating your driver's license tonight. I suggest you get off the road and stay off until you deal with this."

"Okay, thanks," Kibbe said, hurriedly scrawling on the signature line and accepting his copy of the ticket before driving cautiously away.

As he resumed patrol, the deputy kept thinking about the stop, a report of which he would send to Homicide. Roger Kibbe had been nervous, although he seemed to be trying hard to appear calm and nonchalant.

It had been the first time in his career, Deputy Armando Mayoya realized, that he'd ever been thanked for confiscating someone's license.

JANE DOE, found dead on the shore of Brannan Island in Sacramento County three months earlier, reclaimed her identity the first week of December 1986.

She was Lora Renee Heedick, twenty, a petite blue-eyed blonde reported missing in April from the Stanislaus County community of Modesto, an hour's drive south of Sacramento.

Identification of the badly decomposed body had been delayed because the Stanislaus County Sheriff's Department had not gotten around to asking Heedick's family for the name of her dentist until November, then hadn't picked up her dental charts until early December.

Once DOJ's Missing Persons Unit received the X rays, technicians immediately searched their records of more than one thousand unidentified dead. Within days, the X rays were matched to Jane Doe's dental work.

Why the delay by the local cops?

The Lora Heedick disappearance had a low priority due in part to the usual doubt that plagued adult missing persons cases as to whether or not a crime had actually been committed. Another factor: Heedick, according to her boyfriend, had gotten into a stranger's car for the purpose of committing an act of prostitution. No one in authority would ever state publicly that a young woman who placed herself in such jeopardy deserved to disappear, but there had been an apparent casualness about the case ever since she had been reported missing the next day by her boyfriend's mother. Even when there had been no sign of Heedick after weeks, police made little effort to reach out beyond Modesto by reporting it to neighboring law enforcement agencies or DOJ. A single news story, seven paragraphs long, had run in the local newspaper *two months* after her disappearance. All in all, there seemed to be a nonchalance about Lora Heedick's disappearance that would probably not have been present had the missing young woman been a local cheerleader or honors student.

Sacramento County Sheriff's Detective Stan Reed brooked no such nonsense. Murder was murder in his book. What had once been Stanislaus County's missing persons case had become his homicide investigation. Now that the victim had a name, he had a place to start. Even though the circumstances of her death had already strongly suggested that she couldbe a victim of an active serial killer, Reed never wore blinders when he worked a case, preferring instead to go where the evidence took him.

In this instance, it led him to the poor side of Modesto, a dusty, sun-burnt Valley town dominated by agricultural industries whose biggest employer was E. and J. Gallo—endless rows of stainless steel tanks with up to one-million-gallon capacities made the huge winery look more like a refinery—and whose richest residents were Ernest and Julio.

Reed learned that Heedick's ex-con boyfriend, James Driggers, thirty-two, was the last person to see Heedick alive. The detective met the scruffy, tattooed Driggers at a dumpy place on 13th Street, not far from where he claimed his girlfriend had ridden away in an older, white two-door car driven by a middle-aged man.

Driggers, who had gotten the news the previous day of his girlfriend's body having been identified, anxiously told Reed that he'd known all along that something like this had happened.

"Why?" Reed inquired.

"She wouldn't have left like that with some guy she didn't know."

"Let's start at the beginning," Reed said, taking out his notebook. "How long did you know Lora?"

"Three years, off and on."

"Did she have any problems with anyone or any enemies that you know of?"

"No, she got along good with people. She did the prostitution stuff, you know, only once in a while. When we needed the bread."

"How often?"

"Once a month or something."

"What happened that night?"

Beads of sweat began to pop out on Driggers' forehead. He admitted that he and Lora had been using "uppers" in the park that Sunday night. When they ran out about 11:00 P.M., they'd gone down to the strip on 9th Street so that Lora could make some money for a local dope deal. Driggers described her as strolling up the street in designer jeans and tank top while he waited in front of a 7-Eleven, talking to a couple of other "dopers." He eventually lost sight of Lora.

After about forty-five minutes, he started walking up the street in the direction she had gone. Soon, the white car pulled over with Lora inside. "She told me to get in," Driggers said. "That we were gonna get a room."

Driggers explained that Lora scooted over to the middle to give him room in the front seat. He said after he was inside he reached over and shook hands with the driver, whom he described as forty-five to fifty years of age with graying hair, close to 6-foot, with large hands.

"Isn't it unusual for a John to stop and pick up a girl's boyfriend?" Reed asked pointedly.

"She must have told him to pick me up so we could party. We had an open relationship. I wasn't jealous or nothing. We'd partied with people before. I'd take a walk or whatever."

The driver went up to the next intersection and made a U-turn, Driggers continued, then pulled up in front of the Sahara Motel a short distance away.

"The guy said he could score some drugs at his shop. He said it wasn't far away. I asked Lora what I should do. She said for me to wait outside the motel and they'd be right back. Then they drove off."

Driggers said he went to a store across the street and bought a bottle of wine, returned to the motel, then waited next to the phone booth. "Lora knew the number," he added.

"I stayed there until morning, maybe ten or eleven o'clock. Lora never came back or phoned. That's when I went to my mom's and told her."

"Why didn't you contact the police?"

Driggers said he'd asked his mother to file the report because he feared there might be an old warrant out for him. "When I heard there wasn't, I went down and gave them a statement."

"The initial information you gave about Lora's disappearance wasn't accurate, was it?"

"No. I made up that stuff about her going to see some friends and not coming back. What was I going to tell my mom—that Lora was out hooking?"

With only those exceptions, Driggers's story had not deviated from his initial statement to authorities in April, a copy of which Reed had reviewed. Yet, Reed could see that Lora's boyfriend was as skittish as a downed canary in the path of an approaching tomcat. Was it jangled nerves from the finality of her body being identified, or something more sinister?

In trying to check out Driggers' alibi, Reed found no witnesses who saw Lora Heedick get into a white car or any car on the night of her disappearance, nor anyone at the motel who remembered seeing Driggers waiting at the phone booth or anywhere in the vicinity.

Driggers didn't have a car, which worked in his favor since Heedick's body was found 50 miles from Modesto. He occasionally borrowed vehicles, including his mother's. However, after more legwork, Reed was not able to place Driggers at the wheel of a car (borrowed or stolen) that night, leaving the unanswered question: If Driggers had killed Lora, how had he transported her so far?

Heedick's mother reported that her daughter and Driggers had not been getting along recently. Driggers's own relatives reported that he beat Lora. Members of both families told police they feared he might be responsible for Lora's death. An ex-wife of Driggers's came forward to claim she had been physically abused in their marriage, and that Driggers had forced her on more than one occasion to take part in three-way sex with other men.

The FBI's four-page rap sheet on Lora Heedick's boyfriend began in Florida at age eighteen with driving under the influence, reckless driving, possession of marijuana, and attempting to elude police. Arrests for crimes such as prowling, carrying a concealed weapon, burglary, as well as a conviction for petty theft, followed over the next several years. After a 1984 conviction for burglary, he escaped from jail. Recaptured that same year, he was subsequently sent to state prison. In the months since Heedick's disappearance, he had been arrested in Stanislaus County in the theft of a bicycle and shotgun, but avoided prosecution by providing information about a stolen property ring.

While his checkered past did not make him a murderer, Driggers's lifestyle didn't win him any citizenship points with Reed. The detective saw in Driggers a habitual criminal who was more than willing to have his young girlfriend hook for drugs, a good indicator that he considered her not much more than a commodity to be used. Was she also one to be discarded at will?

Reed shared his dilemma with Lt. Ray Biondi. "I really don't think this is a boyfriend-girlfriend murder but I can't get Driggers out of the case."

Even though the DOJ lab had not found any clothes cutting in the Heedick case, it had been included on the list of suspected serial killings due to evidence of bindings, strangulation, and transportation of the victim. Those same factors all continued to suggest that Heedick had been the victim not of a lovers' quarrel but of the same methodical serial killer who had murdered Brown and Sabrah.

"The scene was all wrong," Reed grumbled. "Heedick was tied up. Driggers wouldn't have had to control her like that. And the garrote—that's not heat of passion."

Biondi had been to enough domestic murder scenes to know there are usually signs of tremendous anger directed at the victim, such as beatings delivered with fists or feet or clubs, multiple stab or bullet wounds, etc. Strangulation was too neat, too controlled. The garrote suggested a killer efficiently disposing of someone to whom he had no emotional ties—stranger on stranger, without the disorder typically present at the scene of passion murders.

"And why would Driggers have brought her all the way up to Brannan Island?" Biondi wondered aloud.

"Even if he could get his hands on a car," Reed added.

"It had to be calculated," Biondi said flatly. "The guy who took Heedick all that way had some kind of master plan."

Biondi didn't need to tell his most senior detective what had to be done. Reed knew the drill. He had to find evidence that either implicated James Driggers in the murder of Lora Heedick, or that cleared him.

If Driggers had not done in his girlfriend, then valuable time was being diverted from catching the real killer.

AS LT. RAY Biondi had hoped, the public plea for clues in the I-5 series had resulted in an overwhelming response in the weeks following the joint press conference.

The Sacramento County Sheriff's Department alone received more than 300 leads concerning the murders; most involved possible suspects. The other departments, like San Joaquin, had gotten a flood of responses, too.

Biondi had been talking to his detectives for some time about the importance of prioritizing leads. The way it was now, individual detectives at various law enforcement agencies who happened to answer the phone when a new lead came in would make an on-the-spot decision as to whether or not it was important. If deemed unimportant, the tip likely wouldn't be passed on—Sacramento wouldn't give it to San Joaquin, Vito Bertocchini wouldn't give it to Stan Reed, and so on. Thus, a lead that could have proven vital in identifying the killer when connected to other information might be lost forever.

Now, with an avalanche of new leads, it was more important than ever to find order in the chaos. Biondi had an idea that his detectives, up to their eyeballs in cases, were shining him on with platitudes: "Yeah, Ray, I'll think about it," and "Sure, boss, we'll come up with something."

When Reed and Bob Bell came around one afternoon to see if Biondi wanted to take a late lunch with them, Biondi sprung to the attack.

"Sit down, guys," he said after shutting the door behind his top detective team. "Let's come up with a way to prioritize. Come on, Bob, make us look smart."

Bell, who had a degree in geology, liked a good mental challenge. As he went on about criteria and rationales, Reed threw out pertinent one-liners in his patented growl. With a legal pad on his lap, Biondi caught it all.

Soon, a plan had taken shape; they would prioritize suspect leads based on a point system:

- 20 points if a suspicious person's identity was known or if they had an ability to trace him;
- 10 points if he had access to a dark, two-seater vehicle;
- 10 points if he was known to have a hair or cutting fetish or had once owned Italian scissors;

- 8 points if he was between forty and sixty years of age and had gray straight hair and a large nose;
- 8 points if he could be placed in the I-5 area;
- 8 points if he made a sudden, unexplained departure from the area after Sabrah's abduction or the press conference;
- 6 points if he had a violent background and/or had committed similar crimes;
- 6 points if he was familiar with the areas where the crime scenes were located;
- 6 points if he had ever attempted to pick up females on freeways or other roadways;
- 6 points if he had recent behavioral changes that coincided with the murders, dates of press releases, or at any time during the summer of 1986.

PRIORITY ONE would be considered "most viable leads," which had earned more than 40 points. They would be the first leads worked by detectives. Priority Two leads, which earned 35 to 40 points, would only be worked in absence of any Priority One leads. Priority Three leads, with between 20 and 35 points, were "informational leads" that "lacked significant detail to follow up." And Priority Four leads of less than 20 points were for "information only."

An hour later, Biondi released the two hungry detectives for lunch. Then he picked up the phone and went to work on the computer-literate types at DOJ's Homicide Analysis Unit to set up a program using the criteria. He explained that every lead sheet sent into DOJ would have a point value attached to it. DOJ agreed to tabulate the numbers and print out the names of possible suspects according to their cumulated point total. DOJ would update the list—based on new information—as often as required.

Biondi circulated the proposed criteria to other departments. Within a couple of days, he had the promise of all departments involved in the investigation that they would use the criteria table for assigning a numerical value to each suspect lead before sending the lead sheets to DOJ. Copies of the resultant computer printout would be sent to all departments.

Nobody seriously thought that the list would tell them who the killer was; its main purpose, rather, was to bring some order to the many hundreds of leads that had already been accumulated. The list would be a system, then, that would be used for assignments when and if there were ever enough detectives to work all the I-5 leads.

Biondi's sense of accomplishment didn't last long, for his fears concerning insufficient manpower to follow up on all the new leads generated by the media exposure had already materialized. Having a computerized list of prioritized leads would be fine and dandy, but what if there were no detectives free to work the phones and knock on doors?

Already stretched to the limit, the Sacramento County Sheriff's Homicide Bureau could not spare a single detective to work the I-5 series full-time. Stan Reed had only been able to spend a day here and there on Heedick, and that had been it. Other jurisdictions, Biondi knew, were in the same predicament.

Sacramento County had finished the year (1986) with a record forty-five homicides. In addition to having worked those cases—nine were still unsolved, including Heedick—the Bureau's four detectives were also responsible for the investigation of all the county's suspicious deaths, kidnappings, adult missing persons, and officer-involved shootings that resulted in injury or death.

To support his request for four new detectives beginning in 1987 (he intended to place two on the I-5 series), Biondi discovered that his bureau had an unusually high annual ratio of 11 homicides per investigator. Orange County Sheriff's Department had 7.5 homicides per investigator, while the San Diego County Sheriff's Department had 5 homicides per investigator. Closer to home, the Sacramento Police Department had 7 homicides per investigator.

"Due to a dramatic increase in workload, the Homicide Bureau needs immediate assistance," Biondi wrote in his year-end budget request. He warned that homicides were occurring in the county at such a rate that the Bureau was "struggling just to complete the preliminary investigation. Unsolved murders are not getting the continuous investigation required to resolve the cases."

In addition to the four new detectives—he acknowledged they would have to go through a period of training in order to be brought up to full speed—he requested the immediate temporary assistance of experienced investigators to help "stabilize the current workload." He wanted, in other words, both a tourniquet and Band-Aids.

Biondi was the first to admit that homicide investigations were costly programs for a law enforcement agency to operate. As manager of a homicide unit that never had enough people, office space, desks, cars, radios, tape recorders, and other support equipment, he constantly found himself facing moral-versus-practical questions: What price is human life worth? How far do we stretch our resources to solve a murder case?

While homicide investigations were never cost-effective in any measurable way, murder was a highly visible event that directly impacted the public's perception of a law enforcement agency. He reminded his superiors that the reputation of a law enforcement agency was often based on its handling of murder cases alone. Although the logic was faulty considering the many other accomplishments a well-run department could achieve, the nearly 100 percent blanket coverage afforded murder by the local media made this perception an indisputable fact.

To his bosses, Biondi beseeched: "Do we ignore viable leads in this serial killer case or do we seize the chance to demonstrate the excellence of this department?"

In going public with the I-5 series at the press conference in November, Biondi had an ulterior motive: with the murder series in the public eye, he hoped that administrators would be less likely to drag their feet when it came to providing manpower and equipment to put together a coordinated investigation.

But it wasn't to be. Biondi's impressive statistics and strongly worded memos could have been filed under the heading: NICE TRY. His call for help was turned down by budget-minded administrators with little serious discussion.

In the days of shrinking municipal budgets that affected virtually every public service from law enforcement to education to filling potholes in our roadways, the Sacramento County Sheriff's Department Homicide Bureau would enter the new year with its existing complement of four detectives—unchanged from a decade earlier when the county's murder rate had been about half what it was now.

Biondi was alarmed about what this would mean to the I-5 series investigation, given that his four detectives had been bogged down *before* the series began to unfold in their backyard. Even though his bureau was officially working only one of the suspected serial killer cases (Heedick), the other two dead women had been, after all, Sacramento County residents. Sabrah, as far as Biondi could tell, had already become an inactive case for tiny Amador County. At least the Brown case had been actively worked by San Joaquin, although Biondi knew that the irrepressible Vito Bertocchini was dealing with his own heavy caseload of new murders.

At such times, Biondi tried hard to remember why he had ever wanted to head the Homicide Bureau. He could have finished out his years to retirement as a supervisor in Patrol or Jails with a lot fewer headaches. He was in the midst of such a melancholy moment a couple of weeks before Christmas (1986) when there was a soft rap on his door.

"It's open," he said, not turning around.

"Ray, it's Kay Maulsby."

Glad for the intrusion, he spun around and with the sweep of a long arm invited Maulsby in, even though he knew why she was there and that he didn't have good news for her.

"Hi. Sorry to keep bugging you," she said.

"No problem."

Maulsby sat down across from Biondi. She was, as usual, sharply attired; today, in a blue business suit with white blouse. At forty-two, her only concession to age was the gray she allowed to streak her light brown hair. Her 5-foot-4 frame carried the same weight (123 pounds) as when she had graduated from Sacramento State two decades earlier with a degree in sociology and double minors in psychology and anthropology. Considering stamina important in her line of work, she kept her build trim and sinewy by watching what she ate, without being obsessive, and hour-long aerobics and weight-training workouts three times a week.

She was all business as she sat across from Biondi, not invincible, but definitely a compact force to be reckoned with. She could have been a high-level banker or a successful real estate broker, but she was neither. Maulsby was a cop.

"They turned me down," said Biondi, not given to sugarcoating. "Not even any temps."

Maulsby tried not to look disappointed, but her eyes gave her away.

"I'm sorry, Kay. I'd have you here in a NewYork minute if I could."

"I appreciate that."

Maulsby had wanted to work Homicide for a long time. She had been interested in law enforcement in college, but had been steered away from it by a school counselor because then—in the late 1960s— police work was still a male bastion. Instead, she became a social worker, although she considered those five years to be mostly biding her time until law enforcement opened up for women, as she knew it must. When the Sacramento County Sheriff's Department advertised to fill "deputy-female" positions needed for a new women's detention facility, Maulsby took the test, scored high, and was hired. Three years later, when the department opened up Patrol to women for the first time, Maulsby was among the first wave of what some old-timers in law enforcement considered a noble experiment doomed to fail. Some of the new women patrol deputies were average, some not so good, and some, like Maulsby, outstanding—pretty much in equal proportion to the performances of their male counterparts. She stayed in Patrol for five years, during which time she earned a reputation as being com- passionate when appropriate and fearless when required. She had been known to stop a carload of bad guys alone and wrestle resisting suspects to the ground. She became a detective in 1981, working burglary A year later she made sergeant. Typically, a promotion put the recipient back at square one to build seniority in rank again, and Maulsby was no dif- ferent. She went back to Jails with her new stripes and waited two years before a sergeant detective position opened in Special Investigations, where she worked Vice.

From the day she had taken the test to join the department, Maulsby had wanted to be a homicide detective, generally considered to be the most important position in police work and one reserved for the best of the best. At the time, it had been a seemingly unreachable dream for a young woman. But she had closed in on her goal: with eleven years on the force and having achieved the rank of sergeant detective, Maulsby felt qualified to work Homicide. By then, she had learned that 90 percent of police work was talking to people, and she was good at getting people—suspects as well as witnesses—to open up under the most difficult circumstances. Her tack was never to be disrespectful to even the slimiest of individuals, nor to badger anyone. Instead of spouting angrily, "You're a lying scumbag," she'd be more inclined to say calmly, "I'd rather have it a lot clearer than that and I know you can do it."

Maulsby had long let it be known throughout the department that she coveted Homicide. Ironically, she came to find her success in the ranks to be holding her back. Within the Homicide Bureau, there was one lieutenant position, one sergeant detective spot, and three detective billets to fill. Waiting for that one sergeant position to open up could—and often did—take years. The careers of many qualified detectives ended without their ever working Homicide.

In 1985, reasoning that her chances of getting to Homicide would be three times greater if she wasn't a sergeant, Maulsby had given up her stripes and taken a voluntary demotion—a $300 monthly pay cut, not to mention lost retirement benefits based on an employee's last pay rate. Her husband, Norman, had supported her decision. She had already been a cop when they'd met, and Norman was in law enforcement himself—he worked for DOJ and was a lieutenant in the Sacramento County Sheriff's Department reserve officer program. They did not have children, and he told her that money should not be an issue; she should feel free to take her career wherever she wanted to. Not many of her colleagues in the department thought she had done the right thing, however, as no one was able to promise Maulsby even then that she would ever make Homicide.

Biondi needed no convincing that Kay Maulsby would be an excellent homicide detective. He had enlisted her and several other detectives to do some legwork in a murder series six years earlier when a landscape gardener was breaking into homes and killing elderly women. Maulsby had proven herself a very capable investigator, excelling, in particular, Biondi thought, in interviewing and interrogation techniques, which he considered vital for Homicide. He found her very straightforward, willing to talk as openly about her abilities as about any shortcomings she might have. He was also struck by her eagerness. The fact that she had taken a demotion a year earlier to increase her chances at getting into Homicide still amazed him. It wasn't something he would have done.

Having Kay Maulsby in the unit was a no-brainer for Biondi. Back in the days when he first became a cop, police work had been a male-only world full of military-like camaraderie and closed to outsiders and the opposite sex. The few females allowed in a department—matrons, dispatchers, clerks—were expected to function only in secondary and supporting roles. After all, how could a woman break up a bar fight or subdue a violent criminal? Biondi had his head turned around when he worked as a supervisor in Patrol in the mid-1970s when women deputies first began working the streets. In no time, he came to realize that it was the individual, not the gender, that made a good cop.

Biondi planned to make Maulsby one of the four new detectives, had his request for increased manpower gone through. Already, Detective Bob Bell had requested Maulsby for a partner—she was that well regarded.

Biondi considered Bell and Stan Reed to be the finest homicide team in the department's history. But with such different personalities and ways of conducting business (a plus in that they had all the bases covered no matter what the challenge), both seemed ready for a change. Biondi had an idea that Bell and Maulsby would be a very good fit as permanent partners. Like Maulsby, Bell had had an excellent reputation (working Burglary) before coming to Homicide two years earlier. Bell, whose wife had an important job in state education, didn't have a chauvinistic bone in his body and was meticulous about his work in the way that Biondi knew Maulsby was. He would do well, Biondi had no doubt, teaming with the Bureau's only female homicide detective. But would it ever happen?

Maulsby was always good about not taking up too much of his time. She had stood and was now at the doorway.

"I don't have any reason to be optimistic," Biondi admitted as he came to his feet. "But check back anyway."

She smiled sheepishly. "I will."

Biondi knew she would, too.

CHAPTER EIGHT

At 5:30 P.M. on Monday, December 15, 1986, Harriet Kibbe, a forty-ish blonde whose pale blue eyes and blanched complexion suggested Scandinavian blood somewhere in her ancestry, answered a knock at the door of her ground-floor apartment in northeast Sacramento.

The occupation of the two beefy men at her doorstep was so apparent that they might as well have been sent over by Central Casting.

"Mrs. Kibbe?" asked the big, dark-haired one in the windbreaker.

"Yes."

"I'm Detective Bertocchini of the San Joaquin County Sheriff's Department."

He handed her his business card.

"Yes, we're expecting you." Looking down at the card, she saw it was like the one left on the screen door of their former residence a week earlier.

"This is Detective Reed of the Sacramento Sheriff's Department," he said, gesturing to the poker-faced middle-aged man next to him in a corduroy jacket.

At the time they had found the detective's card with the message "Please call" scrawled across it, Harriet and her husband, Roger, were in the midst of moving from their home of eight years in Oakley—a quiet Delta community about 40 miles from Sacramento. Harriet had no idea what the police could possibly want, and Roger told her he didn't either. Busy with the move, she hadn't called the number for two days. When she did, she was shocked that "Homicide" answered. "What is this about?" she asked Bertocchini when he came on the line. He explained that he wished to set up a time to talk to her husband about an "ongoing investigation." When she pressed for more information, the detective told her that her husband looked similar to the composite drawing of a suspect.

Harriet promised to speak to Roger and get back to the detective. She was shaken by the call. It seemed like a cruel rerun from hell. Eight years earlier, Roger had been questioned in the disappearance of a young woman in suburban Walnut Creek, across the bay from San Francisco. Roger had steadfastly denied knowing anything at all about the incident, but the cops had persisted, going so far as to interview their neighbors about his activities. Apparently, an eyewitness had seen the young woman getting into a multicolored van that resembled Roger's. He had insisted to Harriet that it was pure police harassment—he'd been out of the joint only a few years, and obviously they still had his name on file. *Was this more of the same?* she wondered.

Roger assured Harriet he knew nothing about any murder. Nervous about dealing directly with the cops, he sought advice from his brother, Steve, who lived at Lake Tahoe, on how to handle the situation. Even though Roger was the eldest, he had always turned to Steve, two years his junior, whenever he was in a pinch. Steve urged him to meet with the detectives as soon as possible, and he personally called Bertocchini to set up an interview.

Harriet invited the detectives in. Roger appeared, cup of coffee in hand. After brief introductions, Bertocchini explained that he'd been sent a report filed by Deputy Mayoya after Roger was stopped in Stockton the previous month for a traffic violation.

"I got the report because the deputy thought you resembled the composite in one of my cases."

Roger shrugged, but said nothing.

Without further ado—the cops didn't take Harriet up on her offer to sit down—Bertocchini asked Roger to accompany them downtown.

Harriet was taken aback when the detectives wouldn't let her come with them—there was plenty of room for the four of them in the unmarked car. The detectives told her she could follow, which she did.

For months now, Harriet Kibbe had been extremely worried about her eleven-year marriage. She still loved Roger, but she'd been unhappy for a long time.

It wasn't that he mistreated her; he'd slapped her exactly three times in their marriage. He'd cheated on her only once as far as Harriet knew, although she was aware that he had an eye for the ladies and knew he came off as charming in a cuddly sort of way even though he seldom wore his upper-front denture plate, which he found uncomfortable. On their first wedding anniversary, he'd left her for a woman from work. Their only separation lasted two weeks before he returned, asking Harriet what she wanted to happen next. "I want my husband back," she said. He went out and bought her red roses, which he delivered with a solemn promise never to stray again—"I don't know what I was thinking," he said with bowed head.

Compared with her other spouses (Roger was her fourth), Harriet considered Roger a decent husband. He had a kind side to him that came out especially around children (they were childless; a decade earlier Harriet had lost custody of her young son from a previous marriage, and Roger had a grown daughter from his first marriage) and animals (he adored their three cats). He made friends easily, always had a job, and never failed to bring his paycheck home, too. Because of his steady work they'd been able to save up and buy a home. He wasn't macho, demanding, or bossy. And he was a teetotaler, which meant a lot to Harriet, having been raised by parents who drank a lot. (She and Roger had once ordered iced tea at a pizza parlor and he was mistakenly served beer. So unaccustomed to alcohol was he, Roger had complained, "They gave me vinegar," when he tasted it.) Although they were scrimping these days, they didn't quarrel about finances like many couples she knew.

Harriet understood that she and Roger fulfilled powerful needs in each other. She was dominant and needed to lead and protect, and he was submissive. It was a dynamic that had seemed to work for them. Roger's father had recognized it shortly after their marriage: "Thank God for you, Harriet," he had whispered to her at a family gathering. "You're just the kind of woman Roger needs." Harriet knew Roger wanted her to be not only a wife but a mother to him as well, someone to replace the one he'd never gotten along with, who had died of cancer in the early 1960s.

Harriet knew that whenever anything went wrong, like when their furniture-making business went under in June (1986) and they lost

$35,000, she got the blame. She understood this came with her wife/ mother role. She knew people looked at Roger, the follower, and thought, "How could it be *his* fault?" They didn't know that when things got tough Roger was often among the missing. Like in June when they'd faced the imminent loss of their business: He'd walked out like he didn't have a care in the world, driving up to Lake Tahoe to visit his brother for several days and leaving her with a fully loaded furniture delivery truck broken down on the highway, an unhappy landlord looking for his overdue rent, and a stack of bills to pay. Soon after, foreclosure proceedings began on their Oakley home, avoided only at the last minute by a bargain-basement sale of the property arranged by Harriet. Although Roger was adept at solving mechanical problems, he deferred to her on running everything else in their lives—money, business, property, etc. Typically, it was she who had found their new situation managing a large storage facility, for which they both were paid a salary and lived for free in the managers' apartment. It would, Harriet hoped, give them a needed breathing spell.

Still, their marriage was unraveling. Thinking that Roger surely wanted out, she had asked him the month before to stay with her for another year. He'd agreed with no comment or discussion—not even "Why?" or "What do you mean?" Secretly, she had hoped he'd say something reaffirming like "I don't want us to break up" or even "Let's try to work this out." But he hadn't. And really, she knew he wouldn't.

Her plan favored logic over emotion: they could use the time to get back on their feet a bit financially before parting ways. Harriet, who had previously had her own bookkeeping service, intended to use the inter- vening time to develop a proprietary accounting program she hoped to sell to small businesses in and around Sacramento. At forty-four, she didn't like the idea of being on her own—after leaving an abusive home at age sixteen, she'd gone from one man to another. But if she was to be alone, she was determined to be able to support herself.

It wasn't that Roger came to her and said he was unhappy—that wasn't his style. He expressed it in other ways: by going deeper into his impen- etrable shell, by staying out all night, by not sleeping with her.

The unresolved issues between them had mounted through the years. They remained unsettled because whenever Harriet needed

Roger the most, he would completely disconnect from her and refuse to open up, not even answering her direct questions. He would act like she wasn't even in the room, ignoring her so completely that she felt invisible. Whenever he went inside himself and pulled down the shades, it was as if no one was home. "Are you trying to drive me crazy?" she'd ask in frustration. He didn't seem to understand that normal hurts, fears, and resentments didn't evaporate through neglect, but grew larger and more imposing until they filled a room, and a marriage, like a 900-pound gorilla.

"Please care enough about me to talk to me," Harriet would plead. "Please care enough about me to show some emotion." In response to her cries for spoken acknowledgment, Roger, his face impassive, usually left the room.

Harriet, who had always had a bad temper, now had a backlog of anger she could summon at any moment. With the least provocation, she could fly off the handle and rant wrathfully—but only in Roger's presence, not at work or among friends. She knew exactly what she was doing. Her mantra: *If I'm going to be miserable because he won't talk to me, then by God, I'm going to see to it that he's miserable, too.*

Yet, Harriet was never seriously able to consider leaving the marriage. Even now, with so little marital intimacy left, she was still waiting for him to pack up and leave her. That was the way it worked. Her previous husbands had all been mean-tempered guys who ran around on her until the day they were finished with her. Then they had left.

She had never in her life left a man (or cheated on one). Her worst fear imaginable was being abandoned, and yet it had happened time and again. All she'd ever wanted was to be accepted for who she was—no need to be taller, skinnier, smarter. But from the beginning of her life, things had been out of kilter. Her father had died a month before she was born, and her young widowed mother wasn't ready to be saddled with another child (Harriet had an older sister). She felt her mother hadn't wanted her, and as she grew up her stepfather came to want her in ways he shouldn't have.

The two-car caravan left I-5 at J Street and headed down tree-lined streets bracketed by high-rises.

Harriet followed closely; she didn't want to lose them and have Roger think he'd been—*abandoned.*

Harriet was protecting her husband as she had always wanted to be protected, but never had been.

WHEN THEY arrived at the third-floor offices of the Sacramento County Sheriff's Department Homicide Bureau, Roger Kibbe was ushered into a small interrogation room enclosed by four windowless, whitewashed walls. He settled in a hard chair beside a veneer-topped rectangular table shoved against one wall.

Vito Bertocchini, alone in the room with Kibbe, sat directly opposite him with nothing between them.

The detective began by wanting to know the location of Kibbe's recent residences, where he worked, and what type of vehicles he had driven in the past year.

Bertocchini already had obtained some of this information by way of a thorough records check. However, he wanted to hear it directly from Kibbe.

After Kibbe's recitation, Bertocchini, whose eyes never left Kibbe, asked out of the blue: "Were you soliciting prostitutes in Stockton when you were stopped by Deputy Mayoya?"

"Yeah."

"Had you done this before in the area?"

Kibbe nodded.

"How long had you been doing it?"

"Couple of w-weeks."

The stutter was slight, but apparent. "How much did you usually spend?"

"I don't spend money. I've never really been with a h-hooker. We just talk and they leave."

That's a new one, Bertocchini thought.

The detective asked Kibbe where else besides Stockton he had gone to seek prostitutes.

"Oakland and Sacramento."

"What kind of prostitutes interest you?"

"They have to be white."

"Okay. Anything else?"

"Not really."

Bertocchini asked Kibbe if he'd taken Interstate 5 when he traveled to and from his former residence in Oakley and his business near Modesto—a round-trip of some 120 miles.

"Yeah."

"Do you travel on I-5 to Sacramento?"

"When I visit my brother in Tahoe."

That route would have taken him in the direction Charmaine Sabrah was driving the last night of her life and past where her car had broken down.

"From Oakley," Bertocchini went on, "how would you pick up I-5?"

Kibbe said he'd take the Antioch Bridge, go into Rio Vista, then out Highway 12 east to I-5.

Bertocchini knew that route would have taken Kibbe within a mile of where Lora Heedick's body had been dumped, and only a stone's throw from the ditch where StephanieBrown's body had been found floating facedown.

Bertocchini remembered the pitch-black night five months earlier when he and Pete Rosenquist had stood above the ditch and concluded that Stephanie's killer, in order to find such an isolated spot, would likely have known the area.

The detective asked Kibbe if he was familiar with the Ione area in Amador County—where Charmaine Sabrah's body had been found in a field off the road.

"Yeah, I know it."

"Did you ever drive through there to get to your brother's place?"

"That w-would be the long way to Tahoe."

Kibbe said he used to have a friend who lived in Ione whom he visited occasionally. He said it had been three or four years since he'd been in the area.

"Do you ever stop to pick up hitchhikers or to aid stranded motorists?" Bertocchini asked.

"No."

"Roger, we'd like to take your photograph and get your fingerprints," Bertocchini said. "Would that be all right?"

Kibbe shrugged. "I guess," he said, asking if he could see his wife now. "Sure, I'll go get her."

Summoned from the spartan waiting room where she'd been sitting flipping through year-old fishing magazines for something to do, Harriet thought Roger looked defeated sitting alone in the interrogation room.

"Everything go okay?" she asked.

He seemed to be staring at the tip of his shoe.

"I'm not going home," Roger said flatly.

Harriet was floored. "Of course you are."

"No, I'm not." He hung his head so low she couldn't see his eyes.

A detective suddenly appeared, startling them. They were ready for Roger in the Identification Section. She stayed with him while he was fingerprinted and then photographed. Her mind raced as they went through the procedures she had seen before only on TV crime shows.

She well remembered Roger being taken in for questioning years earlier; how frightened she'd been and how cocky Roger had acted. The year had been 1978. Employed in an accounting office at the time, she'd been working late one afternoon when he called from home—a cookie-cutter tract house they owned in industrial Pittsburg, 20 miles northeast of Oakland—to say that two detectives were in their living room and wanted to take him in for questioning. A few days earlier Roger had told her he thought the cops were following him and taking pictures of his van. He didn't speculate as to why, and Harriet assumed it had to do with his prison record. After that, she'd spoken with a couple of their neighbors, who reported that police were asking questions about Roger and his multicolored van in connection with the case of the missing young woman who had been in the news and the subject of flyers up around town for more than a month. They'd taken Roger to the Contra Costa County D.A.'s office in Martinez, where she had met up with them. When she hadplanted herself in front of the detectives and demanded to know what it was all about, one of them whirled on her and said: "Would you like me to book *you* now?" She had moved aside. As Roger went by, she saw a smirk on his face. He said loud enough for the cops to hear, "We have nothing to worry about." She'd been taken aback at how calm and reassuring he sounded.

Why was he acting so differently this time?

Roger had claimed he didn't know anything about any missing woman back in 1978 or about any murder case now. He said he'd done nothing wrong, and she believed him. She'd never known Roger to hurt anyone— in fact, he always went out of his way to avoid confrontations. There were times when if she'd been a man she would have punched someone's lights out—like when a former employee walked into their office and stole Harriet's Rolex right off a table. Roger saw it happen; he told her about it the next morning when she couldn't find her watch. But what had he done about it at the time? Much to her exasperation: nothing. Roger avoided showdowns of any kind.

She'd begun her life with Roger aware of his troubled past. In fact, he'd been out of state prison only a short time when they met in 1972. That two-year stay behind bars, an earlier conviction (1963–65), and another one in 1974 for which he served a year had all been for property crimes like petty theft, burglary, grand theft. He'd done really dumb things like taking wood from a lumberyard and tools from a garage. It wasn't as if he profited from his thievery, or even needed what he stole. She knew he had sometimes stolen to get even with someone he was mad at—blind-siding rather than confronting *was* Roger's way—but other times he didn't know his victims at all. Like the time years ago back in his hometown when he'd parked a couple of blocks from an army surplus store he intended to loot late one night, broke a window, and waited at the corner bus stop to see if the place had a silent alarm. When the police showed up a few minutes later, Roger had calmly given them a description of "two men who ran that way," then climbed aboard a city bus, which he rode only to the next stop and then circled back to his car. He'd clearly relished telling the story of how he'd "outsmarted the cops." Harriet came to realize that thievery had been a kind of mind game to him. He wasn't motivated by profit—he had no drug or other expensive habits to support. True satisfaction for him was fooling the cops and getting away with it.

In any case, as far as she knew, Roger had never hurt a soul. So why then, she wondered, was he worried about not coming home?

———

BERTOCCHINI **was** still the new kid in Homicide, but as a skilled street cop he knew about judging people by their words and demeanor. And he had a strong feeling about Roger Kibbe, a real *bad* feeling.

Throughout the hour-long interview, Kibbe had remained outwardly calm, although Bertocchini sensed that he was squirming. Kibbe had not made any obvious admissions or slipups or incriminating statements, however, and answered all the questions put to him.

Before Kibbe departed, Bertocchini had asked if he'd be willing to take a polygraph if it could be arranged for the following day.

Kibbe said he wanted to call his brother.

Bertocchini showed him a phone.

When he was done, Kibbe said he'd think about it and get back to Bertocchini.

"You'll call me in the morning and let me know?" Bertocchini pressed.

"Yes, we will," Harriet said.

After the Kibbes had left, Bertocchini went into Biondi's office, where Biondi and Reed had watched the interview on a closed-circuit television monitor.

"What do you guys think?" Bertocchini asked.

Reed and Biondi were noncommittal.

"This is weird, I know," Bertocchini said, running a hand through his mane of thick black hair. "I mean, I'm not exactly Mr. Experienced Homicide Investigator, so tell me if I'm off base here. But sitting across from this guy, he sent chills down my spine. The way he talked about women—it was like they're his playthings. And he's on I-5 a lot and he's familiar with all the locations of our women. He's got the cars, too."

Verifying the information Bertocchini had obtained from DMV, Kibbe had said he bought the Datsun 280Z in June (1986)—two months before Sabrah disappeared in what her mother described as a "dark two-door sports car." Prior to that, Kibbe said he drove a white two-door 1972 Ford Maverick, which he'd sold in July (1986)—three months after Heedick disappeared. The Kibbes had registered a white four-door 1986 Hyundai, apparently to replace the Maverick, in July (1986).

Turning to Reed, Bertocchini asked, "Wasn't Heedick picked up in an older white two-door?"

"That's what Driggers says," Reed answered.

Bertocchini pointed out that Kibbe had had his furniture shop in the truck-stop town of Ceres, "about three miles from the main drag of Modesto." Also, that Kibbe and his wife had rented a townhouse nearby, while subletting their Oakley home to friends at the time of Heedick's disappearance.

Days earlier, Bertocchini had run Kibbe's name through the DOJ for a criminal record and come up with his lengthy rap sheet for burglary and theft. His record was notable, Biondi had thought this evening as he reviewed it, in that there weren't any crimes of violence or previous sexual misconduct listed.

"His wife said something interesting," Bertocchini continued. "When we got here she wanted to know if she should hire an attorney. She said Roger had previously been questioned in Contra Costa County by police in the disappearance of a young woman from a shopping center because his van was similar to a van that was used in the crime. It had caused them a lot of grief and she didn't want to go through that again."

Biondi thought Bertocchini might be getting too worked up about Kibbe. The homicide chief realized that the two detectives sitting in his office were exact opposites. Reed always had his feet planted firmly on mother earth, and evaluated people and information in a careful, almost detached way. Bertocchini, on the other hand, seemed to put substantial weight in hunches and spinal chills.

The fact of the matter was that there had been a deluge of "persons of interest"—or POI's, as Biondi had taken to calling them—in the I-5 investigation. POI's differed from suspects in that there was no evidence or information linking them to a specific crime. A POI was investigated, rather, due to a variety of less tangible factors, such as: They looked like the composite, they drove a similar car, they had a violent criminal history that included rape, they frequented the geographic areas the victims were abducted from or where their bodies were dumped, they had been reported to police by suspicious friends or relatives.

Some weeks earlier, Bertocchini himself had been called to the scene of a traffic stop in Stockton where a look-alike was being detained. John Samples certainly resembled the composite, and was the right age, height, and weight. He was driving a dark red MGB, and a search of the vehicle found a loaded flare gun. Samples admitted he often took "joy rides" on I-5 to Sacramento. Although he was an unemployed mechanic, he denied ever stopping to assist females with disabled cars. Bertocchini had felt so strongly about Samples that he had deputies take him downtown for further questioning, and also had Mrs. Carmen Anselmi brought out to the scene to view the car. Although some things were similar, she finally concluded that it wasn't the vehicle she had ridden in that night. After further questioning, Bertocchini established that Samples had been elsewhere on the date of Charmaine Sabrah's disappearance.

As for the Stephanie Brown case, Bertocchini's sometime partner, Pete Rosenquist, had investigated a Chester Simmons, who had been released from prison in December, 1985, and had been taken back into custody for rapes in the Sacramento area a month after Brown's death. Simmons would stop vehicles at gunpoint and threaten to fire through the window if females did not comply. He also choked his victims while raping them. Simmons denied having anything to do with Brown's death, but without a confirmed alibi he had to be considered a serious contender.

The previous month, Stan Reed had spent several days trying to locate Jack Browner, a look-alike who drove a dark green Triumph, even searching his apartment—the rent was in arrears by several months—before finally locating him. As a traveling salesman, Browner frequently used I-5. He admitted to fifteen previous felony arrests going back to the 1960s when he was a Hell's Angel. On one occasion, he'd been picked up for questioning in a first-degree murder.

Also in November, Reed had spent time investigating Richard Taylor, a southern California airline pilot who had been the suspect (arrested and released) in five female murders in Hawaii. The victims were usually picked up at bus depots, tied up, strangled, and dumped along freeways. Reed could not place Taylor in the Sacramento area for any of the murders; also, he was eliminated as a suspect in the Brown case because he had had a vasectomy and most likely could not have left the sperm detected on the vaginal slide by the DOJ lab.

The first week of December, Reed had brought in for questioning a particularly interesting POI: a Sacramento cabbie named Wayne Welborn, who had kidnapped, raped, and murdered a thirteen-year-old girl a decade earlier. That a convicted rapist-murderer had been freed after serving only five years (he'd raped and sodomized the teenager before shooting her in the chest with a shotgun, for which he'd been allowed to plead guilty to second-degree murder) might have come as a surprise to the head of the local PTA, but not to Reed. He was well aware that rapists and murderers walked the streets; he dealt with them all the time.

Welborn, the son of a prominent physician, had regularly bragged to his state department of corrections staff psychologist at a parole outpatient clinic about his violent fantasies involving women. Welborn had continued to see the psychologist weekly after he'd been released from parole several months earlier. In December, he had appeared to be so agitated and ready to explode that the psychologist had phoned the Sex Abuse Bureau of the Sacramento County Sheriff's Department to advise them that Welborn would be a very good suspect in any unsolved rapes. "I still don't always know when he's fantasizing or telling the truth," she admitted. "He could just be getting off telling me about 'pretend' rapes. I don't know. But he claims to have raped at knifepoint twenty to twenty-five women since he got out of prison three years ago. He said most of them were hitchhikers he picked up." Sex Abuse had passed the information along to Homicide.

Reed had spent an hour interviewing Welborn, a handsome, well-spoken Ivy League type who had a fixation on emergency services—he liked to monitor police calls and make false reports. After killing the teenage girl, he'd even called police to report finding the body, then watched from a distance as officers conducted their crime scene investigation.

Welborn had claimed he was working the nights that Brown and Heedick had disappeared. When Reed asked if he'd submit to a polygraph, Welborn flinched. He told of his girlfriend's recently flunking a polygraph regarding a stolen VCR that she didn't steal. "She had knowledge of the theft and that's what affected the results," he said.

"Are you saying you have knowledge of these murders?" Reed asked, his interest piqued.

"Yes, I might."

"What do you know, Wayne?"

Welborn clearly enjoyed the attention. "The type of personality involved here," he began, as if lecturing to a college psychology class, "fits a guy I did time with. His name is Chuck Anderson, and he's from Sacramento. While I was in prison with him, he attacked a female officer with a pair of scissors. He hates women and he would be capable of doing something like this."

"Do you have any specific information that he's involved in these killings?" Reed asked.

"No, I do not."

Reed suspected Welborn was playing games, but he jotted down the information anyway.

Before he left Homicide, Welborn made a point of stopping to meet Lt. Ray Biondi, whom he said he'd seen a lot of on television. Acting as if it was an honor to be brought in for questioning in a murder case, Welborn noticed a stack of Little League cookies Biondi was selling for his sons, and bought twenty bucks' worth.

It turned out that Chuck Anderson was still behind bars. As for Welborn, his alibi was confirmed by his taxi logs, his manager and fellow drivers, and several fares he had picked up on those two nights.

As far as Biondi was concerned, there were lots of POI's, some much better would-be suspects than Kibbe, given their records of sex-related violence. But suspects were not the first thing on Biondi's mind at this point. Although he always hoped for an easy break like a "magic phone call" identifying the culprit, he knew that without some serious organization in this multijurisdictional investigation, the killer's identity might show up as a lead or in a report but not be recognized as such by detectives. Someone, somewhere might even have interviewed him, but the report might have been buried in voluminous paperwork and unless a new piece of information caused a second look, no one might ever focus on him again.

Biondi considered the main thing that had been done right in the investigation so far had been the centralization of all physical evidence with the DOJ crime lab. But the real payoff in terms of scientific analysis of the evidence would not come until they could get sufficient manpower to follow up on the hundreds of unworked leads and otherwise work the growing number of unsolved homicides in a coordinated fashion.

Bertocchini's enthusiasm was not to be extinguished. "I tell you, this guy is killing women. Everywhere we have dead bodies, this guy has a reason to be there," he told Biondi before leaving his office that night.

Bertocchini drove home on I-5 that night excited, and also frustrated. He wondered if he was out of his depth. Maybe he was better suited to being a street cop than a detective. All this endless jawing and inaction got to him. He much preferred slapping the cuffs on a bad guy and lighting up a cigar to celebrate.

If he had his way, Kibbe's Sacramento residence would have been staked out round-the-clock beginning immediately. But the consensus was that while Kibbe was worth knowing about and his picture should be shown to witnesses, with hundreds of other leads to follow up on, who could get overly worked up?

Anyway, the veteran detectives knew Kibbe's brother, Douglas County Sheriff's Department Detective Steve Kibbe, from the Nevada side of Lake Tahoe, 80 miles due east of Sacramento, as they had all worked cases with him over the years.

What were the chances that the brother of a homicide detective would turn out to be a serial killer?

CHAPTER NINE

The morning after Roger Kibbe was questioned by Homicide, Harriet went into the bathroom to take a shower. When she emerged ten minutes later, Roger had vanished. Checking the bedroom, she found that he had taken most of his clothes with him. He had done so in a great hurry; socks and other items were scattered about the floor.

She could have kicked herself: Roger hightailing it was so damn typical she should have seen it coming.

Still in her robe and with her hair wrapped in a towel, she dropped listlessly to a chair in the bedroom. She sat with arms folded and rocked slowly back and forth.

Upon their arrival home from the police station the previous evening, an obviously shaken Roger said he couldn't trust the cops not to rig the polygraph against him. Chalking up his distrust to his past troubles with the law, Harriet empathized rather than argued. Without the slightest doubt of her husband's innocence, she'd said, "If you don't want to take it, don't. If they bother us, we'll go see a lawyer."

After that, they had gone to bed, sleeping separately, as they had for the past eight months. In the Oakley house they'd each had their own bedroom, but in the new apartment they slept in the same room: Harriet in a king-size bed in the center of the room, Roger in a single bed shoved into a corner.

They had slept together for a decade of married life, and as far as Harriet was concerned their sex life had been just fine. Roger never was a romantic, but once between the sheets he was always sensitive to her needs. Their conjugal bed, in which he functioned well and with obvious confidence, was the one place he took over—much to the delight of

Harriet, who willingly let go. Throughout the years, they had averaged a good three times a week; she was missing it and she couldn't understand how he wasn't.

Whenever she dwelled on the start of their separate sleeping arrangement, she thought it seemed totally unnecessary. However, she blamed the impasse on Roger. Allergic to fleabites, she didn't like sleeping with their cats. At night they customarily put the cats out or closed the bedroom door. One night, however, Roger declined to do so, saying he wanted to sleep with the cats. Feeling that he'd made his choice, Harriet stormed into the spare bedroom. That had been in April (1986), and since then they'd slept separately and had not been intimate. Harriet had wondered if having one bedroom (from which the cats were banned) in the apartment would change things, but it hadn't.

Harriet understood the episode with the cats had been only a symptom, not the disease. She and Roger had been coming undone for so long it was difficult to remember when the first signs of disharmony had appeared. In truth, they had surfaced even before they were married. But after living together for three years, getting married had seemed the thing to do. Besides, she'd had such a troubled family life growing up that a little trouble seemed normal. And now, no one could say she had given up easily. The past summer, she'd even jumped from an airplane trying to save her marriage.

Roger had long enjoyed woodworking in his garage workshop and skydiving on weekends; neither hobby had ever included her. Anxious to find something they could do together, Harriet had signed up for her first parachute jump. Roger had been supportive, and seemed to get a kick out of watching her make practice landings off the couch. She'd made the tandem jump with an instructor from 7,500 feet—frightened to death the entire time—and that had been the end of it. Roger hadn't invited her back out to the jump zone with him, and she hadn't volunteered.

The major disappointments they'd experienced had surely taken their toll—most recently, the collapse of their business, for which Roger had borrowed (and lost) $10,000 from his brother Steve for start-up capital. Such a reversal, followed by the loss of the home they had loved and their general inability to work through everyday problems, had added to their increasing burden.

Restless one night not long after they'd stopped sleeping together, Harriet got out of bed at 4:00 A.M. and found Roger's room empty. She dressed and drove to the shop, where she found him asleep on the office couch. Waking him up, she said, "Tell me what's wrong. I need to know." Without saying a word, Roger, fully clothed, threw off the blanket and walked out. "We need to talk!" she yelled to his departing back. When she heard his car pull away, she broke down.

A month or so later, Roger had not been home for several nights in a row. Around 10:00 P.M. Harriet called the shop. Sounding desperate, she told him that a "Mexican guy" had called threatening to burn down their house. She begged Roger to come home, and he finally did, an hour or so later. By then, the police had arrived. Lying alone in bed that night, Harriet knew she'd reached rock bottom: she'd made up the call and even filed a false police report in an effort to get Roger to come home to her.

Harriet began picking up Roger's mess in the bedroom when suddenly she stopped. Dropping the things back on the floor, she rushed into the small office that adjoined the apartment. She opened the drawer in which she kept the cash deposits from customers. It was empty. Roger had made off with the $375 she'd carefully counted out and for which she'd prepared a bank deposit slip the afternoon before.

In an instant, her depression turned to anger.

Roger obviously didn't give a shit about her and had left for good. His leaving now threatened *her* new job and *her* new home. Luckily, she had just enough money in savings to cover the loss, which she would do right away. But their boss had hired them as a couple: she to handle the office work, Roger the maintenance and upkeep around the rental yard. With Roger gone, who would do the outside work? How long before their employer found out she was alone and fired her? Where would she go? Where would she get the money for another place? How would she support herself?

Cursing Roger's gross ineptitude when it came to living life, she took a roll call of his shortcomings:

He was weak,

—emotionally unstable,

—insecure,

—a latent thumb sucker who stuttered the most when he lied, not when he told the truth,

—a frightened little boy in a grown man's body,

—at forty-seven years of age totally unfit for adult responsibility.

Why had he always been so afraid to reveal himself?

———

SHE PICKED up the phone and dialed Vito Bertocchini's number at the San Joaquin County Sheriff's Department. When he came on the line, Harriet told him Roger had decided not to take a polygraph.

"We have an attorney, so please don't bother us anymore," she said abruptly.

"Mrs. Kibbe, I'm just trying to gather information in our investigation," Bertocchini said. "We have several young women who were abducted, sexually assaulted, and strangled to death. One of them was nineteen years old. Another one had an infant at home she was still nursing."

So quick had she been to disassociate Roger from the entire matter, she hadn't considered the enormity of the crime itself. *Murder* had been committed—lives had been taken, callously snuffed out, leaving grieving families.

Harriet knew the detective had meant to shock her, and he'd succeeded. Yet, she formed the thought—stronger than ever—that Roger could not possibly be involved. If a stack of two-by-fours were missing from a lumberyard or if someone's customized parachute rig had disappeared at the airport, she might have wondered if Roger was up to his old tricks. But *multiple homicides?*

They had lived in the same house, slept in the same bed, eaten at the same table, laughed at the same TV shows, wrapped Christmas presents for each other, gone through the ups and downs of life together for more than a decade. While Roger certainly had his faults, he had never displayed a penchant for violence or a hatred toward women. Harriet had been with men about whom she could not so testify, but Roger wasn't among them. The three slaps, delivered open-handed and during fits of anger over an eleven-year period, hardly counted as violence in her book. As for women, he'd never had trouble making and keeping them as friends. And given the mile-wide streak of passivity that ran through him, anyone who knew Roger wouldn't possibly peg him as a murderer.

Sexual assaults? He'd never been the least rough in bed; not with Harriet, and as far as she knew, not with other women. Years earlier, Roger had told her of making love to his first wife, who he said was quite boisterous in bed, and having to stop occasionally to make sure he wasn't hurting her. How could a man that sensitive *assault* a woman?

Harriet felt very sorry for the victims and their families, but before hanging up on Bertocchini she told him that she didn't see what it had to do with her husband.

As for Roger's sudden departure, that was nothing new. Sometimes, he'd disappear just as Harriet was getting ready for bed. Nothing she could point to seemed to be the trigger—not an argument or words of any kind exchanged. He'd just sneak out and slink away. When he returned—hours later or the next morning—he'd have nothing at all to say about his absence. She had even stopped asking him where he'd gone because he would simply ignore any questions he didn't want to answer. It seemed whenever Roger got antsy these days, he hit the road. In July alone he'd logged 10,000 miles on the Datsun 280Z, which they'd bought the previous month as Harriet's car but which he liked so much he took over. She had bought another car, a white Hyundai, for herself. Once he had the 280Z to drive, Roger had given his old Maverick to a young guy who had been employed part-time at the shop in exchange for $140 owed in back wages when the business failed. (Roger giving away the Maverick—a good-running car they'd owned for three years—for such a pittance had infuriated Harriet. Seeing it as another example of Roger's irresponsibility, she'd dragged him along to their ex-employee's house to try to recover the car. It was too late, however, as the ownership transfer had already been filed with the state, and the young man legally owned the vehicle.)

What had made Roger's departure different this time was that he'd packed his things. He had never done that when he went away before.

As the day wore on, her anger subsided. She stayed busy showing rental spaces (normally Roger's job) and preparing rental agreements for new customers. Their boss showed up that afternoon. When asked about Roger, Harriet said he was running some errands. She had a feeling she hadn't lied well. How long would it be before the truth came out, and she found herself out of a job and a place to live?

That they would part had no longer been in doubt; it had come down to a matter of timing. Roger had obviously decided now was better than later. Thinking about it, Harriet could hardly blame him. She had turned into such a miserable nag she couldn't stand herself sometimes. Why wouldn't Roger want to leave sooner? He deserved happiness, too.

A few months earlier, Harriet, pessimistic about her life changing for the better, had contemplated suicide. She had phoned her sister-in-law, Julie Kibbe (Steve's wife), one afternoon to ask her opinion on the "easiest and most painless" method. Harriet's rationale had been that if she was going to do it, she wanted to do it right, and not suffer needlessly or wind up a vegetable.

Julie had gone right along with the program. "Get in the car and you run the hose."

"Really?"

"Oh, yeah. You drive the car in the garage and start the engine, but first make sure you drink enough so that you're pretty numb. Make sure you lay down on the seat because if you sit up they'll have to break your legs to get you out of the car when you're dead."

Harriet wondered at the time what difference it would make if her legs had to be broken when she was dead, but she refrained from saying anything and logged the advice.

Fifteen minutes later the sheriff's department was at Harriet's door with deputies, paramedics, and an ambulance. She would find out later that Steve, overhearing his wife's end of the conversation, had become alarmed and called authorities. She was kept under observation in the hospital suicide ward until 3:00 A.M. the next morning. When they released her, she had called and asked Roger to come get her. When he arrived, he was angry. She was unable to get him to talk on the gloomy ride home. *I've just left a suicide ward*, she thought. *Why isn't he more concerned about me?*

It had been not so long after that when Harriet, finally beginning to lay plans for life after Roger, had solicited his promise to stay for a year—a promise that she assumed, given his sudden departure, he'd decided not to keep.

The phone awakened her that night. She was surprised to hear Roger's voice on the other end.

"Hi, how you doing?" he asked in his soft, almost hushed voice.

"What," she sputtered, still half asleep. "Why are you calling me?"

"To see how you are."

"You ran off without a word and you call to see how I am?" She had thought she might actually never hear from him again, but here he was calling so soon.

He said he had left just to clear his head.

She wasn't a fool. She knew he could well be cheating on her. But right now Roger's possible involvement with another woman was not a high-priority concern.

She explained that after he left she'd called the detective and told him there would be no polygraph.

"Do you know anything about any of these women who were murdered?" she asked, a new urgency in her voice.

"No."

Two days later Harriet was in the office doing paperwork when Julie phoned from Tahoe. She told Harriet that Roger had arrived at their place the previous night. That didn't surprise Harriet, as Roger often ended up at his brother's whenever he disappeared for a day or more.

"Roger feels bad and wants to come home," Julie said. "But he's afraid to. He's got the crabs."

"The *crabs*?"

Roger had made his admission to Steve, claiming he'd caught them from a motel bed. Steve told Julie, with orders to strip the bed Roger had slept in.

"Roger's afraid to tell you," Julie said, "but I thought you should know."

Harriet also spoke to Steve. The two of them, she had long ago realized, performed very similar roles in Roger's life. Steve was Roger's protector, always trying to make something better for his older brother. In that sense, she and Steve were almost like competitors, and perhaps for that reason their relationship had never been particularly warm. However, it had been Steve and Julie—her then next-door neighbors—who introduced Harriet to Roger in 1972, when he had come to live with them after being released from a halfway house following a prison stay.

Harriet asked Steve if she knew where Roger had been the last three days.

Steve said Roger had called collect from outside Las Vegas the previous day. Before accepting the charges, Steve had asked the operator where the call originated from. He heard Roger say, "Don't tell," but Steve insisted the operator tell him before he would agree to pay for the call. In this conversation, Roger told Steve he was taking a trip across country "to get away." When Steve asked him why he was leaving, Roger said he feared he was about to be framed for murder. Steve had persuaded Roger to take a room for the night and call him back in the morning. When Roger did, Steve had been able to convince Roger not to flee.

Steve said Roger also related having been stopped by the Nevada Highway Patrol for doing 110 mph on U.S. 95 in the desert north of Vegas. Harriet knew that Roger carried Steve's sheriff's department business card; on occasion, when stopped by a cop, he'd pull it from his wallet in the hope that he could get out of a ticket. Sometimes, it worked.

When she spoke with Roger, he sounded apologetic.

In the face of everything—she made a note to call the pharmacy and find out how to get rid of crabs—Harriet found herself strangely relieved that Roger wanted to come back. Things would go easier with the job, and it would make her a lot less crazy about her immediate future.

She agreed to drive up to Tahoe and pick up Roger and bring him home. He'd leave the Datsun 280Z there, with Steve promising to drive it to Sacramento in a week or two.

Although she could get very angry with Roger for his silent and sneaky ways, when he was gone Harriet missed him. She also felt sorry for him.

The next evening, Roger stood naked in their bathtub as Harriet soaped his entire body with a special medicated shampoo, then ran a fine-toothed comb through his body hair. It was a painstaking process, as he had thick black hair covering his chest, shoulders, back, and legs.

Harriet again felt needed.

ON THE morning of December 19, 1986, four days after he had questioned Roger Kibbe, Vito Bertocchini met with Carmen Anselmi at her Sacramento apartment.

He explained he was going to ask her to look at a group of photographs. Then, he went through the admonishments required by law. "The fact that the photographs are being shown to you should not influence your judgment. You should not conclude or guess that the photographs contain the picture of the person who committed the crime."

Anselmi nodded.

"You are not obligated to identify anyone," he went on. "It is just as important to free innocent persons from suspicion as to identify guilty parties."

Anselmi said she understood.

The detective took out six color photographs not much larger than wallet-size. He spread them out on the kitchen table. All were frontal head shots of middle-aged Caucasian men with graying hair. Five were known as "filler photos": pictures of nonsuspects, most of them sheriff's department employees. Photo 3 was Roger Kibbe.

She looked at the photo spread anxiously, with darting eyes. She didn't hit on any of them. "It was so dark in the car," she said, sounding discouraged.

"Please go through them again, one by one, and take your time. It might be helpful to try to eliminate the ones you're sure aren't the suspect."

This time, she went much slower, picking up each picture and studying it intently. In so doing, she eliminated #1, #2, #4, and #6.

Bertocchini asked her about #5.

"He has a fuller face," she said, "but I can't positively eliminate him."

"Okay. What about number three?"

"The hair is right. Color, style, and hairline. The nose is the same, too."

Bertocchini waited.

"I can't be sure one way or the other. I never saw the front of his face. Always the side. His right side. It might be better if I could see them in person."

Bertocchini knew they didn't have enough on Kibbe to bring him in for a lineup. To put together a stand-up lineup, they were required to process a suspect into jail and notify an attorney, who would have to be present; if the suspect couldn't afford one, a public defender would show up.

The detective gathered up the pictures and left.

Although he made a point of not showing it, he was every bit as disappointed as Charmaine's mother.

The detective had not been very surprised when Kibbe declined to take a polygraph. He felt stronger than ever that Kibbe was dirty.

Bertocchini was still haunted by Harriet Kibbe's comment that her husband had previously been a suspect in the disappearance of a young woman. He contacted the Contra Costa County Sheriff's Department to see if they had anything in their files other than what appeared on Kibbe's rap sheet, which by law included only arrests and convictions. A deputy in the records section promised to look. Most police departments routinely kept "field interrogation" cards that documented any time an individual was contacted by officers. An "FIR" card could lead to a treasure trove of reports.

In the mail a few days later came a copy of Offense Report #84-8068, dated April 1984. The crime of "rape by force" had been reported by Janice Evans, a twenty-seven-year-old white female. She initially identified her attacker as "Robert," but investigators soon identified the accused as one Roger Reece Kibbe, age forty-five, who resided in Oakley and worked in a nearby city as a truck driver for Volunteers of America. (She gave the license number of her attacker's white, two-door car as 1SAL700, one letter off from Kibbe's Maverick: 1JAL700.)

Bertocchini refilled his cup with coffee fit for a lube gun and returned to his desk to read the twelve-page report.

Janice Evans had first been contacted by a sheriff's deputy at the county hospital where she was examined. She had met her attacker five days earlier when she agreed to have sexual intercourse with him in exchange for $30. When she told him she had been down on her luck lately, he offered to help. The next day she met him at his place of work and he gave her five dollars for lunch. The following day she returned and he gave her lunch money again. Out of the blue he asked if she wanted to come live with him for a while; he'd offered to pay her $200 a day for sex. As she had a $150-a-day heroin habit, she agreed. They met at 8:00 P.M. that night, ostensibly to drive to his house. They drove on a mainthoroughfare a while, then ended up on a rural road. "Robert" explained he needed gas and that a friend of his had a pump on a ranch that he could use. They continued on the dark road before he pulled over and told her to get out. He came around the vehicle with a 4-inch chrome revolver leveled at her. He ordered her to pull down her pants and lie down on the ground. "Please leave me alone," she said. "Just take me back." The man warned: "If you don't do what I ask, I'll blow your pussy off."

She complied and he kneeled down. He inserted the barrel of the gun in her vagina and moved it in and out for several minutes. Then he pulled down his own pants and ordered her to give him "a blow job." She accommodated, and after he ejaculated in her mouth he told her to stay on the ground until he left. She walked into town and flagged down a motorist who took her to the hospital. (Although she had a few scratches, nothing was found by the attending doctor and nurse that conclusively proved Janice Evans had been raped.)

Another report summarized an interview that a sheriff's department sergeant had with Kibbe at his place of work two weeks later. After the sergeant read the suspect his Miranda rights, Kibbe said he understood his rights but wished to discuss what happened. He said Janice Evans was a prostitute who hung out on the street in front of his place of work. He said he had given her "a few dollars" now and then but denied having sex with her. "I don't know what type of diseases she is carrying," he said. "I'd never touch a prostitute." He admitted to having given her a ride the night in question, but contended that nothing had happened. He said he had dropped her off in the parking lot of a fast-food outlet where she told him she intended to meet a friend.

The sergeant also interviewed a friend of the victim who confirmed that two weeks earlier she had related the same story she had told the deputy at the hospital, and that she had seemed very frightened.

When the sergeant went looking for Janice Evans to conduct a follow-up interview, she was nowhere to be found. Two weeks later, the case was closed, although on its jacket was the note, "Review if victim reestablishes contact."

Bertocchini considered the incident report he'd come across vindication of sorts for his feeling that Kibbe was potentially dangerous, and a viable suspect. This report may or may not have been the "young woman's disappearance" alluded to by Harriet Kibbe, Bertocchini knew. Still, it seemed quite relevant to the investigation at hand. He phoned Stan Reed with the information about the old rape case.

As usual, Reed played it cool, not encouraging Bertocchini's anxious speculation. But he did pull the single-page tip sheet that he'd begun on Kibbe the night he came in for questioning.

Written on the sheet was the following: "Kibbe attempted to pick up prostitutes in Stockton, driving dark two-seat sports car. Had pellet gun. Sold white Maverick this summer. Fled area on 12/16/86."

To this, Reed added a note about Kibbe's history of being a suspect in the abduction and rape. Then, he sent the tip sheet to DOJ. Kibbe's name was in the hopper.

WHEN DETECTIVE Stan Reed showed James Driggers the same photo lineup that Carmen Anselmi had seen, Driggers wasn't able to single out anyone either.

However, Driggers went through pictures of older American cars and picked out the Ford Mavericks for the years 1970 to 1975 as looking like the white car that Lora Heedick rode off in the night she disappeared.

Investigators contacted the individual who received Roger Kibbe's white 1972 Maverick six months earlier in exchange for back wages due him. He reported that he'd sold the vehicle the previous month to someone in Arroyo Grande, 200 miles south of San Francisco. When local police knocked on his door, the Maverick's new owner gave them permission to search the vehicle.

A DOJ criminalist arrived on the scene, and spent two hours examining the car and removing miscellaneous debris with forceps from the floor mats, front and rear. He also took tape lifts from the floor of the car, picking up whatever stuck to lengths of Scotch tape, then vacuumed up whatever remained and sealed the contents in a plastic bag. Two long hairs were taken from under the seat-belt holder on the driver's side; a hair and piece of yellow fiber from the trunk; a length of rope from the trunk; plant material and soil from the passenger-side rear fenders; long, needle-like plant material from the driver's side rear fender and hair samples from the new owner.

The young man who had received the Maverick directly from Kibbe, his former employer, was interviewed by detectives. He remembered the vehicle being very dirty inside when he first got it. Among the items he noticed on the rear floorboards were long fingernails coated with pink fingernail polish, women's hair clips, and a lot of brown hair. He had vacuumed and washed the vehicle several times before selling it. On the front floorboard had been a large odorous stain he attempted to disguise with deodorants and soaps. When this didn't work, he cut out the stained carpet and threw it away shortly before he sold the car.

At the Sacramento DOJ lab, where the samples from the Maverick were analyzed under a microscope, no evidence was found that connected Lora Heedick or any of the other strangulation victims to the vehicle—a major disappointment to homicide detectives in several counties.

At this point, nothing was coming easy. Even the Maverick lead—assuming that Driggers himself wasn't the killer and that his picking out the Maverick hadn't been irritatingly coincidental—was convoluted. Investigators with the Stanislaus County Sheriff's Department reported that they were checking out *another* Maverick lead: two ex-con brothers who lived in Modesto frequented the strip where Heedick had disappeared, and drove an older white Maverick.

Reed decided to ask Driggers to take a lie detector test. Knowing that most guilty suspects avoided the test administered by the authorities, Reed was impressed that Driggers quickly agreed.

On February 3, 1987, Driggers was strapped to a polygraph machine operated by a sheriff's department sergeant who was a trained polygraph

examiner. But then something strange happened. On two key questions—
"Did you yourself cause the death of Lora Heedick?" and *"Regarding the
death of Lora Heedick, did you yourself cause her death?"*—to which
Driggers answered no, the examiner judged him "deceptive."

Driggers could not be arrested simply because he failed the polygraph—in most situations, polygraph results weren't even admissible in
court. When Reed broke the news to Driggers that he had failed, however,
the detective advised him of his Miranda rights.

Driggers said he understood his rights, and that he wished to talk
anyway. He vehemently denied that he had killed his girlfriend.

Reed was well aware that polygraphs were not 100 percent reliable—
one reason the courts frowned on them. Variables such as the examiner's
competence, the wording of the questions, and whether the suspect had
recently imbibed alcohol or taken drugs or prescription medication could
and did influence results. Contrary to popular opinion, polygraphs were
not all black-and-white, pass or fail, but contained distinct gray areas.

Nevertheless, Reed considered polygraphs a valuable investigative
tool. He had always deemed especially weighty the willingness or reluc-
tance of an individual to be strapped to the rather intimidating contrap-
tion via a network of body sensors. Someone determined to prove his
innocence certainly had more reason to take a polygraph than a guilty
person, Reed reasoned. It was known, however, that some sociopaths and
psychopaths could "beat" the machine. It had been explained once to Reed
that these individuals lacked a kind of internal wheel the rest of us have
that spins at warp speed when we know we've done something wrong.
In short: a *conscience.* A lack of conscience confounded the polygraph, a
"scientific" machine built on the premise that people aren't entirely comfortable telling a lie.

Fighting back tears, Driggers explained to Reed that he'd been unable
to shake the feeling that he was partly responsible for Lora's death because
he had taken her to the stroll that night to hook for drug money.

If Driggers had had strong conflicting emotions when he answered
the questions as to whether he had "caused" her death, Reed knew it was
at least theoretically possible that the polygraph had detected a guilty conscience—via rises in blood pressure, pulse rate, etc.—rather than guilt.

Repetition being the art of effective interrogation, Reed took Driggers back over the events of the night in question. The detective had heard it all before until, suddenly, Driggers mentioned something new.

"I called my mom a lot that night."

"From the motel pay phone?"

"Yeah."

"Why?"

"To see if Lora had showed up or called."

Not only had Driggers not mentioned this before, but neither had his mother when Reed interviewed her. He doubted it could be proven, however, as phoning one Modesto number from another would be a local call and probably wouldn't show up on a telephone bill.

"I didn't have much money on me," Driggers added almost as an after-thought. "I called collect."

Reed returned to Modesto and talked to Driggers's mother, Rita, at the cramped rented home where her son lived with her. It was here, with the Driggerses, that Lora had lived the last months of her life.

Rita Driggers remembered her son calling her collect several times the night that Lora disappeared. And yes, she did keep her paid phone bills. Sure enough, her April–May phone bill listed numerous local collect calls throughout the night from a Modesto number.

Reed went by the Sahara and confirmed that the number on the phone bill belonged to the phone booth.

The documented calls meant one of two things to Reed: either Driggers was telling the truth, or as part of a plan to get rid of his girl-friend he had gone back to the pay phone several times to make alibi calls. Which one was it?

Before leaving Modesto, Reed found Driggers at a friend's house and asked him to come to Sacramento the next day. Driggers said he didn't have transportation or any money to take a bus. Reed slipped him twenty bucks.

Driggers didn't show up. When he sashayed into Homicide a few days later, Reed eyed the disheveled young man with his patented steely gaze. There were things about Driggers and his story that still bothered the detective. But suppose everything he said about that night was true?

"James, I'd like you to work with our artist on coming up with a picture of the man Lora drove off with."

Driggers's bloodshot eyes lit up. "No problem. I wanna find that fuckin' guy as bad as you, man."

This didn't mean Reed considered Driggers completely in the clear. But unless he developed new evidence to the contrary, the detective was willing to give Lora Heedick's bad-news boyfriend the benefit of the doubt.

Early in the new year (1987) Reed had a new crime bulletin sent out to other law enforcement on the Lora Heedick murder, incorporating the latest information provided by Driggers. The suspect vehicle was described as a 1970–75 Ford Maverick, white or light color, two-door, with a dirty interior. A picture of that model Maverick was sent with the bulletin. The suspect was described as a "white male, fifty to sixty years of age, 5-foot-10 to 6-foot, needed a shave, large hands, dirty fingernails." The artist's composite Driggers worked on went out with the bulletin, too.

A composite that looked a lot like Roger Kibbe.

CHAPTER TEN

Business was brisk for the Homicide Bureau as 1986 came to a close and the new year began. A drug dealer was found dead in a homemade coffin floating in aSacramento river. All four Bureau detectives jumped on the case, searching the victim's apartment in San Francisco and interviewing family members, friends, and known associates. Within a week, they identified the killer.

At the end of January, Lt. Ray Biondi was out on the streets like a gumshoe again working three different homicides in one twenty-four-hour period. It was his own fault: he'd screwed up and given too many detectives time off.

The following month, DOJ's Homicide Analysis Unit produced a printout of its first "I-5 Investigative Tip List." Using information about known possible suspects as well as the point-based criteria provided by the Homicide Bureau, DOJ put Roger Kibbe in first place with 52 points. He was closely followed by Wayne Welborn—with 48 points—the Sacramento cabbie who had bragged to his psychologist about raping women and who had so obviously reveled at being questioned in connection with the I-5 murder series. A bevy of other undesirables followed: two ex-cons who earned 44 points; two other would-be suspects with 42 points, including one who had been a suspect in three female homicides five years earlier (the bodies had been dumped in the Delta).

No sooner had the printout been circulated to San Joaquin and the other departments than Welborn was charged in the death of a woman unrelated to the unsolved series, although the victim's nude body was found, ironically, in an irrigation ditch off I-5 south of Sacramento.

The victim was a sixty-nine-year-old woman who was last seen alive entering a taxicab outside a bar late the previous night. Her family said she had a history of abusing alcohol and Valium, and had gone to Shelly's, a seedy neighborhood bar. The bartender said she left a few hours later in a cab. The cab company identified the driver as Wayne Welborn.

After at first denying any involvement in the woman's death, Welborn ended up making a "negotiated statement," in which a suspect is allowed to give a statement concerning his culpability in return for reduced charges. The statement was much too self-serving to suit Detective Stan Reed, who pushed for a full confession. The problem was that the pathologist ruled the cause of death was alcohol and Valium ingestion, and exposure. Welborn claimed the woman had taken off her own clothes, which were found scattered at the scene. He admitted to trying to have sex with her, and to leaving the drunken woman and driving away. He was charged with involuntary manslaughter and attempted rape, but the manslaughter charge was eventually dismissed. Convicted of attempted rape of an unconscious person, Welborn was sentenced to three years.

And the beat went on—in early March, a Sacramento store clerk was wounded and a patron killed during a robbery at a convenience store. Six days later the body of a man, shot in the head, was found wrapped in a blanket and dumped at the side of a road. Within weeks, a parolee was arrested for all three shootings.

A few weeks later, Biondi, with some hesitation, went on a brand-new TV show called "America's Most Wanted." After he presented information and pictures concerning a fugitive suspect in the poisoning death of a local beauty queen, the phones began to ring. The show aired on a Sunday, and by Wednesday they had arrested their suspect, who had been working as a chef under an assumed name out of state.

Twice, Biondi and one of his detectives made trips to Salt Lake City in connection with the Unabomber cases—the latest bombing had occurred in that city in February (1987).

If the I-5 series hadn't been forgotten, it had certainly been pushed to the back burner. This was true not only in Sacramento County, but also in San Joaquin, where Vito Bertocchini had picked up a drug rip-off killing on New Year's Eve and had been working it ever since. The problem, as it had been from the very beginning, was lack of manpower to work the series full- or even part-time. Biondi didn't even have the personnel to assign to start at the top of the DOJ "Tip List" printout and work their way down focusing on and/or eliminating possible suspects.

With the new year arrived a newly elected Sacramento County sheriff, Glen Craig, a man with impressive credentials in state law enforcement. Previously, Craig had been commissioner of the California Highway Patrol and director of the California Department of Justice. Also, a new commander of the Detective Division was installed: Frank Wallace, who had been Biondi's patrol sergeant in the 1960s.

Biondi wasted no time in lobbying Wallace for more detectives. It was immediately apparent how overwhelmed Wallace was with the size of the caseloads being carried by his detectives—not just in Homicide, but in virtually every bureau. He directed his lieutenants to heighten their administrative tracking of each and every case (manhours expended, etc.). At first blush, some of the Bureau lieutenants, including Biondi, thought Wallace was burying them in unnecessary paperwork. But before long, Biondi came to understand that the captain needed ammunition if he was to lock horns with the pragmatic bean counters farther up the chain of command who opposed any additional expenses.

While Biondi knew that other bureaus were just as hard pressed in dealing with a tremendous volume of crimes—domestic violence, robberies, child abuse, sex assaults, felony assaults, arson, etc.—then and always his priority was much simpler: he wanted to solve murders. He didn't understand why the new sheriff wasn't clamoring to ensure a well-staffed and well-equipped Homicide Bureau. It would have been expedient simply for political reasons, as nearly 100 percent of homicide cases received some type of media attention.

Captain Wallace was a throwback to an earlier era. Biondi still remembered the sting of being called out on his first homicide in the early 1970s and ordered to respond to the office, while his bosses—a captain and lieutenant—went to the crime scene. He drank coffee at the office waiting for his bosses to come back and fill him in. Biondi had fought this type of higher-up involvement from his first day in Homicide, although it hadn't ended once and for all until the tremendous increase in crime in the early 1980s.

During his tenure in Homicide, Biondi had broken the mold in more ways than one. He was the first head of Homicide to last in the position more than four years, and his longevity led to some revolutionary changes in how murder cases were investigated. But in the beginning, he did what everyone else did when they took over Homicide: lead by example. Always out in front, he pushed himself and his weary band of detectives to find one more witness and bring in one more suspect, no matter how many straight hours they'd worked. It was fun for a time, but the back-breaking pace could not go on. Also, when he saw that some of his detectives were turning into robots waiting for his next move, he realized he was curbing their initiative in the same way his bosses had done to him.

From then on, he worked to create an environment within the Bureau that gave the individual detectives the control they needed to work cases their way and reap the satisfaction of their successes while they learned from their mistakes. It meant he had to protect them whenever they ordered a captain or some other boss to stay behind the rope so as not to contaminate a crime scene, but he did so fervently. The detectives that could accept the challenge—the hours were still unbelievably long— stayed to become career homicide detectives. The department and the public it served benefited from having the most experienced and highly motivated detectives on the job.

In the old days, all available detectives would be assigned to a single murder case until it was solved. The team's boss, whether a lieutenant or captain, would lead the investigation and know as much about the case as anyone. But by the mid-1980s, cases were assigned to field-grade detectives who became the department's experts on individual cases. When Wallace insisted on being briefed in detail about unsolved murder cases, briefings were held. Sometimes they were the cause of much friction. The detectives weren't able to take the time to tell the captain everything, so they hit the surface. Soon, the captain was posing questions and challenging the detectives. The adage that a little information was more dangerous than none proved true. On one occasion involving a fire-related death, Wallace formed an opinion totally different from that of the detective who had investigated the crime scene. The detective thought it was arson-murder, the captain did not. A heated argument ensued, and the loud confrontation added to the tension the detectives already felt about the top brass. Biondi's detectives, accustomed to full autonomy over their cases and knowing that they worked more murders in a few months than Captain Wallace did in his entire career, came to resent the grillings. They soon had Wallace grouped with the rest of the department's administration, which didn't seem to place priority on murder unless the victim was somebody important or the case was otherwise putting heat on the department.

Captain Wallace formed an opinion on the I-5 investigation. To Biondi's disbelief, the captain was openly skeptical that the murders were connected.

For Wallace's benefit, Biondi went over the list of similarities that caused him to conclude that a serial killer was on the loose.

"Even if it is a series, a lot of them are operating in other counties," Wallace said matter-of-factly. "We've got our own major murders to work."

Biondi could feel the steam venting. Women had been abducted and murdered—so they shouldn't work the cases because some damn political boundary was crossed?

Wallace may have seen the eruption coming.

"Look, don't misunderstand me," Wallace added quickly. "I think we should give some attention to these murders. I just see all the other cases that need your attention, too. I don't know how much more you can handle."

Feeling defused, Biondi said, "My point exactly."

KAREN FINCH, age twenty-five, was a true California blonde.

Her sun-bleached hair cascaded several inches below her shoulders, framing a long face that a wide smile warmed instantly. A dedicated sunbather with a golden tan, she had little need for makeup. On weekends she favored shorts and sleeveless tops, and leather thong sandals when she absolutely couldn't go barefoot. Her eyes were a rich mahogany brown, and her teeth as perfectly straight and white as a movie starlet's. Although only 5-foot-5, she seemed taller—it was probably the long legs. Her well-proportioned 122 pounds were ample proof of hours spent at the gym and her daily 3-mile jogs.

A people person, she tended to lead with her heart, and had endured her share of life's disappointments. In fact, she was going through a divorce, and shared custody of her two-year-old daughter, Nicole. But she was also in an exciting new relationship with a twenty-three-year-old man she'd met a few months earlier. She was beginning to feel that they might have a future together; they had already talked of marriage, and about the logistics of finding a place midway between their jobs and close enough to Nicole.

On the morning of Sunday, June 14, 1987, Karen picked up Nicole at her ex-husband Steve Higgins's place in Twain Harte, situated on the western slope of the Sierra only 20 miles as the crow flies from the entrance to Yosemite National Park. Karen had spent the previous night at her boyfriend Larry Blackmore's house in nearby Sonora. A state correctional officer at the Sierra Conservation Center, Larry had to work that day, so it would be just Nicole and her.

Karen was excited about her new job; she had the added responsibility of handling bookkeeping for a dentist as well as working with patients. She had started only a week earlier, and would be making more money than ever before. She loved her new apartment, which she'd been in only two weeks; the complex had a pool and hot tub. With a forty-five-minute commute to and from work and much longer drives to Tuolumne County to Nicole's father's place and to Larry's, Karen had two weeks earlier bought a year-old sporty Plymouth Turismo coupe to replace her older El Camino, which kept breaking down.

After a rough period—Karen had written her mother a while back: "Please keep praying for me as I'm going through some trials"—things were looking up in her life.

When Karen and Nicole arrived at Larry's house, they both changed into their swimsuits and went out back. They had stopped at Kmart and bought a wading pool, which Karen now inflated and filled with water from a garden hose. She positioned herself under the sun and stretched out on a beach towel, watching as Nicole squealed happily in her new pool.

After lunch, Nicole took a short nap. Then, they went back outside until around 4:00 P.M., when they came in and changed. Karen had promised Steve to have Nicole back by 5:30P.M. When they pulled into Twain Harte, they stopped for yogurt cones.

When they got to Steve's—he had kept the house and most of their furniture—Karen mentioned that her car had been running hot. She asked him how to check the coolant level. While Nicole rested on the couch, they went out front. He popped the hood and showed her where to check the coolant without removing the radiator cap. The level seemed fine.

Saying good-bye was difficult, as usual, for mother and daughter. The little girl, in her daddy's arms at the curb, waved weakly, then began to whimper.

"Bye, Nicki. I love you," Karen said, fighting back her own tears.

It was 5:30 P.M. when Karen pulled away. She was facing better than an hour's drive to her new apartment in Lodi, some 30 miles south of Sacramento. A friend had asked her the other day how she could cope with all the driving she did. Driving was therapeutic for her, Karen explained. She especially enjoyed using the long stretches of country roads, but she also used busier U.S. 99, which ran through Lodi, and nearby I-5, which she used to get to work in Sacramento.

At 10:30 P.M. that night, Larry Blackmore came home to find Karen gone. When he'd called her that afternoon to say he was going to work an extra shift, they had left it that she would stay over. Obviously, she'd changed her mind and headed home. He wasn't surprised, given that Karen had to be at work in Sacramento in the morning. He tried calling her apartment, but there was no answer.

He next called his mother, who lived nearby. As it happened, Karen and Nicole had stopped by around 4:30 P.M. to say hello. Sure enough, Karen had mentioned that she was going to head back home that night to rest up for work.

Larry tried Karen's number again around 10:45 P.M. but there was still no answer. He stayed awake awhile hoping she would call, but eventually he fell asleep.

He woke up at 8:30 A.M. Monday, which was his day off. He called the dentist's office where Karen worked, but was told she had not showed up or called in sick or late.

Larry telephoned Karen's parents to get Steve's number. Steve wasn't home, and it took some effort to track down his work phone. When Larry finally reached him, Steve explained that Karen had dropped Nicole off the previous afternoon and left about 5:30 P.M. She hadn't said where she was going but Steve said he assumed she was heading to Lodi.

At 9:45 A.M., Larry called the Tuolumne County Sheriff's Office. A sheriff's deputy arrived at 11:00 A.M. and took a missing persons report.

A worried Larry got in his car and cruised between his house in Sonora and Twain Harte to see if he could spot Karen's car, but came back shortly when he realized he should stay by the phone in the event she called.

The phone rang at 1:30 P.M. It was Larry's sister, Marcia, calling from a pay phone at the Stockton Airport. Marcia had driven their mother to the airport for a trip to visit a relative. Larry had originally planned to do so but had elected to stay home in case Karen called. His sister, who had heard from their mother about Larry's growing concern for Karen, said she could have sworn she saw Karen's car parked on a country road near the airport. She had even jotted down the license number.

Larry didn't know Karen's new license number. He figured it was a long shot—his sister, who had seen Karen's white Plymouth only once or twice in the two weeks she'd had it, had probably seen a similar-looking car. But he took down the number she gave him and called the sheriff's office anyway. He asked them to run the number, which they did while he remained on hold. The license number came back no good; there was no such number on file.

Shortly after 6:00 P.M. Larry made another quick trip to Sonora to see Karen's ex-husband. Not wanting to believe that Steve had anything to do with Karen's disappearance, he was relieved to see that Steve seemed genuinely concerned. They were careful not to discuss the situation in front of Nicole; neither wanted to needlessly upset the little girl.

The phone rang a few minutes after Larry returned home. He raced to it hoping that it would be Karen. She would be all right and have some explanation and that would be the end of it. But it was her parents, Glen and Naomi Finch, who lived in Oroville—where Karen had been raised and graduated from high school—about 60 miles northeast of Sacramento.

Both were worried sick, and took turns talking to Larry about what else could be done.

Larry asked if they happened to know Karen's new car license plate number. Her father, who was a minister, said he did. He went to look it up, then recited it to Larry.

It was only *one number off the* license number Marcia had given him for the car parked out by the airport.

Larry told the Finches about his sister's call.

"Marcia must have taken it down wrong," he said. "I'm going out there myself. I'll call you later."

Larry took Highway 120 west out of Sonora for nearly 50 miles, then turned on French Camp Road, a shortcut to Highway 99 and, just west of the highway, the Stockton Airport. It was pitch-dark by the time Larry reached the car at the intersection of French Camp and Ripon roads. He pulled up behind it, and kept his motor and lights on as he got out.

He shined his flashlight into the car. With a sinking stomach, he realized it was Karen's car—he recognized the things in the backseat that she'd brought to his place.

He tried the driver's door—locked.

That was typical Karen; she *always* locked her car.

The passenger door was locked, too.

As he peered inside, Larry couldn't detect anything out of the ordinary. He checked the tires, but they looked fine. He walked around the car looking for visible body damage, but there was nothing to suggest an accident.

This was a plausible route for Karen to have taken. Highway 120, three or four miles on French Camp, then Highway 99 north for about 15 miles to Lodi. He wanted to believe she had had engine trouble, pulled over, locked the car, and gone for help. But even as he ran that scenario through his mind, he knew it was wishful thinking. If she'd had engine trouble, Karen would have called somebody within the last twenty-four hours.

But she hadn't.

THE FOLLOWING Sunday, a family of four was out for a drive on picturesque Jackson Highway east of Sacramento.

It had been a particularly warm day, and Alex Gutierrez, a campus police officer and reserve deputy for the Amador County Sheriff's Department, had promised his young son they would stop and take a walk along Deer Creek before going home to dinner.

Gutierrez pulled off the highway onto a narrow, shady lane and continued on about a half mile before parking some 30 yards short of a small bridge that crossed the creek.

The entire family got out. Gutierrez was in the lead—his son was busy collecting flat rocks for skipping in the creek—as they approached the bridge.

Gutierrez saw something in the road that looked like a big stain. As he came closer, he saw an article of clothing next to it that had what looked like blood on it. His first thought was that someone had gotten into a fight.

He glanced over to the side of the road. Down in a ditch about 10 feet away was a naked woman lying on her back. She was obviously dead.

Gutierrez spun around and ordered everyone back into the car before they could see anything. He drove to the first house they came to, but no one was home. Farther down the road was a trailer used by an extension school, and attached to it a pay phone. He called 911, and was put through to the Sacramento County Sheriff's Department.

The first patrol unit arrived at 8:00 P.M. After the deputy took one look in the ditch, he went back to his car and radioed for Homicide to respond.

Detective Stan Reed arrived first, his partner Bob Bell five minutes later. Lt. Ray Biondi, who had the farthest to drive from home, showed up ten minutes later with two of his sons along for the ride.

Throughout the years, Biondi had made a point to take each of his five sons to at least one murder scene. He did so not only to show them what Dad does and why he has to work such long hours, but also to give them a reality check; unlike what they saw on TV or in the movies, there was nothing glamorous about murder. Rather, it was ugly, invasive, sickening. It was thirteen-year-old Greg's first trip, and one of his older brothers, Mark, twenty-one, had come along for moral support. His sons took one look at the scene from the bridge, then stayed out of the way and didn't say much. (Eventually, two of Biondi's five sons went into law enforcement, including Mark, who joined the Sacramento County Sheriff's Department.)

By the time Biondi arrived, Reed and Bell were already doing their look-don't-touch close-up of the scene, with Reed dictating into a micro-tape recorder.

"Approximately 8 feet south of the bridge, just adjacent to the dirt shoulder area, are spatters of blood on the blacktop. These spatters encircle an area about 1 foot in diameter. Continuing approximately 2 more feet in a southerly direction, there is another area that appears to be blood, which is approximately 12 inches by 5 inches.

"Where the blacktop meets the dirt area, there is a pair of what appears to be women's shorts, blue in color. Approximately 2 feet to the east of the shorts is a bush. Hanging on the bush are pink panties.

"At this point the shoulder of the road drops off at approximately a 45-degree angle, down about ten feet into the ditch area. There is a pathway adjacent to the blue shorts which leads down the embankment to where the body is located. There are a number of areas going down the embankment that have a red substance which appears to be blood.

"Laying at the bottom of the steps, in the ditch area, is a white female with blond hair. She is laying on her back. Her nude breasts are visible. She has a blouse on that is open in the front. This blouse is white and blue in color. The victim is nude from the waist down and shows a bikini tan line. There are a large number of active maggots around the throat area. I now see that the victim is wearing a pink tank top. The top appears to have been cut up the center. Further description of the body to follow after the coroner arrives."

When Biondi had gotten the call from Dispatch concerning a "female body dump" in a remote area, he had immediately wondered if it could be number four in the unsolved series. When he arrived at the scene, he found Reed and Bell with the same thoughts. After the coroner arrived and the body was pulled onto a stretcher and all the clothes were collected and inspected, they felt even more strongly about it.

They ticked off several similarities:

Clothes cutting

Nude or partially nude victim

Scattering of clothes about the scene

No purse found

Body transported to rural crime scene

Personal identification missing

Although not on I-5, certainly in the general area

Reed had his own entry: *The latest victim had large breasts like all the others.* "This guy knows what he likes."

It was difficult to tell whether the victim had been strangled. More than likely there had been some type of open wound in the front of her neck, as maggots usually went for the first blood they could find on soft tissue before invading other orifices. Further analysis of the neck wound and two puncture-like wounds on the upper torso would have to await the autopsy, but, based on what he'd seen, Reed thought the victim had been stabbed.

Given the amount of blood found on the roadway, it seemed likely she'd been mortally attacked, if not killed, up above and her body rolled down the embankment to the ditch. That the victim had bled extensively was *not* similar to the other crime scenes.

"He may have cut her throat," Reed said.

They knew he hadn't been a slasher before, but they had also seen plenty of cut clothing, meaning he carried a sharp instrument—likely scissors.

"He gets mad at this one," Biondi said, speculating. "Maybe she was able to put up a good fight. He uses what he has in hand to overcome her resistance."

Biondi knew that serial killers generally stuck with what had worked before, but sometimes the manner of death could be dictated by the circumstances.

In collecting the victim's clothing, it was noted that her panties and shorts were stained with fecal matter. As violent death almost always resulted in an involuntary bowel evacuation, Biondi thought it likely that these items of clothing were removed postmortem, or in the very least while she was suffering severe trauma immediately preceding her demise.

The detectives found a 3- or 4-inch length of silver-colored duct tape stuck to the back of the victim's head. To remove the tape and preserve it as evidence, it was necessary to cut her long hair.

Reed and Bell talked about the tape having been used as a gag, due to its position on the head.

Biondi, who had been stooped over the body, suddenly stood up. "Brown's hair was cut, remember?"

"Just below the ears," Reed said.

"He gags them with duct tape," Biondi said. "The tape got caught in Brown's hair so he cut her hair to get it off. He doesn't want to leave the tape behind because he knows we can get prints off it. This time he screwed up or was in a hurry and didn't get it all."

So much for the hair fetish theory, Biondi thought, or that Brown's hair had been snipped off as a "trophy."

"Our guy has a fetish, all right," Biondi said. "A fetish about not leaving behind incriminating evidence."

———

AT HOME early the next morning reading the paper over his first cup of coffee, Stan Reed came across a short article, "Few Clues in Case of Missing Woman," buried on the obituary page of the Sacramento *Bee* about a young Lodi woman, missing for eight days, whose abandoned car had been found a week earlier. A description of the woman fit the blond victim that had gone to the morgue the previous night as Jane Doe.

Reed arrived at the office at 7:50 A.M. and immediately called the San Joaquin County Sheriff's Department. He asked for Homicide, and was told that no detectives were in yet, so he left a message.

Ten minutes later Reed received a call back from a San Joaquin detective who worked with Vito Bertocchini.

"We've got a Jane Doe here who might be your Karen Finch," Reed said. He gave a physical description from memory, and also described her clothing and jewelry.

"I'll get back to you," the San Joaquin detective said.

Reed asked for the number of the victim's next of kin, and was given her parents in Oroville.

First, he phoned the department of motor vehicles and ordered a copy of Finch's driver's license and thumbprint, to be picked up at the counter later that morning.

Next, he called the Finches, and asked Naomi to describe the jewelry her daughter would have been wearing. It was identical to what Jane Doe had been wearing.

Reed was not about to tell a mother her daughter was dead based on jewelry. "I'll call you as soon as I know anything for certain," he promised.

Calling San Joaquin back, Reed informed the same detective he'd talked to earlier that the body they had found was wearing jewelry described by Finch's mother.

"You have dental charts?" Reed asked.

"Yeah."

"Can you get 'em to me?"

While Reed worked the phones, his partner, Detective Bob Bell, was at the morgue. Bell made sure that a complete "rape kit" was done prior to the autopsy.

The victim was found to have multiple contusions to the upper abdomen and chest, as well as the right thigh and forearm. The pathologist also found multiple incised injuries to the front neck, along with secondary insect and predator damage. He described two well-identified slash wounds with secondary transections of major blood vessels of the neck as the primary cause of death. There were also stab wounds to the right chest, just above the nipple, and to the right shoulder—wounds that, in the opinion of the pathologist, could have been made by either a knife or scissors.

At 11:30 A.M., positive identification was made by a sheriff's department technician who compared a driver's license thumbprint with the corresponding thumbprint of the fresh Jane Doe.

Glen and Naomi Finch received a second phone call that morning from the Sacramento County Sheriff's Department.

That's how another set of parents learned their daughter, too, was a homicide victim.

CHAPTER ELEVEN

Four hours after Glen and Naomi Finch had received official notification of their daughter's death, Detective Harry Machen met with them at their residence to get some background on Karen so that the murder investigation could begin in earnest.

The Finches explained how all week long they had been expecting the worst and hoping for the best.

"Every time the phone rang, I was afraid to answer it," Naomi said softly.

From Karen's mother Machen heard about the young woman's failed marriage to Steve Higgins. Karen had had an affair with a coworker of Steve's the previous summer. Shortly after that ended, she had become pregnant, and against Steve's wishes had an abortion. After several tries at reconciliation, Karen had finally filed for divorce. They had made one court appearance, with another scheduled.

According to the mother, Karen and Steve seemed to have been getting along recently, as long as they didn't talk about personal things, like finances or rehashing the marriage. When it came to co-parenting Nicole, they did fine.

"Was there any physical violence between Steve and Karen?" Machen asked.

"Not that we were aware of," said her mother. "We never saw any signs of it."

After the divorce, Karen had gone through a state of depression, according to her mother. "She had gone to counseling and had worked through the depression and guilt. It seemed that she was getting her life back together."

"When was the last time you heard from her?"

Naomi said it had been on the afternoon of Saturday, June 13—the weekend Karen disappeared. "She called just to say that she loved us and to thank her father and me for helping her move the previous weekend. She said she loved her new job and her new apartment. She had Nicole that weekend, and was enjoying her."

On the workdays she had Nicole, Karen drove her into Sacramento and placed her in day care close to work.

"I asked her about her long commute because I was a little concerned," Naomi said. "She said she didn't mind because she had time alone with Nicki, and also that the driving helped her unwind. I wasn't quite as concerned as I would have been if she had still had her old car, which used to break down a lot."

"How did she sound?" Machen asked.

Naomi managed a bittersweet smile. "She sounded really up. She was in a very positive frame of mind about getting on with her life."

"What was her temperament like?"

"Karen had a way of making friends with everybody. All her patients loved her. She never flew off the handle, although she didn't let people push her around either."

Machen asked how Karen might act around a stranger who needed help or seemed stranded on the road.

"She would stop and help anyone that she knew or felt comfortable with," Naomi said. "If it was a stranger she would be very reluctant. I don't think she would stop or go too far out of her way."

"Do you know if she carried duct tape in the car?"

Naomi looked at her husband.

"As far as I know," Glen said, "the only tape she carried was adhesive tape in the first aid kit that she always kept in the car."

Machen asked about Karen's finances, her friends, and where she hung out. When there was nothing further that the Finches could add, the detective handed them his card and asked them to call if they thought of anything.

Meanwhile, Detective Stan Reed was 60 miles away in Sonora interviewing Karen's boyfriend, Larry Blackmore.

Reed knew that Blackmore had been cleared by both Tuolumne and San Joaquin as a suspect in Finch's disappearance. He had an airtight alibi for the night Finch had disappeared—his superior officer at the correctional facility had confirmed Blackmore had worked a sixteen-hour shift until 10:00 P.M. Also, Tuolumne County, as part of its missing personsinvestigation, had routinely asked Blackmore to take a polygraph and he'd agreed. He was found to be telling the truth about having nothing to do with his girlfriend's disappearance.

Reed noted that the young man seemed crushed. Shaking his head sadly, he looked at the detective with glassy eyes that sought an explanation.

They had met five months earlier, Larry began, at a pizza parlor where Karen had worked nights and weekends for a short while to help make ends meet. For the last two months, he said, "we were inseparable."

He told of their last weekend together, then not being able to get ahold of Karen Sunday night. He explained how his sister had called to report she might have seen Karen's car, and his attempts to check the license plate number.

When he had gone out to look at the car himself that night, the boy-friend had done the right thing: As soon as he realized it was Karen's car, he used a pay phone to call the San Joaquin Sheriff's Department. When a cruiser arrived an hour later, Larry told the deputy that his girlfriend was the subject of a missing persons report in Tuolumne County. The deputy asked his dispatcher to call Tuolumne and see what they wanted done with the car. They waited another forty-five minutes before getting an answer that was less than satisfying. No one at Tuolumne seemed to know anything about the case, and they said just leave the car where it was. At that point, the San Joaquin deputy seemed ready to sluff off the whole thing as not being his problem. Larry, however, insisted on having the car towed to the next town; he was afraid it would be stolen or stripped if left at the side of the road. As the deputy made the necessary arrangements, Larry searched as best he could the adjacent walnut orchard but found nothing. When the tow truck arrived, he assisted the driver in jimmying open the driver's door. Then Larry got in and knocked the gearshift into neutral with his flashlight. He even ended up paying for the tow.

"How was the car parked?" asked Reed, who considered it unfortunate that a detective hadn't responded to the scene, and yet he understood what a low priority most departments give to a new adult missing persons case.

"On the shoulder. It looked like it may have stopped quickly. There were skid marks on the asphalt, about three feet long, one skid mark for each tire. The car had rolled past the marks onto the gravel before stopping."

"Anything else?"

"Well, there were some tire marks just in front of her car, like someone had been parked there and spun out in the gravel as they were getting back onto the road."

Reed processed that information. Had Karen Finch pulled up behind a car that had appeared to be disabled, or to talk to someone who had otherwise gotten her attention?

"I saw several large footprints in the dirt around the driver's door. They looked like tennis shoes."

"You said the car was locked."

"Right."

Given something to do, Larry had perked up during the interview. His law enforcement training was obvious, and Reed considered it helpful. The young man was very observant, and able to describe clearly and concisely what he'd seen.

"When you got the door open, what was inside?"

"There was a Wendy's cup in a holder near the gearshift, and a pack of gum. Her sunglasses were on the front dash. She had some type of clothing laid out on the passenger seat, and a baby's bathing suit on top of it. In the back was an emergency roadside kit she always carried, and her sandals."

No shoes had been found at the crime scene, Reed recalled. If Karen had gotten out of the car barefoot, she probably hadn't intended to walk very far—even if she had locked the car door after her, which itself would suggest that she hadn't been forced out of the vehicle but had left of her own free will.

Before he left, Reed had the boyfriend make a detailed drawing of exactly where he'd found Karen's car.

After trying unsuccessfully to contact Karen's ex-husband, Reed drove to the location where Finch's car had been parked. The detective had already called to make sure the vehicle had been impounded, and to request DOJ to process the car—inside and out—for prints and other evidence.

Reed walked the area, searching for footprints or anything else of interest. By now, however, the scene had been trampled by numerous friends and relatives of Karen Finch's who had come out during the week she was missing in search of clues. The amateur sleuths had turned in, he'd heard, a collection of cigarette butts, empty beer cans, and other roadside trash.

Reed found the skid marks on the blacktop midway between two telephone poles where the boyfriend had said Karen's car had been parked. But there was no way of knowing if they had come from Finch's Plymouth.

During its missing persons investigation, Tuolumne County had asked Steve Higgins if he would be willing to take a polygraph. Detectives explained that he was, after all, involved in divorce proceedings with the missing woman. Although Higgins seemed very forthcoming in lengthy interviews with detectives, he expressed reservations about taking a polygraph. He said he'd heard that they were only as reliable as the person administering the test.

Reed would learn that Higgins had a strong alibi: A male friend who had been visiting for several days could account for Higgins's whereabouts the night Karen disappeared. As the friend's fingerprint had shown up in Karen's car—on a piece of mail that she'd picked up at Steve's house that Sunday—he had been asked by San Joaquin to submit to a polygraph. The friend took the polygraph four days after Karen's car was found; he was judged to be truthful in all his responses, including those that cleared Steve Higgins.

Two days after Finch's body was identified, Biondi pulled all four of the Bureau's detectives off their other cases for the day and responded with the entire crew to the Twain Harte–Sonora area to knock on doors, conduct interviews, and retrace Finch's movements on the day she disappeared.

Starting at 10:00 A.M. at the Tuolumne Sheriff's Department, the detectives met with local authorities and learned the identity of two suspicious persons who had come to their attention. Both fit in the "sudden departure from the area" category; fleeing the area after a crime was one indicator of guilt looked for by murder detectives. For good reason, someone who has killed doesn't want to stick around to be questioned. One possibility was a twenty-three-year-old male reported missing from Sonora on the same day as Finch. They were given a copy of the missing persons report. Another was a twenty-nine-year-old weight lifter who had previously been arrested for indecent exposure and who worked out at the same gym as Finch. Initial information was that he had a consistent workout schedule, which he failed to keep the day following her disappearance. In the end, neither man was connected to the Finch case, but in the beginning there was no way to know that without substantial legwork.

After the meeting, the five detectives from Sacramento went off in separate directions, some to Twain Harte and some to its next-door neighbor, Sonora.

Biondi first stopped in at the local newspaper, the *Union Democrat*, and updated a reporter as to the investigation. He asked the paper to help solicit reports from residents of any suspicious or unusual activity that may have occurred around Twain Harte.

Biondi drove into Sonora and interviewed a liquor store proprietor who had called to report having seen Karen Finch in her store on the Sunday she disappeared. She identified a picture of Finch. A little girl was with Finch, said the store owner, and they bought a small carton of milk and a can of soda. The owner put the time at noon.

Next, he interviewed the neighbors of Larry Blackmore; the couple owned the house Blackmore rented. They remembered seeing familiar cars parked out front on the Sunday Finch disappeared, but recalled nothing that aroused their attention. Both identified a picture of Finch—they remembered her visiting their tenant, Blackmore, and jogging in the area on occasion.

The other detectives conducted similar interviews, none of which shed any light on Finch's disappearance. By all accounts, she'd had a relaxing day with her daughter, visited her boyfriend's mother, stopped for frozen yogurt with her little girl, dropped Nicole off at Steve's on time, and left town.

Probably an hour or so later and after driving nearly 50 miles, she pulled her car off the road for some unknown reason. She got out, apparently barefoot and carrying her purse, which was never found, and locked the car with keys that were never found either. The car was full of gas and operable when authorities hot-wired it days later.

A few days after the canvass of the Sonora area, the most viable suspect lead in the case surfaced through a phone call to Tuolumne detectives from a police investigator in Merced, some 40 miles south. The investigator was inquiring about Rick Gerson, a registered sex offender who was believed to have moved from Merced to Sonora. Tuolumne authorities knew nothing about Gerson, and were glad to get the tip on him. If he was in the area, he had broken the law by not properly registering. The investigator mentioned that Gerson had, ten years earlier, used a knife to kill a young woman, for which he'd served time in prison. Tuolumne thought the information interesting enough to pass on to Sacramento.

Stan Reed began a paper background on Rick Gerson. He was in his mid-thirties, 6-foot, 175 pounds, with graying brown hair. A check with the department of motor vehicles revealed that two vehicles were registered to him: a 1986 Nissan pickup and a 1972 Ford Pinto.

After running a criminal check on Gerson, Reed called the Merced Police Department and spoke to a detective familiar with the murder Gerson had been convicted of.

One night around 8:00 P.M., Rick Gerson had entered a small retail business and robbed it at knifepoint.

"A sixteen-year-old salesgirl was working alone," the detective explained. "He went through her purse and took some money. He found a nightie she was carrying for a sleepover that night. He cut it into strips, and bound and gagged her. Then he put her on the floor, took off her jeans and panties, and sexually assaulted her."

"Go on," said Reed, taking notes.

"The pathologist was sure of penetration because of severe bruising," the detective continued, "but Gerson didn't have an orgasm that way. He didn't get off until he started cutting on her, and then he came all over the floor."

"Did he cut her throat?"

"Oh, yeah. Stabbed her six times in the throat and neck. Her carotid artery and jugular vein were severed. Know what the guy does then? Puts a 'Closed' sign out, goes home, takes a shower, and changes. Then he comes *back* and ransacks the place to make sure he got all the money and everything else of value. Just calmly stuffs everything in his backpack. He even cut the bindings off the victim and put them in his pack. Then he strolls out the back door. That's the point we got lucky. Someone saw him that time. When we got our hands on him later that night, we found the money, the murder weapon, and the bloody bindings in his backpack."

The detective told Reed that Gerson had been convicted of murder, served seven years, and was paroled in May 1985. In the year since, Gerson had been a "good suspect" in another San Joaquin Valley town in the rape-strangulation of a twenty-two-year-old woman, although there hadn't been enough evidence to charge him.

Reed next called Gerson's parole agent. As Gerson was no longer serving parole, the agent didn't have a current address on him. When Reed told him of the Karen Finch case, the parole agent said, "Yes, he would be capable of that."

The state department of motor vehicles had an old address on Gerson, too. Nine traffic citations had been issued to him by various jurisdictions in the past eighteen months. Reed contacted the traffic courts to see if Gerson had given a more current address at any of his appearances. In this way, Reed found Gerson's Sonora address, which he'd supplied to the court some months earlier.

The address sounded familiar. Reed flipped through the Finch file until he found what he was looking for. The slasher murderer, Rick Gerson, had lived two doors from the apartment Karen Finch had first moved to after she separated from her husband.

Reed sat face-to-face with Rick Gerson, not long after, in an interview room of the Stanislaus County Jail, where he'd been booked several days earlier on a misdemeanor.

Reed asked the ex-con if he was willing to assist in eliminating himself as a possible murder suspect.

"Yes, I'd be glad to help," said Gerson, a big, muscular guy with Elvis sideburns and tinted glasses.

"Do you remember where were you on Sunday, June 14th?"

"June 13th was my birthday," he said. "On Sunday, I was in Sonora. I dropped my fiancée off at work around 2:30 P.M. I picked her up that evening after work about 10 P.M."

Gerson said that in between driving his fiancée to and from work he was home alone, meaning he had no alibi for the hours during which Finch had apparently disappeared.

Until recently, Gerson had worked for a courier service, which assigned him regular routes that had taken him, at various times, to Modesto, Fresno, and Sacramento on Highway 99 and I-5, sometimes until as late as 2:00 A.M.

Reed went over some other dates, starting with the date Lora Heedick disappeared.

"Were you in Modesto on April 20, 1986?"

"No, I was making deliveries to Fresno then."

Reed asked about July 15, 1986—"Were you driving on I-5 south out of Sacramento late Monday night or very early Tuesday morning?"

"In July I was driving the Fresno route. If I wasn't on the road, I would have been home in Sonora."

Reed asked Gerson if he'd been driving on I-5 toward Sacramento early in the morning of August 17, 1986, even though he looked nothing like the composite of the man whom Carmen Anselmi said her daughter had ridden off with.

"Man, that was a year ago," Gerson said, scratching his head. "August— no, I wasn't going to Sacramento then. I was working farther south. What day of the week was that?"

"Sunday."

"I didn't work Sundays. I don't know where I was."

"Are you familiar with the I-5 series of murders?"

"Yes, it's on the nightly news all the time. I'm an ex-con and with this type of crime, I watch out. If I can mentally place myself somewhere else at the time that these events occurred, it helps."

"Are you responsible for any of these murders?"

"No."

"Were you responsible for the murder you were previously convicted of?"

"No, but the evidence was strong against me."

For Reed, Rick Gerson would be one of those monstrous thorns in the side that periodically came with a case—a guy who could be "good" for the deed but who can't be placed at the scene. For months, his name would keep popping up in connection with Finch. Although no evidence ever built up against him, with so many intriguing coincidences—like his having lived two doors from Finch—he was never really cleared either. He hung around like a freeloading houseguest who arrived for the weekend and spent the summer.

Just one more murderer walking the streets, Rick Gerson would, in the end, prove to be simply another distraction to be dealt with in pursuit of a serial killer.

AS OF June 1987, the Sacramento County Sheriff's Department Homicide Bureau had received five hundred suspect leads in the I-5 series via the media. Of those, Lt. Ray Biondi counted twenty individuals as viable suspects who should be investigated; "should be" were the operative words.

The Bureau was handling, on average, one new murder a week. In the first six months of the year, detectives had twenty-two homicides, all but one of which had been solved. Ten unsolved cases were carried over from 1986, as were eight even older cases that had new, workable leads. The Bureau also received an average of three missing persons cases a day, and at midyear had ten cases that were being investigated.

For nearly a year Biondi had been firing long memos up the chain of command requesting help. He had visions of his memos being folded into paper airplanes and launched out upstairs windows. He was convinced he'd become known within the department as the world's biggest whiner.

Biondi had been promised more than once that help was on the way, only for it not to materialize. But in early July, the promise was finally kept: four detectives from other bureaus were authorized to transfer to Homicide for temporary assignment to work I-5.

He had lobbied so long and hard for reinforcements, when they finally came to pass, Biondi felt neither jubilation nor surprise. "It's about time," he offered grimly. There would be, he knew, other aggravating struggles ahead: Where were the new homicide detectives going to work and what were they going to drive, for example, as no office space was available in Homicide and no spare cars existed in the entire division?

Why was help finally on its way? In retrospect, the big press conference held the same month as the sheriff's election had pinned down the department. After the ballyhoo, and given that the body of another young woman (Karen Finch)—abducted, no doubt sexually assaulted, murdered, and dumped—had since been found in Sacramento County, common sense dictated that something had to be done. Also, to Biondi's pleasant surprise, in Captain Frank Wallace he'd found himself with an irascible if effective new ally who managed to sell the top brass on the fact that the staffing of Homicide was insufficient to handle its cumulative caseload and, at the same time, conduct an aggressive investigation into the rash of unsolved female murders. Too, maybe all the paper planes zinging out the windows had helped. Whatever the reasons, Biondi would finally have the live bodies he needed to launch a serious investigation.

Biondi knew the four new detectives were totally unfamiliar with the cases and would need time to review all the reports and organize the files. Once they were comfortable with the cases, he had some ideas of directions to send them, but he also wanted them to be free to follow their noses. There being no time to train rookie detectives, three of the four selected had previously done stints in Homicide. The fourth, Biondi phoned to give the good news.

"Just wondering," he deadpanned, "you still interested in coming to Homicide?"

"Heavens, yes!" Kay Maulsby said.

A year nearly to the day after Stephanie Brown was abducted on I-5, strangled, and dumped in a ditch 20 miles away, an I-5 task force had finally been born.

The hunt was joined for an elusive serial killer.

CHAPTER TWELVE

When DOJ criminalist Jim Streeter received the clothing evidence in the Karen Finch case two weeks after her body had been discovered, it didn't take him long to recognize that the cutting was the same as what he'd seen in the Stephanie Brown and Charmaine Sabrah cases.

Some articles of clothing were cut completely through, as if to remove them. Other garments were cut in the telltale teasing patterns, or what Streeter had labeled "nonfunctional" cutting in the Brown and Sabrah cases.

Finch's pink tank top was sliced down the front in a series of jagged cuts that would have exposed the victim's breasts. But there were also slits of one-quarter to one-half inches in length coming off the center cut, slits with no discernible function. The top was also cut from under the victim's left arm down toward the bottom of the garment, but stopped short of the hem. At the shoulder seam was another cut—approximately one-half inch in length—that went nowhere. The left shoulder strap was almost cut through, but not quite.

The blue shorts and pink panties were cut in an identical pattern, suggesting that the victim had been wearing them both when cut. They were cut completely through in the front, beginning on the left side seam and running across the crotch down to the hem of the right leg.

The shorts were splattered with blood that turned out to be the victim's type A. To Streeter, it appeared that the victim was wearing the shorts—or at least they were nearby—when she received her violent stab wounds. They had been found on the road, near copious amounts of type A blood.

At the autopsy, no sperm had been detected by the pathologist when he examined the rape kit swabs under a microscope. This didn't deter

Streeter, as it was not uncommon for a trained criminalist to find sperm after a pathologist had failed to do so. At the DOJ lab, specimens were routinely subjected to histological stains, a process that makes different cells easy to identify. In the case of sperm, what was commonly referred to as the "Christmas tree" stain was used; the heads of sperm cells became red and the tails turned green. When Streeter microscopically examined two slides marked "cervical" and "introital"—the latter swabbed from the opening of the victim's vagina—they both lit up in a brilliant red-and-green collage.

The hairs in the victim's pubic combings were similar to her own light brown pubic hairs plucked at the morgue by a coroner's assistant, Streeter noted. And he observed nothing remarkable—no blood, tissue, etc.—in the scrapings from underneath her fingernails recovered at the morgue as part of the rape kit examination.

A piece of duct tape found on the road turned out to be different from the duct tape found stuck to the victim's hair. A latent print analyst could find no fingerprints to lift off either length of tape.

Always, Streeter came back to the cutting. Obviously, the act meant something so important to the killer that he carried scissors to the crime scene and repeated the ritual again and again.

After his initial analysis of the Finch evidence, Streeter called Biondi. "I'm looking at lots of nonfunctional cutting, more than Brown and even Sabrah," the criminalist said. "Cuts that go nowhere—up, down, sideways."

Even when they did find the killer, Biondi knew they might never learn the culprit's inner thoughts and feelings as to why he did what he did. Why he killed whom he killed, why he cut their clothing, why anything. With serial killers, the authorities and the families of victims rarely got answers to those kinds of troubling questions.

Biondi didn't think that the I-5 killer was a rapist who happened to be killing, or even a killer who happened to be raping. He exhibited signs of a true serial killer; his motive was no doubt psychological, with his perverted acts having meaning only to him. At the scene of any serial killing where the victim had been raped, it would be correct to say the motive was sexual assault. But it usually went deeper than that. What was the killer actually accomplishing in acting out his fantasy? Almost always it came down to power and control, with the crimes committed by individuals who were otherwise powerless in their daily lives, or *thought* they were. It was about control of the situation, control of the moment, controlling who would die, controlling how and when. The crime was an elaborate dance for the killer that prolonged his power over the victims. He felt superior to someone, maybe for the first time in his life; his ability to end a life whenever he decided to do so gave him the power so long denied him.

But Biondi wasn't interested in becoming an amateur psychologist. He preferred to get on with the investigation. From a detective's point of view, motive wasn't the most important thing. Sure, in a cop's ideal world it would be nice to know the motive every single time. But much more important was identifying the killer and developing the evidence that linked him to the murder. Cases were solved and successfully prosecuted all the time where motive was never known.

"It's clear to me he's psychologically torturing his victims," Streeter continued.

"Could be a big turn-on for him," Biondi said matter of factly.

Biondi knew that regardless of a serial killer's psychological demons, his reasons for killing might be a lot simpler than forensic experts, psychological profilers, and true-crime writers would sometimes have the world believe.

He'd known plenty of serial killers who had killed simply because they enjoyed it so damn much.

KAY MAULSBY had finally made it.

Life at the Homicide Bureau, however, did not start out as she had pictured. For starters, she and the other three detectives assigned temporarily to the I-5 investigation had no place to work, no desks, no phones, nor were they assigned cars.

First things first: Maulsby made arrangements to borrow an unmarked car from Vice, where she'd previously worked, while the other "newbies" had to borrow a set of wheels every time they wanted to hit the pavement.

With no available work space for them in Homicide, the four new detectives put down roots in a combination conference and storage area down a short hallway. Cardboard boxes filled with old case files were stacked chest-high and three-deep against one wall. Most of the remainder of the floor space was taken up with a conference table, a variety of hard and cushioned chairs, and two old metal desks that were placed top-to-top and pushed into a corner. A window looked out over the Detective Division's parking lot.

The I-5 investigation consisted of several cardboard boxes containing assorted charts, maps, loose documents, and the all-important case volumes, which included crime scene reports, autopsies, and interview reports.

The first thing Maulsby did was to pin the maps on the wall that showed the widespread locations of the abductions and body dumps. Then, she and the other detectives emptied the boxes onto the conference table, and sat down to sort through the files and begin reading.

An hour later, they were busily taking notes and discussing the cases when a group of detectives with their lieutenant in tow showed up to have a scheduled meeting around the conference table.

The I-5 investigation quickly went back into the boxes, and the four nomad detectives making up the special task force to find a killer had to get lost for a while.

So it went, every day, several times a day.

Homicide had been given the extra personnel to work the series, but little else. Everyone knew it was a ridiculous way to run a major investigation. Ideally, they should have had a "war room" equipped with desks, phones, and filing cabinets; a place where all the files were organized and easily accessible and where detectives could sit side-by-side, exchanging ideas, opinions, and observations.

But Maulsby was not looking for excuses. Like the good cop she was, she'd make do with what she was provided.

After she'd read the cases and visited all the crime scenes, she paired up with one of the other detectives assigned temporarily to Homicide: Joe Dean, a forty-year-old sergeant from the Jail Division who had worked Homicide for a couple of years before getting his stripes, which resulted in his transfer. Built like a linebacker at 6-foot-2, 200 pounds, Dean was a hard-nosed Joe Friday kind of cop who tended to see things in black-and-white with no shades of gray.

The last week of July, Maulsby came into Biondi's office to talk about the Heedick case.

In Biondi's opinion, the best homicide detectives were very idealistic, and he had recognized this quality in Maulsby. What drove them forth in nearly impossible situations for extremely long hours had to be their unshakable belief that every murder could be solved. To be comfortable with anything less was unacceptable.

Based on what she'd read, Maulsby explained earnestly, she felt that James Driggers was a viable suspect in the murder of Lora Heedick and he needed to be worked.

Maulsby noted that Rita Driggers's phone bill had confirmed collect calls from the pay phone that Driggers claimed he had waited at that night, but also on the bill was another Modesto number called from the pay phone and charged to Rita's number that had never been identified.

"I think we should get a warrant and go to the phone company and find out who else he called," she said.

Biondi appreciated that theirs was a fresh objective. He told them of the difficulties experienced by Stan Reed—he'd gone back to the rotation and was handling new murders—in getting Driggers out of the case. Driggers had lied to his mother about the circumstances of Heedick's disappearance, caused her to file a police report with false information, failed a polygraph, had a rap sheet as long as his leg, and it went on.

Still, Biondi added, "I've always felt this one was part of the series even without the signature clothes cutting."

The mission Biondi had handed the four new detectives was clear: solve these four murders, whether they were linked or not to the series or to one another. If Maulsby and Dean felt Driggers needed to be worked, then so be it. After all, according to FBI statistics, 28 percent of female murder victims were killed by their husbands or boyfriends.

He advised them not to concern themselves with jurisdictional matters: Stephanie Brown, for example, was as much their case as San Joaquin's, even though her body had been found in the other county. He recommended that they touch base with the other departments, of course, and keep them informed. But everyone wanted the same thing: results. Given that three of the four new detectives had previously solved murder cases—the same three were also sergeants, and of course Maulsby was an ex-sergeant—Biondi believed that the high hopes he was placing in them to make progress in the investigation were not unrealistic.

Maulsby and Dean conducted numerous interviews in Modesto—in some instances reinterviewing people Reed had talked to earlier. If anything, the contradictions surrounding James Driggers only deepened.

When they met with Lora Heedick's boyfriend, it was in an interview room at the Stanislaus County Jail, where he was awaiting transportation to state prison on a strong-arm robbery conviction. "I have nothing to hide," Driggers told them. "I feel this is the loss of a loved one. I don't have no violence in me."

He declined, however, to go over his activities on the night his girlfriend had disappeared, claiming he was too tired from working out in his cell the previous day and not getting much sleep. He promised to talk further if they returned the next day. They did, but Driggers passed word through a guard that he didn't wish to see the detectives.

From the phone company, they got a name and address for the other number that was called from the pay phone on the night of Heedick's disappearance. It turned out to be a house inhabited by a group of dopers; one of them said he knew Driggers, but no one knew or had heard of Lora Heedick.

Driggers remained an enigma.

Maulsby visited, on her own, Carmen Anselmi. The two women hit it off immediately; Maulsby the inquiring detective with a heart, and the grandmother obsessed with seeing her daughter's killer identified and held accountable. They sat across from each other at the kitchen table, sipping iced tea, as Charmaine's little boy napped in the adjacent room.

Carmen told how excited Charmaine had been that night about getting out for a change. "I wanted it to be really fun for her. I bought her some new things to wear and loaned her my earrings and a skirt. I arranged for baby-sitting and paid for it as my treat."

Maulsby had her go over what had happened at the dance and afterward when they went to get something to eat, then their ominous car trouble on I-5. Some new details emerged, such as: Carmen wanted to walk to a house they could see a mile away, but Charmaine was afraid to get out of the car. "I guess she felt safer staying in the car. I didn't want to walk alone, so I stayed in the car, too."

Maulsby figured that Carmen had probably relived the ride with the man in the dark sports car a thousand times or more, but she asked her to recall it once more. As she did, the detective tried to pry out more details.

"He was so quiet that it made me a little nervous," Carmen admitted for the first time. "I was afraid to even turn and look at him. I was afraid he might get mad and ask me what I was looking at him for. I mostly just saw his profile out of the corner of my eye. I think he only turned his face right toward me once. That was when I said something about how my son wouldn't like it when he found out we were out dancing. When I said that, he looked at me with a nasty smile on his face. About the only other conversation we had was when I asked him if he lived around there and he said Stockton. If he lived in Stockton, I asked, why was he on the road to Sacramento so late? He either said he had a business there or had business to do there, I can't remember which. He didn't respond like people normally do. He just answered real short answers and acted like he didn't want to talk, so I didn't say any more."

Carmen admitted to Maulsby how terribly guilty she still felt for letting her daughter get in the man's car.

When the interview was over, Maulsby handed her business card to Carmen and encouraged her to call any time. "If you want to know what's going on," she said, "or just want someone to talk to."

On the way out, Carmen proudly showed the detective her grandson, who had already started walking.

Another afternoon, Maulsby and Dean drove to Lodi on a Sabrah lead—to make contact with a forty-year-old man whom a neighbor reported as matching the description of thesuspect in the Charmaine Sabrah case. He did a little, Maulsby thought, but he had an airtight alibi.

And so went the next couple of weeks, with Maulsby immersing herself in the cases. While she and Dean cleared some leads, none of them turned up anything promising.

Meanwhile, Biondi had assigned the other new detectives, Gary Gritzmacher and Tom Carter, to investigate the possible suspects at the top of the DOJ "Tip List," starting with Roger Kibbe. However, before they could get started, they found themselves tied up for weeks on what seemed like an important lead at the time—if true. Two security guards on foot patrol in a rural commercial area located along the Delta in San Joaquin County reported seeing a man in a blue Nissan 4 × 4 pickup attempting to dispose of what looked like a body. When the man spotted the uniformed guards, he put his suspicious load back in the truck and quickly drove off before the guards could get a license number.

Gritzmacher and Carter obtained a computer printout of all Nissan 4 × 4 pickups registered in the state. Unfortunately, registrations did not indicate the color of a vehicle, so the detectives found themselves with a list of 3,660 late-model (1983–1987) pickups. Due to the volume, the detectives focused on those registered in the San Joaquin Valley, which pared the list down to several hundred. One by one, they tracked the vehicles down, first checking the color, then looking for the special features reported by the guards: a chrome roll bar and a row of lights above the cab. Whenever they found a pickup close to the suspect truck, they interviewed the owner to find out where he and his truck had been on the night of the sighting. Although it was a needle-in-a-haystack lead, a report of someone attempting to dump a body in the general area of the I-5 series had to be taken seriously.

When the term "temporary" had been used to describe the assignment of the four new detectives, Lt. Ray Biondi had no idea how short a period of time some administrators had in mind. By early August—after only one month—he was already having to write memos justifying their continued assignment, explaining that the four were "learning the cases" and "we need to consider this a long-term commitment."

Biondi was summoned by the undersheriff to appear in Sacramento County Sheriff Glen Craig's office on August 20 (1987) to provide the three top officials of the department (including the chief deputy of investigative services) with "an update on our Special Taskforce" and to "review" Homicide's ongoing manpower requirements. Biondi translated the memo's bureaucratic language as follows: "Get your butt up here and tell us why you still need the extra bodies."

Within the opening seconds of the meeting, Biondi's assessment proved only too accurate.

"How many leads are you working, how long will it take to clear up each one, and when can we get our temporary people back?" the deputy chief asked in a single breath.

The three bosses sat looking at him, waiting.

Amazed at the obviously unrealistic expectations of the brass, Biondi sat dumbfounded. He could rattle off an accurate count of the leads, of course, but as to how long it would take to clear up each and every one—he knew he'd be dispensing total SWAG (Some Wild-Ass Guess). Unforeseen variables would greatly impact on the duration of the investigation—like whether or not the actual killer was presently among the suspect leads, whether the killings continued and new cases had to be handled, how many new leads would surface, etc. Didn't the brass hats realize this? Had they been out of the field that long? Or had law enforcement become such a cut-and-dried numbers game to them?

Careful to make eye contact with the sheriff, who would have the final word, Biondi laid out his case for keeping the four temporary detectives indefinitely. He said it was still his hope that other agencies would contribute manpower and resources to a multi-agency I-5 task force.

As to the four detectives, Biondi admitted he didn't know how long he'd need them, "but I don't see this series getting solved without this kind of full-time effort."

"My biggest concern," said the chief deputy, "is that this is summer and we need these people back for vacation relief in their respective bureaus."

Biondi didn't dare respond because he couldn't be certain what might come out if he opened his mouth.

"Now wait a minute," Sheriff Craig said sternly. "Your priorities are wrong. Vacation relief is *not* our biggest concern. Our priority is to solve these murders."

Thank you, Sheriff, Biondi wanted to holler. At that moment, he wished very much he had voted for the man.

"You know, my daughter drives on I-5 frequently," the sheriff went on. "I'm very concerned as a parent. This is a scary situation."

Biondi was promised that everything would be done to allow him to keep the detectives as long as possible.

Two weeks later, Biondi attended another meeting, this one at DOJ, to discuss the feasibility of forming a multi-agency task force to investigate the I-5 killings.

The multi-agency task force Biondi had long envisioned would total four to six detectives, on loan from various departments with cases in the unsolved series. They would work together daily in one room, with one manager in charge, and with all the necessary support, such as lab and clerical. A small, focused group would be far more productive, he knew, than the independent investigations that had been going since Stephanie Brown's abduction and murder a year earlier.

Biondi led off, explaining to the eight other participants that while Sacramento County presently had four detectives assigned full-time to I-5, his department simply didn't have the facilities or resources to "do the job right." His department, he explained, favored forming a multi-agency task force, with DOJ assuming a leadership role.

"We've focused so far on four cases, Brown, Sabrah, Heedick, and Finch, which contain distinct similarities in MO," he explained. "But I would not want to limit the scope of the investigation to these killings. I've got a feeling this guy has done more.

"I'd like to stage another press conference and release new information," Biondi went on, "to regenerate public interest and support. The last press release resulted in nearly a thousand leads combined for us and San Joaquin, and hundreds of persons of interest for us to look at. From them we developed about twenty potential suspects, many of whom we have interviewed at least once. We may have even already talked to the killer, but if we have it was more a matter of dumb luck than anything. There are people out there who have information we need. This guy doesn't live in a vacuum. He has family and friends, and there may be witnesses who have seen things on the road or somewhere but haven't stepped forward for whatever reason. I think we need to go public again in a big way, but doing so would require a task-force approach to handle all the new leads."

Any hope Biondi had of other departments contributing detectives to a task force soon faded:

San Joaquin—a captain of detectives explained that as of September 1 (1987) they had assigned three detectives (including Vito Bertocchini and

Pete Rosenquist) to work I-5 full-time; however, his department did not support the multi-agency task force concept. He went on to gripe about the DOJ lab, which his department used exclusively as they didn't have their own crime lab. He then requested—a bit audaciously, Biondi thought—that DOJ criminalists review fifteen unsolved female homicides that had occurred in his county over the past five years to see if there were any similarities with I-5. (DOJ had already compared nearly thirty female body dumps to known I-5 cases, searching for similarities.)

Modesto Police Department—even though Lora Heedick had disappeared from the streets of this quiet town, only to be found strangled 50 miles away, a sergeant said they had no homicides related to I-5. Therefore, they would not be able to become involved in a task force.

El Dorado County Sheriff's Department—a homicide detective reported that a Jane Doe had been found two months earlier that might be tied to the I-5 cluster. Estimated to be in her twenties, 5-foot-3 and 120 pounds, with long brown hair, she was nude from the waist up and had been dead for six months to a year. Her decomposed body was found in a ravine off Highway 50, a well-traveled route to Lake Tahoe. "It looked like she might have been thrown from a car or the shoulder of the road," he explained. Due to the condition of the body, the cause of death could not be determined. The detective asked for DOJ's help in identifying the victim; however, he said his department would not be able to participate in a task force.

Department of Justice—DOJ was willing to do everything but lead a task force. DOJ would continue to act as a clearinghouse for all the information sent to it by the various departments, and provide skilled lab support.

Although Biondi would keep pushing every chance he got for a multi-agency task force, at this and subsequent meetings between various agencies it became obvious that, at best, there would be two or more I-5 investigations running simultaneously from within different departments. He couldn't help but feel that ego and politics had derailed good law enforcement. The problem was not at the field detective level, where guys like Vito Bertocchini and Pete Rosenquist wanted very much to work on I-5 with other professionals like Stan Reed and Bob Bell. The juggernaut went farther up the chain of command, where bosses worried that another manager, another department, another sheriff would get all the publicity, and eventually, once the killer was caught, all the credit.

Without a major coordinated effort, the brunt of deciding what information to send DOJ, whom to interview, and which leads to follow up on would fall to the detectives working the cases, with veto power given to their bosses, who might or might not know anything about the unsolved series. It would continue to be, Biondi knew, haphazard at best.

As if he needed further proof of just how bad it could get, he returned to the office to discover that he was about to lose two of his four temporary detectives. Gritzmacher andCarter had been ordered by the chief deputy to return to their former assignments—Gritzmacher back to Narcotics to work on a big drug case and Carter to the Jail Division for vacation relief. They had worked on the I-5 series for exactly six and a half weeks—just long enough to become familiar with the cases—and had spent an entire month running down the blue Nissan lead that never panned out.

For now, Biondi could keep Maulsby and Dean.

From upstairs another compromise had come down in a seriously compromised investigation.

How many more young women would die by the same hand, Biondi worried, before they got their act together?

KAY MAULSBY looked forward to her lunches with fellow detective Bobby Armstrong. And now, in early September (1987), it would be their first since she'd started Homicide.

If the department had given an award for the friendliest detective, Armstrong would have won hands down. Slender, with a full head of salt-and-pepper hair and a ready-made smile, Armstrong, fifty-three, already had thirty-three years' seniority on the department, and professed no intention of retiring until forced to do so by county regulations at age sixty. He was one of those rare individuals who made a point of never saying anything bad about anyone. In his case, living by the Golden Rule had reaped huge dividends. Everyone liked Bobby Armstrong, really *liked* him, even the bad guys he'd arrested over the years, many of whom still served him loyally as informants two and three decades later.

Armstrong worked Vice, which is where Maulsby met him when she worked the same detail. He spent lots of time dealing with prostitutes on the stroll in the shadows of the state capitol building. Even though Armstrong regularly busted them and their pimps and Johns, Maulsby knew that he had earned the trust of many working girls because he cared.

Picking at her salad while Armstrong dug into a thick pastrami and rye with gusto, Maulsby talked about having gotten her feet wet on the I-5 investigation.

"We're looking for a guy who picks his victims based on opportunity," she explained. "He comes across a stranded motorist, someone who is lost on the highway, whoever he can find that he likes. I can only guess how much time he spends driving around window shopping."

Armstrong, intent on his sandwich, nodded.

"So I'm thinking, Bobby, who are the greatest victims of opportunity?"

"Working girls." He was paying attention.

"Right.

"We've had only one possible prostitute victim so far, but it makes sense we might have more. If he sees one he likes, you know, they'd be easy enough to get in his car. I'm wondering if you've heard anything on the stroll?"

"Just the usual. You know, a John who doesn't pay, an out-of-control pimp, that kind of thing."

"Do me a favor, Bobby. Let me know if you hear anything from the girls on the street or if anything comes across your desk that seems out of the ordinary. You know, some weird guy they're having troubles with."

"Happy to, Kay." The sandwich had mysteriously disappeared. He asked how she liked Homicide.

Maulsby tried to stifle a schoolgirl grin but was unsuccessful. "As much as I always knew I would. I feel like there's nothing I can be doing that's more important."

Armstrong found the grin highly contagious.

IN THE wee hours of September 14, 1987, Debra Ann Guffie, a willowy blonde who had turned twenty-nine two days earlier, stood on the curb at the corner of Auburn Boulevard and Howe Avenue in

Sacramento. Wearing tight blue jeans and a red T-shirt, she had no trouble attracting attention as she boldly made eye contact with male drivers passing by.

Business had not been good the past couple of nights. She had a "trick pad" at the Ritz Motel down the street, but was not making ends meet. She'd gone seven or eight hours without banging her arm; her nose was starting to run, her legs ached, and she was having the cold sweats. After a decade of working the streets to support her heroin habit, she knew the signs. She needed to get some money fast.

Shortly after midnight, a light-colored compact car pulled over. The middle-aged male driver reached over and opened the passenger door for her.

She peered in.

"You dating?" he asked.

"Yeah," she said. "I have a room nearby."

He shook his head. "No room. I've had bad experiences. I know a place up the road where we can park."

"Okay with me."

She climbed in, figuring she'd give the old guy some head—that's all you could really do in a small car—and make enough to buy a $25 bag of heroin from a regular supplier, and use his rig to shoot up. If she was lucky, she could be back on the corner ready for business in an hour, feeling a whole lot better than she did right now.

They drove down Auburn Boulevard a short distance, then crossed over the freeway.

Debra always made a point of being sociable with her Johns. She could hear herself babbling now—she talked fast normally, but when she was in early withdrawal her words sped up even more. The conversation was one-sided, however, as the man said nothing until they entered a darkened golf course parking lot and he'd parked and turned off the lights.

He took a long look at her.

"I'm into photography," he said softly. "Will you pose nude for me tonight?"

"All depends. How much?"

"Fifteen hundred."

As ill as she felt, Debra wanted to crack up. *Fifteen hundred dollars* to photograph what she gave away for fifty bucks every night? Right, and his name is Hugh Hefner and he's going to make her Playmate of the Year. She thought she'd heard it all, but this guy really took the cake.

She called his bluff. "I need fifty bucks up front," she said, fully intending to take whatever money he handed over and stiff the old guy. She knew he would have done the same to her after taking his dirty pictures.

"I've only got twenty-five."

"That's not enough."

"Is twenty-five enough for a blow job?"

Now he was getting down to business.

"I usually get thirty. But yeah, why not?" As much as she needed the money—she had less than three dollars to her name—she wasn't going to quibble and lose the John.

She was sitting so close to the dash that she leaned forward to find the release and move her seat back. She had her hand on the handle, but couldn't get it to budge.

She swore, as she was going to have to operate in tight quarters. "Guess that's as far as it goes."

"No, it goes back more."

He leaned toward her as if to help. But instead, his left hand in one swift motion grabbed her right wrist and twisted her arm painfully.

At the same instant, she heard a metallic click that scared her as much as the sudden violence.

She said, "No!" in the assertive yell of a dog trainer, and in a sharp reflex found the strength to break his grasp and pull her arm back. As she did, she turned toward him and saw he had handcuffs in his other hand.

Her right hand flew for the door handle. It was locked. She knew she hadn't locked it when she climbed in—she never did that in case she wanted to bail.

In the next instant, he grabbed a handful of her long hair and slammed her face hard into his lap.

She felt the coarseness of his jeans against her cheek, and could smell urine and stale sweat.

"Please—don't hurt me." She was begging now. "You don't need to do this. I'll do anything you want. Just don't *hurt me.*"

He had been so timid before he turned, with no sign of weird or hostile behavior, that she hoped he could be reasoned with.

"Don't struggle and you won't get hurt, cunt."

A chill cut through her. His voice had taken on a completely different sound. It was the voice of someone who meant business; a mean voice she could never trust no matter what it told her. If she stayed here, she knew she *would* get hurt. Real bad.

Fuck begging. She exploded with all the manic energy that had been coursing through her for hours, screaming hysterically, flailing legs and arms—her right hand had not stopped clawing for the door lock—squirming and jerking her head, shoulders, and body like a human bronco.

At that moment her fingers found the lock. She pulled the lever and the door handle below it. Feeling the door give way, she pushed it open with all her might.

His hold on her hair was so strong that she thought he would pull out a hunk, but she didn't care. Ignoring the searing pain, she pulled against him in a tug-of-war for her life. At the same time, she thrust her feet and legs out the open door and willed the rest of her body to follow.

The man kept his death grip on her hair as Debra Guffie's screams pierced the night air.

CHAPTER THIRTEEN

Sergeant Charles Coffelt of the Sacramento Police Department was cruising slowly through the darkened maintenance yard in the rear of Haggins Oaks Golf Course.

Coffelt wheeled into a narrow alleyway between two metal buildings, heading quickly for the front lot. He radioed his location and reported that he was investigating loud screaming.

A field supervisor on the graveyard shift, Coffelt had a patrol team working under him. Still, whenever possible he led by example. As a detective earlier in the year, he knew about nighttime thefts from the golf course's maintenance buildings, so he made a point of cruising through the area several times a week to check on security.

As Coffelt swung his cruiser into the front lot, he saw a light-colored, four-door compact vehicle parked in the dimly lit lot about 150 feet away with its passenger door flung open. A figure was half in and half out of the car.

He headed his patrol car straight for the compact. It appeared to Coffelt as if a woman was struggling to pull herself out of the car as a man behind the wheel was trying to keep her inside. As they fought, she continued to scream.

When he had closed to within 75 feet, the beams of his headlights lit up the car. Coffelt could see that the man was holding the woman by her long blond hair.

Suddenly, she came flying out of the vehicle, with her momentum carrying her several feet away from the car. She fell hard on the pavement on her hands and knees.

The white car shot ahead, its passenger door ajar.

The decision to go after the car or first check on the woman's condition was made easy for Coffelt by the fact that the car was heading toward the rear of the parking lot, where the patrol sergeant knew there was no exit.

Coffelt rolled up next to the woman.

"You all right, ma'am?"

"He—he"—she was hysterical and crying—"tried to *handcuff* me! He's—crazy!"

She picked herself up off the ground.

"Get that *sicko!* He would've killed me!"

The driver of the white car had realized his dilemma and whipped a U-turn near where Coffelt's patrol unit had charged through the two maintenance buildings like the 7th Cavalry.

The white car zipped past them, accelerating as it headed for the only way out of the parking lot.

"Stay here," the patrol sergeant barked.

Coffelt went after the car, which after clearing the lot turned onto the surface street and headed for the freeway overpass. Activating his red lights, he tucked in behind the fleeing car at the overpass.

The car turned right at the first intersection they came to, pulled over to the shoulder, and stopped, with Coffelt right behind.

Coffelt illuminated the suspect car—a new Hyundai bearing California plates—with his spotlight. He put out on the air the license number, their location, and a request for backup. He could see that the driver had remained upright behind the wheel.

Given the circumstances of the chase, Coffelt decided to conduct a high-risk vehicle stop. He opened his driver's door, crouched behind it, and drew his service revolver. Aiming his gun at the Hyundai, he would stay where he was until other units arrived.

It didn't take long.

This was a busy location, with the freeway a dividing line between Sacramento city and unincorporated county—everything on one side belonged to the city and everything on the other to the county. Two sheriff's patrol cars, monitoring Coffelt's transmissions, happened to be closest and arrived first.

One unit pulled up to the left of Coffelt's patrol car, throwing more light on the Hyundai. The other unit came up behind him and turned his lights out so that Coffelt would not be silhouetted.

The deputy on the left crouched behind his door, with his weapon pointed at the Hyundai. The deputy in the back was watching the opposite side of the Hyundai with his gun drawn, too. In this way, each deputy had a line of fire that did not go through Coffelt.

In this situation, it was standard procedure that the officer initiating the stop, regardless of rank, was in command and directed the activities of the other officers. It kept things safer that way, rather than having someone new to the situation arrive and start making wrong decisions.

Even though none of his own troops had arrived yet, Coffelt was ready. Over his loudspeaker he ordered the driver of the Hyundai to turn off the engine and throw the keys out, then keep his hands in sight outside the window.

The driver obeyed.

"While still keeping your hands out the window," Coffelt's voice boomed through the rooftop speaker, "open up the door using the outside handle."

In this way, Coffelt would not lose sight of the suspect's hands. He didn't want the guy reaching down into the darkened car and coming up with any nasty surprises.

When the door was open, he told the driver to exit the car and walk up the street for about four or five feet.

The driver did as he was told.

"Now get down on your knees and lie on your stomach with your hands extended out to the sides of your body."

Coffelt started his approach, not taking a direct route to the suspect but walking alongside his own unit, then going to the rear of the suspect's car, where he could see inside the vehicle for anyone else.

In a crouch, he came around the driver's side. As he did, he dragged the palm of his hand across the trunk lid to feel for movement inside.

When he reached the suspect, Coffelt ordered him not to move. He took one of the man's hands and held it behind his back, which would aid him in controlling the suspect should he try to get up off the ground. He then directed the man to put his other hand behind his head.

Coffelt slapped the cuffs on the suspect.

By then, several of Coffelt's patrol officers had arrived. Coffelt helped the suspect up off the ground, and patted him down for weapons.

"What's your name?" Coffelt asked.

The suspect, a middle-aged man with graying hair, kept his head bowed and said nothing.

Coffelt handed him off to another officer to place in the secured rear seat of a patrol car.

The sergeant leaned inside the Hyundai, sweeping the powerful beam of his flashlight across the seats and floorboards. When he turned around, he was surprised to see the young woman from the parking lot.

"I was afraid to be alone back there," said Debra Guffie, nervously eyeing the man in the backseat of the patrol car.

She explained that she had run from the lot and followed the flashing lights. As she spoke, she was trying to light a cigarette but her hands trembled so much that she was having great difficulty. Finally, she got it lit and took a couple of puffs, which seemed to steady her a bit.

"He pushed me out of the car when he saw you," she explained. "Threw my purse and jacket out, too."

"You said he had handcuffs," he said. "You sure?"

"What do you mean?" Her voice cracked, and she seemed ready to cry again. "He was gonna put 'em on me! Fuck, yes, he had handcuffs!"

Coffelt brought one of his officers over to take a full statement from the shaky victim. Then, he directed another officer to go back to the parking lot and search it.

"What am I looking for, Sarge?"

"Handcuffs."

UNDER GAUDY chandeliers in the main ballroom of a Nashville, Tennessee, hotel, Lt. Ray Biondi stood at the podium beside several display boards with poster-size pictures of StephanieBrown, Charmaine Sabrah, Lora Heedick, Karen Finch, and articles of cut clothing, along with maps showing the locations of the abductions and dead bodies.

In his presentation to more than 200 homicide detectives from thirty-five states attending the National Conference on Serial Killing, Biondi laid out the pertinent facts of the unsolved series, including the peculiar "nonfunctional" clothes cutting found in three of the four cases.

Biondi showed the hefty printout of the computerized suspect list recently compiled by DOJ. "The identifiable suspects we've been able to find have been interviewed at least once," he said. "Some more than that."

Suggesting that the computer was a good way to organize and prioritize suspect leads in a series that lent itself to thousands of tips called in from the general public, he reviewed the criteria that were developed to give weight to various factors relevant to the murder series.

"Of course, these are only suspects we *know* about. I'm sure there are other viable suspects we don't know about. Is our killer on this list? I can't tell you. Check with me after we catch him and I'll let you know."

Biondi made his presentation on the first day of the four-day conference, and the I-5 display stayed up along one wall of the ballroom for the next three days. He also attended a workshop involving female murders associated with freeways, and heard of an unsolved series along Interstate 10 in a southern state in which all the victims were redheads. He also learned of a couple of cases in which clothing had obviously been ripped or cut for quick removal from the victim. However, he never once came across similar nonfunctional clothes cutting—not during other presentations or countless coffee breaks or over evening cocktails in the hospitality room, where the most valuable inside information was always dispensed at cop conventions over free drinks. Nowhere in the country had there been a case with the consistent and baffling signature of the I-5 killer.

Biondi boarded a plane to return home on the afternoon of Thursday, September 17, 1987.

Although he wouldn't know it for another twenty-four hours, that same day a fifth body was found.

FIRST THING the next morning, criminalist Jim Streeter received a call from a deputy in the South Lake Tahoe substation of the El Dorado County Sheriff's Department, which didn't have its own crime lab and contracted its forensic science work to DOJ.

Streeter was told that an unidentified nude female homicide victim had been found the previous afternoon off a closed service road adjacent to Highway 50, four or five miles west of Lake Tahoe. He was asked to respond to the sheriff's substation in South Lake Tahoe, and from there he'd be taken to the mortuary. They wanted him to check the body, before the autopsy, for any fibers or hairs that at some point might be matched to a suspect.

El Dorado was Sacramento County's immediate neighbor to the east. From downtown Sacramento to South Lake Tahoe it was 100 miles on U.S. Highway 50, with the first portion of the drive through the suburban sprawl of Sacramento County and the rest through rugged El Dorado, a 65-mile-long county that extended from rattlesnake-rich foothills where gold was discovered at Sutter's Fort nearly 140 years earlier into pine-studded High Sierra country, ending at the western and southern shores of Lake Tahoe, the largest alpine lake in North America.

On a Sunday drive with his family, Streeter would have taken his time and enjoyed the changing scenery—most of it national forest—but not today. With thoughts of murder and dead bodies on his mind, he made the trip in under two hours, walking into the South Lake Tahoe sheriff's substation at 11:30 A.M.

Told by a lieutenant that he'd have to wait for the arrival of the detectives, who were still at the crime scene, Streeter cooled his heels for half an hour.

When the detectives showed up, they explained that the nude body of a young adult female was discovered in the woods by a woman jogger who decided to investigate a strange odor she'd been noticing in the area for several days. The victim had obviously been strangled with a ligature that was still around her neck.

Streeter was told that the victim's clothing had been strewn about the area. He was shown several garments that had been recovered from the crime scene.

Each article of clothing was sealed in a plastic bag, and Streeter left them in place so as not to lose any possible trace evidence prior to a more thorough exam at the lab. He moved the material around under the plastic until he found what he had hoped he wouldn't, and yet exactly what he expected to find. A chill went down his back.

"Heard of the I-5 series?" he asked, his eyes riveted on the plastic evidence bag still in his hands.

The answer was no, even though a detective from El Dorado's main office in Placerville, the county seat 40 miles west of South Lake Tahoe, had attended the I-5 meeting held a month earlier at DOJ. It was another instance of miscommunication, even in such a small department as El Dorado (120 sworn officers), which had only eleven detectives total to handle all types of investigations: eight assigned to Placerville and three at the South Lake Tahoe substation.

"This killing appears similar," Streeter said, not looking to get into a lengthy explanation.

The criminalist, however, picked up the nearest phone and called the Sacramento County Sheriff's Homicide Bureau to speak to Lt. Biondi, whom he found out to lunch. He left word that he would call back.

Streeter was taken to the nearby mortuary where Jane Doe was due to be autopsied later that day.

The body, greenish in appearance due to decomposition, was lying on a gurney in an embalming room.

After a visual examination of the body, Streeter plugged in a hand-held laser, which was really just a fancy black light. He slipped on a pair of yellow goggles and snapped off the overhead light. Under the pale gray beam of the light, the body was bathed an eerie yellowish green.

The object of the laser examination was to try to find objects that under normal light would not be seen. In a head-to-toe examination of the corpse, Streeter found three fiber fragments—they showed up in various fluorescent colors under the black light. He collected them from the victim's right arm, right breast, and pubic hair.

Whitish stains were illuminated on several areas of the body, possibly indicating semen. Streeter used a black felt pen to outline the areas on the victim's right breast, across her chest extending down toward her left hip, and on her left leg shin. None of these areas, however, would test positive to acid phosphatase, the medium used to detect the presence of seminal fluid.

All the while, the mortician, who with his comically dour expression and all-black outfit looked like he should be cast on "The Addams Family," had been hovering over the body like an overly protective parent.

Streeter told the mortician to have the autopsy physician swab the areas he'd encircled in black ink. "They need to use swabs moistened with distilled water and only one swab should be used for a single area," he added, knowing how country bumpkins could screw up scientific evidence.

The criminalist made a point to look at the victim's wrists to check for any hair loss, indicative of tape having been wrapped around her wrists at some point as bindings, but found none.

With help, Streeter rolled the stiff body onto its side. Examining the buttocks, he noted what appeared to be fecal matter on and around the rectal area. There had not been fecal stains on any of the garments he'd seen, leading Streeter to conclude that Jane Doe had been killed at some point after her clothes were off.

Streeter told the El Dorado detectives what other evidence he needed from the autopsy. "Her entire head of hair should be collected, if at all possible, so that I can examine it for any traces of duct tape. As for fingerprints, I'd like for her hands to be removed and delivered to our Latent Fingerprint Section."

One of the detectives arched an eyebrow.

"Some of the items recovered at the scene may have palm prints on them," Streeter said, by way of explaining his unusual request. "I want us to have a complete set of impressions for elimination purposes. And an X ray might help us in identifying her."

Streeter had noticed something strange about the four fingers on her right hand: they were missing the last joint, and had no fingernails. He thought X rays could determine if the shortened fingers were the result of postmortem animal activity or a birth defect.

Streeter called Sacramento from the mortuary, this time reaching Biondi.

"I'm in South Lake Tahoe. I've just seen a Jane Doe found here yesterday that you may want to see before the autopsy. Nude female body dump off Highway 50, ligature strangulation."

"Think it's our guy?"

Streeter had saved the best for last.

"Ray, her clothes are cut."

DETECTIVES Kay Maulsby and Joe Dean arrived at the South Lake Tahoe mortuary at 4:00 P.M. After looking at the body, they went to the sheriff's substation to see the clothing. Then, they returned to the mortuary for the 6:00 P.M. autopsy.

They all wore masks, and for Maulsby, her most outstanding memory of her first autopsy would forever be the terrible stench that emanated from the decomposing corpse.

The pathologist began by making a cursory physical inspection of the body. He noted numerous scrapes and bruises on her arms and legs and a deep bruise on her right hip.

The ligature around her neck, a black material, turned out to be one of several pieces of a chiffon jacket recovered at the scene. At the back of the victim's head, the ligature was entwined around a section of tree branch. Strands of the victim's medium-length, slightly curly blond hair were caught in the ligature. The placement and tightness of the ligature, the pathologist remarked, was sufficient to cause death.

The victim had been gagged with a piece of her own pantyhose. A portion of nylon had been stuffed into her mouth, then tied so tightly behind her head that when it was removed it left a deep furrow in her skin.

With the ligature and gag off, facial photos were taken in the hope of having an artist reconstruct a likeness of the victim.

It would take someone with a good imagination, Maulsby thought. She worried about becoming nauseous and making an embarrassing spectacle of herself. She maintained her composure by staying intently focused on everything being said by the pathologist, who explained each of the invasive procedures he performed in a dispassionate play-by-play narrative.

Her partner, Joe Dean, left the room early; to go to the crime scene while it was still light out, he said. It was a good out, one Maulsby would have liked to have thought of first. Instead, she made it her mission to learn every possible detail she could about the murder of Jane Doe.

As for the rape-kit exam, pubic and scalp combings were taken and her fingernails were scraped, although no apparent debris was found underneath them. It was impossible to check for evidence of rape. The vagina and cervix were completely gone, testimony to the fact that insects first attack available body openings.

Examining the victim's head, the pathologist found a subdural hematoma 3 inches in diameter.

"She received a hard blow to the head before death," he commented. "It wasn't fatal, but it may have caused unconsciousness."

The pathologist attempted to cut off the scalp intact, as requested by Streeter, but the condition of the deteriorating skin prevented its complete removal. Sections of the scalp were removed, however. The victim's jaws and teeth were also removed so that her dental work could be X-rayed for identification purposes. Inked prints were taken of each foot and her hands were amputated above the wrist bone.

An internal examination revealed that Jane Doe had a healthy heart and other major organs, and no natural, preexisting conditions that had led to her demise. Toxicology results would come back negative for drugs and alcohol.

The pathologist estimated the victim's age at between sixteen and twenty-one. She was 5-foot-3 and about 115 pounds. She'd been dead two to four weeks. The cause of death was listed as "ligature compression of the neck."

"You know, the ligature was constructed so that it could be tightened and loosened with the stick," said the pathologist, removing his soiled rubber gloves and stepping to a nearby sink. "It could have been tightened down until she blacked out, then released to bring her back."

Maulsby tasted bile.

"You mean he could have *toyed* with her?"

The pathologist looked over his shoulder at Maulsby as if that thought hadn't occurred to him.

"You could say so."

"How long do you think—"

"No way of knowing," the pathologist said, working up quite a lather with the disinfectant soap that momentarily overpowered some of the unpleasant odors in the room.

It was too dark to stop at the crime scene after the autopsy, so Maulsby and Dean headed directly back to Sacramento. They were both starving, neither had eaten since breakfast, but they were not tempted to stop. The smell from the autopsy room had permeated their clothes.

Maulsby returned first thing Monday morning to South Lake Tahoe, where she met El Dorado's lead investigator in the case: Detective Jim Watson.

In his late thirties, Watson was a six-footer with a compact build, sandy hair, and ruggedly handsome features out of an L. L. Bean catalog. Although he had a pleasant personality and was considered easy to get along with, Watson was the conscientious type who went through the day exuding an intense commitment to complete whatever tasks had to be done. His okay-we've-talked-about-it-now-let's-do-it attitude tended to brush slower-moving objects aside, although he usually managed to do so without offending or making waves.

Watson took Maulsby to the crime scene.

Old Meyer's Grade Road was a remnant of the old highway used decades earlier before a new section of U.S. 50, which it roughly paralleled, had been completed. Three miles long, the sloping two-lane paved road was gated at each end and locked. It was opened to vehicular traffic only when the state road department occasionally used it as a bypass during avalanche control on U.S. 50. Local residents in the sparsely populated surrounding hills used it daily for walking and jogging.

Jane Doe's body had been found in a woody area off the road about 600 yards downhill from the top gate, where Watson parked.

"He either parked here or down at the other gate, which is more difficult to find," Watson said. He explained that there weren't any highway patrol units patrolling on this section of Highway 50 at that time of night.

As they walked down the road, Watson pointed to white evidence cards with numbers on them stuck in the earth alongside the road. Articles of clothing had been strewn along the way; first her panties, then her black jacket, her dress, a black patent leather high heel.

"I think he took her down to the scene alive and made her walk," Watson said. "It's too far to carry a body. I checked the bottom of her feet. They weren't scratched at all. She obviously had her shoes on."

"Undressing her as they went?" Maulsby asked.

"Or he undressed her at the scene and then walked back to his car, throwing her clothes along the way."

Watson led them off the road to a clearing about 35 feet into the tall pines. Amid scrub brush and large boulders, evidence cards dotted the landscape like so many craters on the moon.

"We found her over there," Watson said, pointing to a small clearing next to a rotted-out log. A rudimentary outline of the body had been made in the matted-down grass.

An inhospitable place to die, Maulsby thought. In the dark, alone with a serial killer, forced to walk down a deserted road to what she had to have known would ultimately be her death. Doubtless, the end had not come quickly for her. The killer had brought her to this godforsaken piece of ground so that he could take his time.

"She was face up on her left side," Watson said. "Her right arm was behind her back and her left arm was draped across her left thigh."

"Right here," he said, pointing to a spot about 2 feet away from the outline of the victim's head, "we found a short piece of white cord. Two more pieces of the same cord were found back up the road. One piece next to her dress and the other one near her panties."

Found near the body, Watson went on, was a pack of Newport cigarettes, a white lighter, and two condom packets.

Maulsby wanted to know if the condoms were used. When she worked Sex Assaults, she'd heard of savvy rapists who used them to avoid leaving semen evidence.

"One package was open but not used," Watson said.

It was her first murder scene since working Homicide, and Maulsby made notes and took in all the information she could. Still, she was happy to leave. As they returned to the car up at the gate, she wondered how in the world the killer had found such a desolate place.

Later that week, Maulsby went to see Jim Streeter, who had received and was evaluating all the physical evidence from the Jane Doe crime scene.

Streeter was in his lab taking tape lifts off a piece of the latest victim's jacket—it had been found cut into four sections, including the one used as a ligature. The material was laid out on a lab table atop a single sheet of white butcher paper. Holding a piece of Scotch tape between his fingers, Streeter tapped it on the garment two or three times, then suspended the length of tape across a small plastic dish. He pressed the ends of the tape down on the sides, then placed a lid over the dish, which would later be placed under a microscope for examination of hairs and fibers. In this way, every square inch of each garment from the crime scene would be methodically covered by tape lifts.

When his hands were free, Streeter took Maulsby to the opposite side of the lab. There, he introduced her to his mute assistant, long retired from the retail business, now serving a higher calling. A bald mannequin used to help examine damaged garments was wearing Jane Doe's pink, sleeveless dress, which Streeter had already processed for tape lifts.

"Here's a classic example of what I've been calling nonfunctional cutting," Streeter said enthusiastically. "Assume the attacker wanted to get to her breasts and pelvic areas immediately. What would be the best way?"

It was a quiz, Maulsby could see. She pointed to the zipper that ran diagonally across the front of the dress from the left shoulder down to the lower right hem.

"Uh-huh. But what does this guy do? He cuts up from the bottom seam a couple of inches on the left side, then stops. It accomplishes nothing. Then he cuts along the shoulder seam on the left side and down the back about six inches. He cuts likewise along the other shoulder. See what I mean? They serve no obvious purpose."

"So he didn't cut her dress off?"

"Not in my opinion. See, the cutting is just the way he plays. I think he cuts the dress while it's on her, then unzips it when he's good and ready. Several teeth are missing at the bottom, as if the zipper was forced."

Streeter moved toward another lab table.

"This is her pantyhose."

Maulsby counted five pieces of nylon, including a section that contained the reinforced crotch liner. Each was inside its own plastic evidence bag.

"This section here—it's a foot and part of a leg—was used as the gag. They look cleanly cut to me, not ripped or torn. If I had to guess, I'd say she was wearing them when they were cut."

Streeter asked Maulsby if she was familiar with the Sabrah case.

"I've read the file."

"You remember her pantyhose was cut?"

"Yes." Maulsby also recalled that Sabrah had been found with her wrists still bound by pieces of her nylons.

"Well, it's the same artist at work here. Sabrah's pantyhose was cut in the same exact fashion."

"What about her panties?" Maulsby asked.

"They aren't cut. But I can tell you they came off her while she was still alive."

"How do you know that?"

Streeter told her.

The criminalist next showed Maulsby the three pieces of white cord found at the scene. They measured between 17 inches and 23 inches, he said, and appeared to be a common nylon cord available at any hardware store.

The detective picked up each piece of cordage, looking for stains or marks, but saw none.

Before she left, Maulsby asked Streeter if there had been any progress on identifying Jane Doe.

"So far, no match on dental with any of our missing persons," he said. "I had her hand with the short fingers X-rayed yesterday. It's a birth defect. Maybe that'll help. El Dorado is planning to send out a flyer."

Jane Doe had been Maulsby's first face-to-face murder victim. The detective couldn't shake the overpowering remorse she'd felt at the morgue, and again at the scene.

If the hills could only talk, she had reflected at Old Meyer's Grade, what tales would they have told of the screams and struggles and crimes of a fortnight ago?

To Kay Maulsby, rookie homicide cop, Jane Doe was more than another female body dump.

That had been someone's child lying there.

Somebody was surely worried sick about her.

CHAPTER FOURTEEN

Judy Frackenpohl feared the worst.

It was unlike her seventeen-year-old daughter, Darcie, not to call home every week or so—a curious contradiction considering Darcie had been a chronic runaway for the past two years.

Judy, forty, a short brunette with green eyes, was a single mom of two: Darcie, and her younger brother, Larry, two years her junior. Her two kids couldn't have been more opposite: Larry, the good boy, quiet and appreciative, and Darcie, the wild seed, affectionate but rebellious.

Judy had a good job and rented a home in a middle-class suburb of Seattle. She'd been on her own financially and in most every other way since her divorce thirteen years ago. Her ex-husband had not been very good about paying child support but he'd been around for the kids on birthdays and holidays until his death, at age thirty-four, eight years earlier. He had been married for a third time but was living alone when diagnosed with terminal cancer. As he became sicker, he had no place to go. Judy had him move back in for the last months of his life, bringing in a hospital bed and caring for him. When he died, it had been difficult on both the children, then nine and seven years old. However, losing her father seemed to hit Darcie the hardest. Always a daddy's girl, she remembered his promise to her after the divorce that he'd never leave her.

Darcie had not only her mother's eyes and light complexion, but also her outgoing personality. Her nickname as a child was "Little Miss Big Enough" because she wasn't afraid to do anything. In large crowds, Darcie would approach and talk to anyone. In the third grade, she was walking home from school one day when she had to go to the bathroom; she knocked on the door of the next house she came to and asked to use the toilet. A parent could worry about a willful child like that, and worry Judy did.

As Darcie turned fourteen, mother and daughter fought incessantly. Judy saw in her daughter an inability to come to terms with the major event of her young life: losing her father. On an emotional level, she seemed to resent that he'd broken his promise not to go away. Her mother was the first and best target of Darcie's smoldering anger. Darcie went into counseling—individually as well as family—but nothing seemed to help. Darcie refused to accept her mother's rules, cut school, and at fifteen began running away. Whenever she came back home, she seemed more impatient than ever with her mother's values. The friends she brought home, misbehaving and troubled truants, were a parent's worst nightmare. Darcie's boyfriends were always black; Judy was convinced her daughter did this for shock value, as it hadn't been occasional or gradual, but 100 percent all the time. Once, Darcie's beau turned out to be an intelligent, college-prep student whom Judy liked. Perhaps it was an acceptance Darcie wasn't seeking, as her very next boyfriend was the worst yet. Judy had the feeling that Darcie was dropping down the social ladder until she got to a level of society that she could be sure her mother would never approve of. Eventually, she stopped bringing anyone home. By the time she'd turned sixteen, Darcie was running away for weeks at a time, living in the streets, and becoming involved in prostitution.

A Seattle police officer called collect at 2:00 A.M. one night to tell Judy he'd just had a long talk with Darcie on the street and let her go. "I know she's a listed runaway," he said, "but I can't force her to go home. We talked for more than an hour, and I have to tell you I don't know why your daughter is out here. She's not a heroin addict with caved-in veins. She just doesn't belong on the streets."

Judy was at a loss to understand it, too. The three of them had always been a tight little family, camping out of their 15-foot trailer that Judy hauled to national parks behind an old pickup, and vacationing every summer in Alaska, where Judy's parents lived. Judy was proud of the stability she'd single-handedly given the kids—living in the same house their entire childhood, going to the same school, having plenty of extended family nearby.

After Darcie's rebellion, Judy's efforts had run the gamut: from driving around frantically looking for her, to angrily locking Darcie out of the house when she ran off, to finally accepting Darcie's absence as her decision.

Over a period of time, "tough love" won out. Judy stopped giving Darcie money and footing her bail on charges ranging from vagrancy and shoplifting to prostitution. "I do not condone what you are doing," Judy told Darcie, "and I will not contribute financially to your lifestyle."

At the same time, Judy never hesitated to reinforce to Darcie that she was free to come home any time. She always had a home and the door was always open, but with one caveat: she had to abide by her mother's rules. These rules included getting back into school, not doing drugs (Darcie was a dabbler), helping around the house, and otherwise being a responsible member of the family. It was Darcie's choice.

More than not, Darcie opted to stay out.

The previous Christmas (1986) Darcie had spent in a Seattle jail cell on a loitering charge. A local television station did a story on the unfortunate souls spending Christmas in jail. They handed out gifts on Christmas Eve to prisoners, and interviewed some of them live on camera. Darcie looked into the camera and said she didn't have a home and, flashing her baby blues, how she didn't have anywhere to go. It was an Oscar-worthy performance, and Judy had been mortified, even more so when friends and relatives started calling to say they'd seen Darcie on TV.

At times when Darcie became desperate enough—like when she had to be hospitalized on her mother's insurance for an acute venereal disease shortly after the Christmas she spent in jail—she returned home. But she never stayed for long; usually two or three days, a couple of weeks at the longest. When she left again, it could be in the middle of the day or night, without notice, and usually she didn't even pack a bag. Rain or shine, she would walk out the door with the clothes on her back.

Still, she had *always* called home regularly, never going more than two weeks without touching base.

Darcie's last call had been on August 23 (1987), a Sunday afternoon—collect from Sacramento. She was checking in, telling her mother that she and James planned to go to Disneyland, then maybe to Texas in a couple of weeks.

Judy had never met James Brown but she knew from Darcie he was her twenty-year-old black pimp-boyfriend. They'd met several months earlier in Seattle when Darcie was on the streets and Brown had just gotten out of jail on a pandering charge. He had recruited her on the spot. As far as Judy was concerned, nothing good would come to Darcie from this symbiotic relationship or from her traveling farther away.

"You feel like coming home?" Judy had asked tentatively. She was disappointed that Darcie wasn't already home—a week earlier, she called from Oakland and reported that she and James were fighting and that she was thinking of coming home. Obviously, they'd made up.

Judy told Darcie she didn't like her being so far away, and that Larry was missing her, too. "I'll wire you a ticket to come home," Judy said.

Darcie had said she would "think about it."

The last thing Judy said was "I love you." She certainly didn't like what her daughter was doing but she'd raised her kids to know that her love for them was never conditional. How could she love them less for their mistakes?

"I love you, too," Darcie had said.

A month earlier, Darcie had been placed on a Trailways bus and sent home by the San Francisco Police Department after a prostitution bust. She'd stayed for Larry's fifteenth birthday in late July. Darcie had dinner out with them, then left the next afternoon for California, saying she needed to go back and get James out of jail. As Larry had walked her to the bus stop two blocks away, she confessed she didn't really want to go back to California but that she was afraid of what James would do to her if she didn't. Darcie had always found it easier to confide in her brother than her mother. For his part, Larry heard more about his sister's wayward life than he really needed to, but he always listened. When the bus came they hugged good-bye. It was the last time Larry saw his sister.

Judy was accustomed to her daughter's leaving, but Darcie's return to California had bothered her a lot. It was so far away, and Darcie's hustling life only increased the odds that something bad would happen.

Six days after Darcie's last phone call home, Judy received a collect call from James Brown in Sacramento. He wanted to know if Darcie had called or come home. Judy told him she hadn't. He said he didn't know where she was.

Initially, Judy took heart in the news, thinking that Darcie had left the guy and might be on her way home.

Then, a few days later, she received another collect call from Sacramento. This one was from someone who identified herself as Lily. Claiming to be a friend of Darcie's, she said that Darcie had disappeared and that James had been arrested for "suspicion of a missing person."

Judy called the Sacramento Police Department to see if they had arrested anyone named James Brown. She checked the jails, too, but no one had heard of him.

The next day—September 4 (1987)—Judy called the King County Department of Public Safety to file a missing persons report. King County covered all the unincorporated areas of greater Seattle.

After taking Darcie's age and description, the officer, obviously going down a form, asked questions.

Did she have a history of running away?

"Yes," Judy said.

"About how long has she been running away?"

"Two years."

"She's a chronic runaway, then?"

"Yes."

"To your knowledge does she use drugs?"

"Sometimes."

"Is she involved in prostitution?"

"Yes."

The officer was obviously filling in the blanks on the form, but the entire process seemed to Judy very dehumanizing. She felt that Darcie was being placed into a category that would result in no one taking this seriously.

"Listen, I've had a lot of trouble with my daughter," Judy said. "But she never goes more than a week or so without calling, no matter what she's involved in. It's now been almost two weeks since I've heard from her, and then I get these calls from California that she's missing. I'm very concerned that something has happened to her. I want her name put into the system as a missing person."

The officer duly wrote down the information, but Judy had the distinct impression that this missing persons report was not going to be his or anyone's high priority.

"Tell me, Officer, should I file a missing persons report in Sacramento?" she asked.

The officer said no. "She lived here and left from here, so this is where the report should be filed.

"We'll need the name and address of her dentist."

Darcie had had extensive orthodontic work; in fact, she was still wearing a retainer that had been soldered into place by the dentist on her last visit. Judy gave the officer the name of their dentist. She also explained that Darcie had an unusual birth defect.

"On her right hand," Judy said, "my daughter is missing the tips of her four fingers above the top knuckle."

THE MISSING persons report on Darcie Renee Frackenpohl collected dust for more than a month before being reviewed by a King County detective.

The report finally landed on the desk of Detective Mike Hatch, formerly of the Green River Task Force and recently assigned to a new squad formed to track missing persons and teenage runaways who fit the profile of Green River victims.

The first bodies in the local unsolved murder series had been discovered in July and August 1982, when the remains of five young women were found in and near the meandering Green River in southern King County. Two of the bodies had heavy rocks placed on them to hold them underwater. The press dubbed the unknown suspect as the "Green River Killer." Since the grisly discoveries that summer, a total of forty-one young women had been killed in what was to become one of the largest serial murders in U.S. history.

A majority of the bodies were skeletonized by the time they were found, but most of the victims were thought to have been strangled, and usually with their own clothing, although in numerous cases no clothing was found. After being abducted, the victims were transported to rural dump sites.

Over time, a clear profile of the victims had emerged. The majority were young—or young-appearing—females last seen on Pacific Highway South near the Sea-Tac Airport, the Rainier Valley area of Seattle, or downtown. The majority had some connection with a street-type life-style (although thirteen victims did not), either as known prostitutes or through having friends or associates involved in the illicit trade.

The special squad—consisting of Hatch and two other detectives—had been formed to investigate a growing backlog of some 200 missing persons cases in King County, including about two dozen young women with street lifestyles. One of the goals of the squad was to determine if the Green River Killer was still active. A similar effort three years earlier that evaluated reports on missing persons and teenage runaways had given police their first understanding of just how prolific this serial killer was.

Hatch called Judy Frackenpohl on October 8, 1987, to see if she'd heard from her daughter in the thirty-four days since Judy had filed the report. She told him that she had not.

The next morning, Hatch checked King County Vice records and found several contacts his department had had with Darcie, including a prostitution-related arrest in June (1987). That same morning, he called Judy and asked for copies of her phone bills showing the collect calls from Sacramento. Judy said she would copy the records, and be available to meet with him. Hatch said he wouldn't be able to sit down with her. Three days later, the detective picked up the bills from the receptionist in the lobby of Judy's office. He called the California numbers, finding them to be pay phones.

When she heard nothing more from Detective Hatch, Judy telephoned him as the two-month anniversary of Darcie's disappearance approached. She called to say she still hadn't heard from Darcie, and to remind him that someone cared.

"You know, the typical runaway will call home during the holidays," he offered.

"But look at her pattern," Judy said. "Darcie is not a typical runaway."

Hatch made the following notation of her call in the missing persons file: "10/20/87, 0930 hrs. I received a phone call from Judy Frackenpohl. She states that she still has not heard from Darcie Frackenpohl as of yet."

Then, the detective closed the file.

A month would pass before he made another entry.

With no reason to be optimistic, Judy was filled with an eerie sense of apprehension and impending danger. It hit home that her daughter's lifestyle had become increasingly dangerous, and not conducive to growing older.

Darcie had, as far as her heartsick mother was concerned, dropped off the face of the earth into the dark nether world of the missing. She had been gone before, of course, but she had never been *missing*.

Her mother knew that Darcie would not go this long without being in touch; not unless she couldn't call or come home. Not unless she was being held against her will.

Or—unless she was dead.

"THE SUSPECT you're looking for is probably white, male, mid-twenties to early thirties, unmarried, either never married or divorced, works with his hands and is dexterous with tools, and has a reason to be outdoors, like a job or hobby."

The words of the profiler from the FBI's vaunted Behavioral Science Unit left the three detectives from the Sacramento County Sheriff's Department Homicide Bureau stuck somewhere between awe and amusement.

"Do you have his phone number?" someone asked.

Lt. Ray Biondi had first been exposed to the psychology end of murder investigations when he attended a school taught by instructors from the FBI's Behavioral Science Unit back in 1976. At the time, he'd thought it was fascinating stuff, and had come back eager to view murder scenes with this cutting-edge training in mind. As with most new things, the eagerness soon wore off, although his fascination with reading the signs of a scene remained.

What Biondi came to realize over the years after countless murder investigations was that the experienced homicide detective is a profiler in his own right, even without a single psychology course to his name.

In fact, the detective had an advantage over the professional profiler, Biondi believed, in that he interacted with the murder through the investigation and developed intuitive feelings as to who, how, and why. The detective also experienced the crime scene through all his own senses, and had a similar intimacy with the unique cast of characters—victim, witnesses, suspects—that showed up in each case.

The profiler, on the other hand, generally developed his information from afar, through a cold study of written reports and other documentation. As a result, most profiles ended up being drawn with ambiguous borders, with even the most detailed suppositions carrying frustrating qualifiers like "could be," "probably," "more than likely."

In Biondi's mind, there was no way that profiling could be compared with forensic evidence. Profiling was much more of a last resort. In fact, he did not know of a single murder or series of murders in which the profile was instrumental in the resolution of the case, or even played an important part in the case. Profiling went wrong when it was oversold, sometimes through the direct claims of the profilers themselves to having solved murders. Like psychics, profilers only talked about the ones they were right about.

No matter how good the profile or how skilled the profilers themselves, you could not eliminate a viable suspect because he didn't fit the profile, and likewise, a profile most certainly should never be used as the sole reason to focus an investigation on someone.

While Biondi believed that profiling research was valuable training for detectives and helped them open their eyes to look at things in a different way, he considered a detective's feelings and opinions more useful toward solving a case. These feelings and opinions guided a detective from the moment he visited the crime scene until a suspect was arrested. Biondi strongly held that detectives were better off identifying suspects not through complicated personality profiles but with simple, old-fashioned police work: interviewing witnesses, following leads, collecting evidence, etc.

That said, Biondi wasn't about to pass up an opportunity to discuss the I-5 series with the FBI's expert profilers, who were in Sacramento the first week of October (1987) to speak at a homicide investigation school put on by DOJ. The popular two-week course was attended by detectives from various northern California departments, including Kay Maulsby, who had learned, among other things, the difference between an "organized" and "disorganized" serial killer. The I-5 killer would be considered "organized" due to the obvious planning and preparation that went into his crimes. The "disorganized" category was reserved for "frenzy" killers.

The profilers had graciously accepted Biondi's invitation to come over after a long day in the classroom and meet with him, Maulsby, and Joe Dean. The FBI agents and the detectives had gone out for a quick dinner first, then returned to the Homicide Bureau and settled around a conference table with loosened neckties and mugs of coffee.

The detectives briefed the profilers on the unsolved cases, including the latest one in El Dorado, with Maulsby providing details of the Jane Doe crime scene, autopsy, and physical evidence that had been gathered.

Biondi realized that they had a serial killer who was becoming decidedly better at what he did. His killings were impulsive only in the way he chose his victims, for the crimes themselves were obviously planned at great length. He was bringing nylon cord now, probably to use as restraints instead of making do with pieces of the victim's clothing. He'd changed his strangulation method; by twisting a piece of wood into the ligature he could asphyxiate them in a more controlled manner. He was learning and progressing all the time, finding what worked best, discarding that which didn't. The scenes screamed out a kind of arrogance on his part, as if he had all the time in the world to taunt and torture his victims and to cut and remove their most intimate apparel. He had become a hideously effective killing machine; no doubt he was better at murder than anything. He was enjoying himself, really enjoying himself. He would never stop on his own. Not ever.

Concluding that a murder series did exist and that it was improbable there were two or more killers acting independently and duplicating the same type of crimes, the profilers agreed with a general profile of the I-5 suspect that Biondi had prepared for an upcoming press release that he hoped would reignite the public's interest in the case.

- The killer was a frequent lone traveler of major highways in the San Joaquin Valley, including Interstate 5 and U.S. 99, as well as the U.S. 50 corridor from Sacramento to Lake Tahoe.
- He was a *probable* resident in one of the above areas, more likely the Valley as he was familiar with the rural areas and back roads.
- He has owned or has access to several vehicles during recent years.
- He was *probably* familiar with and frequented prostitution strolls in San Joaquin Valley cities.
- He *probably* had a nonthreatening demeanor and appearance upon first contact.
- He *could be* a loner type with relatively few close friends, living a quiet lifestyle. He was *probably* known to neighbors as a "quiet nice guy" and kept to himself.
- He *could* live alone, or *may* live with family, such as parents, brothers, sister and his wife.
- It *could be* he is familiar with the difficulty law enforcement agencies experienced in multijurisdictional investigation.

Some of the recommendations of the profilers the locals had already done, such as making a concentrated media plea to generate hard suspect leads and also to increase the pressure on the killer.

But there had been no major media coverage in months, Biondi pointed out. "I think we need to keep more pressure on him."

"Yeah, he might be getting comfortable again," the FBI's Bill Hagmaier said. "He might think he can kill without fear of the cases being connected."

Maulsby wanted to know if there was a danger in more media coverage. "Will it result in more murders?"

Hagmaier said that although some serial killers were known to have coveted media attention, there was no reason to believe that the frequency of the I-5 murders would increase in proportion to the media coverage. The profiler suggested it was more likely the opposite would happen. "Increased public awareness would mean he would have to work that much harder to find his victims along the roadside."

"In the real world," Biondi said, "the more leads we get, the more man-power we need to work them. Not having enough people has been a prob-lem for us all along."

Biondi explained he had only two detectives, Maulsby and Dean, working on I-5 full-time, and that San Joaquin had its own investigation going with three detectives assigned full-time for the past month.

"Green River is doing it right," one of the profilers said. "Their task force is from five jurisdictions and under one roof."

"How many people do they have now?" Biondi asked.

"Right now, forty."

Biondi was momentarily speechless. He was thinking what he could do with half that.

"By the way," Hagmaier said, "your actual body count could be three or four times greater than it is now."

"You mean there could be twenty bodies out there?" Maulsby asked incredulously.

"I certainly *do* think there are others out there you haven't found," Hagmaier said. "And may never."

Biondi agreed with Hagmaier. "Considering the rural dump sites, we were lucky to find some of the ones we did."

Biondi's beeper went off; it was Dispatch. He went to his office phone, and found out about a new homicide that looked like a gang murder but would turn out to be a well-staged domestic killing (wife killed by hus-band). He called Stan Reed and Bob Bell, asking them to respond.

When he returned to the conference room, Biondi explained what the call had been about.

Hagmaier, his interest piqued, started asking questions about the fresh murder that Biondi couldn't answer.

Finally, Biondi said, "Look, Bill, you wanna go take a look?"

Hagmaier had the expression of a Little Leaguer throwing out the first pitch on opening day. "I sure would."

Off they went, the "real world" detective to show the expert profiler from Quantico that murder looked a lot different up close and personal than it did on paper.

Late the next afternoon when Maulsby stopped by the office after having spent the day in the classroom, she found a Sacramento Police Department report on her desk, along with a note from Bobby Armstrong saying she might want to take a look at the attached report of an assault on a prostitute.

The report, dated three weeks earlier, started off routinely enough. Hooker gets into a guy's car, agrees to give him a blow job for $25, then the guy tries to handcuff her. They struggle, she gets away, guy drives off but is pulled over by a city unit. He's booked on assault with intent to commit rape and driving without a valid driver's license. He refuses to make a statement to the arresting officer. At the end of her statement, the victim says: "That guy was weird. He would have killed me if that policeman hadn't come along. I want to press charges even if I have to go to jail for my warrant." She had signed a complaint form, and was placed under arrest for an outstanding warrant.

The name of the suspect didn't mean anything to Maulsby. He was listed as being forty-nine years old, 5-foot-11, 180 pounds, brown eyes over black graying hair. At the time of his arrest, he was wearing a T-shirt, blue jeans, and white sneakers. He had given a Sacramento address and no phone.

Maulsby kept reading. Listed under the physical evidence recovered at the scene were some very curious items. At that point, the report stopped being routine for Maulsby.

She called the Sacramento Police Department and spoke to a clerk in the property room. She gave him the crime report number and explained that she was interested in seeing all the booked property as soon as possible.

Maulsby appeared at the Sacramento Police Department's property room at 8:00 A.M. the next morning. After showing her ID, she waited at the counter as the property clerk behind the wire cage went back to search the stuffed shelves. When he came back, he was carrying a large manila evidence folder, which he gave to Maulsby.

She checked the evidence tag to make sure it was from the right case, then opened it where she stood.

The first thing she saw was an empty plastic Ziplock Baggie with chalky smudges still on it; obviously it had been dusted for prints.

Everything else had been put into a separate evidence bag. She opened it and let the contents slide out onto the Formica-covered counter-top. Each item was secured in individual plastic bags and tagged.

Maulsby caught her breath.

Even though she'd read a description of the items in the crime report, seeing them with her own eyes made her feel very much like a voyeur parting a dark shroud and peering into a secret, filthy place she wasn't meant to be.

First, there were the handcuffs found by officers in the golf course parking lot. They didn't have a serial number, but "Taiwan" was stamped into the metal.

Next came the items from the plastic Baggie that had been found in the parking lot near the handcuffs.

Two handcuff keys, said to fit the cuffs.

White plastic vibrator, the battery-operated type.

Scissors, about 6 inches long with blunt ends, the kind that nurses use when bandaging wounds. Examining them, Maulsby could see remnants of tape adhering to the blades, and what looked like fibers stuck to the tape.

Two rubber hair bands.

Two identical pieces of wooden doweling, about 6 inches by one-half inch, and strung between them white nylon cord about a foot and a half in length, each end looped around a dowel and knotted.

Another longer piece of the same cord.

With chills chasing each other up and down her spine, Maulsby realized she'd seen the cordage before—

It was the same type of nylon cord that had been found lying next to Jane Doe at the El Dorado crime scene.

CHAPTER FIFTEEN

Minutes after recognizing the cordage in the sadistic "crime kit," Detective Kay Maulsby sprang into Lt. Ray Biondi's office with the news. She first summarized the circumstances of the assault case and all the other physical evidence recovered before telling Biondi about the cord.

"What's the suspect's name?" he asked.

Maulsby looked down at the assault report.

"Kibbe," she said. "Roger Kibbe."

"He's number one on our hit parade," said Biondi, sounding like his usual unflappable self. Inside, however, a voice was screaming, "Holy shit! Is it possible the criteria worked beyond our wildest dreams and the killer is actually at the top of the list?"

Biondi told Maulsby how Kibbe had received the highest score on the DOJ "Tip List" printout months earlier. "I had Gritzmacher and Carter ready to work their way down from the top," he said, "before they got hung up on blue Nissans."

Maulsby remembered having seen the DOJ list early on. She went to the I-5 boxes, found the printout, and returned to Biondi's office, reading along the way.

"Kibbe was a suspect in a female abduction three years ago in Contra Costa County," she pointed out.

"That's something Vito found," Biondi said.

He told her of Bertocchini's bringing Kibbe in for questioning the previous December after he'd been stopped by the San Joaquin patrol deputy who thought he resembled the composite.

"Vito thought Kibbe was dirty from the get-go," he went on, "but there really wasn't anything to connect him. He was driving an older white Maverick at the time of Heedick, but Driggers and Carmen Anselmi didn't pick him out of a photo lineup."

Biondi knew how important individual initiative was when it came to working a murder series. Without it, important leads and tips had a way of falling by the wayside. The way that Maulsby had alerted Vice and then made sure not to let the assault report slip through a crack was more than rookie luck.

They agreed to get the cordage over to the DOJ crime lab right away so Streeter could take a look at it.

"But based on what I saw with my own eyes," Maulsby said with conviction, "that cord was the same. This is the guy."

VITO Bertocchini was not a happy trooper.

Displeased it had taken his department so long to establish an I-5 task force to work the unsolved series, he was also frustrated that a heavy workload had kept him away from the Stephanie Brown and Charmaine Sabrah cases for months. He hadn't forgotten the faces of those innocent victims and their grieving loved ones, nor would he any time soon.

Most particularly, Bertocchini was highly vexed that he hadn't been able to spend any appreciable time investigating the man he felt certain was the I-5 killer.

In a meeting with fellow homicide detectives Pete Rosenquist and Larry Ferrari and their sergeant, Bertocchini laid it on the table.

"I want to work Kibbe *real* hard," he said, turning up the bass. "I think we should set up surveillance on him."

The sergeant looked uncomfortable. Surveillance meant long hours and overtime, which meant budget overruns.

Just an hour earlier, Bertocchini had talked to a deputy district attorney about whether they could get a search warrant for Kibbe's home and vehicles. The D.A. heard him out but nixed the idea of going to a judge until they had more probable cause as to Kibbe's involvement in murder. They would also need a list of what specific items they'd be looking for, as no judge would give them carte blanche.

Another detective stuck his head in the room.

"Phone for anyone working I-5."

Ferrari got up to take the call.

Bertocchini was glad to have Ferrari on the team. He was only in his late twenties; however, he was a seven-year veteran of the department and a skilled interviewer. Likable and enthusiastic, he genuinely cared about people and struck up friendships easily. Although of Italian ancestry, the 6-foot-1 blonde had the fair features of a California surfer and the slender build to match. A stylish dresser, he wore all the latest fashions and came off very debonair for a cop.

Ferrari returned showing a boyish grin. "Vito, Christmas is early. That was Kay Maulsby. Guess what she found this morning on your old friend Kibbe?"

Bertocchini perked up as Ferrari told him about Kibbe's assaulting the prostitute and having thrown from his car the crime kit that was found to have his fingerprints.

"Kay says it's the same cord she saw two weeks ago at a murder scene up in South Lake Tahoe," Ferrari said.

Bertocchini pounded the table with gusto.

"Goddammit! I *knew* he was killing women!"

He jumped up and left the room.

Vito Bertocchini had a deputy D.A. to find.

IN THE MONTHS since Roger had been brought into the Homicide Bureau and questioned by detectives, he and Harriet Kibbe had not seen or heard from the police.

Life had gone back to a kind of dysfunctional routine for them. In May (1987), they had moved to another Public Storage facility, also in Sacramento, and were living in its one-bedroom managers' apartment adjacent to the rental office. By day, they ran the business. In his spare time, Roger, who had grown a full beard, did odd jobs around the place. Harriet continued to work on the accounting program she hoped would bring her financial independence.

They were living together like platonic roommates with no claim to the other. On Roger's nights out, he returned late or sometimes not until early morning. Only once did he offer any information as to where he had gone. He came home one morning in late August (1987) and stood outside the bathroom, which Harriet was busy cleaning. When she looked up from the tub, she saw he had a black eye. Standing there like a child explaining his tardiness at school, he said he'd been at a video arcade and gotten in the middle of a fight between some guys. There was a time she would have scolded, but that time had passed. It seemed odd to her that Roger would become involved in any kind of a physical altercation, which she knew was much too confrontational for his liking. But she shrugged it off and went back to scrubbing the tub.

At this point in their relationship, she didn't much care what Roger was doing on his own time after work, or even whether he was or was not cheating. She preferred not to think about Roger being with other women, of course, but she'd lost all interest in resuming sexual relations with him. Their boundaries had been well defined: They were still together only as a matter of accommodation.

Although Harriet and Roger didn't subscribe to any newspapers and only occasionally watched TV news, she was aware that the toll of the I-5 killer was mounting. It gnawed at her that Roger had been questioned as a possible suspect. By now, the police had obviously realized their mistake or they would have been back, right? The man responsible for those killings was a monster, the type that Harriet had only read about in the true-crime books she devoured. She knew that vicious, cold-blooded killers existed, of course, but she didn't know what one looked like in real life. She was certain, however, that they didn't look and act like Roger. Still, the fact that the police had had some reason to question him in connection with the series of terrible crimes continued to trouble her.

One night in the summer (1987), they were lying in their separate beds shortly after turning out the lights. She asked the question she'd asked him before and would continue to ask him—the question she couldn't shake.

"Do you know anything at all about these dead women?"

Without the slightest hesitation, Roger answered, "No," then bade her good night.

Harriet noticed some changes in Roger that summer. He seemed more withdrawn than usual, and at times outright morose. Thinking it had to do with their deteriorating marriage, she couldn't blame him. She was feeling similar hopelessness. A marriage that once seemed to have a future had turned into a leftover carcass with no sustenance for either of them. Who could be joyous about it?

Roger had sold his custom-made $2,300 parachute rig, too—for only $800. He'd had it less than a year, and had worked weekends for months packing chutes at the Antioch skydiving center to build up enough money on the books to buy it. The chute was a rectangular para-foil in Roger's favorite colors: red, white, and blue. He had a jumpsuit to match.

Harriet was bewildered that Roger had parted with his beloved rig. A veteran of more than four thousand jumps since 1966, he now seemed reconciled to giving up the one thing he seemed to enjoy above all else in life. When she asked him why he'd sold the rig, he told her because they needed the money, even though she never saw a penny of it and she paid all the bills. Things were tight and parachuting was not a cheap hobby, but Harriet would not have asked him to sell his rig—it would have been like asking a weekend fisherman to sell his favorite rod and tackle.

On a hot August evening as they sat in the living room watching a TV sitcom, Roger cleared his throat during a commercial and out of the blue said: "There will come a day when we'll part company and you'll be grateful for it."

It was a veritable speech for him these days.

"What do you mean?" she'd asked.

Harriet was sitting on the couch across from Roger, who was in an easy chair.

"You'll see," he said.

On the night of Roger's arrest for assaulting the prostitute, Harriet was in the hallway outside the bathroom when he casually announced, "I'm going out."

She turned to look at him down the long hallway; he was already at the front door with his hand on the knob. In faded blue jeans, T-shirt, and sneakers, he looked like a regular guy heading out for bowling league night—only it was nearing midnight and she'd come to think of him more as a prowling tomcat.

"Oh?" she said as casually as if he'd told her he was going to stay up and read. She'd long given up questioning him about his comings and goings, and all the mileage he put on thecars, or even caring what he did as long as he didn't use credit cards or otherwise run up debts.

He turned and left, and she went into the bathroom to brush her teeth for bed. The next time she heard from him was his collect call from jail the following morning.

"What did you do to end up *there*?" she asked.

"I'll tell you later. Call Steve and let him know."

She inquired about the car, and Roger said it had been impounded by police.

They'd sold the Datsun 280Z in February (1987)—deciding to get rid of it because Roger said it looked too much like the car driven in some of the I-5 killings—but not before he'd logged 27,196 miles on it in only seven months. (He'd put 26,755 miles on their previous car, a red Honda, in just eight months.) Since then, their main form of transportation—they also had an old pickup that barely ran—was their white four-door 1986 Hyundai that they'd purchased in the summer of 1986 for Harriet to drive.

"The car is *impounded*?" she said. "That's just great. What am I supposed to do without a car?"

Harriet realized that to an outsider it might have sounded as if she was more worried about the car than Roger.

She called Steve and broke the news, explaining that Roger wouldn't tell her what he was in jail for.

Steve promised to make some calls.

When he rang back, Steve told her straight out that Roger was in jail for attempted rape of a prostitute.

Harriet's legs went weak, and she felt her heart pounding. She had to sit down. *Rape? This* was the guy who wasn't interested in it at home, and he was going out picking up prostitutes and trying to *rape* them! For a moment, she saw the morbid humor in it: *You don't have to rape prostitutes, you big dummy, you only have to pay them.*

Then, she began to cry.

Steve outlined the steps she needed to go through to get the car out of impound, which she did that afternoon when their relief Public Storage employee gave her a lift downtown.

Later that afternoon when Roger called again from jail, Harriet threatened not to bail him out. But after she hung up she got to thinking that questions would be asked by their regional supervisor if Roger was gone too long. As it was, she had signed up with an agency for temporary bookkeeping work from time to time as a way to bring in more money. Roger would need to cover for her double dipping, as Public Storage considered her a full-time employee. But a few days in jail wouldn't hurt him, she decided. Anyway, after his behavior he deserved to cool his heels awhile.

Four days later, she bailed Roger out after a municipal court judge set bail at $15,000, which they met by signing an agreement to pay a $1,500 premium to a local bail bondsman. She said nothing to Roger inside the police station when they first brought him out like a stray needing a home.

They walked silently to the car.

Harriet was still furious about the arrest and the fact that he'd been with a prostitute, and normally she would have been ranting and raving. But she knew that in the best of times, yelling at Roger was like screaming at a brick wall; a sore throat was all she ever got out of it. Why bother now?

She drove from the jail parking lot with Roger slouched over in the passenger seat. When they hit the first red light, they sat mute, both staring straight ahead.

Harriet was rolling over in her mind questions she would have liked to ask Roger: *How many prostitutes had he picked up? How long had he been doing this? Had he been with prostitutes when they were still sleeping together?*

Finally, without looking at him, she hissed: "Can't you keep that thing in your pants?"

Roger said nothing.

For the next two weeks, Roger stayed close to home. It seemed the ordeal had knocked the wind out of him. He didn't use the car or go out a single night, and was content to putter around the place, cleaning out and showing storage spaces, doing some painting, and otherwise keeping busy.

On a Saturday morning the first week of October (1987), Roger and Harriet took a leisurely drive to Lake Tahoe on U.S. 50, passing right by

Old Meyer's Grade Road, where the unidentified young woman had been found nude and strangled seventeen days earlier.

Steve was to receive an award from his department at a special dinner and had invited them and other family members to attend the ceremony. Roger wouldn't have missed it for the world. He and Steve were close; about as close, Harriet thought, as two brothers could possibly be. What they talked about and had in common when they were alone she couldn't guess—the older brother who had been on the wrong side of the law so much of his life, and the younger brother who was the law.

She knew the brothers had opposite opinions about their late mother, Lorraine, a hospital nurse who had died of melanoma at age forty-three in 1963. By all accounts, Steve worshiped her memory, while Roger, who long felt he was his mother's least favorite of her three boys, did not. Many of Roger's stories about his mother had to do with her anger and ridicule directed his way. According to Roger, she always "yelled and screamed" at him, finding fault in everything he did. She hadn't liked his tendency to stutter when nervous, his disinterest in school, his difficulty with reading, his slow-moving gait, and seeming scores of other minor and major faults she found with him. He remembered her being quick to discipline him and let fly with an open hand. One of Roger's earliest childhood memories was of his mother beating him until he couldn't walk for playing with his army toys in her monthly supply of flour—this during World War II rationing. He also had memories of being locked out of the house, naked, as a boy by his irate mother and hiding in the bushes until his father came home. That night he issued his first threat to run away from home. Before long, he was sneaking away in the dark for hours on end; he soon found he enjoyed peeping into neighbors' windows. His sneakiness grew, and before long he was burglarizing those same homes, and eventually stores.

The third Kibbe son, Jonathan Jr., who worked in the aerospace industry in San Diego, was five years younger than Roger. When their mother took seriously ill, her two youngest sons—then grown men—had come to her bedside, but not her eldest. And when Lorraine Kibbe died, Roger had a good reason for not making his mother's funeral: he was in state prison serving a two-year hitch for burglary.

Seemingly without an ounce of envy or resentment, Roger idolized Steve, who, in turn, appeared very comfortable in his role as the stable, responsible brother who was always there when his hard-luck older brother needed a lifeline.

It was a Kibbe family reunion of sorts at Tahoe, with Roger's father, Jonathan "Jack" Sr., and his second wife, Susan, whom he married a year after Lorraine's death, and who was also a nurse, coming up from San Diego. Only the third Kibbe brother, Jack Jr., failed to make it.

At the "Law Enforcement Appreciation" dinner given at the Carson Valley Improvement Club in Minden, Nevada, that night by the Elks, the Kibbes all sat together.

Steve was not as tall as Roger, who himself was not as tall as their father. More stocky than his father and Roger, Steve had a full head of hair sprinkled with gray and a closely cropped beard. He had a soft and deliberate way of speaking, not unlike Roger. For the occasion, he wore a blue blazer, white shirt with tie, pressed jeans, and, like every Nevada cop worth his weight in sagebrush, cowboy boots.

When Steve's name was called, he moved to the front of the room where his boss, Douglas County Sheriff Jerry Maple, waited at the podium. As the sheriff handed Steve his award and shook his hand, polite applause began. Everyone at the Kibbe table, including Roger, beamed with pride.

Homicide Detective Steve Kibbe had been named "Officer of the Year" the same week that Roger Kibbe had become the prime suspect in the I-5 serial murders.

CHAPTER SIXTEEN

When criminalist Jim Streeter received the pieces of white cord found at the Jane Doe murder scene in El Dorado and in Roger Kibbe's crime kit, he studied them under a microscope, finding all five pieces to be the same in several important respects.

Type of fiber: nylon

Number of fibers running through cord: six

Color of fiber: white

Type of weave and pattern size

Threads per cord: 32

Shape of cord: hollow

Streeter could not say that the cordage found at the two locations had once been part of the same length of line. The closest he could get—and all he could testify to in court—would be that the pieces were similar.

In examining the scissors from the crime kit, he saw the tiny pieces of duct tape on the blades that Kay Maulsby had noticed but was unable to match the fibers stuck to the tape with any of the victims' clothing. If the fibers were from the last victim Kibbe had killed, they had not yet found her.

Streeter spent that afternoon checking various hardware and sporting goods stores around Sacramento looking for similar white cord, but found none. On a hunch, he stopped at the Lodi Airport and showed the cordage to the owner of the Parachute Center, who recognized it.

"What's it used for?" Streeter asked.

"Suspension and reefing lines."

Streeter had a blank expression.

"In the construction of parachutes."

AT THE wheel of a lurching, smoking motor home, Detective Vito Bertocchini pulled into a shopping center parking lot adjacent to the Public Storage facility on Tupelo Drive inSacramento. Heading for the end of the lot closest to Public Storage, he parked the beast that would be his home away from home for the next two weeks.

In the passenger seat, Pete Rosenquist studied the terrain through binoculars. "This is good," he said. "I see the office and the front door. There's a walkway in back that leads to the storage spaces. We're covered on both ends."

"Pete, do you know where we're at?"

"Shit, you're right!"

They were around the corner from the beauty shop they'd gone to a year and a half ago to interview Stephanie Brown's hairdresser about her chopped-off hair.

Bertocchini knew that Roger Kibbe had not lived on Tupelo Drive then, and he recognized it as simply a strange coincidence. Kibbe had come across Stephanie lost on I-5 south of Sacramento; he didn't follow her from the beauty shop. Still, it made the detectives feel as if they'd come full circle.

They checked in by radio with two unmarked cars, driven by Sacramento detectives Bob Bell and Harry Machen, that had followed. After they found parking spaces nearby, Bell and Machen joined the party in the Winnebago, owned by the San Joaquin County Sheriff's Office for use on major drug surveillances that had been known to last for weeks.

The morning went by quietly with no activity.

At 1:30 P.M., they sent a sheriff's department records clerk into the Public Storage office to make contact with Roger Kibbe. She did, pretending to be interested in renting space, and came back out to report that the suspect worked from 9:30 A.M. to 6:00 P.M. Although the white Hyundai was parked in front, Harriet did not appear to be on the premises.

The detectives had met earlier that morning at the Sacramento County Sheriff's Department Homicide Bureau to establish ground rules in their attempt to keep an eye on Kibbe during his every waking moment until a search warrant could be served.

Luckily, there was a window between new murder cases in Sacramento—the last one, ten days earlier, was solved right away with the arrest of the victim's boyfriend. As a result, Lt. Ray Biondi was able temporarily to divert the entire Bureau to the Kibbe investigation.

Biondi put Stan Reed to work on the crucial affidavit in support of a search warrant, which would be reviewed by a judge prior to a warrant's being issued. The key new development in terms of probable cause was, of course, the nylon cordage. Reed would describe, in addition, other physical evidence, each crime scene, the criminal acts that had occurred, list the specific items they would be searching for at Kibbe's residence, as well as offer his learned supposition as to what he thought had happened ("Based upon my training and experience, it is my opinion that …"). The affidavit would take a week to write, and run nearly seventy pages.

The Sacramento detectives had joined forces with Bertocchini, Rosenquist, and Larry Ferrari from San Joaquin in setting up the Kibbe surveillance, considered essential if for no other reason than to keep the I-5 suspect from killing again. However, the detectives all hoped to develop new promising leads in the process—perhaps Kibbe would unwittingly lead them to where he'd stashed the victims' purses?

The detectives had discussed that morning how far to let Kibbe go before stopping him. What if they saw him pick up a potential victim and drive off with her?

"You'll have to stop him right away," Biondi said.

They couldn't take any chances trying to follow Kibbe and possibly losing him, Biondi counseled. After all, they were after more evidence, not more victims.

On the first day of surveillance, October 16 (1987), Kibbe didn't leave the facility all day. At 6:00 P.M., Harriet arrived home in a Chrysler with another couple, who came inside the residence. An hour later, the two couples came out and left. They were followed by Machen and Bell to a nearby restaurant, where they had dinner. They arrived back at 9:00 P.M. The other couple stayed until after midnight, then left. Lights in the residence went out at 1:34 A.M. Forty minutes later, with Roger Kibbe home in bed, surveillance was concluded.

The next day featured more of the same, with Roger home alone and Harriet gone. The detectives whiled away the time in front of a 10-inch TV watching the opening game of the World Series between the St. Louis Cardinals, whom they all hated for having beaten the San Francisco Giants for the National League pennant that year, and the power-hitting Minnesota Twins. Someone went out for cold beer and munchies.

Harriet came home at 3:30 P.M.

The Twins won 10–1.

Roger and Harriet left at 5:30 P.M.

As detectives ran to their parked cars and tried to set up on the Hyundai, they lost it in traffic. Although their pride was injured, the cops took some consolation in the fact that Roger was not alone. They returned to the motor home and awaited the couple's return. Roger and Harriet came home at 10:00 P.M., and their lights went out an hour later.

The following afternoon, a Sunday, Roger took a walk over to the shopping center. Detectives followed him on foot. He picked up a few things at Payless, then stopped at Taco Bell for a Coke before returning home. Later, he and Harriet went grocery shopping. They turned in at 11:00 P.M.

The next morning a unit followed Harriet to a cellular phone company, where she spent the day working in the office. When she got home that night, she and Roger went clothes shopping. Their lights went out early, at 9:00 P.M.

Detectives had noticed some things in the hours they'd spent watching Kibbe. Obviously, he really wasn't going anywhere. Whenever he did go somewhere, it was with Harriet, and she always drove. Of course, Roger's driver's license had been revoked, although that hadn't stopped him from cruising the stroll the previous month when he'd picked up Debra Guffie. Still, when they walked together Harriet always led, with Roger lagging behind a step or two.

Having a lot of time on their hands, the detectives batted around various scenarios. Concluding that Harriet was the dominant one in the relationship, they wondered if she had grounded Roger since his arrest. Speculating further, they theorized that perhaps it took a big fight with

Harriet for Roger to make his move. Could they orchestrate such a donnybrook?

The next morning, Kay Maulsby, who had completed the two-week homicide school, was briefed on the surveillance effort. Biondi shared with her the conclusions of the detectives who had been watching Kibbe, and directed her and Joe Dean to drop in unexpectedly on Harriet at the cellular phone company and "jack her up."

Their purpose, Biondi made clear, was to irritate her. "She might be the trigger that sends Roger off. She comes home and takes her anger out on him. We'll watch to see what he does."

Maulsby and Dean dropped in on Harriet after lunch.

They first talked to her boss, finding out that Harriet had been employed for two weeks as an accountant through a temp agency. Maulsby explained they wanted to speak to Harriet "about her husband," and made a point of saying that she was not the subject of their investigation.

The detectives were shown into a private office, where Harriet soon joined them. They showed her their badges.

"Are you married to Roger Kibbe?" Dean asked.

"Yes, I am."

"Do you reside at 6380 Tupelo with him?"

"Yes, I do."

"We've got some questions about your husband," Maulsby said in her best tough-guy voice.

Harriet glanced out the plate-glass wall; a couple of office employees quickly turned away.

"You came *here* to talk to me about Roger?" Harriet asked, her cheeks reddening. "I've just started working—"

"Your husband was recently arrested for assault on a prostitute," Dean said, cutting her off. "This is serious."

"We want to know about his comings and goings," Maulsby said, even though she felt they were sailing steerage on the *Titanic* without a life jacket.

Although Maulsby was new to Homicide, she knew about getting information out of people. This was no way to proceed. Coming here plainly to embarrass Harriet and get a rise out of her so she would go home and lambast Roger was shortsighted. Suppose Harriet had valuable information about Roger to share with them? No one believed she was a serial killer, only that she was married to one. Her life could be hellish right now. A much better tack, Maulsby thought, would have been to approach Harriet in a quieter way, coming to her sympathetically, not confrontationally.

Harriet lifted a shaking hand. "There's the door."

"We told your boss you aren't in trouble," Dean said somewhat lamely.

"Get out!" Harriet barked, a fury in her voice. "You think I don't have any feelings or any rights here? Don't come back either because I won't tell you a thing."

Maulsby and Dean looked at each other, and left.

In terms of pissing off Harriet, Maulsby knew they could consider it mission accomplished. But if they'd really accomplished something, why did she feel so lousy?

That afternoon on surveillance at Tupelo Drive, detectives eagerly anticipated Harriet's arrival home.

It was Bertocchini's thirtieth birthday, and he was hoping for a special present that Roger Kibbe could best give him—a slipup of some kind, new physical evidence, maybe Roger going cruising for another victim. Bertocchini would dearly have loved to slap the cuffs on him in the act.

Harriet came home at 5:10 P.M.

Half an hour later, Roger came out and walked to the back of the lot holding a white plastic bag, which he dropped into the garbage can, and went back inside.

"Harriet must be really pissed," Bertocchini deadpanned. "She made him take out the garbage."

At 6:22 P.M., they observed Roger mopping the floor of the office.

The detectives howled.

Roger then went to work cleaning the countertops.

As Kibbe went about his chores, the cops watched the third game of the World Series. At one point, Rosenquist ran over to Payless with a roll of film he had previously shot of Roger walking through the parking lot. When he turned it in for developing, the salesgirl told him he could get two prints for the price of one, and also a free pair of nylons.

Rosenquist picked up a pound cake, and back at the motor home they celebrated Bertocchini's birthday. Rosenquist gave him the nylons, which Bertocchini complained weren't his size.

Even though the lights in the Kibbe residence went out before 10:00 P.M., the surveillance team stayed in place until after midnight before reluctantly calling it a night.

So much for the Harriet-as-a-trigger theory.

AT 10:00 A.M. the next morning, Detective Kay Maulsby picked up Carmen Anselmi at her apartment for a tour of a dozen Public Storage rental businesses.

In setting up the tour, Maulsby had explained to Carmen that she was going to be shown a group of people working in storage rental businesses around the city. In viewing these individuals, Maulsby counseled, it was important to keep in mind that the man who drove off with Charmaine might or might not be in this group of people.

In the car, Maulsby went back over everything, as Carmen, obviously nervous, nodded her assent.

"You're in no way obligated to identify anyone today," Maulsby said. "Study each person carefully. Remember that hairstyles change and beards can come and go."

Maulsby further cautioned Carmen that if she saw anyone who looked like the suspect, she should wait until they were back in the car before commenting. The detective had Carmen bring a hat and dark glasses to disguise her own features so that recognition wouldn't be a two-way street.

"Remember now, you may not see anyone who looks like him and that's okay, too," Maulsby said before they got out of the car at the first location on Folsom Street.

After they spoke to a man who identified himself as Frank and he showed them a storage space, they got back into the car to debrief. "His hair has too much gray," Carmen said. "And he's heavier."

At the second stop, on San Juan Avenue, the man behind the counter, Ken, was "too pudgy."

At the next stop, a woman was working the counter.

At the fourth location, on Vernon Boulevard, the manager's name was R.J. "He doesn't look like him at all."

Women were managing the next three locations.

On Howe Avenue, George came next. "No, no."

Tony, on Auburn Boulevard, was "out of the question" because he was "too dark and too fat."

Then another woman.

They arrived at Tupelo at 2:15 P.M. Working behind the counter was a soft-spoken man with a closely cropped salt-and-pepper beard. He identified himself as Roger, and answered their questions about space sizes and prices. He took them out back and showed them a few storage spaces.

Back in the car, Carmen said the man who took her daughter away had straighter hair and a lighter complexion.

"This guy is not the one."

THAT NIGHT, Kay Maulsby was awakened by the phone.

As she reached for the bedside phone, she saw on the illuminated clock dial that it was past midnight.

A deputy was calling to advise her that Debra Ann Guffie had been arrested and was being processed at the downtown county jail facility.

"Thanks very much," said Maulsby, whose feet were on the floor by the time she hung up.

Anxious to speak to Guffie, who had gone back out on the streets since her run-in with Roger Kibbe, Maulsby had asked the warrant bureau to contact her in the event Guffie ended up back in custody. Guffie had failed to appear for a court date on a medical fraud misdemeanor involving her using someone else's insurance card for medical treatment, and a bench warrant had been issued for her arrest. Maulsby had given them not only her office and pager numbers, but her home number as well, with instructions to call day or night. It had been a long shot—Guffie might or might not be arrested in the near future, and some deskbound deputy might or might not notice the flag to call Maulsby before Guffie was kicked back out the revolving jailhouse door.

After the booking process was completed, Maulsby signed for Guffie and drove her the two short blocks to the Homicide Bureau. It was 1:45 A.M. when they sat down in an interview room.

Guffie, who on the ride over easily admitted to supporting herself through prostitution, had the wasted heroin junkie look Maulsby had seen so often working Vice. The emaciated blonde with sunken cheeks and a pointed jaw didn't look at all well, and Maulsby knew she'd be feeling even worse in a few hours. Nevertheless, as Guffie recounted the incident at the golf course parking lot a month earlier, her memory proved sharp and detailed. There were no obvious inconsistencies with what she'd previously told police.

"Did he make any threats?" Maulsby asked.

"When he slammed my face down he said, 'Don't struggle and you won't get hurt, cunt.' He said it only once but he said it real hateful-like. He didn't raise his voice, but it was *hateful*. He said it very slowly and calmly and pronounced each word distinctly."

Individuals who had been on the street as long as Guffie could easily become hardened and cynical about what life threw in their direction. But Guffie was obviously still very shaken by the experience in the parking lot, and well aware of what a near miss it had been. She was motivated to help the police and even testify, she explained to Maulsby, because she didn't want to see other women go through what she went through, or worse.

"Was there any sexual touching or talk?"

"We didn't get that far," Guffie said. "He hadn't even unfastened his pants yet so I can't tell you if he had an erection or not."

Maulsby understood why the district attorney's office hadn't filed assault with intent to commit rape, the felony for which Kibbe had been arrested. As he hadn't had time to make any overt attempts to rape Guffie, it would be an uphill battle to pursue felonious assault, which by statute required an "overt intent" to commit a further crime, such as rape, great bodily harm, robbery, etc. Instead, the D.A. had filed two misdemeanor counts: battery and soliciting prostitution—each punishable by up to a year in jail.

"You know what I think was going to happen?" Guffie said, biting her lip. "I think he was going to handcuff me there in the parking lot and drive me off somewhere else. It was dark there but we weren't hidden. The way he acted and the way he looked, I think he's really sick and that he probably has hurt or killed someone before."

Maulsby knew Kibbe had pleaded not guilty to the charges and that a trial was scheduled for the following month in Sacramento Municipal Court. As they still lacked the evidence necessary to link him to murder, the Guffie assault case was shaping up as their best shot for getting Kibbe off the street quickly. Assuming he was convicted, his subsequent stay in county jail would give them the precious time they needed to try to build a winnable murder case.

The detective could see that Guffie would make an articulate and credible witness despite her lifestyle. But it had taken an arrest warrant to round her up for this interview, and she'd soon be back in her element on the street.

What were the chances that Debra Guffie would show up at trial and point an accusatory finger at Roger Kibbe?

FOR THE surveillance team, the days came and went.

One evening Roger Kibbe went for a stroll through the shopping center. As he exited the store, an attractive young woman passed by. He turned and gave her a long look.

There was a break in the boredom one afternoon when Vito Bertocchini, who happened to look down into a car in the lot, suddenly bellowed: "You son of a bitch! I'm going to fuckin' bust your pervert ass!" He flew out of the motor home, gun in hand, with the other cops scrambling to follow.

Bertocchini had noticed a young man, who turned out to be a police officer's son, sitting in the car masturbating to the sight of women walking through the parking lot.

The detective already had the embarrassed man up against his car. "Zip up and get your hands in the air," he said. "I'd shoot it off but it's too small a target."

Another evening, Kibbe walked to a video store in the shopping center. Larry Ferrari followed him inside. He watched as Kibbe showed keen interest in the adult movie section, frequently going close to the area but never close enough to pick up a film. He left the store empty-handed.

On October 25, Kay Maulsby joined the stakeout team. Wading into the midst of a bunch of bored male cops stuck inside a motor home watching the seventh game of the World Series, she felt like the token "girl" allowed to play a pickup baseball game only because she had a big brother. But after a while, she too put her feet up, grabbed a beer, and started rooting for the Twins, who ended up winning 4–2.

In the meantime, Roger spent the afternoon mopping and cleaning and fussing around the office, all to great hoots from the guys: "His wife puts an apron on him during the last game of the World Series? No *wonder* he kills women."

Early the next afternoon, there was an inspection of the facility by Public Storage supervisory personnel. After they left, Harriet departed, too. Roger walked to the video store and rented a war movie. He went to Taco Bell, then back home.

Four hours later, detectives noticed Kibbe pacing the floor in the office. He walked back and forth to the front door, opening and closing it several times, and kept looking out the window every few minutes.

The watchful detectives agreed:

Roger Kibbe was acting very restless.

AT 12:20 P.M. the following afternoon, detectives Kay Maulsby, Joe Dean, Vito Bertocchini, and Pete Rosenquist walked into the Public Storage on Tupelo armed with a search warrant duly signed by a municipal court judge.

Roger Kibbe was alone in the office. He showed a flash of recognition when Maulsby stepped up and explained the purpose of their visit.

When she handed him a copy of the search warrant, Kibbe expressed no surprise, nor did he inquire as to what they would be searching for.

"Okay, go ahead," he said.

Maulsby turned to the other detectives. "Call in the troops," she said.

They were joined by detectives Larry Ferrari (San Joaquin) and Jim Watson (El Dorado), and several investigators from the Department of Justice, including criminalist Jim Streeter. Someone was designated the recorder, who would write down a complete inventory of all the evidence seized, and another had a camera to photograph pieces of evidence in place before they were picked up.

As the others spread out to conduct a thorough search of the office and adjoining residence, Bertocchini had more bad news for Kibbe.

"The warrant empowers us to take your fingerprints," he explained to Kibbe, "and to get samples of your hair, saliva, and blood. We'll be taking you downtown."

Kibbe shrugged as if this kind of thing happened to him all the time. He stepped forward meekly and was escorted to an unmarked car by Bertocchini and Rosenquist.

A six-page list of "items to be searched for" was attached to the warrant. It included: unaccounted personal belongings of Stephanie Brown, Charmaine Sabrah, and Karen Finch (Lora Heedick was not included because it was believed her clothes had not been cut); hair, blood, body fluids, fibers, and latent prints from the Hyundai and the old pickup; white nylon cord; knife or scissors; duct tape; photos of the victims and any sexually explicit photos of women involving bondage and/or sado-masochism (justified to the judge by Kibbe's having asked Debra Guffie to pose for nude pictures); rental records of storage spaces to determine if Kibbe had his own spaces that might contain "souvenirs" of his crimes; records of gasoline purchases that might provide dates and geographic locations; telephone toll records in the event Kibbe called his wife from different locations to explain his absences from home; checkbook and charge receipts; and—from the person of Roger Kibbe—blood, saliva, pubic and head hair, and fingerprints.

The detectives split up for the scavenger hunt; each was wearing a new pair of gray funeral gloves used by pallbearers.

Watson took the bedroom. He found in the closet a "peep show" key ring, a copy of *Adam* men's magazine, and two X-rated films entitled "Pretty Girls #68 and #28," and numerous reels of old 8mm home movies.

In a hallway closet, Dean found some traveler's check receipts and Kibbe's U.S. Parachute Association card.

In the kitchen, Ferrari found a pair of black-handled scissors with blades about 5 inches long. He also found two rolls of tape; neither was duct tape.

A detective going over the rental records in the office—he called customers listed in the books to verify their locker numbers—determined that Kibbe had two lockers in his own name. With the help of Dennis Kissinger, the Public Storage general manager who happened to show up in the middle of the search, the keys were located in the office.

Dean took locker 428. Inside, he found several cardboard boxes and some old clothes. Going through the boxes, he found an X-rated striptease video entitled "Fleshdance," and several books, including *Parachuting, The Parachute Manual,* and *Sport Parachuting.*

Maulsby opened storage locker 427. Inside, she found a shoe box filled with receipts and tax records. Her next find was more interesting: four pieces of wooden doweling. To Maulsby, they looked exactly like the pieces of doweling she'd seen in the crime kit.

A piece of tree branch had been used to tighten the garrote around the neck of El Dorado's Jane Doe. Had Kibbe fashioned the smooth, solid dowels since then as a procedural improvement? The theory around the cop shop was that the dowels and nylon cordage represented a devilish "progression" by the killer. Several pieces of cordage had been brought to the Jane Doe scene for some other reason—as bindings?—but by the time of the attack on Debra Guffie, cordage had been strung between two dowels, ready for use as a sophisticated garrote that could be easily tightened and loosened around the neck of the victim.

The doweling was photographed and bagged.

A few minutes later, bent over digging through a cardboard box, she suddenly straightened up. "We'll need a picture of this," she announced.

Maulsby had located two coils of white nylon cord that looked similar to the cordage found at the murder scene and in the Guffie crime kit.

DETECTIVES Vito Bertocchini and Pete Rosenquist transported Roger Kibbe to the Sacramento County Sheriff's Department. On the way, he refused to answer any questions.

Not about to give up so easily, the detectives led him into an interview room at the Homicide Bureau.

Although cops on television and in the movies seem to have almost unlimited power to question and hold suspects before an arrest, real-life police officers are required to observe the rights of citizens, or suspects, as guaranteed by the U.S. Constitution. Unless someone is under arrest, for example, he can refuse to go to a police station to answer questions.

In Kibbe's situation, the search warrant compelled him to come to the station for the collection of various bodily evidence, but he was not required to speak to detectives. Most suspects, however, did volunteer to speak—innocent ones, in particular, to clear matters up, but also a surprising number of guilty suspects, many of whom believe they're smarter than the cops. Detectives like nothing better than the talkative, deceitful ones, who before long will usually be well trussed up by their own tangled webs.

They all took seats and the veteran, Rosenquist, began by explaining to Kibbe that additional investigative work had been conducted since he'd come in and talked to Bertocchini the previous December.

"You wouldn't be here if we didn't have something," Rosenquist said bluntly. "It's that simple. Now, we want to go over a few things. How do you feel today? Are you ill?"

"No," Kibbe said.

"Are you under a doctor's care?"

"No."

"On any medication at all?"

"No."

"Do you take drugs?"

"I've never taken drugs," Kibbe said. "Don't smoke, don't drink. Never have."

Rosenquist read Kibbe his Miranda rights. "Having those rights in mind, do you want to talk with us?"

Kibbe shrugged. "There's nothing to-to discuss."

"Do you mind if we talk to you?"

"You can talk. Name and address, that's all I can give you."

Unlike Kibbe's previous interview in December 1986, which had been voluntary on his part and did not require a waiver of his Miranda rights in order to gather admissible information from him—the theory being that he was free to walk out any time—this visit was not voluntary. Most of what is seen on TV police dramas about Miranda is wrong: reading a suspect his rights is not required at the time of arrest but only before the suspect is questioned while in custody. The search warrant allowed for the search of Kibbe's person for the purpose of collecting hair, blood, and other samples, and therefore he was properly taken into custody. As a result, the only way police would ever be able to use in court anything Kibbe said to them now would be in the event he waived his rights to remain silent and have an attorney present. Clearly, by his response, Kibbe had not done so. The detectives proceeded knowing that anything he told them would most likely be inadmissible in a court of law. They did so for a couple of reasons. First and foremost, if he confessed, they would know they had the right person—case solved. Second, if Kibbe ever took the stand at trial, the prosecutor *could* use what he'd told the detectives for impeachment purposes on cross-examination. Therefore, the interview proceeded, and was tape-recorded.

"That's all you can give us?" Rosenquist said.

"There's nothing to talk about."

"How about parachuting?" Bertocchini said.

The detectives had already cooked up a plan to try to draw Kibbe into a conversation on skydiving, which they knew, from comments he'd made in December, to be a favorite hobby. Once they had him talking, they would try to switch him to other topics.

"I signed up for jump school when I was in the service and then chickened out," Rosenquist said. "How did you get started? In the military?"

"Never in the military," Kibbe said.

"Oh, you weren't?" said Rosenquist, who knew full well that Kibbe had been in prison at the age many young men were in the service. "Then how did you get started in jumping?"

"Curiosity."

"How many jumps you make?" Bertocchini asked.

"Pretty close to forty-two hundred now."

"So, you'd be qualified as an expert."

"Yeah." Kibbe's chest seemed to expand.

Bertocchini could see they were was making progress.

"Did you ever think about being an instructor?"

"I didn't want the responsibility."

"Did you ever have your main chute not open?"

"I've had four of them not open. The first one on only my twenty-sixth jump."

"How high up?"

"About four thousand, I guess."

"Did you panic?"

"Yeah, a little bit."

The detectives talked back and forth about parachuting—Bertocchini had had one rip-cord jump with a bunch of other deputies and no desire to ever do it again—but Kibbe spat out the bait and went quiet.

"Where were you born, Roger?" Rosenquist asked.

"I can't say anything."

"Pardon?"

"I'm not going to say anything."

"You're married now?"

"Yes."

"How long you guys been married?"

"I don't remember."

"Can you tell me why you think we're talking to you today?"

"I have no idea."

"No idea why we would be serving a search warrant at your home?"

"No."

"The main reason we're here is about Charmaine Sabrah. The gal that disappeared on I-5."

"The name's not familiar."

"A gal's car broke down along the road."

"I heard about it on TV."

"It happened over a year ago. You say you don't know anything about her?"

"Right. I heard something on TV several times. It's been quite a while."

"You don't remember ever stopping and helping out a gal with her mother? Do you know what happened with her? What eventually became of her?"

"I don't believe I ever heard anything more about it. I don't know."

"She was killed," Rosenquist said evenly. "Are you the kind of person that could do something like that?"

"I don't think so."

"Have you ever thought about doing anything like that?"

"No."

"Never at all?"

"I walk away from things."

"Do you?"

"I've never been in a fight in my life."

"Would you be willing to take a polygraph?"

"No. No reason to."

"If you were to take one, what would it show?"

"I don't know what it would show."

"Is there any reason why somebody is going to tell us that they saw you out riding around that night down in our county where Charmaine Sabrah disappeared?"

It was a bluff by Rosenquist. Their only eyewitness, Carmen Anselmi, had passed on two chances to finger Kibbe—once in a photo lineup and once in the flesh.

"I don't know."

"Do you go riding around at night?"

"Yeah, but I'm usually home by eleven o'clock or midnight. I don't go far."

"Is there any reason why somebody would have seen you down that far south on I-5 near Stockton?"

"Not really. There's no reason to go down there."

"I don't know what your travels encompass. Maybe you were going down and looking for different jobs."

"Why should I look for a job when I have one?"

"I don't know."

"Makes no-no sense."

"Maybe you had to go down there and buy furniture or something."

"When I had the furniture business I never transported. I h-had a truck driver wh-who did that."

"Can you think of any reason why somebody would say they saw you down there the night she disappeared?"

"I h-have no idea."

The detectives sat quietly, looking at Kibbe.

"You guys got no intention of taking me back, do you?"

Too bad, Bertocchini thought, *that Kibbe's concern about being arrested for murder wasn't a valid one.*

"You're probably going back," Bertocchini admitted. "The thing is, Rog, there's so many things that need explaining. Like Sabrah broken down on the freeway. Maybe you did give her a ride and maybe you're afraid to say you gave her a ride and dropped her off somewhere."

"I don't give anybody a ride."

"Everything seems to be indicating you did," Bertocchini went on. "I think what we need to do is to talk and eliminate you if you didn't do anything. Obviously, you'd be benefiting yourself, and also benefiting us. We need to get rid of you one way or another."

"You're-you're telling me that I killed somebody."

"No, we're not. I'm not telling you that, Roger."

"You're accusing me of killing somebody."

"No."

"That's the way I look at it."

"I'm not telling you that, Roger," Bertocchini insisted.

"I know, but that's the way I look at it."

"Well—"

"You-you got to understand my point."

"Yeah."

"I understand where you guys are coming from. This is your job. You guys are polite and you're kind. But you got to understand my side."

"We do," Bertocchini said.

"I see that you guys are accusing me of murder. That's what I hear. And that's a low blow."

"We're not accusing you."

"Y-you may not be, but that's what I hear."

"Obviously, your name isn't the only one that's ever come up."

"Probably not," Kibbe said, relaxing some.

"We're not sitting here accusing you. We're here to discuss things so we can go ahead and get to the bottom of this. Maybe you dropped her off at a phone booth. That's why we're here talking to you, Roger."

"You've got to get-get in my shoes and behind my eyeballs and listen to wh-what I'm hearing and what you're saying."

It was Rosenquist's turn. "There's a lot of things that point to you," he said. "Otherwise, we wouldn't be here. Did you give her a ride someplace?"

"I don't even know the girl. I just told you I don't pick anybody up off the freeway and give them a ride."

"Rog, we know you pick people up. Okay? You've recently been stopped for doing that but we don't want to get into that. We just want to know what happened to Charmaine Sabrah. If there was a problem between you and her, if she created a situation, that's what we want to hear. We'd like to hear your side of the story."

It could be tough to sympathize with a suspected killer, but Rosenquist was trying hard to do just that.

"I don't know her."

"I'm sitting here trying to think of explanations. You just gave her a ride and dropped her off at a phone booth or you gave her a ride down the road and she tried to rob you or she spit in your face or hit you with her elbow. I don't know. I mean, we weren't there. We don't know. I don't want to sit here and say Roger just decided to kill her so he just killed her. You're the only one who knows what happened. Is there a problem here?"

"With what?"

"With Charmaine Sabrah?"

"I don't know. I don't know her."

"You don't remember picking a gal up and driving down the freeway and dropping her off someplace?"

"No, I don't."

"This was on I-5."

"I've been on it many times. I've been on Highway 101 and 80, too."

The baton went to Bertocchini. "Do you remember giving Charmaine a ride?" he asked.

"I don't even know the name."

"I realize you probably wouldn't have known her name at the time. It was about four in the morning."

"I think that's a little bit too early," Kibbe said.

"Too early for what?"

"Like four in the morning—hell, I'm home."

"Oh, you're home by then?"

"Yeah. I would be sleeping."

"How often do you go out at night? Once a week, twice a week, three times?"

Kibbe shrugged.

"Where do you go?"

"I don't know. Just go."

"The last time we talked, last December, you told me that you went out and looked for prostitutes. Do you still do that often?"

"No."

"Obviously, you don't go drinking."

"No, I don't."

"You just drive around wherever you feel like?"

"Yeah."

"No particular place, you just drive around?"

"No particular place."

"When you take off, how long would you be away?"

"A couple of hours at least."

There was some noise outside the interview room, and Rosenquist slipped out for a minute, then returned.

"They're working on a new homicide right now," he said.

"Where at?" asked Kibbe, noticeably perking up.

"Huh?"

"Where at?"

"I don't know." Rosenquist knew that some killers had an intense interest in police work, and he wondered how often Roger talked to his detective brother about it. "When we're through here we'll take your blood and urine and hair samples," Rosenquist said.

"That's all I know." Kibbe was anxious to move on.

"Vito has your rap sheet. All that's on it are property crimes like burglary."

"That's all," Kibbe agreed.

"Way, way back. You have nothing recent?"

"No, I've been clean for thirteen to fourteen years. Except for a f-few tickets."

Rosenquist, noting that Kibbe had previously admitted to trying to pick up women in Stockton, read off the names of some young women missing from the area. He asked Kibbe if any of them sounded familiar.

"I never picked up a girl in Stockton. I-I wanted to but never did."

"Why not?"

"I thought that I could but when it'd come right down to it, it's hard to do."

"Hard to talk to them or what?"

"It's just hard to do. I thought that I'd just waste a lot of gas driving around trying to."

"Did you ever stop and talk to them?"

"A couple of them, yeah. Some of them thought I looked like a cop and they would move on."

"Oh, really?"

"Yeah."

"When you are driving back and forth going no particular place, what would you do if you saw a stranded female?"

"Probably keep right on going."

"You wouldn't even stop to help her?"

"No."

"Why not?"

"Too dangerous."

"Even if it was just a gal? You look like you're big enough to handle yourself."

"I don't do that. I don't stop for anybody."

"This isn't a trick question," Bertocchini said. "Obviously, you're attracted to women, right?"

Kibbe nodded.

"Okay, you're attracted to women. Your marriage isn't so good right now, is it?"

Kibbe froze.

The next several questions went unanswered.

"Roger, you're starting to get hinky on us," Bertocchini said.

Rosenquist again asked if Kibbe would take a polygraph.

"No, no."

"Absolutely not, huh? Can you give me a reason?"

"There's nothing to-to discuss."

"Going back to what I said in the beginning," Rosenquist said patiently, "we have a lot of information or you wouldn't be here."

"I take it from you that in a roundabout way you are saying that I'm a little crazy," Kibbe said.

"I don't know," Rosenquist said.

"But this is what you're saying, basically."

"No. What I'm saying, Roger, is that I don't know. We come to you hoping you can give us some explanations."

Bertocchini piped up. "If you were in our shoes, Roger, you'd be doing the same thing."

"Probably."

"The same exact thing."

"Probably."

Rosenquist surmised aloud that Roger's detective brother, Steve, would be doing the "same exact thing, too, if he was in my position."

Kibbe nodded in agreement.

"We're only trying to do our job," Rosenquist went on. "We're not trying to say you're crazy. I'm not trying to say that you're the murderer, okay?"

"This is what I'm hearing from both of you."

"I've interviewed other people, too."

"How many have you talked to?"

"Several."

"I know that's a lot of bull."

"No, it's not."

"Roger, remember there was a composite picture of a suspect put in the paper?"

"Yeah, I—I—I think so, yeah."

"Our office received hundreds of calls and Sacramento County received even more. We've interviewed hundreds of people. And we've given polygraph tests to other people, too."

Rosenquist wanted to know if Kibbe had anything else to tell them.

The suspect shook his head.

The detectives walked Kibbe to the sobriety clinic next to the jail, where a male nurse took samples of hair from several areas: arm, back of the hands, head, and pubic. The nurse also took a saliva sample and withdrew a vial of blood.

On the ride back to Tupelo, the suspect spoke up. He told the detectives that he had no hard feelings toward them and knew they were simply doing their job.

"But I have to do what I'm told to do," said Roger Kibbe, looking out the window at the passing urban scenery. "And my brother told me not to take a polygraph."

CHAPTER SEVENTEEN

Carolyn Jean Redman was an attractive twenty-five-year-old brunette with long hair, high cheekbones, and soft blue eyes.

She seemed surprised when Detective Pete Rosenquist knocked at the door of her apartment the first week of November 1987, inquiring about her father, Roger Kibbe.

A resident of Eugene, Oregon, until her move to Stockton the previous year—Rosenquist had located her through driver's license records—Carolyn said that she hadn't seen or talked to her father in years.

The detective advised her he was seeking background on her father, who had "recently been found in the company of a prostitute and was arrested for trying to handcuff her."

Carolyn seemed neither surprised nor concerned, explaining that she didn't know her father all that well, as he and her mother had divorced before her second birthday and her mother had raised her in Oregon.

"My mother talks as if he never paid child support and never tried real hard to keep in contact with us," she explained. "When I got a little older I would write him letters once in a while but he never answered them."

"Did you see him while you were growing up?"

"A few times. The first time was the summer that I was thirteen. My mom and I flew down to San Diego and stayed with her parents. One afternoon we went over to see my Grandfather Kibbe and my dad was there."

Carolyn said she next saw her father in 1979, when she was seventeen years old and had just had a baby. She stayed with her father and Harriet for a month and a half that time. She recalled he gave his first grandchild a lot of attention.

Rosenquist asked what she thought of Harriet.

"I didn't care much for her but I think it had more to do with the fact that she wasn't my mother and she was living with my father."

"What kind of marriage did they seem to have?"

"While I was with them it seemed like they had a major crisis at least once a week. Harriet would call a meeting to discuss it. She did most of the talking."

"Do you remember anything specific?"

"No. It just seemed like a lot of things bothered her. She was pretty uptight all the time."

"How would your father respond to her concerns?"

"He'd just listen and not say much. He and Harriet seemed to get along, though. They never had a big fight in front of me. They seemed to be living well—I remember they had nice furniture and didn't want for much."

Rosenquist asked how he could contact her mother, Marjorie.

Carolyn showed him a return address on a letter her mother had sent her from Washington State, and he jotted down the information. When he came to the state, she'd written "WAWA."

"WAWA?" he said.

"Oh, that's a joke between us. That's how you pronounce Washington if you stutter. See, that's one thing I do have in common with my father. I stutter sometimes."

Rosenquist was surprised; he hadn't noticed a single hesitation, and told her so.

"I have better control over it than he does."

"Tell me, Carolyn, do you think of your father as a good guy or a bad guy?"

"A good guy, I guess. This is the first time I've heard about anything bad that he's done."

"I need to ask something that might be difficult for you, Carolyn. Did your father ever abuse you?"

"No," she answered without faltering in the slightest. "I have no memories of ever being abused."

"Did your father ever complain about being abused as a child?"

"We never discussed anything like that. We usually had nothing much to say to each other because we really didn't know each other very well. He's very quiet, you know."

———

VITO BERTOCCHINI finally found the missing persons case that Harriet Kibbe had alluded to when he'd first brought Roger in for questioning a year ago.

Methodically checking one by one with police departments throughout Contra Costa County, he had come across the case of Lou Ellen Burleigh, a twenty-one-year-old brunette with shoulder-length hair and hazel eyes who disappeared on Sunday morning, September 11, 1977, from a shopping center parking lot.

Bertocchini talked by phone with Walnut Creek Police Detective Jerry Whiting, who remembered the more-than-a-decade-old case and the suspect, Roger Kibbe.

Whiting explained that the victim had been a student at a local secretarial college. One day a male subject, identifying himself as John Brown and claiming to be a representative of the Helena Rubinstein Co., called the college wanting to hire a young secretary with no experience for $1,200 a month, with lucrative benefits and short hours.

Burleigh went on the job interview, which was to take place in a new office at the shopping center still under construction. When she arrived at 1:00 P.M. Saturday afternoon, she was met by a man in his early forties, about 5-foot-10, with graying hair and several front teeth missing. The man explained that since his office was not yet finished, he'd have to interview her in his van. They were seen by several construction workers getting into a multicolored van. They talked for about half an hour, after which the man asked Burleigh to return for a second interview the next day.

"She did," Whiting said. "On Sunday, there were no construction workers or other witnesses around. We found her car in the parking lot that night when her boyfriend reported her missing. He told us she'd expressed some reservations about returning for another interview, as the man made her uncomfortable. She'd asked her boyfriend to come with her, but he was unable to do so. Since things had gone okay the day before, she decided to go back."

Bertocchini wanted to know how Walnut Creek had gotten the lead on Kibbe.

Whiting explained that a police detective in neighboring Pittsburg had called after reading about the missing woman. "He had a case on his desk involving a prostitute who was picked up by a guy in a multicolored van about a month after Burleigh disappeared. She'd had some trouble with him and jotted down his license number. When she was arrested for prostitution a few nights later, she handed the license number to police. It came back to Kibbe. He matched the description of the suspect in Burleigh, and his van was like the one she was seen getting into on Saturday. We took a picture of the van and got one of Kibbe. The problem was that the eyewitnesses at the shopping center couldn't positively identify or eliminate either of them. He was as good a suspect as we had but we didn't have anywhere to take it. One problem was that it was a missing persons case, not a homicide. We were a small department, and didn't have the detectives to spend a lot of time on the case."

"Was Burleigh ever found?" Bertocchini asked.

"No, she never was."

Bertocchini asked for a copy of the Burleigh file. When it arrived, he was able to glean more details. The prostitute who had connected Kibbe and his van to Burleigh, Gina Reilly, thirty-four, said she'd received a phone call in response to a personals ad she had placed in the *Berkeley Barb*: "Playboy Bunny seeks supportive relationship." The man who met her outside a Black Angus restaurant on a Friday night, October 7, 1977, said he wanted to make "a date" with her and would pay $200 for sex. She was apprehensive when he said he wanted to drive into the country; she agreed only after he doubled his price to $400 and showed her his identification. She would tell police a few days later that his name began with an "R," and was "something like Richard." She said his last name had a double "ee" sound in it. She recalled his date of birth as 1939.

According to Reilly, they drove into the country a considerable distance and parked across from a small airport. The man asked her to step out of the van, which she did. He began to walk her across a dark field, at which time she became alarmed. She was cold and asked him to put his arm around her, which he did. She said she wanted to go back to the van where it was warmer. The man complied. They had intercourse in the back of the van on a sleeping bag. Afterward, they drove around some more until he pulled over and asked to have sex again. Reilly said she would rather not. When the man became "very persistent," she agreed. Then they drove some more. As they crossed the Benicia Bridge over San Pablo Bay she noticed the clock on the bridge showed 3:30 A.M. She said it was late and she wanted to get back. He turned the van around in the middle of the bridge and headed back toward Walnut Creek. At one point, he pulled up a dark hill and parked by an empty field. He claimed his two sisters lived in a house up on the hill and that he wanted to check to see if they'd left their lights on, as they often did. When she refused to get out, he went around to her side, opened the door, and pulled a knife from the glove box. He stuck it to her throat and ordered her out. As they walked up the hill, Reilly said she became "totally submissive." She said, "There is no need for you to pull a knife. I will do whatever you want. You can have sex with me again. You can have my purse." He said nothing, and they kept walking. Then she said, "I thought you were a nice guy." The man answered, "I'm a fucking asshole." He repeated it several times. Having been in tight spots before, Reilly decided that the best thing to do was "act very cool and undisturbed by the threats." The man finally asked her, "Aren't you scared? Aren't you scared?" She answered, "No, I'm not. I know you're a nice guy and you won't hurt me." At that point, the man removed the knife from her neck and they returned to the van. He agreed to take her back to the Black Angus. On the way, she asked him if he'd done this before. The man said, "Yes, I've done it with girls three times before." He dropped her off in the restaurant parking lot, and she got his license number as he drove away. Police ran Kibbe's rap sheet, saw he was heavily involved in burglaries but had no sex-related offenses. The prostitute declined to press charges.

In spite of the inability of the shopping center witnesses to identify Kibbe in a photo lineup, Bertocchini saw that he was brought in for questioning in the Burleigh case by Walnut Creek detectives on January 19,

1978. The report noted that he was accompanied by his wife, Harriet, who waited outside the interview room. To detectives, Kibbe denied any involvement with Burleigh, both before and after being shown her picture. He also denied any involvement with Gina Reilly, even though detectives went over the incident in detail and explained that she'd gotten the license number of his van. He claimed not to know about "either of these girls." He gave police permission to search his van for any possible evidence, including the knife. Nothing was found.

Based on the facts of the case and what he knew about Kibbe, Bertocchini had little doubt that he was responsible for Burleigh's long-ago disappearance. He wondered just how many more women had gone missing through the years after crossing his path.

The detective marveled at Kibbe's ability to remain a moving target for so long. He had some luck, certainly—even when he had the bad luck of someone taking down his license number, key witnesses couldn't identify him. That had happened a decade ago in Walnut Creek, and it had repeated itself in the I-5 investigation. Kibbe wasn't careless, either; he was good at not leaving behind incriminating evidence. He confounded police by crossing jurisdictional lines; hadn't it happened too many times to be coincidental? He also knew enough when confronted by authorities to deny, deny, deny. He could certainly have picked up some of this information over the years from listening to his cop brother. In hearing the warstories that every cop accumulates throughout a career, had Roger deduced how bad guys fooled good guys?

On the same afternoon that Pete Rosenquist was visiting Roger's daughter in Stockton, Bertocchini and Larry Ferrari walked in the door of the California Rehabilitation Center at Norco, a state prison located in Riverside County east of Los Angeles.

During the search of Tupelo, detectives had found an envelope addressed to Roger and Harriet Kibbe from an inmate at Norco. A subsequent phone call to the prison revealed that their correspondent, Helen Pursel, was Harriet's older sister and only sibling.

In their rapidly expanding investigation of Kibbe, Bertocchini and Ferrari had flown into L.A. that morning and rented a car for the drive to Norco.

After the confrontation Kay Maulsby had had with Harriet two weeks earlier, Bertocchini and Ferrari weren't sure what kind of reception they would receive from Helen. They were pleasantly surprised when she greeted them in a private interview room at the prison with a smile and an open manner.

Like her sister, Helen, forty-eight, was a light-complected blonde with curly hair, but unlike Harriet she was laid back and had a natural gift for putting others at ease. Married with three children ranging in age from twelve to twenty-nine, her current prison stay—she was midway through an eighteen-month sentence—was her second in five years for theft. The detectives found her more than willing to discuss her brother-in-law "in connection with an ongoing investigation."

Helen said proudly that her twenty-four-year-old daughter, Susan, was an Alameda County Sheriff's Department deputy, and that her daughter was married to a sheriff's deputy.

A regular cop family, Bertocchini mused, *were it not for Mom the con.*

"Where do you want to start?" she asked cheerfully.

"At the beginning," Bertocchini said.

Helen explained how Roger and Harriet had met some fifteen years earlier, married in Lake Tahoe, and settled in the Oakland East Bay community of Pittsburg before buying a home in Oakley in the late seventies.

"Harriet started her own bookkeeping business called Check Mate and Roger was working at the time for the Volunteers of America. In 1984 or so, they borrowed some money and purchased a furniture warehouse south of Modesto. Roger manufactured furniture and Harriet managed the books. Is this what you want?"

"Keep going," Bertocchini said.

"Last spring [1986] the business went under. During the time she'd been helping Roger run his business, Harriet had neglected her bookkeeping service. They had to look elsewhere for another source of income, and that's how they became involved in the Public Storage business last winter."

Bertocchini asked when she'd last seen Roger.

"Before I came here," she said. "Summer of '86. Roger and Harriet have never visited me here but I call them collect once in a while. I talked to Roger a month ago."

"What do you think of their marriage?"

"Well, my sister has been married and divorced three times. Her ex-husbands were all strong, macho-type men. Her marriage to Roger has a better chance of lasting because he's a lot different than the others."

"How so?" Ferrari asked.

"He doesn't drink," she said. "Besides that, Roger is incapable of hurting anybody."

"You should tell that to the prostitute he assaulted last month," Bertocchini said solemnly.

Helen's eyes widened in surprise as Bertocchini went on to describe Roger's recent assault arrest. It was sometimes good to surprise someone in an interview.

"That's a side of him I've never seen," Helen said. "I know he's very naive sometimes. Maybe he got in over his head."

"Does Harriet dominate Roger?" Bertocchini asked.

"Oh, without question. She makes all the decisions. Although he was the one who wanted to go into the furniture business, she made it work for as long as it did. He would have been nowhere without her."

"Do they argue?"

"Harriet's anger is extremely explosive but it doesn't last long. I've never heard Roger argue in any way with Harriet or raise his voice to her even when she's screaming at him."

"What would he do?" Bertocchini asked.

"Leave. At least a couple of times a year, after Harriet has yelled at him, he'll jump in the car and go away. Typically, he'd be gone for two or three days at a time, and end up at Steve's."

As he and the other detectives had first suspected while on surveillance, Bertocchini was hearing from someone who should know that Roger's relationship with Harriet could be, at times, the catalyst that sent him forth.

"Harriet would phone Steve to make sure Roger had shown up," Helen said. "Then he'd drive home and things would return to normal."

"Why do you think their marriage has lasted?"

"My sister is a very insecure person. Always has been. She relies heavily on Roger, and I know he relies on her. I don't think she'd leave him for any reason. She didn't leave the others and they treated her like a doormat."

"What else can you tell us about Roger?" Ferrari asked.

"He's an extremely artistic person who likes to paint and draw," she said. "You should see some of the beautiful furniture and wooden toys he's made. But I've always found him to be a little strange."

"In what way?" said Bertocchini.

Helen seemed a bit embarrassed. "His background is not unlike mine. He's spent considerable time in institutions. That does something to someone. He's so quiet you don't know what he's thinking. I've always felt a little sorry for him."

"Do you think he'd stop for a stranded motorist?" Bertocchini asked.

Helen looked quizzical for a moment. "I doubt it," she said. "Roger's not the type to get involved."

Bertocchini explained they were heading to San Diego to do further background interviews on Roger.

"You should talk to his other brother, Jack, who lives there," she suggested. "And his father, of course.

"Roger adores his father."

"YOU'RE THE one who called a few days ago?" asked the Chula Vista Police Department records clerk.

Before leaving for southern California, Detective Vito Bertocchini had phoned to see if the department still had a file on Roger Kibbe.

Kibbe's rap sheet revealed that three of his first four arrests as an adult—starting in 1957 when he was eighteen years old—had been made by his hometown police force. Old reports might contain valuable history on him.

Without even checking, the clerk had told him that the department didn't keep records that ancient. When he got off the phone, Bertocchini was chastised by Pete Rosenquist. "It's easier to say no over the phone than to someone's face," he said. "The best way to deal with clerks and bureaucrats is to go in person."

So, the first stop on their first day in Chula Vista—the day after he and Larry Ferrari had interviewed Helen Pursel in prison—was the local police station.

"Like I told you on the phone," the clerk said, "there's no way we're going to have records that old."

"I was just hoping," Bertocchini said. "We've got this multiple-murder investigation going."

She nodded understandingly. "I saw this big pouch of old microfiche reels a while back. I can look."

"I'd sure appreciate it."

She returned half an hour later with a sheaf of papers in hand. "I don't know why we still had this. Those reels should have been thrown out ages ago."

The clerk had copied all forty-one pages of Roger Kibbe's file from microfiche.

On their way out, Bertocchini said to Ferrari, "Remind me to thank Uncle Pete for this."

They jumped in the car and headed for nearby San Diego, where they had an appointment to interview Kibbe's father. Bertocchini drove, and Ferrari read the reports.

The packet contained juvenile contact reports going back to the mid-1950s, arrest and booking reports, and various supplemental reports. It was a vivid portrait of a young life going astray from which there would be no return.

"The earliest one is dated July 17th, 1954," Ferrari said. "Suspect: Roger Kibbe. Address: 545 Casselman. Hair: dark brown. Height: five-foot-four. Weight: One forty. Age: fifteen. Report of crime: Received call of theft of clothes from clothesline located at 447 Casselman. On arrival victim stated she had been ironing in front room and had made several trips to check clothes on the line. At approximately 4:30 P.M. she discovered clothes missing from line. Description of missing clothing: one orchid dress, two bathing suits, four pairs of hose."

Ferrari paused.

"Keep reading," Bertocchini said eagerly.

"Officers were contacted by a nine-year-old girl who saw the suspect entering a park carrying the box, which he buried. Officers found the box and recovered the missing clothes. They contacted Roger and his parents. Report submitted to the juvenile division."

Ferrari flipped a page.

"Here's a juvenile contact report," he said. "Officer Leo Kelly goes out to the Kibbe house. Roger admits he's been taking women's clothes off clotheslines in the area near his home for the past year. Does not know how many times but states 'once or twice a week.' Takes them off the line and puts them in his pockets or under his shirt and carries them either to the park or throws them in the first trash can he comes to."

Ferrari read silently for a minute.

"Jesus Christ!" he exploded.

"What?"

"Roger hands the juvenile officer a box of stolen women's clothes hidden in his closet. They're *cut up!*"

"No way."

"Oh, yeah."

Bertocchini practically wrecked the car getting over to the side of the road so he could read the report himself. When he finished, he was certain they'd just made a key connection in the I-5 serial murder case.

"Cutting up women's clothing was a ritual for Roger at fifteen years of age for Christ's sake," Bertocchini said incredulously. "And thirty years later he's still at it. Only now he's graduated to cutting up clothes while the women are still in them."

"ROGER'S been in trouble most of his life," said his father, Jack Kibbe Sr., seventy-three, a tall, Ichabod Crane—type with sagging jowls and sloped shoulders.

Detectives Vito Bertocchini and Larry Ferrari were seated on a lumpy couch in an add-on room at the back of Jack Kibbe's San Diego home on a quiet suburban street, where he and his wife, Susan, had lived for more than a decade.

The detectives had told the senior Kibbe that they were investigating his eldest son in connection with his recent arrest for assaulting a prostitute.

"Roger had a miserable childhood," he said, reclining in a black vinyl La-Z-Boy. "His mother was a bad influence in his life. She didn't like him very much.

"Lorraine was a nurse and she usually worked the twelve-to-eight shift at the hospital. When she came home at night she would scare Roger just by her presence. She had beaten him when he was young. I was in the Navy and away a lot during the war, and I didn't know what was happening until I came home.

"I'd been away for nearly two years when I got dropped in front of the house by a taxi in '45. We were living in Navy housing at the time on 32nd Street in San Diego. During the war that area was the biggest whorehouse in town with all those young, lonely Navy wives. Roger was out front. He was about six years old. He looked at me with big eyes and said, 'Are you my daddy?' That shook me up."

The senior Kibbe was reminiscing about a period of his son's life that was of minimal interest to the detectives, but they weren't about to cut him off.

"A week or so later we were taking a drive. Roger was standing up on the backseat looking out the window. We passed 28th Street and he said, 'Here's where we picked up Uncle Howard.' Lorraine never came out and admitted it but I found love letters. I would have divorced her but I didn't want some other guy bringing up my children. So we stayed together. I don't know if Roger knew what was happening.

"Whenever I was around I'd intervene between Roger and his mother so he wouldn't get hit. But I made the Navy a career and didn't retire until 1953. I was gone a lot."

"What about Roger's school days?" said Bertocchini, realizing he was being drawn into the life story.

"He had difficulties in that department. He was a poor reader. The other kids called him 'dumbbell.' In high school, he'd get up in the morning, get dressed, and after breakfast head out the door like he was going to school. The first we knew he wasn't going to school was when we went for a parent-teacher night. They thought we'd moved away. Roger quit his junior year of high school. But he was talented in other ways. He's real good at woodworking and drawing. One night he was sitting at the kitchen table drawing a plan for a building. I was impressed with his detail. His mother arrived home from work. Without saying a word, Roger gathered up some of his papers and left the room. He was always trying to steer clear of her. As he was leaving, she began to yell at him for the 'mess' that he'd made."

"Did he have close friends?" Bertocchini asked.

"No, he was a loner. Other children picked on him a lot. I remember dropping him at a matinee and before I even pulled away the other kids had started in on him. When he'd get to stuttering, the kids teased him even more. I did as much as I could with the boys. Used to take them camping. Roger especially really enjoyed the outdoors."

Asked when he'd last seen Roger, the senior Kibbe told of going to Tahoe for Steve's ceremony the previous month and seeing Roger and Harriet there.

"What do you think of Harriet?" Bertocchini asked.

Harriet's father-in-law said at first he thought she would be good for his son. "But marrying her has turned out to be the worst thing that ever happened to Roger. Harriet blames him for everything that goes wrong. She's domineering and mean."

"Before Tahoe," Ferrari asked, "how long had it been since you'd seen Roger?"

"A year ago. Maybe a year and a half. I remember it was hot so it must have been summer [1986]. Roger drove down and stayed four or five days. His furniture business had just shut down. He told me he was going to start working out of his garage, making wooden toys and whatnot."

"What was he driving?"

"Some kind of dark sports car."

"Could it have been a Datsun 280Z?"

"Yeah, that's what it was."

"What did Roger do while he was here?"

"Stayed around. Several nights he went out."

"Did he say what he was doing at night?"

"He was trying to find some woman he'd known years ago from skydiving. Told me he never found her, though. After four or five days, he left for home one night around ten o'clock. Said he wanted to drive when it was cooler."

"Could you come up with the dates he visited?"

"I don't know. I'll ask Susan when she gets home."

"Sir, we thank you for your time," Ferrari said, standing. "I'm going to leave my card."

Bertocchini stood, too. "Just one more question, Mr. Kibbe. As his father, how would you describe Roger?"

"Timid. Not a mean bone in his body."

That same day the detectives met Jack Jr., forty-three, the youngest of the three Kibbe boys. He was bigger than his brothers and sandy-haired.

The detectives met him at his suburban San Diego home shortly after he'd gotten in from work. He operated an assembly machine that drilled holes and shot rivets into the wings and fuselages of new aircraft, a job that had to be done right the first time and took considerable skill and concentration. He'd worked for Rohr Industries, the largest employer in Chula Vista, for two decades and planned to stay until retirement. Every bit as settled in his home life, he was happily married and the father of two children.

In a statement concise enough for an epitaph, Jack Jr. said: "Roger is a kleptomaniac. He stole stuff of no value just to be stealing, and he lied a lot."

Bertocchini nodded. "He got in trouble early."

"Yes. We had no discipline in the family. My brothers and I could come and go as we pleased. There wasn't any type of curfew."

"What's Roger like?" Bertocchini asked.

"Calm, quiet, slow-moving. He used to stutter a lot when he was young. He still stutters when he begins to lie."

Jack explained that he'd last seen Roger the previous summer. "He called first and I gave him directions to the house. When he got here he told me he'd come down for a visit because he'd gotten into a fight with his wife."

Bertocchini asked if there were any old friends of Roger's in the area to whom they might want to speak. Jack gave him the name of an ex—police officer from Chula Vista with whom Roger was friends growing up.

"Anything else you can tell us about Roger?"

"I know he's got a weak stomach and doesn't like the sight of blood," Jack said. "To this day he won't go into a hospital and refuses to see a doctor or seek medical attention of any kind."

Perhaps to balance his other comments about his brother, Jack made a point of saying that shortly after Roger left on the day of his visit, their daughter, Denise, called from the paint store where she worked.

It seemed Uncle Roger had stopped by with a beautiful bouquet of fresh flowers for his young niece.

"THE CASE of Roger Kibbe will be forever etched in my memory," said Leo Kelly, the former Chula Vista juvenile officer who had confronted Roger Kibbe, age fifteen, three decades earlier over the clothesline theft of women's clothing.

"Not only were the circumstances of the crimes so bizarre," said Kelly, a tall man with receding steel-gray hair, "but I was certain that this type of behavior from a youngster would result in a lot more serious acts down the road if something wasn't done."

Kelly told the detectives about making the psychiatrist appointments for Roger, and then the boy's parents not continuing with them.

When Detective Vito Bertocchini let Kelly know that Kibbe was suspected of being a serial killer of young women, the ex-cop nodded sadly. "That's the type of thing I feared might happen. Even as a youngster, he was very sneaky, and I thought he was capable of doing harm to someone."

Kelly confirmed that Kibbe became a habitual truant. "He'd leave in the morning like he was going to school, then sneak back to the house after his mother left for work and spend the day there. His father didn't seem to be home much, so Roger was able to take advantage of the situation."

"When we caught Roger with the stolen clothes, he told me he knew he was doing wrong," Kelly said. "I asked him why he did it and he said he didn't know."

Bertocchini asked what type of clothing he took.

"Ladies' hose, bras, panties, and some slips. Mostly underclothes, you know. He didn't bother with anything else."

"He told you he cut them with scissors?" Ferrari asked.

"Yeah. He admitted he cut them up. I always thought it was interesting that he used his mother's medical scissors. He was an angry boy who grew up, I guess, to be an angry man."

"Is there anything else you can add?"

"The time to help Roger Kibbe has long passed," Kelly said. "I certainly hope you take him out of circulation."

Kelly explained he'd left the police department a year after his run-in with Kibbe. He suggested the detectives contact Jack Dowell, who worked Juvenile during and after Kelly's tenure.

They found the slightly built, mustachioed Jack Dowell living in a motor home in a Chula Vista trailer park. Dowell said he well remembered Roger Kibbe, too.

"I arrested that boy several times," he said. "He didn't like me and would refuse to talk to me."

Bertocchini asked about the clothes-cutting incident.

"I remember that. The clothing wasn't cut into individual pieces but each garment was still intact. The cutting went through the material in random patterns."

Nonfunctional cutting, Bertocchini thought.

"But what really sticks in my mind," Dowell went on, "are two occasions sometime after that. Each time, Roger was discovered in the garage of a different vacant house. He claimed to have been kidnapped, brought to the house, tied up, and molested by unknown assailants.

"The really strange thing about it," the retired cop continued, "was that the boy was tied up with women's clothing—slips, bras, that sort of thing. It was obvious he'd tied himself up and fabricated the whole story. It had to have been some sort of sexual fantasy. At the time, I also got the impression that he didn't like women and was acting out something."

Contained in the old files of the Chula Vista Police Department had been a two-page report by a San Diego Sheriff's Department polygraph examiner concerning a test he administered to Roger Kibbe in January 1970. Bertocchini and Ferrari located the retired examiner, A. G. Van Ravestyn, living in San Diego. He, too, recalled Kibbe.

"He'd been arrested for burglarizing the jump center at the airport," recalled Ravestyn, who had retired as supervisor of polygraph examiners five years earlier. "He was suspected of stealing a number of parachutes and selling them to a surplus store for something under a hundred dollars. At first he denied everything, but after I told him he was deceptive on the test, he confessed. I asked him why he committed a theft against people he parachuted with and who trusted him. He was unable to offer an explanation and finally said he didn't know."

Roger went on to tell the examiner that since his release from county jail two years earlier, he'd attempted many burglaries and committed at least two—a beauty shop and a residence.

"He described how he had stood for as long as an hour in front of many buildings trying to decide whether or not he should enter. His only explanation for these acts was that he felt angry or just felt that he had to do it. He said he'd committed 'hundreds' of burglaries in his life."

Kibbe was subsequently convicted of the airport burglary and sent back to state prison for two years.

What interested the detectives most, however, was the other information contained in Ravestyn's detailed report, which thoroughly dissected both the history and psyche of Roger Reece Kibbe:

Roger presently resides at the San Diego residence of his father and stepmother. His natural mother died in 1963. Roger feels that he gets along quite well with his father, but has an intense dislike for his stepmother. He felt that his relationships with his natural mother were strained and that she did not care for him.

Roger attended Chula Vista High School until the eleventh grade. He did poorly in reading and writing but was adept in mechanical engineering and shop work, and enjoyed art class. He was married in 1961 to Margie. Their marriage lasted eighteen months. There was a daughter born to the couple, but Roger has not seen the child for a number of years.

For the past eight months Roger has been on unemployment compensation. He went to an adult high school and is a certified welder, but he has been unable to obtain work in this field. He worked for a two-year period for National Steel as a welder, but he was fired from the job for committing theft, and they will not re-hire him. Roger has a extensive criminal record. He has been arrested over twenty times for burglary, grand theft, receiving stolen property. He has done time in state prison and county jail.

Roger says he has been a "loner" all his life. He has no close friends, and admits that he really trusts no one. He has a girlfriend but describes her as cold and unfeeling. He talked about a possible marriage, but with no apparent feeling. Under the least distress, Roger becomes agitated and inarticulate, manifesting many physical signs of his mental distress. Roger claims he has never received any form of psychiatric treatment during his incarcerations. He knows his kind of behavior is not normal and feels he needs help, but has difficulty expressing his desire for this help.

When one considers his record as a juvenile and as an adult, a pattern of reaction to stress emerges. At the present time, he has hurt no one during his crimes. This may not be the case in the future if this subject is merely incarcerated and released. It is the opinion of this examiner that Roger should have the advantage of psychiatric evaluation both for his own sake and that of the community.

Yes, it was unusual, Van Ravestyn told the detectives, for him to delve as deeply into a subject's personal life as he did in this instance. But for some reason Roger Kibbe, after failing the polygraph and most assuredly realizing that he faced another conviction and prison term, had been willing to talk that day. And Van Ravestyn, with a B.A. degree in psychology and an inquiring mind, was there to listen.

Van Ravestyn would join the ranks of the Chula Vista officers in recognizing that Roger Kibbe was a potent threat to himself and to society. Most chilling was Van Ravestyn's final paragraph:

It is not inconceivable that Roger could take the life of another. He has an intense dislike, almost a hatred, for women. If this were coupled with his anger, he might someday do great harm to an individual. Roger is potentially one of the most dangerous men that this examiner has ever encountered.

ON THEIR last day in southern California, the homicide detectives found and interviewed Roger's ex-cop friend, Hector Hendershon.

Hendershon was a friendly, olive-complected, middle-aged aerospace worker who still lived in Chula Vista and also worked for Rohr Industries, which had started back in the 1930s in the garage of Fred Rohr, who built the fuel tanks for Charles Lindbergh's *Spirit of St. Louis*. (When the city fathers told Rohr in the 1950s that he wasn't as powerful as he thought he was, he began paying his workers in silver dollars. It soon became impossible to find a paper bill in Chula Vista.)

"How'd you first meet Roger?" Bertocchini asked.

"Through his mother," Hendershon said. "I met Lorraine at Chula Vista Hospital while I was working as an attendant on the police ambulance. After delivering someone to the hospital, I'd often stay around and have coffee with the nurses. One night when Lorraine and I were in the break room she told me that her oldest son was having some problems. She wondered if anyone could help. I volunteered to talk to the boy and see what I could do for him.

"I got together with Roger and liked him right away. He was a quiet, strong, healthy kid. He was an introvert and sometimes sullen but all it would take was a friendly word or pat on the back to pull him out of it. I found that if he wanted to talk to you, he'd talk your ear off. If he didn't want to talk to someone, he wouldn't say a word or stutter terribly. He started coming over to my house, playing with my two young daughters. He became like a member of my family. If he had two dollars in his pocket, he'd go out and spend a dollar fifty on toys for my kids."

"What about Roger's home life?" Ferrari asked.

"I think Lorraine did a good job of raising the three boys considering the circumstances. The father, Jack, was never around when the kids needed disciplining. He was away in the Navy during most of their formative years."

The detectives realized they were getting a different take on Lorraine Kibbe than they had from her husband.

"Lorraine was an unforgettable character," Hendershon went on. "She was very kind and had a good sense of humor. She was concerned about her kids and worked hard. She was a good person, the type who would do for people. One night, I brought a woman in by ambulance who was going to have a baby any minute. She didn't have any medical insurance. The administrator told me to take her to the county hospital. I knew we'd never get there in time. Lorraine and I delivered the baby on the back steps. She got into a lot of trouble and almost lost her job over that."

Bertocchini asked Hendershon to describe Lorraine.

"She was a slight woman, about a hundred and fifteen pounds," he said. "Sandy-colored hair, bright eyes. Perky and witty. She was very feminine but not flirty."

Hendershon explained that when he quit the police force he bought a convenience store and hired Roger.

"I knew about the malicious mischief Roger had gotten into because I saw the police reports. But Roger never stole anything from me. He even kept track of the free Cokes he drank while at work, so I'd know where they went. After work, I'd drive him home on the back of my motor scooter. Nothing I wanted Roger wouldn't do for me."

"Do you remember Roger ever stealing ladies' clothes?" Bertocchini asked.

"Yes, I do. More than once. When I asked him about it he admitted it. He told me he cut them up. I asked him why he would want to do that. He said because he'd been mad at somebody and this was how he took out his frustrations. I was never clear on who exactly he was mad at. I suggested there were better ways to handle his anger. He did have a problem with his temper, although I never considered him capable of harming anyone. He wouldn't ever confront. He'd go behind someone's back to get even. Unless you knew him, you couldn't tell if Roger was a friend or a foe."

Asked when he'd last seen Roger, Hendershon said it had been five or six years.

"Roger drove up to my house and called to me. 'Come on, Hec, let's go.' I asked him, 'Go where?' He opened up the trunk of his car. Inside were two parachutes. He knew I'd been a paratrooper in the Army, but that I'd never jumped in civilian life. I told him, 'No, Rog, I'm too old for that.'"

Bertocchini grinned. "Me, too."

Hendershon held a faraway look. "You know, I always felt sorry for Roger. I think he got shortchanged in life. He had difficulty reading the label on a can of beans. I think they pushed him along in school until at some point he just stopped going. When it came to teaching him things, I found him to be a smart hombre. If Roger wanted to learn something, you could teach him anything. He showed an interest in fishing and everything I did—except for one thing."

"What was that?" asked Bertocchini.

"Hunting. He wasn't interested in killing animals."

CHAPTER EIGHTEEN

Kay Maulsby's journey to the Nevada side of Lake Tahoe early in the afternoon of November 19, 1987, was a kind of professional courtesy call. She wouldn't even write a report about her face-to-face with Detective Steve Kibbe.

She'd never before met Roger's younger brother, although the guys who'd been around longer at the Homicide Bureau knew him. Ray Biondi remembered Steve Kibbe and some other Douglas County detectives dropping by the Bureau the previous year on a murder case they were working. There had been the usual amount of shoptalk on various cases, and Biondi was sure they'd even discussed the I-5 killings. After Roger had developed as a suspect, Biondi had made a point of calling Douglas County to let them know. The Bureau had always had a good relationship with Douglas County, and the turn in the investigation could impact not only on Steve Kibbe but on his entire department. At some point, they might have media inquiries to deal with. The undersheriff he spoke with had called Biondi back to say they'd had a "discussion" with Detective Kibbe—"I just want you to know that Steve was told he's going to be a cop or a brother."

After a curt handshake, Kibbe showed Maulsby into his office and closed the door.

Maulsby saw the family resemblance in the casually attired man across from her. The cop brother was a slightly younger, shorter, huskier version of the killer brother.

"If my brother was a murder suspect," Maulsby began, "I'd very much appreciate the detectives sitting down and telling me what they had. That's why I'm here today."

Kibbe nodded.

Their first conversation had been a week earlier, when Steve had telephoned Maulsby to offer his assistance. He made it clear in that conversation, however, that he had serious doubts about his brother's guilt. "I've known Roger about forty-seven years longer than you have," he said. "I think I know him a lot better than you do." Roger had called him the week before on the "verge of suicide," Steve explained. "He and Harriet had been at each other's throats since you served the search warrant. They were fired and evicted by Public Storage as a result of your investigation. Harriet had driven Roger up to a friend's cabin outside Placerville and left him there with no car and no phone."

Maulsby had already known about Placerville. She'd joined other detectives earlier that week for two days of surveillance at the rustic cabin, located off Highway 50 midway between Sacramento and Tahoe.

Steve had gone on to explain that Roger "couldn't handle" being alone at the cabin. "He falls apart when he's not within arm's reach of Harriet. They really feed off each other. He called from a pay phone and asked me to come pick him up. I did and brought him home. We had some long walks and talks. I got him stabilized, and in a few days took him back to Harriet. He's still very frightened and insecure."

On the ride up to meet Steve at his office—they had arranged the appointment at the end of their phone conversation—Maulsby had struggled with a dilemma. She wanted to provide Steve with enough information to show that Roger was a viable suspect, but also, having heard about the brothers' "long talks and walks," she didn't want to give Steve too many details to pass on to Roger. She realized it was a fine line she'd have to walk—trying to convince Steve of his brother's guilt and enlist his cooperation without giving away important details of the ongoing investigation.

In his office sitting across from Steve Kibbe with his desk between them, Maulsby began her careful recitation.

If Steve was surprised or disturbed by any of the information, he didn't show it.

Of course, he was a homicide detective, Maulsby reminded herself. That's how he was trained to react.

Maulsby realized that this was a difficult situation for him—another cop detailing why his brother was suspected of committing multiple homicides. She wondered how she would have reacted if the tables were turned.

As Steve began to open up, it was clear that he was quite concerned about his brother, whom he described as "without a mean bone in his body." Roger had long tried to emulate him, he said. When Steve would grow a beard or mustache, so would Roger. When Steve would shave it off, Roger would follow suit. There was even a time, Steve said, when Roger had wanted to be a cop. Now, the loyal brother in Steve made it clear he stood ready to give Roger a place to live and help in finding a job when he got out of his "present difficulties."

Maulsby plowed on. "Can you give me some dates that Roger has visited you?" She was interested in determining whether Roger had found victims along the road to or from visits to Steve's—the Jane Doe murder scene, after all, was just a few miles down the road on Highway 50.

Steve checked his desk calendar and reeled off a couple of dates, none of which matched any known abductions. The effort struck Maulsby as very casual, almost perfunctory, and she couldn't believe the veteran homicide detective didn't offer to roll up his sleeves and help them get to the bottom of things.

On the drive back to Sacramento, Maulsby replayed the session. Even with a fellow homicide detective laying out the mounting circumstantial evidence pointing to his brother's involvement in a series of murders, Steve had acted rather unimpressed. He seemed able to turn his back on the evidence. Indeed, his attitude came off as: Roger is my brother and you're wrong about him. As an experienced homicide detective, he knew the score. Where was the cop in him? Did he really believe his line about Roger's harmless ways, delivered with full knowledge of Roger's troubled past? Or was he dying inside at the suspicions building against his brother, and was he harboring his own doubts about Roger?

Detective Steve Kibbe was in a very tough spot.

"I FELT a chill. I knew I was gonna die."

"What did you do then?" asked Sacramento County Deputy District Attorney Jeanne McCullough.

The eyes of everyone in the hushed courtroom were on the prosecution's first witness in the *People of the State of California* v. *Roger Kibbe* in Department G of Sacramento Municipal Court, with the Honorable Alice A. Lytle presiding on November 20, 1987.

"Then I started fighting," answered Debra Guffie, her blond hair long on the sides and cut butch on top.

"When you say 'fighting,' can you describe what you did?"

Guffie answered not in words but with body language, mimicking how she desperately fought to free herself from her assailant that night in the golf course parking lot.

"Let me see if I can describe for the record what the witness is indicating," said Judge Lytle. "You sort of half rose out of the seat flailing your arms in front of you. Is that what you did?"

"Yes."

"Were you making any sounds at the time?" asked McCullough.

"I screamed once or twice."

"And while this whole process of screaming and the flailing of your arms was going on," McCullough continued, "what else were you doing?"

"Your Honor, I object." The voice belonged to short, rotund Bart Wooten, deputy public defender, seated at the defense table next to his client, Roger Kibbe. "She said she screamed once or twice, and it assumes a fact not in evidence."

"That question is acceptable," the judge said.

"Thank you, Your Honor," said McCullough.

Since well before the start of trial, the thirty-one-year-old brunette prosecutor had been fighting over the smallest issues in what should have been a routine matter. But there was nothing run-of-the-mill about this misdemeanor case that might well have been settled by a plea bargain were it not for one juicy piece of information that the twelve jurors would never hear: that the middle-aged defendant was a suspected serial killer.

McCullough, who had been in the D.A.'s office only eight months and had been handling jury trials for even less time, had found herself at the controls of a critically important case.

Weeks earlier, Kay Maulsby had come to McCullough's office to say that homicide detectives in several counties were confident that Roger

Kibbe was the I-5 killer. She mentioned the similarity of the white cordage, which seemed to connect Kibbe with the latest murder, but admitted
that they didn't yet have the hard evidence they needed to charge him.
Maulsby had gone over this with Biondi more than once. They could make
an arrest on the basis of probable cause—and the white cordage *did* con-
stitute probable cause—but that only meant Kibbe could be held for forty-
eight hours unless the district attorney filed charges. Filing formal charges
required a much greater burden of proof: beyond a reasonable doubt.
Many district attorneys, including Sacramento's, tossed another ingredi-
ent into the mix: they would not file charges unless there was a likelihood
of conviction.

"We don't have enough to file murder charges and we don't
have enough detectives to watch this guy indefinitely twenty-four hours
a day," Maulsby had explained to the new prosecutor. "Our best shot at
getting him off the street for a while and buying ourselves some time is in
your hands."

"You mean if he walks on this assault charge," McCullough had said,
"more women may die?"

Maulsby nodded. "I'm afraid so."

It was the most pressure that McCullough had had yet as a prosecutor; plainly, it was up to her alone to get a bad guy off the street. If he was
acquitted, not only would it be her fault but others would pay the ultimate
price for her mistakes or incompetence.

The judge and defense counsel were also made aware of the ongoing
murder investigation, and everyone turned up the intensity level several
notches. Since then, McCullough had battled opposing counsel at every
step. It had taken two days to seat a jury in a trial that would feature only
a handful of witnesses and a few days of testimony. The case required
conscientious jurors who would not be put off by the victim's occupation,
McCullough had realized.

The case was viewed by McCullough's superiors as a tough one that
had to be done, but there was no talk of replacing her with a more experienced litigator. The reason the case was considered tough by even veterans
in the D.A.'s office was because no one had known for certain until Debra
Guffie walked into the courtroom whether she would in fact show up. If

she hadn't, the trial could have gone on with the police witnesses, but it would have been difficult to convict. Jurors might well question why what happened in the parking lot that night was serious enough to send a man to jail when it wasn't serious enough for the victim to show up.

As it was, Guffie was a no-show at an early pretrial hearing. Partly as a result, a felony attempted-rape charge was reduced down to three misdemeanors: battery, soliciting prostitution, and false imprisonment (for Kibbe attempting to handcuff Guffie). After that missed appearance, Maulsby went looking for Guffie. The detective found her living at her disabled mother's home and served her with a subpoena. Maulsby talked to her about the importance of prosecuting the man who had attacked her, although without telling Guffie that Kibbe was a suspected killer. A couple of days before trial, Maulsby picked up Guffie at her mother's house an hour away and brought her to Sacramento. At the county's expense, she was put up in a hotel close to the courthouse. One evening after preparing her witness to testify, McCullough gave Guffie a ride back to the hotel. She had from their first meeting been impressed not only with Guffie's expressed motivation for testifying—not wanting other women to be hurt—but by how articulate she was. The young prosecutor had decided that this strung-out, heroin-addicted prostitute would do fine on the witness stand. "You know, I have a dream," Guffie told McCullough as they pulled up in front of the hotel. "Someday I'd like to have my own small house with a white picket fence where I can live undisturbed." McCullough was touched by the sweet, innocent dream of such a hardened street person. "I hope you find your dream, Debra."

One of the first questions asked by McCullough after Guffie had taken the stand was whether she could identify the man who picked her up that night and drove her to the parking lot. Guffie answered in the affirmative. With a steady hand she pointed to the defense table at Kibbe, who was wearing a red-and-blue jacket over a sports shirt open at the neck. With identification out of the way, McCullough had focused on taking Guffie through her ordeal, step by step.

"And in making those flailing motions," McCullough continued, "what were you trying to do?"

"Get the door open," Guffie said.

"That would be the passenger door?"

"Uh-huh."

"Did you have any problems getting that door open?"

"Yes. It was locked the first time I tried."

"Had you locked the door?"

"No."

"And did you get it unlocked?"

"Yes."

"What did you do then?"

"I opened the door and went to jump out."

"Did you jump out?"

"Uh-huh. I was also pushed."

"Who pushed you?" asked McCullough.

"The defendant."

"What part of your body did he push?"

"My lower back."

"How did you land?"

"On my hands and knees."

"What were you feeling at that point?"

"Thanking God he didn't want me and that he'd pushed me out and I'd gotten away."

Guffie told of the defendant quickly driving off, and the police officer showing up before she'd even picked herself up off the ground. She described running after the police car as it chased after the white car, and next seeing her assailant in the back of a police car a few blocks away.

Being careful not to leave any damaging information for the defense attorney to use to impeach her witness on cross-examination, McCullough had Guffie explain how she had first given a phony name to police because she was afraid of being arrested on an outstanding warrant.

"You eventually told them your real name?"

"Yes."

"And you were arrested?"

"Uh-huh."

"And what were you arrested for?"

"For fraud of a medical card."

"You spent the night in jail?"

"Yes."

McCullough had Guffie explain that the charge resulted from her using someone else's medical card. The D.A. couldn't imagine the jurors being too concerned about it.

"What happened with this charge?" asked McCullough.

"I recently did two and a half weeks in jail on it."

"No further questions."

The defense attorney, who was also fairly new, did no damage to the witness on cross.

After Guffie's testimony—McCullough thought she had come across very well—the prosecutor called six more witnesses, all of whom worked for the Sacramento Police Department, over the course of the next two days.

At each break in the proceedings, McCullough fretted over whether Kibbe, who came and went daily of his own accord, would return to court. Knowing he was the subject of a murder investigation, he might flee, she feared, if he thought he was going down on the misdemeanor charges and headed for lockup. Or would he hang around, willing to do some county jail time and counting on the cops not being able to make a murder case stick?

Four patrol officers, including Sergeant Charles Coffelt, testified to events leading up to the arrest of Kibbe, and to finding the handcuffs in the parking lot.

Another officer, Robert Gillis, a trained crime scene investigator, testified to his own search of the parking lot, during which he found the sealed plastic Baggie containing the crime kit. He detailed for the jury its contents.

The last witness, Penny Hummel, a civilian identification technician, testified to finding a latent print on the handcuffs that matched Kibbe's right ring finger.

By the time McCullough rested her case, she thought it would be real stupid of the defendant to take the stand. Why would he testify and pin himself down one way or the other—truthfully or not—as to the circumstances of a case that could well be the linchpin in a subsequent murder prosecution, where the stakes would be so very much higher?

Sure enough, when it was time for the defense to present its case, Wooten informed the court that they had no witnesses to call.

"Do you have any evidence at all to introduce?" asked the judge.

"No, Your Honor."

Following final arguments by the lawyers—McCullough felt she'd delivered the case neatly wrapped with a ribbon on top—the jury returned a swift verdict on November 25, 1987.

As to one count of battery: guilty.

As to one count of soliciting prostitution: guilty.

As to one count of false imprisonment: not guilty.

The jurors were thanked by the judge for their service and dismissed. Later in the hallway, several jurors would tell McCullough that they convicted on the first two counts because a police officer had corroborated Guffie's testimony on these points, but not on the last charge because no one else had seen Kibbe attempt to handcuff her.

McCullough requested that the judge have the defendant remanded to custody pending a probation report and sentencing hearing. Such a request was not so unusual given the facts of the case.

With Kibbe and his lawyer standing, the judge ordered that the defendant be taken into custody immediately Two bailiffs moved behind Kibbe; one handcuffed him.

At that moment, McCullough saw the first outward sign of emotion from Kibbe, who throughout the trial had remained stoic. He smiled, actually smiled. She had the strangest feeling that Roger Kibbe was relieved.

Kibbe is off the street; it was a satisfying thought for McCullough. She turned slightly, her eyes finding Maulsby in the front row of the spectators' section.

A smiling Maulsby, who was thinking, *Roger will be eating Thanksgiving dinner in jail*, gave the prosecutor a dignified thumbs-up.

Three weeks later, Kibbe would be back in court for sentencing. During an interview with a probation officer, Kibbe had been asked about his crimes against Debra Guffie. He said he knew he was wrong for picking up a prostitute, but that the rest of the case had been "blown out of proportion."

The judge gave him eight months in county jail. With time served and credit for work and good behavior, Roger Kibbe would be out in five months.

The clock was now ticking on the I-5 murder case.

A FEW minutes past 8:00 A.M. on her first day back to work after the Thanksgiving holidays, Kay Maulsby received a call from a booking officer: Debra Guffie was back in custody.

Maulsby realized she'd forgotten to remove the flag on Guffie's name. She was being held on a variety of drug charges, Maulsby was told, including possession of crack cocaine and being under the influence of a narcotic.

The detective was sorry to hear that.

"Can you put her on the phone?" she asked.

It took a minute or two, but finally a faint voice on the other end said tentatively, "Kay?"

"Yes, Debra, this is Kay. Are you all right?"

"I guess."

Maulsby had feared that the pressure of testifying at the trial would add to the monkey Guffie was already carrying on her back.

"Do you know how the trial turned out?"

"No," Guffie said sleepily. "Never heard a thing."

"Roger Kibbe was convicted."

"He was?" Guffie had perked up. "He really was?" She sounded as if she didn't believe that twelve upstanding citizens could possibly view her as anyone's victim.

"Yes," Maulsby said. "He's in jail right now. What you did, Debra, was very important."

"It worked out okay, huh?"

"It sure did."

"Can I ask a favor?"

"Absolutely."

"Could you call my mom and let her know. She was real scared about me testifying."

"I sure will."

"Kay, you're a real peach. Thanks for everything."

It sounded as if Guffie was saying good-bye for good. Maulsby kept her on the line awhile, just chatting. She ended the conversation with a sincere offer.

"If there's anything I can do to help, Debra, like get you into a treatment program, let me know."

If Roger Kibbe was ever going to be tried for murder, Maulsby had an idea that Guffie, the one victim who had gotten away, would once again be an important witness against him. This was certainly not something that Maulsby would burden Guffie with now; she was too busy taking life one day and one step at a time, and faltering even at that.

Of the four Sacramento detectives who had been assigned temporarily to the I-5 case, Maulsby was the last one left. It was funny, she reflected, how things worked out; she, the only one who hadn't worked Homicide, outlasting them all. Lt. Ray Biondi had even let on that he didn't intend to give her back but was going to fight to keep her in Homicide permanently. She had her own desk, phone, and office cubicle now, and was feeling right at home. She had even been confident enough to take on the department's administrative lieutenant when he had recently suggested she solicit funds from other departments involved in the investigation to pay for overtime in connection with the surveillance of Kibbe. "Is that *really* the job of a homicide investigator?" she demanded angrily. "I'm trying to catch a killer. Your job is to get the financing for the investigation." She had warned Biondi that he might hear repercussions from her insubordination but he'd only laughed, "Good for you."

The best part, she reflected that morning as other Bureau detectives scurried about busy with their own caseloads, was that there was no one in close proximity with which she had to have interminable meetings about I-5. *Hallelujah and let's hit the pavement.*

With their prime suspect behind bars for a few months, Maulsby understood that the investigation had taken a new turn. Gone were the distractions of the past couple of months since she'd discovered the Guffie case: the focus was now on Kibbe's background, the surveillance operations, getting Guffie to the witness stand. What was needed was a renewed concentration on all the murder cases, a review of the evidence in each and how they tied together. Something that didn't appear important in one case might show up in another and provide a critical connection.

The investigation needed to return to basics. The best place to start, Maulsby figured, was to have all the physical evidence laid out before her. Other than the Jane Doe crime scene in El Dorado County, she hadn't viewed any of the evidence firsthand. That trip to Tahoe had certainly paid off with her later recognition of the white cordage in the crime kit, but what else was buried in the pile of evidence obtained in the cases? So far, she'd mostly read descriptions in reports, not the same as seeing evidence with her own eyes.

Maulsby called Jim Streeter and asked him to set aside time for her to view in his lab all the victims' clothing and other physical evidence in the cases. On the phone, they went over a list of what he'd accumulated from the various departments. When they got to Lora Heedick, Streeter explained that he'd examined her blue jeans, panties, and socks a year earlier and found no cutting. He'd returned the clothing to the Sacramento Sheriff's Department as he wasn't convinced it was an I-5 case.

"Been down that road myself," Maulsby said. "We spent a lot of time looking at her boyfriend. I'd like to see her clothes, too. If you sent them back, our property warehouse should have them."

Before tracking down Heedick's clothes, Maulsby reviewed the autopsy report. In addition to the garments Streeter said he had previously examined, there was also mention of a pink tank top. She called Streeter.

"I never saw a tank top," he said. "Was one found?"

"It was wrapped around her neck as a ligature, and apparently looped around her wrists, too, as bindings."

"I'd like to see it."

It took Maulsby one phone call to her department's property warehouse to find the clothing Streeter had returned a year ago: Heedick's jeans, panties, socks, and loafers.

"No pink tank top?" she asked.

"Nope," the clerk said. "Don't have that."

Maulsby next called the county crime lab. She gave a criminalist the case number, and explained that she was looking for a tank top that had never made it to DOJ or the property warehouse. "I don't find anything but I'll keep looking," he said. "Have you tried the coroner?"

Five minutes later, a deputy coroner was explaining to Maulsby that they had no reason to keep any of Heedick's clothing. "We sent all of it to the crime lab," he said.

During her lunch hour, Maulsby went to the property warehouse. She reviewed the paperwork and checked the shelf upon which the clothes had been stored since their return from DOJ. There was no sign of Heedick's tank top.

She checked out the clothing Streeter had earlier examined and took it back to him because she wanted the garments part of their evidentiary show-and-tell.

The next morning she called the county crime lab again and spoke to the same criminalist. She told him her thinking: that if the coroner no longer had the tank top and it wasn't at the property warehouse and had never shown up at DOJ, it *had* to be at the crime lab. The search widened.

That afternoon, the criminalist called to say he had located the top in the freezer compartment, where a colleague had placed it a year ago. "It had 'ligature' marked on it, which is why it didn't go to DOJ with the rest of the clothes," he said. It was a lame excuse because all the physical evidence in the I-5 was supposed to go to DOJ.

Maulsby went to the lab and peeked inside the manila envelope. She saw rolled-up pink fabric sealed in plastic. Closing the envelope, she signed for it and made a beeline to DOJ, where she placed it in the hands of Jim Streeter.

Maulsby finally located an old 8mm projector and sequestered herself in a broom closet–size room to view the Kibbe home movies confiscated during the search of Tupelo. There were eleven movies, some dated 1976, 1977, and 1978. In grainy, flickering black-and-white images, the movies depicted a younger-looking Roger, with a neatly trimmed beard, and a thinner Harriet vacationing with an assortment of other people who appeared to be family and friends. There were outings on a lake with a boat, and a Little League game. There was dramatic footage of skydiving— no doubt, Roger had carried the camera out the door of the plane. Also, he filmed a wild ride in a parachute while being towed behind a boat.

Viewing the two "Pretty Girls" pornographic films last, she found them curiously repetitive. In each, a male and a female were engaged in various sexual acts. The women wore nylons, had long hair, and were very busty. Both movies ended with the man ejaculating upon the woman's breasts. Maulsby couldn't know if the movies provided a window into any special desires of Roger's, but she did recall that his victims all had long hair and most had seemed to be busty.

When the I-5 evidence was ready to be reviewed, Maulsby drove over to Streeter's lab. When she walked in, she was nearly staggered by the stench of death from the victims' clothes. Streeter had set up several large electrical fans and vents, mostly to no avail. He was already wearing a surgical mask, and handed one to her.

Streeter commented that he'd been inundated with dozens of unsolved cases sent in by various agencies wanting him to review all the physical evidence in the murders—some old, some new—for possible linkage to the I-5 series.

"Did you get a chance to look at the dowelling and the white cordage from the search of Tupelo?" Maulsby asked.

Streeter said the four pieces of dowelling from Tupelo were the same color and diameter as those in Roger Kibbe's crime kit. He told of also comparing the two new pieces of cordage from Tupelo with the cordage in the crime kit and, most important, to the cordage found at the Jane Doe murder scene. "They're all alike in size, color, weave, type, number of threads. I've had several conversations with the manufacturer trying to come up with more uniqueness, but all we can really say is that they're a similar type of common cordage used in the construction of parachutes."

Maulsby winced.

"Still not enough," she said under her breath.

The physical evidence, spread out on long lab tables, was segregated by victim. For good reason, Streeter had made Lora Heedick first up.

"I have something to show you," Streeter said, quickly moving to and hovering over the pink tank top that had spent a year in deep freeze.

"You see how it's in three pieces and tied together with twine? I went back and checked the autopsy report. The pathologist made two cuts removing it—one at the loop around the neck and the other at the wrists.

That's why we ended up with three pieces. Then he tied the pieces together to show how they were connected. Look here."

Streeter pointed to the shoulder straps.

Maulsby saw that both straps were cut through.

"And here," he said.

Both side seams were cut open several inches.

"The pathologist didn't make these cuts, Kay."

Twenty months after she had disappeared from a Modesto street, Lora Heedick, following much investigation and debate, was finally and unequivocally added to the I-5 body count.

TWENTY-NINE top officials from six law enforcement agencies—in fact, Lt. Ray Biondi, who had been pushing for such a high-level meeting, was outranked by all but one participant—met at the Department of Justice on December 21, 1987, to hear a detailed, scientific presentation on the I-5 murder series by criminalist Jim Streeter.

Streeter utilized photo boards of clothes cuttings and other visual aids to illustrate the similarities in the murders of seven young women. In addition to Stephanie Brown, Charmaine Sabrah, Lora Heedick, Karen Finch, and El Dorado's Jane Doe, found on Old Meyer's Grade, Streeter had recently discovered similarities in two other cases:

• An unidentified white woman believed to be in her twenties, dead six months to a year, who had been found nude from the waist up in El Dorado County on June 11, 1987, in a ravine off Highway 50 about 75 miles west of Lake Tahoe. Although the cause of death could not be determined, there was "neck trauma," leaving open the possibility of strangulation. Streeter found cuts in the crotch of her designer blue jeans.
• An unidentified black woman, about twenty-six years old, found May 19, 1987, in Nevada's Virginia City highlands, some 15 miles southeast of U.S. 395 and 30 miles south of the Nevada shore of Lake Tahoe. The victim had been dead for several months; the cause of death could not be determined. Her bones had been scattered over a wide area by animals—the victim was

found only when a dog brought a human leg bone home to his master and a police search ensued. Her bra, blouse, and jeans all had extensive nonfunctional cutting.

When Streeter finished, the meeting was thrown open to general comments. The tone of the room, Biondi observed, ran from mildly supportive that an active murder series was working to outright skepticism.

The biggest skeptic was the elected sheriff of San Joaquin County, who, after Streeter's presentation, had the temerity to ask: "How do we know these cases are linked?" It was particularly ironic coming from Vito Bertocchini's top boss—Bertocchini, the first detective who suspected Roger Kibbe of being a serial killer.

Hellooo, Mr. Sheriff, are we at the same meeting? Biondi dearly wanted to respond. *Have you been listening for the last hour or doing the Sunday crossword?*

Instead, Biondi coolly reiterated some of the factors just outlined by Streeter. "We can't say there is a direct link of physical evidence at each scene," he admitted. "We don't have matching fingerprints, tire impressions, bullet casings. What we have is a combination of similarities, including, but not limited to, cutting of the victims' clothes."

Certain if he added his own "gut feeling" that a series was at work he'd be drummed out of the corps, he left it at that.

The stated purpose of the meeting was to discuss Biondi's suggestion that there be more press coverage—the most important reason being perhaps to pick up additional eyewitnesses and other information the public at large might have without realizing its importance—as well as some firm commitments from other agencies to help with the sweeping investigation.

From the beginning, Biondi sensed a resentment in the room directed at him; like it was his fault they had to drive all this way and sit down for a couple of hours. And hey, it probably was.

The issue of added press coverage met with nearly total resistance, which dumbfounded Biondi because three of the murders—Brown, Sabrah, and the Jane Doe later identified as Lora Heedick—had been publicized a year ago as part of a series, even though at the time they did not have evidence that Jane Doe's clothes had been cut. He began to suspect the revolt had more to do with bruised egos than sound law enforcement. His department, and he personally, had been out in front of the cameras for the last news conference. If someone else wanted to carry the ball on the evening news, that was fine with him.

Biondi went quiet, letting his boss, Sacramento County Sheriff Glen Craig, who supported a joint press release on the series by all the agencies, run the show.

Some of the comments against going public:
- "We don't need to because we aren't sure about the cases being linked."
- "We don't have to tell the press anything. We can just wait and answer their inquiries as they come in."
- "Our agency isn't allowed to talk to the media."

In the interest of reaching peace among the warring factions, Sheriff Craig worked out the structure of an agreement. Its centerpiece was the judgment that it was "premature" to go public with the seven linked cases at this time. However, if the press inquired as to any of the murders, certain information would be given out, including the fact that there were "similarities" in the cases, "but we will not discuss those similarities." Also, it was decided that, should the media push individual departments for further information, each department could hold its own press conference and "discuss only their own cases."

So much for asking for help from the top, Biondi boiled inwardly. He was glad he'd decided beforehand not to talk about suspects, and had kept mum about Roger Kibbe.

From where Biondi sat, the brass, through its collective wisdom, had come up with an unbelievably stupid way to handle the series of murders that now counted seven victims.

Why was he not so terribly surprised?

CHAPTER NINETEEN

With 1987 coming to a close, Judy Frackenpohl knew deep down that her daughter was dead.

It had been four months since Darcie's last phone call from Sacramento. As the acceptance of her daughter's likely fate crept farther into her very being, Judy found the singularly most trying part was not knowing what had happened. Were her daughter's remains lying somewhere as yet undiscovered? Or had she been found with no identity and did she lie unclaimed? What would they *do* with her?

Darcie's pimp, James Brown, had called the Frackenpohl residence in suburban Seattle a week or so after Judy had filed the missing persons report. Darcie's brother, Larry, was home alone at the time. Brown wanted to know if they'd heard from Darcie, and Larry said no. After the short conversation, Larry had hung up, then quickly picked up the phone to call his mother at work. Brown hadn't yet been disconnected—he was whining to someone, "That bitch is probably hiding from me," before the line went dead. His complaint, obviously unintended for their ears, made both Larry and Judy feel more confident that Brown had had nothing to do with Darcie's disappearance.

Seattle Detective Mike Hatch of King County's new missing persons bureau wasn't so sure about James Brown, even when Brown initiated a call to the detective three months after Darcie's disappearance to find out whether there was anything new in the search for her. In truth, there was no search under way for Darcie—just a file that Hatch hadn't opened in a month. When Brown said he was in Seattle, Hatch tried to solicit information about the last time he'd seen Darcie, but Brown said he didn't want to talk about it over the phone. He refused to give his whereabouts but promised to come to Hatch's office four days hence. He also consented to Hatch's request to take a polygraph that day. When the day arrived, Brown was a no-show. Thirty minutes later, Hatch had a superior court subpoena issued in Brown's name.

The first week of December, Hatch called the Sacramento Police Department and asked for the records section. Since the city was Darcie's last known location, he requested any arrests or contacts that the department had with her, but they came up empty-handed. He spoke with a Sergeant Meadors in the homicide unit and gave him a full description of Darcie. The sergeant said there had been no homicide victims or Jane Does fitting her description within the city limits; he suggested Hatch call the Sacramento County Coroner's Office. Hatch did, speaking to coroner's investigator Laura Synhorst. Hatch asked if they knew of any unidentified female murder victims that fit Darcie's description, adding that she was missing the four ends of her fingers on her right hand. Synhorst said no. She took down all the other pertinent information, and promised to call if an unidentified female victim fitting that description came in.

A few minutes after he'd gotten off the phone to Sacramento, Hatch received a call from Kim Quackenbush, a prostitute friend of Darcie's from Seattle who said she'd been with her on the night Darcie disappeared in Sacramento. The last time she saw Darcie, Quackenbush reported, was around 9:00 P.M. on August 24, 1987. They were both working on West Capital Avenue, a popular stroll area in West Sacramento. At the time, Darcie was wearing a sleeveless pink dress, pink pump heels, and a thin black chiffon jacket. Hatch asked Quackenbush if she thought Brown might have harmed Darcie or if she might have voluntarily left him. Quackenbush was positive neither had happened. Darcie's disappearance was a shock to everyone, she said, Brown included—although within a few days he'd recruited a new blonde to whom he gave Darcie's clothes.

On December 8, Hatch was having his teeth cleaned and his dentist happened to be adjacent to Darcie's dentist. He had the receptionist go next door and retrieve Darcie's dental records, which had been ready for him to pick up since September. The following day, he sent the dental charts to the King County Medical Examiner's Office. The first thing chief investigator Bill Hagland of the medical examiner's office did was to send a copy of the records to the Washington State Police in Olympia for them to enter into the National Crime Information Center's missing persons system, to which many states—including California—contributed information about missing persons and unidentified dead on a voluntary, if somewhat delayed, basis. There was no hit in NCIC.

On Christmas Eve day, Judy Frackenpohl received a surprise phone call from Detective Hatch.

"Have you heard from Darcie?" he asked.

"No, I haven't."

The question irritated Judy. When Hatch had previously told her that the "typical runaway" calls home during the holidays, she had responded that Darcie wasn't a typical runaway because she called home "all the time." *Had he not worked the case seriously,* Judy now wondered, *because he expected Darcie to call over the holidays?*

"Well, in that case, since there haven't been any new leads," Hatch said, "I'm deactivating the case."

"What does that mean?"

"We won't be actively investigating it. Since your daughter apparently disappeared from Sacramento, I suggest you call and file a missing persons report with them."

Judy saw red. "I asked you people *four months ago* if I should do that," she said furiously. "I was told I had to file it here since Darcie lived here."

The detective calmly offered to give her the number of the Sacramento Police Department.

"Merry fucking Christmas to you, asshole!" Judy Frackenpohl yelled into the receiver before slamming it down.

LT. RAY Biondi had a wild idea as to how to get some dialog going with Roger Kibbe: send in a woman detective to visit him in jail.

In the process of persuading detective Kay Maulsby that she should be the one, Biondi found himself answering her cautionary questions.

"You sure we can do this?" she asked. "He's made it clear he doesn't want to talk to us."

"Then he'll tell you to leave."

Biondi's hope was that Kibbe would be less threatened by a lone woman and more willing to open up than he had been to other detectives who had spoken to him.

"Try to establish rapport," he said. "Become his friend. If he is ever going to vent and come clean, be the person he'll talk to. It's lonely sitting in jail. Show him that you care enough to come see him."

"Before or after I read him his rights?"

Biondi laughed. "Don't worry about that. He can go back to his cell or tell you to leave if he doesn't want to talk to you."

"What if he tells me something or even confesses? How can we ever use it, Ray?"

Now *that* was a good question.

A few years earlier, Biondi had been interviewing a guy about a murder. Funny thing was, he thought the guy's wife had committed the nasty deed. But as the guy was going through his alibi he grew noticeably more nervous. Biondi decided to run a bluff. "Tell me how you killed him," he asked, poker-faced. The guy broke down and confessed everything, explaining he'd thrown the murder weapon in a river. Biondi read the suspect his Miranda rights at that point, and had the guy repeat the whole story. The trial judge allowed the confession but a higher court ruled that everything Biondi had learned in the interview was the "fruit of a poisoned tree." Without other evidence to tie him to the crime, the guy walked.

"If Roger confesses, it would be tainted," Biondi admitted. "Let him know that nothing he has said up to that point can be used against him. Then read him his rights and start over. Try to keep him talking. It's up to the D.A. to fight legal issues. Our job is to solve the case."

"You're thinking we don't have anything to lose?"

"Right."

"In that case, I don't have a thing to fear."

Biondi cocked his head, looking at her quizzically.

"All his victims were so busty."

It was a twenty-five-minute drive from Sacramento through long miles of green fields alive with wild flowers to Rio Consumnes Correctional Center, the branch jail that housed 1,200 sentenced prisoners doing county time. The first view of the huge facility was a tall guard tower that jutted up from the middle of the complex and was visible for miles.

At the main entrance, she signed in as an official visitor under the date, December 30, 1987, and gave her badge number. She didn't have her 9mm service revolver to turn in because it was where she always kept it: locked safely in the trunk of her work car. She waited in a deserted hallway for Roger Kibbe to arrive from "B barracks."

She had purposefully not given Kibbe any notice, and wondered if he would even leave his cell when he was told who was here to see him. But she soon saw him sauntering down the hall, next to his escort. When they reached her, Maulsby identified herself. She asked him if he remembered her from the day the search warrant had been served at Public Storage.

"Yeah."

"I'd like to talk to you, Roger."

Kibbe shrugged.

The escort officer unlocked the door to a private conference room, and they all entered.

"You can uncuff him," Maulsby said.

Kibbe's strong hands, manacled in front, came free.

The escort looked at Maulsby.

"It's okay," she said. "You can leave."

He did, swinging the door shut behind him. A few seconds later, the bolt lock clicked in place.

They sat down in metal chairs facing each other.

"I went to Tahoe last month and talked to Steve," Maulsby said.

She had Roger's attention.

"We spoke again over the phone a couple of weeks ago. Steve is concerned about you."

"I know."

"I promised him I'd check with you to see how you're doing. He's concerned that you might need some psychological help. Are you having any problems here?"

"No, everything's fine. I just don't know if they're going to leave me in the same barracks."

"Would you like to stay where you are?"

"Yes, I would."

"I'll try to arrange that."

They discussed general conditions at the jail—Kibbe liked the food but thought it unfair the way the TV room was run—and segued into some of his personal background. It wasn't anything revealing, just droplets of information, but at least he was talking. When he told her about his childhood troubles in school, she empathized. When he spoke about how much he enjoyed woodworking, she smiled.

She thought about how normal it all seemed, Roger talking to her so calmly in such a controlled setting. Yet, she knew the evidence was mounting that he had killed, more than once, with those same thick hands that he so skillfully used to build furniture. He was probably not so calm then, she surmised. He was probably very excited, maybe enraged; no doubt he was fiercely demanding and terrifyingly cruel. In fact, she'd seen the proof of it. That he could do such horrifying things to someone he held no grudge against—women he didn't know but used like an archer aiming at a bull's-eye—was what she found most incomprehensible.

Yet, she sat discoursing with him as if he were her kindly next-door neighbor or corner greengrocer.

Forty minutes later, they parted, the ice broken.

On the drive back, she reflected on how ordinary the soft-spoken, almost grandfatherly man before her had seemed. That must have been the man whom his victims had seen minutes or seconds before he flipped a switch and became somebody, or something, very different.

It had been eerie.

Still, she would return. As long as he kept talking, she'd come back to him for as long as he'd let her.

THE FIRST week of January 1988, Detective Vito Bertocchini located, through a check of motor vehicles records, the Datsun 280Z formerly owned by Roger Kibbe.

Bertocchini picked up Kay Maulsby and Jim Streeter on the way to Rocklin, 20 miles northeast of Sacramento. The new owner, Donald Udell, twenty-three, had purchased theDatsun six months earlier from a Sacramento used car dealer.

The only change he'd made to it, Udell explained, was mounting a new audio-stereo system in the dashboard. In doing so, he made some adjustments in the face plate of the dash, then painted the dash when he finished. During the installation, he told the detectives that he'd found a gold loop earring under the driver's seat.

"Did you find anything else?" Bertocchini asked.

"No, but you know, every once in a while there was a real rotten smell in the car," he said. "I always thought it was the ventilation system."

Maulsby explained they would like to process the car inside and out for trace evidence. "We'll be looking for hair, fibers, and other evidence," she said.

Udell gave detectives permission to search the vehicle believed used in the abduction of Charmaine Sabrah and possibly other I-5 victims.

Streeter started to work, but soon found the power source at Udell's residence inadequate to run his laser machine. Detectives got permission to drive the car to DOJ.

It took Streeter three hours to process the vehicle. In the course of his examination, he took samples of fibers from the seats and floor mats, recovered some animal hairs, and swabbed a stain on the passenger seat while a DOJ latent print examiner dusted the vehicle, lifting a partial palm print from inside the rear window of the hatchback.

Streeter would, however, find nothing to connect Sabrah or any other I-5 victims to the Datsun 280Z.

Roger Kibbe's luck was holding.

TWO WEEKS after the big powwow at DOJ, the secret deal between six California and Nevada law enforcement agencies to keep the lid on the I-5 murder cases fell apart when Sacramento County Sheriff Glen Craig and Lt. Ray Biondi stepped into a room of newspaper, radio, and TV reporters.

Various media outlets had been calling, almost immediately, wanting updates on the I-5 investigation. Biondi convinced his boss they had to go public with the full series and "let it all roll out."

The deaths of four more women had been linked to the I-5 murder series, Sheriff Craig announced, bringing the known total to seven victims.

As far as the public was concerned, the new victims were: Karen Finch, El Dorado's two Jane Does, and Nevada's Virginia City Jane Doe.

The only thing Craig held back was the clothes cutting. "I cannot be specific about what evidence links these seven women to the same killer," he said, "other than they were all traveling on or found near the interstate or intersecting roads and highways. For that reason, we believe the person responsible is mobile and spends a lot of time in his vehicle seeking his next victim. The real tragedy is that he may not look any different than you or me. You might not be able to tell that he has horns and is the devil."

The sheriff, in his frankness, broke another agreed-upon rule by discussing each case in detail, even those that "belonged" to other jurisdictions.

Asked by a reporter for the latest description of the suspect, Craig said they believed him to be white, in his forties, and a frequent lone traveler along Interstate 5 south of Sacramento and on U.S. 50 to the Lake Tahoe basin.

Craig acknowledged Biondi, who stepped forward.

Biondi had been thinking long and hard since the disastrous council at DOJ. All those bosses not wanting to go public had to have been for a reason other than ego. He decided it had to do with the more sinister fact that when they finally did, they'd simultaneously have to commit to doing whatever it took to *stop the killings*. It had to do with politics, budgets, manpower resources, and all that unholy crap. He was damn disgusted, but he'd keep it buttoned up this day.

"Investigators are seeking information from women who may have encountered and then refused to go with a man who offered them a ride," Biondi said. "Anyone who saw anything suspicious that might be connected to these or other related crimes, please come forward. We need your help."

This was not a charade for Biondi—until they had a nailed-down murder case against Roger Kibbe, they would continue to search for evidence and seek information. The veteran had learned not to hang his hat on the first strong suspect that came along. He'd seen plenty that "looked good" before the bottom fell out and they had to start over.

The next day's front-page headlines in the Sacramento *Union* told the general public what a lot of high-ranking coppers hadn't wanted to let out of the bag:

'I-5 Strangler' Expands Trail of Death
Cops Link Slayings of 7 Young Women
to Man Who Prowls the Highways

What the public and many top law enforcement administrators with other agencies didn't know, however, was that the prime suspect was tucked safely behind bars—

—for now.

DETECTIVE Kay Maulsby went back to Rio Consumnes the day after the press conference.

She and Roger Kibbe settled into the same interview room as before, and she asked how he'd been getting along in the week since her last visit.

"Okay," he said.

"Are you aware of the news concerning the homicides?" she asked, touching for the first time on the real reason why she was making these pilgrimages.

"No," he said, a bit warily.

"There was a press conference yesterday. It was on TV last night."

"The inmates switched to another channel when the news came on." It had the sound of a dismissal.

"Listen, Roger, I'm still investigating these cases," she said earnestly. "So are other detectives. You're one of the suspects being looked at but I'll work just as hard at proving your innocence as your guilt if you can help eliminate yourself by giving me something to go on. Like your activities and whereabouts on certain dates."

There was no response.

"Do you think we might ever get to the point where it would be possible to discuss such specifics?" she asked.

He seemed to consider the question. "I-I think so."

"If you are in fact innocent, it's important to the investigation that we eliminate you as soon as possible so that we might concentrate on finding the real suspect."

His nod was barely perceptible.

She decided to back off.

They discussed Harriet and his concerns as to how she was getting along without him.

"I worry about her," he said. "She's still working as a bookkeeper and driving in from Placerville every day. She's going to be trying to find a place for us to live in Sacramento, closer to her work, when I get out."

When I get out.

Maulsby willed herself not to react.

"What are your plans?" she asked, then quickly added: "When you get out, I mean."

"I'd like to find something in woodworking." He was relaxing with the lady cop across from him; his stutter had disappeared. "Maybe I can find someone with a shop who can afford to take on a helper."

After thirty-five minutes, she asked if it would be all right for her to come see him again.

"I thought I didn't have a choice," he said.

"You do, Roger." She wanted to sound firm but friendly. "I'll come back to see you or I won't. It's entirely up to you."

He didn't take long.

"It's okay to come back."

JUDY Frackenpohl answered a knock on the door of her Seattle home at 5:30 P.M. on Tuesday, January 12, 1988.

A man in a brown suit stood at the threshold.

Judy knew without being told—

—This was the detective she'd been dealing with over the phone for four months but had never laid eyes on—

—He was here to tell her that Darcie was dead.

"Mrs. Frackenpohl, I'm Detective Hatch."

"Yes," she managed weakly.

"May I come in?"

She stepped back, turned, and went into the living room. The detective, who was alone, followed, closing the door behind him.

"I'm sorry to have to tell you that Darcie is dead. Her body was found in California. She's been identified."

Judy was listening, but she didn't want to hear any more. What more could there be to say?

Hatch was apologizing for dropping in unannounced, as if that really mattered. "We don't call ahead because we don't want to give false hope," he was busy explaining.

Judy wanted to tee off on the detective and tell him what a lousy job he'd done trying to find her daughter these past four months, but instead she broke down.

She'd filed, by phone, the belated missing persons report with Sacramento on Christmas Eve. For months she had pushed and prodded in every direction she knew, but no one seemed to be listening. Her runaway teenage daughter had never been at the top of anyone's priority list.

With no pair of arms to run to for comfort, Judy stood in the middle of the room sobbing quietly. She'd already cried so many tears over Darcie she was astonished by how many were still left.

"I need to tell you that your daughter was murdered," Hatch said. "But you can't tell anyone. Two detectives are coming up from California in a couple of days to talk to you."

At that point, Judy went numb all over.

Darcie was murdered and she couldn't tell anyone?

Judy knew that in many ways she'd lost Darcie long ago. The memories she had of her only daughter these past years were not cherished ones. But she'd secretly kindled the hope that Darcie would start to figure things out—as some of her schoolmates were doing—and begin to rebuild her life. Get back into school, find a vocation or career path that interested her. Get married one day, have her own children, drive a station wagon to soccer games. The interlocking hopes: Darcie as an attentive mother with her own kids to raise, herself one day as a doting grandmother, the two of them drawing closer in future years.

Hopes that were now dashed forever.

CHAPTER TWENTY

Where was Darcie found?" Judy Frackenpohl asked.

"On the highway to Lake Tahoe," Detective Jim Watson said. "In the woods just off the road. She had no ID."

Judy looked perplexed. "How far from Sacramento?"

Detective Kay Maulsby spoke up. "About a hundred miles. We think she was picked up in Sacramento and driven there. Against her will."

The day after Darcie Frackenpohl was identified, Maulsby and Watson started working together on the case. She had liked the soft-spoken detective when she'd first met him at the autopsy months earlier; calm and deliberate, he wasn't easily stampeded. In fact, at the time, Watson had let her know that he was not convinced the Old Meyer's Grade Road murder was part of a series. "Could be a local thing," he'd told Maulsby, who could see that the handsome, square-jawed El Dorado detective was a cop deep in the bone; he would draw his own conclusions in his own time. In the months since, the similar cordage had moved him, as well, in the direction of Roger Kibbe. Still, Watson took things one step at a time. Through the phone company they were able to get the address of the pay phone from which Darcie had made her last call home. It turned out to be in front of a low-rent West Sacramento motel where Darcie had spent her last days; lounging poolside by day, hooking by night. They conducted interviews at the motel and had the DOJ's Jim Streeter process for evidence the room she was known to have occupied.

Three days later, the pair of detectives had flown to Seattle. Before sitting down in Judy Frackenpohl's living room, they'd already interviewed Darcie's pimp, James Brown, who needed to be eliminated as a suspect. He admitted to having hit Darcie a few days before she dropped out of sight, but denied any involvement in her disappearance and seemed genuinely upset at the news of her murder. They also talked to her prostitute friend, Kim Quackenbush, who reported that Darcie had been beaten and robbed by a 6-foot-4 Indian in a white pickup the night before her disappearance.

"The Seattle detective told me not to tell anyone that Darcie had been murdered," Judy said, bewildered. "How am I supposed to go on like nothing happened?"

"I'm sure what he meant was not to tell James Brown or any of the other people around Darcie until we had a chance to come up and interview them," Maulsby said.

"I still don't understand why it took so long to identify her," Judy said.

"We sent out bulletins and press releases giving a complete description," Watson explained. "Unfortunately, I guess they didn't get to the people who had the missing persons report you filed."

"The *two* reports I filed," Judy said. She told of having filed the second one on Christmas Eve.

Maulsby would later learn that the Sacramento missing persons report, which she never saw, had been filed with the Sacramento Police Department. No one there was aware of El Dorado's Jane Doe, although news stories concerning the unidentified body had run in Sacramento's two major daily newspapers.

Watson knew that Darcie Frackenpohl should have been identified sooner. Seattle police should have sent her dental records to California much sooner than they did. El Dorado had held up its end: DOJ received Jane Doe's complete dental records from a South Lake Tahoe dentist only five days after her body was found. However, DOJ's identification section that kept dental and X-ray records on the state's unidentified dead had not received Darcie's dental records from the King County medical examiner until *110 days later*—on January 11, 1988. That same day, a DOJ technician noted that the missing girl had deformed fingers on one hand and matched her dental records with El Dorado's Jane Doe. Watson had no idea why it had taken Seattle—which was supposed to be the most effective police agency in the country at finding missing persons due to its "Green River" experience—so long to move.

Judy Frackenpohl should not have had to wait four months to learn of her daughter's death.

Judy told about Darcie's final call and her last trip home. Also, about her daughter's teenage rebellion and, before that, the jolt of having lost her father.

"Where's Darcie now?" Judy asked.

Watson wrote down the name and number of the mortuary in South Lake Tahoe. "If you need help with the arrangements or have any questions," he said, "please call me." He gave her his office and pager numbers.

Watson's concern seemed genuine. For the first time in four months, Judy felt she was dealing with detectives who truly cared about her loss.

"My daughter was murdered." It was a statement, not a question, from a mother still trying to come to terms.

Watson confirmed Darcie's death had been a homicide, although he made no mention of the killing being part of a murder series or of their having a viable suspect.

She pursed her lips and looked up with steely eyes.

"I don't want to know who did this. Not ever."

The next day, she called the mortuary.

"The county buried your daughter just after Thanksgiving," the funeral director said.

"Buried?"

"Six weeks ago. Middletown Cemetery in Placerville. You'll be able to have the body exhumed and brought home."

"She was buried with no name?"

"As Jane Doe. We held her longer than usual because she didn't fit the homeless/runaway profile. She was well nurtured and had extensive dental work. We knew she belonged to someone."

"Yes," Judy Frackenpohl said. "She does."

"OUR investigation into the disappearance and murders of several women is continuing," Detective Kay Maulsby told Roger Kibbe during her third visit to Rio Consumnes in as many weeks.

"We haven't been able to eliminate you as a suspect, Roger. It's difficult for me to understand, if you're innocent, why you don't help us clear you."

He remained silent.

"Give me some dates. Tell me where you were. I'd like to know about the vehicles you've driven the last couple of years. Where you've gone."

"I know you have a job to do," he said softly. They were the first words he'd spoken this day other than "hello" and "okay" since she'd been here. "It's just I can't answer your questions about th-those things."

"Is keeping everything inside you something that you've done most of your life?"

He nodded.

"It's become a lifelong habit to deal with your problems by not talking about them?"

"I've never been real good at talking," he admitted. "I usually keep things to myself."

"You think that's a good way of handling things?"

"No."

"Your problems aren't going to go away by not talking about them. Have you been thinking about them?"

"I do think about them."

Maulsby hoped he would continue, and he did.

"But I shouldn't be talking to you about any of this stuff. They told me not to talk to anybody about anything. I'm not even supposed to talk to you about whether the grass is green outside."

"Who are 'they'?"

"I can't tell you."

"Let me guess. Is it a family member?"

No acknowledgment.

"Advice from an attorney?"

Nothing.

"Can you talk about the offenses you've been convicted of? What happened in the golf course parking lot?"

He had previously intimated that the "entire truth" had not come out in court in the Debra Guffie case since he didn't take the stand and tell his side of the story.

"Tell me your side," she said. "I'm willing to listen to whatever you have to say."

"No, they told me not to discuss anything about that either."

She stood suddenly, went to the door, and rapped hard. Spinning back toward him, she said in her most detective-like voice, "If you ever want to talk, you should remember my name and give me a call."

She had wearied of the emotional hand-holding.

Maulsby had believed at times during their sessions that he might at some point open up and allow her to peek inside. But those cracks in the wall quickly closed up almost as soon as they appeared. Most of the time, she felt as she did now as she walked out the main gate of Rio Consumnes.

Roger Kibbe was going to keep his evil secrets.

WHEN criminalist Faye Springer transferred to DOJ's Sacramento lab in late January 1988, her colleague Jim Streeter saw it as a lucky break for the I-5 investigation.

As a trace evidence specialist, Springer was a legend—not just within DOJ or California, but throughout the rather elite community of forensic scientists in the United States.Streeter concurred with his brethren: Springer was among the best in a very specialized field.

Criminalistics was divided into three distinct fields: *serology*, Streeter's specialty, which was advancing almost daily through rapid DNA technological advances; *ballistics*, the analysis of firearms and their ammunition; *trace evidence*, a catchall category for everything else, so named because of all the tiny things that were hard to see with the naked eye.

Streeter, well versed in the I-5 evidence, knew that neither blood typing nor DNA analysis would solve the murder series. Most of the bodies had been too decomposed for biological evidence to be recovered. In the two cases with semen evidence—Stephanie Brown and Karen Finch—there had been problems. All that had been determined with the minute amount of semen in Brown was that it could have been provided by 4 percent of the Caucasian population, a relatively wide net that included Kibbe. There hadn't been enough of a sample to do a full complement of tests to further narrow the genetic characteristics. In Finch, matters were complicated by the fact that she'd had consensual sex with her boyfriend their last night together; Kibbe "could not be excluded" as a second semen donor. So much for DNA.

As for more generalized blood typing, Kibbe had type O, the most common blood type, which he shared with 50 percent of the U.S. population. He was also a nonsecretor—along with 20 percent of all Caucasian males—meaning that his bodily fluids such as semen and saliva did not contain blood-type indicators. As a result, it wasn't possible through blood typing to include or eliminate him as a possible donor.

Streeter had done everything he knew to do with the evidence. Serology had proved inconclusive, as had fingerprinting; forensic science had come up with no direct physical link between any of the dead women and Kibbe. As the criminalist had reported to Kay Maulsby, he was "winding down on the evidence" and had "nothing positive to report."

Streeter had telephoned Springer several times seeking advice on I-5 while she had still been working at DOJ's Riverside lab in southern California. What she did better than anyone was "particle analysis" of trace evidence; she could find the puniest pieces of evidence when no one else could, then figure out their origins and significance. It was tedious, time-consuming work done under high-powered microscopes that took experience, knowledge, and patience—before Springer's arrival, not a single criminalist at DOJ Sacramento was doing what she did best.

Streeter had mounted some slides from I-5 tape lifts and looked at them under a microscope but hadn't gotten very far. With limited trace evidence experience, he had no idea what he should be looking for or, at times, even what he was looking at. He'd found before him a magnified view of microscopic debris from countless sources—how could it be sorted out, separating the junk from the gems? At 500 mag power—things looked different in size, shape, color. It was not his world.

With Faye Springer working in the same lab, Streeter hoped it would be possible to draw her into I-5, an investigation that, from an evidentiary standpoint, was dead in the water. In fact, he had a plan for just that: He'd requested that Springer—in her first week on the job before she was assigned her own cases—work with him preparing tape lifts off some of the victims' clothing. "She's a valuable resource," he'd told the lab director. "It would be a shame for us not to use her."

He greeted Springer on her first day in the large, hospital-white criminalistics lab they'd both be working in. Several items of clothing were laid out on the lab tables.

"Welcome to I-5," Streeter said enthusiastically. "We've got a task force going."

"How many guys?" she asked.

She had brown eyes and shoulder-length hair to match. Her complexion was pallid from so much time spent indoors in windowless laboratories. At 5-foot-4, she was solidly built and carried herself with the gait of someone anxious to get where she was going. Makeup and hairdressers were low on her priority list, and she wore sensible shoes. Her one indulgence: a lick of hair on her forehead that she was constantly whisking back. It was difficult to know what kind of dresser Springer was because whatever she had on was always covered, as it was today, with a white lab coat.

"One full-time detective," Streeter said. "Kay Maulsby of Sac County. San Joaquin had three guys, but they're shutting down this month. DOJ is really behind this."

A bit more skeptically, Springer wanted to know how many criminalists were assigned to the case.

Streeter grinned. "Me. I'm almost full-time."

They worked side by side that day. A few minutes before quitting time the lab director came in to say that the lab could ill afford to have two of its thirteen criminalists on one case when there was so much other work to do. Streeter would follow I-5 to completion, with Springer consulting as needed.

It was no big deal to Springer. In fact, she had burned out on serial murders, which was one reason she had sought a transfer to Sacramento. Riverside seemed to be a veritable dumping ground for L.A. killers. Besides the "Hillside Strangler" case, she had worked the "Trash Bag Murders" and "Freeway Killer" series, with more than twenty victims each, and countless smaller series of two, three, and four victims. She had worked on more than 300 homicides.

Springer's forte was the collection and analysis of "exchange evidence" that could link a suspect to a victim or a crime scene. Under the Locard

Exchange Principle, the basis for the study of trace evidence, it's not possible for someone to come in contact with an environment without changing it in some small way, whether by adding to it or taking something away. When an individual came into contact with a person or location, certain small, seemingly insignificant changes occurred. The longer and more extreme the physical contact, the more exchange evidence would be left behind. Sherlock Holmes had known this; modern-day forensic criminalists like Springer who studied trace evidence had simply gone one better in their sleuthing for tiny evidence, replacing a handheld magnifying glass with high-powered microscopes.

In one Riverside case, she had testified against a drug dealer who was subsequently convicted, largely through trace evidence. As a result, she ended up number three on his hit list, after his own attorney and the prosecutor. When the list was discovered, Springer had found it a bit unnerving that the guy actually had her home address. But it was not the first time she'd been on such a list, and she'd noticed that the prosecutor was always ahead of her. She figured as long as the prosecutor was still breathing, she was probably okay.

Nevertheless, Faye and her husband, Fred, who also worked for DOJ, had decided on a change of scenery. They had opened the Riverside lab together in 1972. It had been a two-person operation in the beginning, so cozy that Springer told friends she was "either going to have to file sexual harassment charges against my co-worker or marry him." She did the latter in 1975; they now had three children ranging from four to nine years of age. Together they had sought the transfer, and together DOJ had moved them—in the process, kicking Fred upstairs to administration. They had bought and settled into a large English Tudor home in a suburb of Sacramento, and commuted twenty minutes to work—in the morning, she drove while he read the newspaper aloud, and in the evening he drove.

As Springer went to work on other cases, Streeter was undeterred. So much for the direct approach; he'd just have to be more subtle. He had an idea that if the I-5 case ever got Springer's attention, she'd work on it no matter what the higher-ups decreed.

One afternoon after Springer had already left for the day, Streeter placed a slide under her microscope; it was a tape lift off an I-5 victim.

When he came in the next morning, Springer was studying the slide. He didn't say anything. A few hours later, she asked to see more.

She was amazed at the amount of physical evidence in the I-5 investigation—all those clothes that could potentially be so rich in trace evidence—and at the same time astounded that nothing had yet turned up. Experience had taught her that the most critical aspect of any trace case was deciding which of the hundreds, even thousands, of fibers, hairs, and other debris picked up in the tape lifts were relevant to the case. It was a long process of elimination that could take weeks, even months.

Streeter delivered to Springer's lab station several boxes of tape lifts. The lifts had been taken with 3-inch lengths of Scotch tape, then each had been secured to its own petri dish, sticky side down with the ends taped over the dish and covered with a glass lid. One by one, she began to slip the small, carefully labeled dishes under her $15,000 stereomicroscope, which gave her a startling, three-dimensional image of the evidence.

As Streeter had hoped, Springer soon had I-5 in her grasp—a serious flirtation, so far, while continuing to work her own expanding caseload.

Her first step in any trace evidence case was to take inventory of everything that had come off the victim, and group these materials into broad categories that could later be narrowed down. Since they had a strong suspect, she would next compare these findings with anything they had from the suspect and his environment, seeking exchange evidence.

She worked like a machine, with little wasted motion. She first viewed the I-5 tape lifts at low power—40 mag or so—to get the lay of the land. When she saw something that caught her eye, she used a tungsten needle and tweezers to remove the fiber and slip it onto its own microscope slide. Then, she really went to work, using increased power settings—she did most of her work between 200 and 400 amplification—and varying types of microscopes. She spent anywhere from four to eight hours analyzing a single fiber, but when she was finished she usually knew all there was to know—its burning point, its chemical makeup, the name of its manufacturer, etc.

In her third week on the job, Springer, who had that afternoon been examining the dozen or so tape lifts from Darcie Frackenpohl's dress, asked Streeter about the car Roger Kibbe was believed to have been driving at the time of the victim's abduction and murder.

"It's a white Hyundai," he said, not bothering at first to look up from his own work.

"Do you remember if the interior carpet was blue?"

Springer, unbeknownst to Streeter, made a habit of looking first for carpet fibers, which were easily recognizable because they were bigger than other fibers. When she looked at the end of a carpet fiber, its cross-section looked distinctly triangular, like a three-cornered block.

Streeter, with a look of astonishment, reacted as if his colleague had uncorked a dinner club magic trick and levitated the heavy lab table between them.

"Yes, it *was* blue," he said, his brow crinkling.

"I thought so," said Springer, turning back to her trusty microscope.

DETECTIVE Kay Maulsby hadn't heard a word from Roger Kibbe in the almost two months since she'd last visited him. Still, she returned to Rio Consumnes Correctional Center on March 23, 1988.

In their private interview room away from guards and other inmates, he seemed pleased to have the undivided attention of the attractive woman detective.

"Have you had any other visitors?" she asked.

"Harriet comes but she hasn't been this week yet," he said. "Steve doesn't visit me. He stays pretty busy with his work, you know."

"Are you depressed?"

"No, I'm not depressed."

"Have you thought about whether you're going to ask for any counseling while you're here?" she asked.

"I know I have some problems and it would probably be good for me to talk to someone. But I'm just gonna put in my time."

Maulsby told of driving to Ceres, south of Modesto, and seeing the location where his furniture-making business had been.

"What route did you use to commute?" she asked.

"I can't remember the name of the road." His guard had gone up. "I d-don't want to answer that."

She asked whether Harriet had found a place for them to live yet.

"No, she's gonna wait until I get out now. We'll find a place together in Sacramento."

Maulsby nodded casually as if the thought of that happy day didn't nauseate her. She waited until she could trust her voice.

The detective had visited another inmate three weeks earlier: Lora Heedick's boyfriend, James Driggers, who was serving out his robbery sentence at Norco, the state prison where San Joaquin detectives had interviewed Harriet Kibbe's sister, Helen Pursel, four months earlier. Lt. Ray Biondi insisted that Maulsby show a single photo of Kibbe to Driggers, who had previously failed to pick out the suspect from a photo lineup. She argued against showing one photo; if Driggers made the ID this time, it could be argued in court as being highly suggestive. Biondi said he didn't see Driggers ever being much of a witness, explaining he just wanted the assurance that "Kibbe is the guy who did Heedick even if we compromise Driggers as a witness." Maulsby had done as she was ordered. She explained to Driggers that she was going to show him a picture of a man and wanted to know if he'd ever seen him in the Modesto stroll area. Driggers looked for a few seconds at the image of a bearded Kibbe, and said he "looked a lot like the guy" who had taken his Lora but he couldn't be certain. "He has a beard and I don't remember the guy having a beard," said Driggers.

Since nothing else was working, Maulsby decided she'd try another approach with Kibbe.

"I know you've talked to a lot of detectives," she said. "Has anyone ever asked you straight out if you killed these women?"

She had heard stories of convicts claiming they would have confessed if only someone had asked them the question. She didn't want Kibbe at some point down the road to be able to say such a thing.

"No," he said. "They always beat around the bush."

"I'll ask you. Did you do it?"

Neither of them broke eye contact, and soon it became a colossal staredown.

Maulsby, determined not to be the first to look away, lived with the silence, his eyes boring into hers.

A minute passed, then two; they seemed like an eternity. Someone was mowing the lawn out in front of the administration building, and somewhere inside the walls a steam pipe hissed.

He broke first. "I can't answer that."

She leaned forward in her chair, closer to him than she had ever been. His face was an impassive mask.

"Roger, you can't even say that you *didn't do it?*"

His expression softened. The corners of his mouth curled as if he was going to smile, but then he caught himself. The moment was gone. He was unreadable again.

The interview was over.

Roger Kibbe was due to be released in thirty-six days.

———

AFTER criminalist Faye Springer found two blue carpet fibers in tape lifts from Darcie Frackenpohl's dress, Jim Streeter produced a floor mat that he had confiscated from Roger Kibbe's Hyundai.

Streeter had taken the mat—under authority granted police by the search warrant—because it had a dark red stain on it. When the stain tested negative for blood, Streeter had stored the mat with other I-5 evidence.

Springer plucked a fiber from the carpet mat and mounted it on a slide. Placing it under her stereomicroscope, she dialed in a magnification of 4x, its lowest power, and brought her eyes down to the binocular eyepiece; by focusing both eyes on a single image, she gained good depth perception and saw a distortion-free image.

Her first microscopic view of the car mat fiber caused a familiar stirring inside—one that she always got whenever she was close to finding a needle in the haystack.

She dialed 10x, then 20x, and worked her way up to the highest power, 65x. As she spun through the mag powers, she made handwritten notes and drawings; a running commentary of her observations would be critical documentation in the event that her testimony was required at a criminal trial.

When she was ready to study a cross-section of the fiber, she took it off the slide and impeded it in a swirl of clear, soft polypropylene substance that hardened almost immediately. Then, monitoring her work through the microscope, she made a thin slice with a special tool, cutting first through the epoxy and then the fiber. That slice she then placed on a separate slide and put it under a microscope to examine the fiber's internal structure.

She conducted the same examination of the blue fibers from Darcie's dress. When she got to the cross-section, she could see they were the same blue trilobular nylon weave developed years ago by Dupont because it hid dirt so well.

Springer was alone in the lab, so it was easy for her to do what came natural: stay quietly focused. In fact, unlike other criminalists, who sometimes donned headsets and listened to music or talk shows while working, she preferred quiet so she could concentrate. She credited her ability to remain at a microscope for so long without feeling motion sickness, as other researchers sometimes did, to having worked her way through college sorting tomatoes and cherries on a fast-moving assembly line. She had her sea legs.

By the time Streeter returned, late afternoon, Springer had worked for several hours on the fibers and knew exactly what she had.

"We have a match," she told Streeter.

She placed the slides containing the fibers in side-by-side microscopes. Streeter first looked at the one from the Hyundai mat. When he looked through the microscope with the fibers taken off the dress, he let out a low whistle.

"You can see they're the same color, shape, and type," she said, "but there's something else. The mat fiber and one of the fibers taken off the dress both have the same dark particles, shaped like footballs, on them."

Streeter hadn't noticed the particles.

"Do you know what they are?" he asked.

"Not yet."

"I also see on the fiber from the dress what might be a speck of red paint, although it's so tiny I can't be certain." Springer explained that the equipment at the DOJ lab couldn't get enough light into the particles or magnify them enough to analyze them sufficiently. She judged the dark particles to be something under 100 microns—smaller than a micro-chip—and the possible paint only two or three microns. What she was working with might well have been called *trace* trace evidence.

"But we have a match?"

Streeter wanted to be clear, as he intended to call detectives with the news.

"Oh, yeah," she said. "The fiber off the victim's dress matches the fiber from the Hyundai."

What Streeter had hoped would happen when he'd first heard that Riverside's famed trace evidence expert was coming to DOJ Sacramento was unfolding before him. Faye Springer had already gone several steps farther than anyone else had been able to with the I-5 evidence.

In the process, she was building a murder case.

CHAPTER TWENTY-ONE

Two weeks before Roger Kibbe was due to be released from county jail, Lt. Ray Biondi and Kay Maulsby showed up at criminalist Faye Springer's lab to review the evidence.

It was the first time Biondi had met Springer. He could see right away that she was totally absorbed in her work and not given to chitchat. While he griped about the bureaucratic snafus in the I-5 investigation, she waited him out. When he finished his whining, she launched into her forensic briefing.

Maulsby had had her first dealings with Springer ten days earlier when they visited several I-5 crime scenes; Springer had wanted to see them firsthand. In overalls and wearing latex gloves, she had collected dirt and plant samples, and they searched for clothing and any other evidence that might have been overlooked. Springer had told Maulsby during their *tour de murder* how she wished she could have been at the scenes while the bodies were still in place. Mistakes had been made by people who didn't know squat about trace evidence, Springer complained, not only the debacle with the pickup autopsy of Charmaine Sabrah but other careless screwups—like laying out Darcie Frackenpohl's dress on the road to better take a picture of it. Trace evidence lost at the scene, Springer explained, was trace evidence lost forever.

Since her success with the fiber evidence, Springer had been assigned to the I-5 investigation full-time, as her higher-ups realized they now had a trace case on their hands. Streeter, who had gladly stepped aside, had switched places with Springer—he was now consulting as needed.

Springer explained to Biondi and Maulsby that the strongest case they had against Kibbe, from a scientific standpoint, was the

Darcie Frackenpohl murder. She'd looked at tape lifts from the other cases and so far found no fibers or other significant items of trace evidence linking Roger Kibbe to the victims. Therefore, the criminalist had focused her efforts on Frackenpohl.

Lined up on a long lab table was an impressive stack of petri dishes containing tape lifts; Biondi thought there must be hundreds of them. The criminalist had separated out some to show the detectives. They looked at a magnified view of the similar blue fibers—the one from Kibbe's car mat and the two recovered from Darcie's dress.

Springer explained that the fibers off the dress were consistent with the fibers from the Hyundai. She told of the dark particles on two of the fibers that she'd not yet identified and the possible red paint speck on one of the fibers found on the dress.

As for hair evidence, Springer said she found two strands of hair that were similar to Kibbe's. She'd found a dark foreign hair among Stephanie's lighter pubic hairs combed out during the rape-kit exam by the pathologist. This hair proved to have several similarities to Kibbe's pubic hair samples. She'd also found a dark foreign hair on Darcie's dress that was similar to Kibbe's body hair exemplars.

"It could be a limb hair, which is too bad."

"Why's that?" Biondi asked.

"Limb hair has less inner structure and is harder to compare," Springer said.

Biondi knew that hair evidence was not at all like fingerprints because hair couldn't positively identify an individual. Forensic evidence in the Brown case, then, came down to the single hair and inconclusive blood typing, insufficient to persuade a district attorney to file murder charges. Every D.A. he'd ever met liked to file winning cases, not sure losers or even close calls. The fiber evidence in Frackenpohl was stronger, but was it enough?

As if Springer read his mind, she said, "Now for the really exciting stuff, guys."

She reloaded a microscope. "Take a look."

Biondi had no idea what he was looking at. Silvery and shiny, it had distinctive grains in alternating squares.

"That's a piece of the white cordage from the Frackenpohl scene," Springer said.

Once her eyes were focused, Maulsby saw what looked like tiny red spots on the glistening threads.

"Is that blood?" she asked.

"No," Springer said. "Paint. Lots more than on the fiber. See the way it's in little globs? You get that when paint is sprayed."

Biondi wondered where this was going.

Springer placed another slide under the other microscope, and stepped back.

Biondi saw more shiny threads and tiny red dots. For a moment, he thought that he was seeing the same cord.

"What's this, Faye?"

"A piece of the cordage from Tupelo," she said.

Maulsby and Biondi looked at each other.

"There's red paint on both?" Biondi asked.

"Not just red paint," said Springer. She explained that she had taken these slides down to her old lab in Riverside to use a very expensive ($275,000) piece of equipment not available at DOJ Sacramento: a scanning electron microscope so powerful it showed atom spacing in molecules. "I was able to determine that these particles are identical in both organic and inorganic composition. It's the same *identical* paint, and it's on all the cordage. All these cords were in the same environment when someone was spray-painting."

The detectives returned to their office elated; Springer had strengthened the cordage evidence about 1,000 percent. Biondi and the other older hands were amazed at the type of evidence she had developed. They all knew about trace evidence from training and textbooks, but it was something they rarely got from their own crime lab. The majority of murder cases went to court with only the basic physical evidence—the murder bullet matched the suspect's gun, fingerprints, blood type, etc. In a sizable number of successful cases, there was no lab-analyzed evidence at all.

In the I-5 investigation, all they had been able to say heretofore was that the pieces of common parachute cord were similar; now, Springer could show that the cordage from a murder scene and Kibbe's residence had been in the exact same place—perhaps a garage or storage locker—when someone was spraying red paint.

Early the next morning, Springer called Biondi with later-breaking news: Although the paint spill on the car floor mat—it was circular, suggesting someone had transported a dripping paint can—had proven not to be the source of the paint on the cordage, she'd found red paint on the two pieces of cordage from the Debra Guffie crime kit that identically matched the paint on the other pieces of cordage.

"I'm sitting here hugging my microscope," she said.

Biondi laughed. "Hug away. The next call I make is to a district attorney to see about a filing."

Biondi realized that this intense and dedicated criminalist, in town for all of two months, had managed to do what a dozen detectives hadn't been able to do in years.

Through microscopic evidence invisible to the naked eye, Faye Springer had deftly slipped a cord—actually, seven cords—around the neck of Roger Reece Kibbe.

"THIS ISN'T a good idea," said Detective Vito Bertocchini, warily eyeing the single-engine airplane being wheeled out of a garage attached to a custom ranch-style home at upscale Cameron Park, an El Dorado County mountaintop suburban enclave 30 miles west of Sacramento where home ownership also bought access to a private airstrip.

Detective Pete Rosenquist had been hearing Bertocchini complain the entire drive from downtown Sacramento, and he thought it was hilarious that such a big, tough guy could be humbled at the idea of winged flight.

"It's just a small airplane," Rosenquist said. "Nothing to worry about."

"I'd rather drive," Bertocchini said for the umpteenth time.

"We're here, partner. Let's do it."

It was early afternoon on April 27, 1988—D-Day for the I-5 investigation, with multiple operations set to go off simultaneously in various locales in two states.

Bertocchini and Rosenquist's assignment was to surprise Steve Kibbe, who was attending a cop school in Fallon, Nevada, with news of his brother's pending arrest in the murder of Darcie Frackenpohl. They were to solicit Steve's help—he was, after all, not just Roger's brother, but a sworn law enforcement officer. The hope was that Steve, with his brother's arrest for murder now imminent, would shore up what they already knew with information as to Roger's activities over the past couple of years, and also persuade Roger to talk to detectives about the I-5 murders.

At a strategy meeting held that morning in Sacramento to determine exactly who would do what and when that day, the El Dorado sheriff had offered to set up a flight into Nevada for the two San Joaquin detectives on a friend's plane. It would save them considerable driving time.

An El Dorado deputy had met them at the airport, and introduced them to the pilot who would be taking them to Fallon. Estimated flight time: forty-five minutes.

When the plane was ready to board, Rosenquist looked at Bertocchini and said, "Piece of cake." He climbed in the back and Bertocchini, less enthusiastic, joined him.

The pilot and El Dorado deputy climbed in front.

As the engine was warming, Bertocchini looked over the pilot's shoulder and saw he was flipping through a book. He caught the title: *Learning How to Fly a Cessna 172.*

"You're kidding, right?" Bertocchini asked.

The pilot turned toward him. "Oh, let me explain something to you guys. This isn't my plane. This is my neighbor's plane. My plane is about the same. I just have to get familiar with some of the controls."

"Where's your neighbor?" Bertocchini asked.

"He's down in Mexico on vacation. I don't think he'd care if we used it for this purpose."

"We're in a stolen plane," Bertocchini whispered.

"What the hell," said Rosenquist.

Rosenquist, a veteran flier, noticed when they took off that the nose was unusually high and the pilot seemed to be correcting for a strong crosswind.

"Pete, something's not right," Bertocchini said.

Rosenquist saw his partner had gone pasty white.

"Just a crosswind," he said reassuringly.

"Fuck! We're popping a wheelie and flying sideways all at once. We gonna go like this all the way to Fallon?"

A few minutes later they were flying over Lake Tahoe. Rosenquist tried to point out the beautiful view but Bertocchini was too busy helping keep the plane in the air.

"Look, look," he suddenly exclaimed, applying a death grip on Rosenquist's arm. "A red light!"

Sure enough, a console light had flashed on.

"What's up?" Bertocchini asked the pilot.

"What the hell is that?" the pilot said.

"Fuck, you don't *know?*" Bertocchini exploded.

"It says 'low voltage indicator,'" the pilot said calmly. "Could you look it up in that book behind my seat?"

Bertocchini found the owner's manual, and went to the index. He could hardly hold the book steady. After reading aloud a sentence on "Emergency procedures for the electric system," he gave up and practically flung the book up front for the pilot and El Dorado deputy to figure out.

Rosenquist couldn't help it; he was cracking up.

Bertocchini looked at him with a menacing stare. "You know what, Pete? When we go down, the first bullet is gonna go in this shit dump that's called a plane. The second bullet is going in you for making me get on it, and the third is going in El Dorado up there so they'll know who did it."

The red light stayed on the rest of the way. Shortly before landing, the pilot quietly explained—no doubt for Bertocchini's sake—that because Fallon was surrounded by restricted military airspace, they would have to "dive rather steeply" to the airport.

Bertocchini, his lips fixed, shook his head in utter disbelief.

On the ground, the burly detective somehow was the first one out.

The pilot got out with the engine still running.

"Why don't you guys go do what you're going to do and get back as soon as you can," he said. "I'm going to leave the plane running because the alternator is out. I don't know if I can get it started again if it shuts off."

Bertocchini, who had regained his confidence now that his feet were back on solid ground, swaggered up to the pilot and glared down at the shorter man.

"Fuck that plane," Bertocchini hissed ominously, "and fuck you. I ain't gettin' back on. I want nothing to do with you or your fuckin' neighbor's plane. And if you don't get out of here, I'm gonna arrest you for plane theft."

With that, Bertocchini spun on his heels and headed for the terminal, where they were to be met by the sheriff of Churchill County, Nevada.

"You serious?" Rosenquist asked when he caught up.

"Yes, I'm fucking serious."

"We might have a hard time getting back."

"I'll walk before I get on another plane today."

ANY HOPE Roger Kibbe may have had about going home early had to have been dashed when he saw an unsmiling Kay Maulsby and another stern-faced detective waiting for him. In no way could their presence be mistaken for a social call.

It was 4:20 P.M. on D-Day—a day before Kibbe was to be released from jail, and sixteen months after detectives had first brought him in for questioning in the I-5 murders.

An hour earlier Kibbe had been told by a guard to "roll up your stuff." He'd done so, and waited. A guard finally came and escorted him to the holding area, where Maulsby introduced him to El Dorado County Sheriff's Detective Jim Watson, who nodded curtly, then instructed Kibbe to put his hands out in front, palms down.

Kibbe did so, and Watson snapped on cuffs.

The detectives had already decided that if Kibbe pressed them as to where they were going, they'd simply say "downtown to talk." But the only thing Kibbe wanted to know was if he could call his wife.

Watson refused.

"Maybe later," Maulsby added. She didn't want him to go into complete shutdown as she knew he could do.

They exited the jail into the brilliant sunshine of a crisp California spring day; a homicide detective on either side of Roger Kibbe, who wore jeans, a royal-blue polo shirt, brown corduroy jacket, and tan boots. He had kept his salt-and-pepper beard, which was neatly trimmed.

Few words were spoken during the twenty-five-minute drive to downtown Sacramento, none by Kibbe. They parked, entered the sheriff's department building through a locked back door, and went up the three flights of stairs to the Homicide Bureau.

Kibbe was placed in interview room 3. A remote video camera was activated along with an audiotape machine.

After a few minutes alone in the room, Kibbe was joined by Watson, who had come in from South Lake Tahoe that morning. Because it was his case—a first-degree murder charge had been filed by the El Dorado County district attorney and an arrest warrant signed by an El Dorado judge—he was given first shot at the suspect.

The detective advised Kibbe of his Miranda rights. Kibbe acknowledged he understood his rights, but did not waive them. He again asked to call his wife. He explained that Harriet was planning to visit him that night at Rio Consumnes. He didn't want her to make the drive for nothing. "She has the number of a lawyer, too," he added.

Watson and the other detectives had already discussed the likelihood that Kibbe would invoke his rights as he had previously. Aware that once an attorney came into the picture they would have no more opportunity to learn anything from Kibbe, the detectives had decided they would proceed with their questioning anyway. Once again, however, anything he told them would probably be inadmissible.

Watson was unsuccessful in getting Kibbe to talk.

The proceedings aired on a closed-circuit television in Lt. Ray Biondi's office, where Biondi, Maulsby, and Stan Reed huddled around the monitor, watching the show and discussing strategy.

Biondi offered, "Roger's a real RV"—cop slang for a self-contained suspect who stayed calm and didn't say much. The veteran detective had seen it before: When a murder suspect is brought in for questioning, an innocent man will pace and fret, while a guilty suspect will look like he's about to fall asleep.

When Watson emerged from the interview room, Biondi informed him that Vito Bertocchini had called. "Steve is willing to talk to Roger.

They're a mile or two away from a sheriff's substation. They'll call when they arrive."

Maulsby decided to give it a try. She went into the interview room, closed the door, and sat down opposite Kibbe. It was a familiar position for them both, but the dynamics had changed. Previously, he had seemed bemused and coy, as if he thought he could get away with something. Now, he looked solemn and worried.

"I know you want to get in touch with Harriet," she began. "I tried but can't reach her."

Kibbe perked up.

"Would your second choice be Steve?"

Kibbe nodded; he looked suspicious, but also cautiously hopeful it was a genuine offer.

"We'll bring a phone in here for you," Maulsby said. She stood and opened the door. "We're ready for the call to Steve whenever you are," she announced.

Then she sat back down.

"You want the house number?" he asked.

"I think they have the numbers. As soon as they get him on the line, they'll bring a phone in."

"You can stand next to me," Kibbe said.

Maulsby looked at him. He was doing his "Sad Sack" routine, seemingly so inept and vulnerable that it was difficult seeing him as a smart, conniving, smart-as-a-fox serial killer.

Roger Kibbe was handed the phone at 5:55 P.M.

"Hey, Roger," said Steve Kibbe.

"Yeah."

"I'm at the Fallon Police Department."

"You're where?"

"Fallon. In the middle of the desert. I was contacted here by two detectives. I know what's happening. I know what went down."

"Okay."

"How you doing?"

"I'm doing fine."

"You know what's happening?"

"They already more or less pointed the stick at me."

"What room are you in right now? I mean, are we talking alone or do you have people there with you?"

"I got Kay right here in front of me. She said she can't wander very far. I'm in one of those little rooms. I don't know if this is being taped or what."

"Is Kay listening to you talk to me?"

"Yeah, she can hear me."

"You know what we talked about at the very beginning of this thing?"

"Yeah."

"I'm going to ask you one more time."

"Okay."

"And I want you to tell me straight up. Don't fuck with me, Roger."

"Right."

"Tell me straight up and you don't have to tell her what we're talking about. Just talk to me."

"I know what you're going to say."

"I gotta know," Steve said. "I told you this before."

"I know that."

"Just answer me yes or no. Don't screw with me, Roger. No matter how bad it is, I've got to know."

"Okay. Well, the answer is no."

"I've seen the reports, Roger."

"I know you have."

"And I've seen the evidence."

"Uh-huh."

"And I support you no matter what. I want you to know that."

"I realize that."

"No matter what, we're still family."

"I know that."

"I'm heading home now. I'm about two hours away. I've gotta have some game plan. I'm going to need your help. Don't make a blistering fool out of me. I don't want to be blindsided."

"Okay."

"Roger, talk to me. I'm your brother."

"Will you tell me something?" Roger asked.

"Yes, I'll tell you anything."

"What do you know?"

"I know what's going before the judge. I know the evidence that they've recovered. I didn't know until this afternoon that they've got physical evidence."

"Do I or do I not get an attorney?"

"Yep, you'll probably have a whole row of attorneys in front of you. I'm talking to you as your brother, and it doesn't look good."

"One more thing," Roger said. "You remember a while back I told you about a credit card? Think about it."

"My mind is in a fog."

"About cashing it in."

"Yes."

"Remember what we discussed about it?"

"Yes. Don't"

"I don't think I have to say any more then."

"Don't do it, Roger. Don't do it. You're going to hurt everybody."

"They're already hurt."

"You're going to make it worse. Do you hear me?"

"Yes."

"Goddammit, if you do it, I'll come down there and I'll dog-shit kick you up alongside the head. Don't you do it."

"Am I going to have a chance to see you?"

"No, you're not going to have a chance to see me as long as you're thinking and talking like that."

"I'm not talking like that right now."

"If you're even thinking about doing it, no, you're not going to see me."

"Okay."

"If you're going to stand tall and be a man about it, I'll be there. But if you're going to take the coward's way out, I don't want nothing to do with you, Rog. You can't do that to me. You don't go up there and goddamn swing by the light. Don't do it. That's foolish and stupid and all you're going to do is prove to everybody that you did it."

"All right. I understand."

"Don't let me down, Roger. I love you."

WHEN detectives Vito Bertocchini and Pete Rosenquist had pulled Steve Kibbe out of a classroom at a Fallon community college and advised him of his brother's pending arrest formurder, he had not acted surprised.

He had known about the murder investigation from the beginning, of course. Beyond that, the detectives thought Steve must surely have harbored his own suspicions. However, they found him still believing in his brother's innocence.

"If all you have against Roger is a circumstantial case," Steve said, "then I don't think he did it. I just don't feel Roger is the type to murder anyone."

Steve said he and his other brother, Jack, used to "always beat up" Roger when they were growing up, and that Roger was never one to fight back. Steve couldn't see such a passive kid growing up to be a serial killer.

Bertocchini asked Steve if he knew about Roger, at age fifteen, stealing women's clothing in the neighborhood and cutting up lingerie.

Steve denied any knowledge of the incidents.

"Do you recall Roger having a black eye last year in the latter part of August?" asked Bertocchini. It had come out in several background interviews that Roger had sported a shiner around the time of Darcie Frackenpohl's abduction. Detectives theorized that she had fought hard for her life.

Steve remembered Roger's black eye but not the exact date. "He said he'd gotten involved in a fight at a video arcade place."

Steve went on to say that he and Roger had taken long walks together since Roger had become a suspect in the I-5 investigation. "I've asked him if he was responsible for these murders and he denies it. If Roger did these things, I think he'd tell me."

Bertocchini decided it was time to lower the boom. "Look, we don't have strictly a circumstantial case," he said. "We've got strong physical evidence."

Only after Bertocchini detailed that evidence—specifically, the cordage and fibers—did Steve Kibbe seem ready to accept the unthinkable.

It was, Bertocchini and Rosenquist would agree, as if Steve Kibbe was straddling a fence, caught between wanting to be a good cop and a loving brother.

The detectives were convinced that the murder of Darcie Frankenpohl—as well as other I-5 victims—had been committed by Roger on the way to or from visits to Steve's place on the eastern shore of Lake Tahoe. Steve confirmed that Roger visited his residence "every now and then," and that when he did, he spent the night.

A murder investigation had taken Rosenquist to Lake Tahoe years before, and he'd met Steve. He remembered Steve's offhanded comment at the time about all the Jane Does in the area: "We find dead girls alongside the road all the time." Rosenquist now wondered how many of them had been Roger's work—cruel amusement for him on his way to see Steve or on the way home. Rosenquist also couldn't help but wonder if the homicide-detective brother had even unknowingly investigated a murder that had been committed by his killer brother.

Bertocchini had thought about what it might be like to have evidence of murder pointing to his own sibling. He'd decided he could still love his brother, but that he would not confuse love with the urgent need to get a serial killer off the street and behind bars. He was sure he'd feel that way even if he wasn't a cop, but because he carried a badge and was sworn to protect life, he didn't know how he could do otherwise. Bertocchini had no doubt: he would give up his brother in a heartbeat if he believed him to be a murderer.

In view of the physical evidence, Steve had agreed to speak to Roger on the phone and ask him once more whether he had committed murder. After their talk, Steve told the detectives it hadn't been a private conversation on the other end, and speculated that Roger might feel freer to speak his mind if Kay Maulsby wasn't in the same room. They arranged it, and a few minutes later the brothers were back on the phone together. Their second conversation, like the first one, was taped at the Homicide Bureau.

"Roger?"

"Yeah."

"I was halfway out the door and I told them it wasn't a private conversation," Steve said. "So, they told me they'd get Kay out of the room."

"Well, the door is shut right now and I'm in the room by myself."

"Okay. Now talk to me."

"What do they have?" Roger asked.

"They have physical evidence. Enough to go to court and convict you."

"You know, I was just saying to myself, as much as I love you and care about you—and I'm proud of you—"

Roger was weeping.

"Don't start crying," Steve said. "Talk to me."

"But I sat there telling myself, dammit, he lied to me."

"I didn't lie to you. They lied to me."

"That's all I could tell myself. I couldn't think of anything else."

"I didn't lie to you, Roger. I told you everything I knew right up till I called you today. I'm in this class down in Fallon. They made contact about three o'clock to bring me down to the station. Okay?"

"What's going to happen?"

"You're going to be charged with homicide. I don't know how many counts."

"Yeah."

"I saw it in black and white. They opened the books and they just let me have it. It's not defendable, Roger. Remember I told you a long time ago, no matter how bad, we'll stand together on this damn thing? I just don't want to be blindsided. I don't like surprises."

"What do I do?"

"Roger, now I got to talk to you like a brother. What I want you to do first of all is get rid of that silly notion about your credit card. I want that gone."

"Okay."

"That'll just muddle everything up."

"Yeah."

"In my own mind, I've got to know," Steve said. "I know you couldn't talk earlier, but I gotta know. I don't know if I could hold it back if I know. I don't know what I'm going to do with it once I know, but you and I've been through too much shit in the last forty-some-odd years to let this go by."

Roger sighed heavily.

"You've never held back before," Steve said.

"How soon can I see an attorney?"

"I don't know. I don't know when you're going to be arraigned. Probably tomorrow. They'll read the complaint and it'll be all documented. Once you're before a judge, because of the seriousness of the offense, they won't even allow you to enter a plea but they'll go ahead and appoint you to the public defender. You ain't got no goddamn money, I know that. I ain't got no money."

"I know that."

"And we can't go to Dad."

"No."

"So, it will be back to the public defender's office and hopefully it won't be the same swizzle dick you had before."

"Dad will get ahold of this somehow," Roger said, "and it'll kill him."

"I know it will. I'm not going to call Dad yet."

"I gotta ask the detectives here if I can see Harriet tonight."

"From what I understand, Harriet is not in the best frame of mind right this minute."

"Of course not."

"She's going to be ricocheting off the wall."

"I'm the only one who could calm her down."

"I've seen the reports," Steve said. "I know what the evidence is. Yes, I was deceived. I did not lie to you. I revealed to you a lot of information that I was privy to that they should have told you but they didn't. I kept you posted. Everything I knew."

"I know that."

"So when you said that I lied to you and I let you down—wrong, wrong."

"I'm sorry that I said that."

"What can I do to help you now?" Steve asked.

"I don't think there's anything you can do."

"What can I expect?"

"You want me to be honest with you?"

"Yep."

"I don't know, Steve."

"All right. You know where I'll be."

"Where?"

"I'll be at home. I can't go back to work because they've already called my boss. I'm going to take a leave of absence."

"For how long?"

"I'm taking a month."

"I hope this doesn't endanger or ruin your career."

"I'm afraid it has, Roger. I'm afraid it has."

"Is that why you're taking a leave of absence."

"Yep."

"You were asked to?"

"Yep."

"I'm sorry. I know that doesn't do any good. All I can say, Steve, is that I'm sorry."

"I'll talk to you later."

Detective Steve Kibbe had done all he was going to do to aid the I-5 serial murder investigation. He went home to his wife and children, took his leave of absence, and struggled to come to grips with what his brother had done.

EL DORADO Detective Jim Watson was the first to go back into the interview room with Roger Kibbe after his telephone conversations with his brother.

"Roger, I hate beating around the bush. I'll come right to the point. After we're through here, I'm going to take you to Placerville and place you under arrest for the murder of Darcie Frackenpohl, a young lady who these past few months I've learned just about everything there is to learn about."

Kibbe showed no reaction.

"At this point, we've developed enough evidence to charge you and take you to trial for her murder. I need to know, for myself, about Darcie. She's got a mother and a fifteen-year-old brother who need to know about her, too. I'm sure you don't know Darcie by name. She's someone who got taken by the sights of the big city and by a young man who influenced her into coming down here and working the streets. For some reason, she happened to be out in the street that particular night in August. For some reason, you happened to be on the same street. I just want to understand how this young lady ended up dead on the side of a hill outside South Lake Tahoe. I need to understand this."

"Do you know where my wife is?"

"At this particular time, I don't," Watson said. "I can tell you we are serving a search warrant on the Hyundai as we speak. I'm sure your wife is worried about you."

"It's not so much that she's worried about me. I need to talk to her."

"Tell me what you're feeling right now, Roger."

"I'm not like that. I'm not gonna tell you that. That's not my way."

"What is your way, Roger?"

"I'm thinking about my wife. There's some things I'd like to get straight with her, so she can understand what's going on."

"Is she going to be able to understand this?"

"I don't know. But I want her to hear it from me."

"I don't need your confession to go to court," Watson said. "We have evidence you left behind at the murder scene. Evidence at your house. Evidence we found at the golf course. I'm just here to get some answers so that I can tell Darcie's mother what happened."

Silence.

"Give me something to tell her, Roger."

"Before I say anything, I want to talk to my wife."

"I understand."

"Can I talk to her privately? Somewhere we can't be heard or taped? Just a private conversation?"

"It can be arranged. Give me her number."

He handed over a slip of paper with two numbers.

"They're both at work, one at her desk and the other on a recorder when she's gone."

"It's almost seven o'clock," Watson said. "Is she normally at work this time of night?"

"Yeah. She's a workaholic."

Ten minutes after Watson left, Detective Stan Reed, the most experienced and dogged interviewer in the Bureau, entered the room. They were playing tag team and Reed was up.

The detective held the slip of paper with Harriet's phone numbers. "Talking to Harriet is going to benefit you and your wife, not us," he said. "The officers who've been in here talking to you have been up front with you."

"Yeah, they've been more than nice."

"They arranged a phone call to your brother."

"I appreciated that."

"We'll be more than happy, if we can get something in return, to arrange a phone call to Harriet."

Kibbe paused. "That'd be nice."

"What could I get in return, Roger?"

Long silence.

"Probably what you want," Kibbe finally answered.

"Okay, let's explore this," Reed said. "How about admitting that you're guilty. If, in your opinion, you are."

"What do you want me to say?"

"I'm going to show you some photographs, Roger. Tell me if you recognize these people."

Reed laid out photographs of seven young women; most were smiling, almost all had long hair, every one of them was dead and gone.

"No, I don't."

"You're presently under arrest for the murder of this young woman," Reed said, holding up a high school yearbook picture of Darcie.

"That's what you say."

"I'm certain there's more than these seven people, but these are the cases I'm interested in. You're going to have to commit yourself to telling me the remainder of the story once you've talked to Harriet. I might even consider a face-to-face meeting for you with her."

"You're showing me pictures I don't recognize."

"Well, that's not true. Let me show you the face of an angel." Reed reached for another snapshot. "This is Stephanie Brown. She was beautiful, wasn't she?"

The detective found another picture in a stack he'd brought into the room with him. "Do you recognize this area here, down off Highway 12 next to a cornfield?"

"Doesn't look familiar to me."

"How about that drainage ditch?"

"Never seen it before."

"Never seen it before? You're having difficulty making any kind of commitments here. How about this isolated road along Highway 50? Do you recognize the spot?"

"Uh-uh."

"This is where you left the body of this young lady," Reed said, holding up Darcie's picture again.

"Doesn't look familiar."

"Do you recognize this?"

Reed was pointing to a picture of the nylon cordage found at Tupelo during execution of the search warrant.

"That's 550 nylon cord," Kibbe said without hesitation.

"Which is used for what?"

"Can be used for anything."

"What did you use it for?"

"Fixing and repairing things."

"Then it's true that you had some of this cord at your home when we did the search warrant?"

"Sure."

Another picture.

"You had this piece of cord tied between two dowels when you assaulted the prostitute," Reed said.

"I don't think I did."

"It's just positively factual. I mean, there's no denying it. It was in your crime kit that had your fingerprints on it. You've been convicted of that. And is it not true that you used to be or still are a sky diver?"

"Used to be."

"Is that when you came by this cord?"

"Uh-huh."

"You also, Roger, used this very same rope on Darcie." He held up a picture of cordage from the Frackenpohl scene. "And that rope that you left there is identical to the rope we took from your house during the search warrant. Absolutely, positively the same rope. We're way beyond where we were when we talked to you the first time. It's to the point that you need to come forward and be honest.

"Now give me something, Roger, and I'll arrange for you to talk to Harriet. Give me everything and I'll arrange for you to have a contact visit with her. I'm willing to give you something in return. But I want a lot from you because you owe us a lot. You owe the families of these girls a lot. That baby that was waiting to be nursed by his mother, Charmaine. You owe that baby a lot, too. This pretty lady, Karen, who had just kissed her little daughter goodbye before you took her out and did what you did to her and cut her throat. You owe her, too."

Kibbe seemed unmoved by the speech.

"Let's talk some more about the cord. There is microscopic evidence on the cords, things that can't be seen with the naked eye. All the cords had been in contact with red paint. The red paint is identical, okay? These criminalists nowadays can do amazing things."

Kibbe was listening, but not reacting.

Reed wasn't deterred. Part of his strategy was to let Kibbe know just how dead-bang they had him so he'd begin to think that he had nothing to lose by filling in the gaps.

"You don't appear to be a violent individual," Reed said. "Just speaking to you, I would say that Roger Kibbe could not do this. But we have the physical evidence that says Roger can and did do these things."

Reed sat back. He'd noticed that even when Kibbe wasn't responsive, he kept eye contact.

"Are there two sides to Roger Kibbe?" Reed asked. "Everybody, I think, has two sides. They have a side that's acceptable to society and a darker one that's not. Most of us, fortunately, can control the side that's not acceptable. We suppress our fantasies. We suppress a lot of anger. But I think at some point, maybe on April 20th, 1986, when you picked up Lora Heedick in your white Maverick, or maybe a long time before, you lost it. You could no longer control that dark side."

This whole exercise would have been more frustrating for Reed had he not known what it was that Kibbe very badly wanted, what it was that he would deal for.

"Okay, give me one of the cases," Reed said. "At least admit your guilt, because there's no doubt about it, is there? Give me that. You give me that and I'll arrange a phone call with Harriet. You give me the thirty-five cases or whatever it is that you're really responsible for and I'll arrange for you to stay in this room alone with Harriet."

Thirty-five was probably a pretty good number, Reed figured. Given Kibbe's age it could be higher. A man didn't suddenly roll out of bed one morning at forty-eight years of age and become a serial killer; not when he'd done his clothes-cutting apprenticeship at age fifteen. No, this one had crossed the line a long time ago.

"I'm not prepared to go out of my way to bring Harriet here if I don't get what I want. Are you prepared to make that commitment? Are you prepared to be totally honest with me? Are you clear in your mind what I want?"

"Yeah."

"And it's clear in my mind what you want."

"I wanna see her."

"I know you want to see Harriet. I can deliver that. Can you deliver what I want? Do you have the heart to be honest with me?"

"Yeah, I do."

"Okay. You could give me the missing property of one of these women. Tell me where to find it."

"If I tell you where something is and you go out and find it, that's it. I'm not gonna get my visit with Harriet."

"That's wrong. Put the carrot out in front of the rabbit. I'm the rabbit, and believe me, I will want the rest of it. I want the whole story. I want the truth."

Reed waited, but Kibbe stayed quiet. The detective sensed some back-sliding. It seemed a good time to take a break.

"I'm going to go talk to my lieutenant to see what he thinks about a visit from Harriet. Can I bring you some coffee or water?"

"No."

"Okay, you sit here and think about it."

Reed sauntered into the office, where Biondi, Maulsby, and Watson were watching the television monitor.

Kibbe seemed to be staring at the floor. Then, he leaned over and placed his head heavily into his hands. It was a defeated, exhaustive motion. He was wearing down. It was going on 9:00 P.M.—they'd been at it for four hours.

"Want to come in with me, Kay?" Reed asked.

"Sure," she said.

It was a special invitation. Reed, who liked working alone, recognized her special relationship with Kibbe after all her jailhouse visits.

The business Reed had handed out about going in to check with his lieutenant was pure moonshine—the way a car salesman goes to "check with the sales manager," then comes back and employs imaginary edicts to try to shape the best deal. It was all about posturing and dickering and endurance. Stanley Reed would have made one hell of a car salesman.

Back inside, Reed broke the bad news to Kibbe.

"The lieutenant says no."

"Fucker," Kibbe said.

"He says I can't bring Harriet in to see you because you haven't given us anything yet. Let me ask a stupid question. Why do you want to see Harriet?"

"I want to talk to her."

"Do you feel an obligation to tell it first to Harriet?" asked Maulsby.

"Yeah, I do."

Maulsby's next question was a gem. "Do you feel like once you've opened up and been honest with her then it might be easier to be honest with us?"

Kibbe looked at them both before answering. "If I can have her, you can have the whole can of worms."

"Will you give us that commitment?" Reed asked. "You sure as hell haven't got anything to lose."

"I have nothing to lose."

Reed was glad Kibbe agreed. They had made progress.

"All you have to do is give us something."

"You have what I want," Kibbe said, "and I have what you want. It's a Mexican standoff."

"I need some commitments from you. Can you tell me where the rest of the cord is? Can you give me that?"

"Yep, I can do that after I see Harriet."

"Can you give me the source of the red paint on the cords?" Reed asked.

"Yeah."

Interrogation was tedious, tiring work, especially with someone who didn't open up or talk much. But Reed was feeling a second wind now that Kibbe seemed to be moving in the direction of giving something up to get his visit with Harriet.

"Okay," Reed said. "Can you identify these girls?"

The photos were spread out on the table.

"There are two of them in there that I don't even know," Kibbe said. He'd looked at the images before when Reed had first put them down on the table, and now he looked again.

"I-I never saw her before in my life," Kibbe said, taking a quick stab at one of the photos.

"So you won't be able to give me that?"

"I can't give you something I don't know."

"Okay, I was simply asking. What is the other one you can't give me?"

"Did you say there was a black woman?"

"Black or Asian. A Jane Doe from Nevada. This is an artist's reconstruction of her face since she was so decomposed."

"I've never had any dealings with a black or Asian woman," Kibbe said in his monotone voice that never wavered no matter what the topic. "White girls only."

"White girls only," Reed repeated sans inflection. "Will you be able to give me details about this girl?"

Reed pointed to Stephanie Brown.

"After I see Harriet."

"Will you be able to give me details of this girl?"

Charmaine Sabrah.

"After I see Harriet."

"Will you be able to give me details of this girl?"

Lora Heedick.

"After I see Harriet."

"Will you be able to give me details of this girl?"

Darcie Frackenpohl.

"After I see Harriet."

"Will you be able to give me details of this girl?"

"She's in Nevada?"

"No, this one's in Nevada."

"I thought you said—"

"Excuse me, I'm confused now. This one was Nevada. But this one was along the freeway outside of Placerville."

"Look, this one and this one," Kibbe said a bit impatiently, jabbing at two photos to clear up the confusion, "I know nothing about."

"Okay, but the other five pictures here you can tell me about?"

"You said there was one girl that had her throat cut?"

"Right."

"Which one's that?"

"Right here."

Karen Finch.

"I know nothing about that."

"Okay, you know nothing about this girl."

"Yeah. Never saw her before."

"Are there other cases we haven't talked about that you can give me?"

"What have you got—four?"

"Yes. Brown, Sabrah, Heedick, and Frackenpohl."

"No, those are the only ones."

"So there aren't others I don't know about?"

"No."

"Are there rapes or other crimes involving women we haven't talked about?"

"Rape?" Kibbe seemed a bit offended. "No. I picked up I don't know how many girls, but I always let them go."

"So, there's four victims you'll be able to tell me about after you talk to Harriet?"

"That's right."

"I have your word on it."

"You have my word."

"And can you give us the personal property of any of these women?" Maulsby interjected.

The IDs and purses of these four women had never been found. Also, in Sabrah, there was jewelry missing. Maulsby remembered Carmen Anselmi's description of her daughter's jewelry: dangly black earrings, an imitation pearl necklace, and a diamond ring—a solitary stone attached to a thin gold band.

"I can give you one," Kibbe said.

"I'm really tempted to take your word," Reed said. "I really am. Tell me again, Roger. We have your word that once you have your visit with Harriet, you will discuss in all honesty and the greatest detail as possible these things that you say you know about."

"That's what I told you."

"You're not gonna just say that you read about them in the paper or some bullshit? It's got to be all the way."

"And the property of at least one," Maulsby said.

"Uh-huh."

"May I have your hand on it?" Reed said.

The detective and killer shook hands.

A FEW minutes past 10:30 P.M. that night, Harriet Kibbe climbed into the backseat of an unmarked police car, where Roger was waiting for her.

They were alone—surrounded by detectives sitting in and standing around other unmarked cars—in the parking lot of Bradshaw's family restaurant at Madison Avenue and Highway 80 in northeast Sacramento, ten miles from downtown.

Harriet was exhausted, sad, and angry. It had been that kind of day since detectives descended on her at work around 3:00 P.M. with a search warrant for her car. Her Hyundai had been impounded; she was told it was going to be processed for evidence again and returned in a day or two. She had found a friend to take her home; the same friend had brought her to the rendezvous with Roger.

She had, in the last seven or eight hours, come to the realization that she'd seriously deluded herself into thinking things would return to some kind of normalcy when Roger got out. She had reasoned it would be possible because detectives hadn't been knocking on her door these past months. Things had settled down. Maybe they had other suspects; maybe they'd even found the real killer.

She had missed Roger during his incarceration, and had enjoyed their twice-weekly jailhouse visits. He had seemed determined, after his latest run-in with the law for his shameless stupidity in picking up a prostitute, to get back on track with a good job and stay out of trouble. She had intended to give him, and their marriage, another try, and had been counting the days until he would be released.

They had observed, apart, their thirteenth wedding anniversary six days earlier with a promise to celebrate in person when he got out. She would make a nice dinner. They might even take in a show. She had so desperately wanted things to be normal. For her to take him in her arms, tell him everything would be all right. To have him take her the way he used to, strong and virile; it was the only time she could really let go and be completely submissive. Yes, she had missed him. They had been through a lot the past couple of years, but she thought there was still time.

Roger's handcuffs had been removed.

They clasped hands like frightened children.

Then, without any adornment at all, he told her. He named names but they meant nothing to Harriet. Four, maybe five. By then, he was bawling. He added at the end, "I'm sorry," like a bad boy who had been caught with his hand in the cookie jar before supper.

Harriet went limp.

She had believed his lies, every single one. She had continued to ask him, in her darkest moments, whether he knew anything at all about the dead women. Always, even in jail, he had said no. He had denied everything, until this very moment.

She had believed his story about the prostitute—he claimed she had lied to police and committed perjury. Harriet had not attended the trial because Roger wanted it that way, therefore she'd known none of the sordid details. She had simply taken his word. For the last year and a half she had believed in his innocence with all her heart.

And now he had told her the awful truth.

He was a killer, and she felt like a fool.

When he had gone to jail, she had come to visit him early on with a plan: she and Steve would team up and go out and find the real I-5 killer. She would pretend to be a broken-down motorist, alone, and Steve would be nearby to catch the guy. Roger had said, "Don't do that." She thought he had said so because he didn't want her to get hurt.

She had never known anyone who had killed. What did a murderer look like? The only vision she could conjure up was the wild-eyed Charles Manson. He was a murderer, yes. He *looked* like one. But Roger? Her shy, timid husband had driven around, picked up women, and killed them with his bare hands?

She tried to release his hand but wasn't even sure if she'd done so because she couldn't feel her limbs.

Harriet broke down, and cried with her husband.

LATER that evening, Roger Kibbe reneged.

"Where's the victim's property you said you'd be telling us about?" asked Detective Kay Maulsby.

"I have no idea," Kibbe said.

"Do you have any intention of telling us anything?" Detective Stan Reed asked.

"No."

Reed was doing a slow burn. They had fucked up, all of them, by not setting up a tape recorder in the car where Roger and Harriet had talked for forty minutes. It had been a huge mistake because now Kibbe was backing out of the deal.

"You're telling me that you're not a man of your word and that your word didn't mean diddly-squat?" Reed asked.

"I guess that's what it comes down to."

"None of this is admissible in court," Reed said. "Tell us about Lora. Or about Stephanie or Charmaine or Darcie. Tell us so we can tell their families."

"I don't know anything."

It was midnight. Except for the trip out for the meeting with Harriet, Kibbe had been in this room for seven hours. He had gotten what he wanted, and now he was back to being an RV. He knew what most guilty suspects didn't know: the less you tell the cops, the better off you are.

Reed stood, looking down on Kibbe.

"Well," the detective said, "I hope they punch your fucking ticket, because obviously you have no remorse."

At 3:15 A.M. on April 28, 1988, Roger Kibbe was booked into El Dorado County Jail on the charge of murder.

HARRIET KIBBE paid the fee and drove into the landfill dump not far from the cabin she had just cleaned out on her way to live with old friends who would have her.

Her life was in shambles. She had already visited Roger in jail in South Lake Tahoe barely forty-eight hours after his backseat confession. She was drawn to him like a moth to the flame; wanting and needing more information, but uncertain as to whether it would help or hurt. Roger had orchestrated their tryst in the police car for her benefit—she realized and appreciated that. After he had so clearly spoken the truth to her, perhaps for the first time in a long time, she had many questions she wanted answered. Or did she? Did she really want to know? Would the details help rid her of all the ugly pictures that kept running through her mind, or would they only make for more horror movies? She had sat studying his face through the glass partition that separated them. He looked drawn and tired; his color was not good.

Since his confession, her worst fear was that she had done this to him. Had he become who he became because of her? Because of their marriage? He hadn't killed anyone before they met; he said not. She accepted his word on it, which meant she hadn't been so blinded when they first met as not to see something that important. But that he became a killer during their time together only added to her feelings of guilt. She had been angry, she had been stubborn, she had been a miserable wife. She had failed him, that much was clear. Had she also helped push him over the edge?

"I'm sorry," she had said tearfully.

It wasn't her fault, he said.

Where did things go so wrong? she wondered aloud.

She had a vision of them living as husband and wife in one room, a room she knew about, but a room where their life together had become a sham because Roger had another room where he lived a major part of his life alone; a secret room filled with violence, murder, and ghosts. He had thrown open the door now, allowing her to peek inside for the firsttime. But did she want to go any further? Did she really want to see what he had done in that other room?

She assured herself she would have left him in a minute had she known he was a murderer. And yet, knowing what she now knew, she had sat there on the other side of the glass, looking into his eyes, talking to him through a telephone receiver, trying to figure things out. If she wouldn't leave him now, when would she? When she wasn't crying, she had gone quiet for long periods, which was unusual for her, and then the opposite: rambling about small things. In between, she asked her questions.

"How did you kill them?"

He had lifted his leg and pointed to his calf.

She interpreted it to mean he'd used their nylons.

"How did you take them such a long way in the car?"

"Tied them up and gagged them."

He admitted to her that he had been so quick to give away their Maverick because it might link him to murder.

"So then you used the Hyundai," Harriet said. "*My* car."

They had managed such exchanges in small doses, remaining, for the most part, fairly detached. The next minute, she was telling him her plans to clean out the cabin and their storage space. It was then he had asked her to do something for him. She couldn't recall him asking her for a favor in a long time. *If only he had asked for what he needed sooner*, she had thought, *things might have ended differently*.

Harriet pulled up next to a mountain of trash, then backed up as close as possible. She stepped from the car, opened both back doors, and popped the trunk lid.

She unloaded quickly, trying not to look at the stuff she was throwing out. Each item represented, in a way, another dead dream. They had all been part of a life, *their* life, and now were no longer needed or could no longer be tolerated. In only a few years, she had gone from owning a home and running her own business to a small apartment that came with a menial job to now living out of suitcases so as to stay mobile and be less of an inconvenience to others. She was living life backward.

She'd first cleaned out the storage space on Drake's Hill Drive in Rancho Cordova, 20 miles east of Sacramento. It was there they had stored a lot of their things after they'd been fired from Public Storage five months earlier. The space had not ever been searched by police because they didn't know about it. She'd found what she was looking for right away. He'd told her it would be in the red pouch where he kept his skydiving records.

At the bottom of the bag had been the solitary diamond ring he wanted her to get rid of. She held it in her palm. The diamond was about half a carat, although it looked larger because it was set in a thin gold band. He claimed he had stolen it from neighbors in Oakley who had given him the key to their house while they were away so he could water the plants and feed the dog. Was that the truth?

She turned, and threw it into the trash heap.

When she got to his sneakers, she hesitated. They were his favorite, a two-tone gray. He used to wear them all the time but hadn't in a while. She had found them in a camper shell not far from the cabin, which had been searched by police shortly after Roger's arrest for murder. But the cops had missed the camper shell, and the shoes were in the narrow closet, right where he said to look for them.

They had two or three red spots on them. Was it paint or blood? She couldn't tell, and didn't want to know.

She was running on instinct now, the powerful instinct to protect, and was not consciously thinking about her actions but simply performing a necessary function.

She heaved them as far as she could.

CHAPTER TWENTY-TWO

JANUARY 1991

Harriet Kibbe hadn't seen Roger in two years.

She walked into the familiar visiting area at the South Lake Tahoe Jail, where he was still awaiting trial, an event delayed repeatedly by a string of pretrial motions and hearings but now scheduled to start in less than two weeks.

After signing in, she located her assigned cubicle and waited for him to be brought out. She was perspiring and felt weak; it wasn't nerves, although she was uneasy.

For eight months after his arrest she had shown up here almost weekly. Both were needy in different ways. They had made an unspoken deal: his information in exchange for her company. Without volunteering anything, he had continued to answer her questions. He did not tell her, however, what he'd done with the women sexually, although she'd asked.

It was odd the things she had thought of.

"What about your black eye?"

Darcie Frackenpohl kicked him.

"And the time you had the crabs?"

He caught them from a victim he picked up in Sacramento when he left home in December 1986, ending up in Las Vegas and at Steve's. Along the way, he'd dumped her in El Dorado. This one, he said, had not yet been discovered.

Harriet thought Roger was perfect in jail. With the discipline, routine, and defined parameters jail afforded, he was more relaxed and communicative than ever. He seemed more trusting, too—of himself, as well as others. After one of her early visits, it had come to her why he'd always wrapped the front porch of every house they lived in with tightly spaced latticework. In retrospect, it had looked like bars.

When she finally had her fill, she had been able to disconnect from him abruptly, with no good-byes. She was back now only because of a call from his lawyer; Roger had asked to see her before trial. The request had surprised her.

She had been subpoenaed by the district attorney the previous month. When she walked into the courtroom, Roger, heavier than she had ever seen him, hadn't even bothered to turn around and look at her. Roger's lawyer explained to the judge that Harriet was going to invoke spousal immunity, and she had been dismissed without being called forward. Immunity ensured that Harriet, who had refused all interview requests by detectives, would not have to testify for either side. However, she had privately promised the prosecutor in a face-to-face meeting that if he couldn't make his case without her, she would do whatever she could to help. She dreaded ever being called upon to do so, and it wasn't something anybody could legally make her do, but she knew she must, even if it meant one day telling the world what she had done at the landfill. In all their long talks, Roger had never once shown a smidgen of remorse for his victims or their families. Harriet knew now that killers came in all sizes and shapes, and could look like, well, somebody's husband. She understood that Roger was capable of killing again, and behind bars was where he belonged.

A diabetic, Harriet had been under doctor's orders to avoid stress. Two weeks after her court appearance, she suffered a heart attack. Hospitalized for a week, she'd been recuperating only a few days at home—she had a steady bookkeeping job and was renting a small house—when Roger's lawyer called. She had explained her health situation and put off her decision for a week, then decided to come, even though she hadn't yet been able to return to work.

Roger came out, sat on the other side of the glass partition, and picked up the phone.

"Hi," he said.

"Hi. I understand you wanted to see me?"

"I didn't ask to see you."

She realized how accomplished he was at making her feel like a sap. He just sat there looking at her, not bothering to inquire as to her health, although his lawyer must have told him about her recent problems.

"Why am I here, then?" she asked with a bite.

It finally came out. He wanted her to get the proper form for him to sign so Steve could dispose of his body. Roger said he was planning to kill himself before trial.

The threat didn't push a button in her like it would have at one time. Now she just thought: *How cowardly.*

"I'm thinking you should face the music," she said.

The past two years had given Harriet some perspective. Although she certainly didn't consider herself blameless for the mess they had made of their marriage and life together, she had come to the realization that no one could turn someone else into a serial killer. A person had to be wired to kill in cold blood, perhaps from childhood, maybe from birth. She had devoured relevant and conflicting articles and knew the popular themes presented by defense attorneys and sociologists, but the bottom line remained unchanged: Roger had murdered those women. She hadn't, and his mother hadn't either, no matter how wanting his childhood relationship with her had been. Still, Harriet couldn't help but speculate as to the root of what she realized must be Roger's great hatred for women. Else why would he have done what he did? Even after the months he'd talked to her about his crimes, there remained that unanswered question: *"Why?"*

She seized the moment. "You said this wasn't about me or our marriage. Have you given any thought to what it is about?"

He didn't answer.

She knew she was playing amateur psychologist, and probably none too well. She figured she'd earned the right.

"Do you think it might be about your mother?" she asked. "Do you think maybe you've been trying to kill her all this time? If that's the case, look where it's gotten you thirty, forty years later. I mean, here you are talking about killing yourself. Haven't you destroyed enough lives in the sake of trying to get back at her?"

His stare was ice-cold.

"No," he finally said.

She departed for home not long after.

ON VALENTINE'S DAY, 1991, *The People of the State of California* v. *Roger Reece Kibbe* began in South Lake Tahoe.

As he stood before the jury to deliver his opening statement, tall, fair-haired, even-tempered Robert Drossel, assistant district attorney for El Dorado County, was well prepared for the task at hand.

In the California criminal justice system, Drossel had done it all: eight years as a prosecutor; seven years as a defense attorney, both in private practice and as a public defender; two years as an investigator for the public defender's office; ten years as a police officer.

El Dorado was the fourth rural northern California county Drossel had worked in, and he knew that cases like the I-5 murder series did not come along very often. For local residents, the fact that serial killers were a rarity in this backwater county was good news. As a litigator, however, Drossel, who had successfully prosecuted two other murder cases and was a veteran of seventy-five felony jury trials with a 90 percent conviction rate, very much appreciated the challenges he knew this largely circumstantial case would offer.

One important decision had been made prior to Drossel's assignment to the Kibbe case. El Dorado District Attorney Ron Tepper and his chief assistant, Walt Miller, had elected not to seek the death penalty. They decided that none of the "special circumstances" required by California law in death penalty cases were applicable. Multiple murders was a special circumstance, but El Dorado had jurisdiction in only one case: the murder of Darcie Frackenpohl. Therefore, additional murder counts could not be filed in El Dorado. It was a loophole in the law that benefited, unfortunately, marauding serial killers. The facts also did not support a charge of kidnapping, another special circumstance, since prostitutes willingly got into strangers' cars all the time. Obviously, at some point it had become a kidnapping when Darcie resisted, but there was no way to determine where that took place. For instance, if the kidnap had occurred as Kibbe was driving her through Sacramento County, then El Dorado did not have jurisdiction. Assuming that Kibbe would eventually be convicted of killing Darcie Frackenpohl, the prosecutors knew that if and when other counties with I-5 murder cases ever filed murder charges against Kibbe, they could go for the death penalty due to Kibbe's prior murder conviction in a related case. This prosecutorial decision had not been affected by the shocking suicide of D.A. Tepper a year before trial. His top assistant, Miller, who had been planning to prosecute Kibbe himself, stepped in as acting D.A. and, with all his new administrative duties, decided to hand the case over to Drossel, in charge of the D.A.'s South Lake Tahoe office.

"Ladies and gentlemen of the jury, this case involves the murder of Darcie Frackenpohl," Drossel began. "During the evidence portion of this case, you'll hear evidence of four murders and an assault, all on young women. You'll hear how Roger Kibbe, the defendant, is responsible for this additional criminal activity. You'll hear how this additional criminal activity becomes relevant to the murder of Darcie Frackenpohl."

Drossel had a relatively laid-back courtroom style, and before a jury was soft-spoken and deliberate. His normal demeanor did not change for this case, even though he was wearing a microphone for the TV show "48 Hours," which planned to air a story on serial killers. In the early days of the trial, however, he was keenly aware of the mike—any miscue had the potential of being seen by 20 million viewers—and wondered why he had ever agreed to such a stunt.

Drossel had fought critical pretrial skirmishes with Kibbe's court-appointed attorney, Phil Kohn, himself a former cop and El Dorado prosecutor. In fact, Kohn had, with Kibbe's permission, placed his name in contention for the acting D.A. post, which he lost to Walt Miller on a 3–1 vote of the county commissioners. (Had Kohn won the appointment, Kibbe would have had to find a new lawyer.) The two sides had tangled over Drossel's intention to present to the jury uncharged crimes—three other murders believed to be part of the I-5 series. Through the other victims, Drossel hoped to show motive, opportunity, and modus operandi, thereby opening the door to the heart of the serial killer theme of the case. In separate pretrial hearings that had the look of court mini-trials, Drossel had to prove to the presiding judge, Superior Court Judge Terrence M. Finney, that Kibbe had a unique modus operandi or "criminal signature" that was present in each killing, and also that there was physical evidence that tied Kibbe to each killing.

Judge Finney—known by the local bar as the "King of the Mountain" because he was the only superior court judge in South Lake Tahoe—ruled in Drossel's favor. As a former D.A., Finney was viewed by some defense attorneys as pro-prosecution, although he was considered extremely bright on evidentiary issues and a strong supporter of open discovery for the defense—a prosecutor who didn't hand over everything to the defense could be in big trouble. In Judge Finney's court, every lawyer won some and lost some.

After the judge's ruling allowing the other uncharged murders to be presented, Kohn, a feisty bantamweight in and out of court, asked for help to investigate the other cases, and was assigned a second lawyer, studious Tom Kolpacoff, who would handle most of the scientific evidence, while Kohn did everything else.

"I'll proceed with the Darcie Frackenpohl murder first because that is the case that gives rise to jurisdiction in El Dorado County," Drossel told jurors. "And then I'll proceed to theassault of Debra Guffie, a young prostitute, because you'll see from the evidence how this specifically and immediately ties in Kibbe to the Frackenpohl murder. Then we'll proceed to the other victims. Stephanie Brown, a young stranded motorist who was murdered. Charmaine Sabrah, a young stranded motorist who was murdered. And Lora Heedick, a young prostitute who was murdered."

Drossel had decided to drop Karen Finch from the roster of victims because her throat had been slashed—a different MO than ligature strangulation—and also due to the fact that there was no physical evidence linking Kibbe to the crime. The prosecutor knew that if the defense was able to knock Finch out of the box at trial, it might place a question mark in the minds of the jurors as to the other uncharged crimes. With more convincing linkage evidence in Brown, Sabrah, and Heedick, he didn't need Finch; so, why take the chance?

"This, then, is the story of the person who has been dubbed 'The I-5 Killer' or 'I-5 Strangler.' It's a story of the defendant, Roger Kibbe, covering a period of two years in his life from 1986 through 1988. This is also a story of a serial killer; that is, Roger Kibbe killed four people and assaulted a fifth and in doing so left his criminal signature at each crime scene. There will be another phrase you will hear in this case which will become as apparent as 'The I-5 Killer.' That is, Roger Kibbe as 'The Cordage Killer.' I don't mean to be flippant here. But you will see how evidence of cordage becomes very relevant and very specific and how it ties Roger Kibbe to murder and eventually delivers a fatal blow."

In presenting the People's case, Drossel promised to take jurors "on a bus tour and I'll be your guide. We'll be traveling through various locales—to the San Joaquin–Sacramento counties area, the Sierra foothills, and the mountains of Lake Tahoe, our own backyard. This will not be a scenic tour. Quite the contrary. It will be a roadway trail of the most repugnant behavior by a human being."

Those were some of the things the jury would hear in the trial. What the jury would *not* hear was also substantial. No evidence would be put forth concerning Kibbe's juvenile arrest record; his stealing and cutting up women's clothing at age fifteen; his tying himself up with women's clothing, then telling police he'd been molested; an adult arrest and conviction record that escalated from minor offenses to more serious ones through the 1960s and 1970s and the opinion expressed by the San Diego polygraph examiner in 1970 concerning Roger Kibbe's "intense dislike, almost a hatred, for women."*

Although Drossel was sometimes frustrated—as were most prosecutors—by how much a jury does not know about a defendant, he accepted that the law was clear: this kind of information was too prejudicial to be allowed into the record. Although it was certainly relevant as to the kind of person the defendant was and whether someone might invite him over

---

* In Roger Kibbe's prison file was a "Social Evaluation" written by a prison psychologist six months after the polygraph examiner's report. It read, in part: "Kibbe's initially fearful manner and stuttering speech completely disappeared once he was certain he had the counselor's full attention. Relaxed, he stopped gripping one wrist with the other hand and displayed an unexpected sense of humor. There was then no evidence of an 'intense dislike, almost a hatred for women' that was commented upon in a January, 1970, polygraph examination, or the basis for the same examiner describing Kibbe as 'potentially one of the world's most dangerous men' ever encountered. Kibbe's lack of self-confidence is apparent ... so is his superior intelligence." Another evaluation was written by a parole officer in August, 1974: "Kibbe does not appear to be a danger to himself or to others. As reflected by his background, subject's latest criminal endeavors (grand and petty theft) once again are of a relatively petty nature and indicative of poor judgment."

for Sunday dinner with the family, it was irrelevant to the charge of murder in the Darcie Frackenpohl case.

When Drossel sat back down, Kohn told the court he would reserve the defense's opening statement until the beginning of their case.

Detective Jim Watson was the prosecution's first witness.

Under Drossel's questioning, Watson told of arriving at the Old Meyer's Grade Road crime scene at 3:00 P.M. on September 17, 1987, and finding the body of a nude female lying in a small clearing some 35 feet off the road.

"Was there any identification on the body?"

"No. She was a Jane Doe."

Watson told of finding several pieces of nylon pantyhose near the body. One piece of pantyhose was used to gag the victim, he explained, and was wrapped up in the ligature around her neck. He described the ligature as part of the victim's lightweight, black chiffon jacket, which had been fashioned into a garrote controlled by a 12-inch stick.

The detective testified to finding three pieces of white cordage, one a few feet away from the body. A second piece was located 950 feet up the roadway from the body, along with the victim's pink dress. A third piece of cordage was found on the narrow road 1,350 feet from the body, he said, along with another piece of the black chiffon jacket and a pair of lacy panties.

On cross-examination, it came out that Watson thought the perpetrator and victim had entered the chained-off roadway at the top of its incline and walked down to the crime scene. And when the killer had finished, that he'd walked back up the hill, disposing of the victim's garments along the way.

"There was no cordage of any kind around the victim's neck, is that correct?" asked Tom Kolpacoff.

"No, just the black fabric."

"How did you first become aware that there was a series of homicides that had been termed the I-5 series?"

"Through my discussions with criminalist Jim Streeter and Detective Kay Maulsby the day the body was found."

The pathologist, Dr. Richard Sander, who estimated he'd conducted 8,500 autopsies and testified "well over four hundred times," told of unwrapping the cloth ligature from around the victim's neck. "Her hair had been caught up in the ligature," he explained. "As the garrote had been tightened around the neck, her hair had looped around and around."

"When you removed the ligature, what did you find?"

"A deep furrow in the neck, or area of the skin that had been compressed by pressure from the ligature."

"What do you think the significance was of the stick in the garrote being located at the back of her neck?

"From a forensic pathology standpoint, I'd say it represented the assailant trying to subdue the victim when she was active. The assailant would be behind her, trying to hold her down or keep her still."

The pathologist testified to finding a 5-inch contusion on the top of the victim's head.

"What could have caused that wound?"

"Most likely a blow to the head, probably in an effort to subdue her."

"Not enough to cause death in your opinion?"

"Oh, no."

The pathologist testified he had been unable to determine if the victim had been sexually attacked due to decomposition and insect activity.

"Do you have an opinion as to the cause of death?"

"Ligature strangulation."

On cross-examination, Dr. Sander was asked by Phil Kohn if the victim's hair had been cut in any unusual manner.

"No, I didn't notice anything like that."

On the second day of trial, Drossel began with fingerprint testimony to document how Jane Doe had eventually been identified. After he'd asked only a few questions, Kohn announced that the defense was prepared to stipulate as to identification.

"All right," said Judge Finney, dismissing the fingerprint expert on the stand.

In the eyes of the law and for the jury's benefit, Jane Doe was now Darcie Frackenpohl.

The next witness, Kim Quackenbush, a slight blonde with short hair, testified that in the summer of 1987 she'd known Darcie for about five months, and that they were working together as prostitutes in Sacramento in August of that year. At the time, Quackenbush was sixteen years old.

Quackenbush told of last seeing Darcie between 8:00 and 9:00 P.M. on August 24, 1987, standing in an alley on West Capitol Avenue between Bank of America and Raley's supermarket—where Darcie "always worked."

"Did you ever see Darcie again?" Drossel asked.

"No, I never did."

Quackenbush identified the pink dress and black chiffon jacket as what Darcie had been wearing that night.

Another prostitute friend of Darcie's, Carol Stockton, a big-boned redhead, took the stand. She, too, had seen Darcie in the alley around the same time, talking to someone in a parked vehicle.

"Can you describe the vehicle?" Drossel asked.

"A small, white car. It looked foreign and new."

She had recognized the car, Stockton went on, because she had exchanged words with the male driver, whom she considered a possible customer, a few minutes earlier.

"What happened with this potential customer?"

"I started to walk up to the window and he told me to get away from the car."

"And where was his car located?"

"In the same alley."

"What exactly did he say?"

"'Get away from the car, bitch.'"

"And what was he doing?"

"Just sitting there, watching. He was looking up and down West Capitol."

Drossel brought out that two years later, in August 1989, Stockton was shown a photo lineup by police.

"Did you pick out a person whom you thought was the person in the vehicle?"

"Yes."

"Is that person in the courtroom?"

"Yes."

"Would you point him out, please."

She pointed to Roger Kibbe.

On cross-examination, Kohn wanted to know if Stockton had seen a picture of Kibbe in a newspaper or somewhere else before she picked him out of the photo lineup.

"No, I hadn't."

"A year earlier, in June 1988, didn't an investigator from the D.A.'s office interview you?"

"Yes."

"Did he show you pictures?"

"Yeah. Of Darcie and her boyfriend."

"That was it?"

"Yes."

"Did he show you a picture of a small, white car?"

"No, I don't remember."

"Did he show you a picture of an older man?"

"He might have. I don't remember."

"Do you remember asking the investigator if the picture was of the man that raped and cut off that girl's arms?"

"Yes, sir."

Kohn had the investigator's report in hand, and was using it to chip away at Stockton's eyewitness credibility. If she had been shown a picture of Kibbe *before* the photo lineup and told this was the man responsible for Darcie's murder, then Carol Stockton's fingering him in the lineup and dramatically in court could just about be rolled up and drop-kicked down the courthouse steps.

"Then he did show you a picture of an older man?"

"He might have."

"Do you remember him telling you that the man whose picture he showed you was in custody?"

"He said somebody had been arrested."

"Going back to what you testified to—did you see Darcie get into the small, white vehicle?"

"No, I did not."

"You went on to do something else?"

"Yes, sir."

"I have no other questions."

The next day's testimony began with two employees of Public Storage. First up was Public Storage General Manager Dennis Kissinger, who testified to hiring Roger and Harriet Kibbe to manage the Tupelo facility. He confirmed that they had a residence at the facility, and also had the use of storage units 427 and 428.

Doris Sampson, a relief manager for the Kibbes on their days off, testified to Roger's having access to the white Hyundai, and also to Roger's black eye in late August 1987.

"How do you happen to remember that particular time period?" Drossel asked.

"On Labor Day that year, I fell over a ramp and got a black eye. Roger and I had black eyes at the same time."

"Did Mr. Kibbe tell you how he got his?"

"Said he'd been drinking in a tavern and was jumped by a couple of fellows."

In his testimony, Kissinger had said he'd noticed Kibbe's black eye, too. Kibbe's explanation to him, however, was different: he'd gotten into a fight at a truck stop.

Judy Frackenpohl was called to the stand next.

As she was sworn in, Judy hoped that the tranquilizer she'd taken would see her through. From the moment Jim Watson had called her in late April 1988 to say they were arresting a suspect in Darcie's murder, Judy had dreaded this moment. In the intervening years, she'd learned more about her daughter's death than she ever wanted to and was still trying to find a way to deal with her loss. And now, she had to face Darcie's killer.

"Do you know Darcie Frackenpohl?" Drossel asked.

"She was my daughter."

Judy looked for the first time at Roger Kibbe, who was sitting at the defense table with his head bowed. From what she could see, he seemed ordinary enough. A graying middle-aged guy working on a potbelly. If she'd passed him on the street she would have taken him for a tradesman of some kind who drank beer and watched weekend sports on TV.

"When was the last time you personally saw Darcie?"

"On the 30th of July, 1987."

"And was there a special occasion?"

"It was her brother's birthday. We all went out to dinner."

Judy tried to stay focused on the prosecutor, but her eyes kept wandering to the defense table. The man they said had murdered Darcie hadn't moved. She wanted him to look at her, dammit—to see a grieving mother.

"In August of 1987 did you receive a telephone call from Darcie?"

"Yes, I did. She called home collect on August 23rd from Sacramento."

"And what was the topic of the conversation?"

"She just called to let me know she was okay because she did that frequently."

"After August 23rd, did you hear from her again?"

"No."

Judy knew she wasn't going to lose it emotionally now because she had too much anger boiling inside her. She was pissed that the defendant was sitting there like a stone statue, not giving her or her testimony any notice.

"Did you think it unusual not to hear from her?"

"Yes, I did."

"I have no further questions."

On cross, Phil Kohn asked her a couple of questions about James Brown, obviously hoping to point a finger of suspicion at him.

Then it was over.

She was excused, and stepped down. She walked slowly between the two tables—one manned by the prosecutor and the other by the defense lawyers and their client.

She slowed, hoping he would look up.

Roger Kibbe never did.

UNTIL Debra Guffie walked into the courtroom the morning of the third day of testimony to point her finger at Roger Kibbe in another criminal proceeding, prosecutor Bob Drossel did not know if she'd even show up, or if she did, what shape she would be in when she took the stand.

Guffie was in an outpatient drug treatment program, but there had been telltale signs not all was well in her life. For one thing, she'd constantly leaned on Drossel for money, which he refused to provide, knowing that would transform her overnight from victim to paid informant.

Drossel approached his own witness with some trepidation.

"I would like to draw your attention to the early part of September 1987."

"Yes."

"Is it correct to state that in 1987 you were a prostitute?"

"Yes."

"How long had you been a prostitute?"

"For about ten years."

"And in 1987 you were supporting a drug habit?"

"Yes."

"What type of drug?"

"Heroin."

"You were an addict?"

"Yes."

"What is your present addiction status?"

"I'm in a crisis program. I'm with child and I want to have a drug-free baby."

Guffie testified that around 3:00 A.M., "after the bars closed," on September 14, 1987, she'd been picked up by a lone man driving a small white car and taken to the golf course parking lot.

"Is the driver of that vehicle in the courtroom today?"

"Yes."

"Would you point him out, please?"

"The gentleman with the blue-and-white-striped shirt."

Roger Kibbe.

Drossel had noticed that Kibbe seldom looked at the witnesses. Whenever his attention wasn't riveted on the top of the table where he sat, he was openly staring at the court reporter, an attractive woman in her late thirties. The prosecutor wondered how that made Sylvia Falkenstein feel.

On the short drive, the man "hardly said anything" and "seemed angry." She said she tried to cheer him up.

"What did you say?"

"'How did you do today? You can't be mad today.'"

She described the attack once they had parked: his grabbing her right hand and trying to handcuff her; grabbing her hair and smashing her face down, then telling her, "Don't struggle and you won't get hurt, cunt."

When she finished, she was choking back tears.

"Would you like some water?" the judge asked.

"No, thank you."

"What happened then?" Drossel asked.

"I was just—I was very frightened because of the tone of his voice when he told me not to struggle."

"What was his tone?"

"It was very cold, like a monotone. It was very frightening."

Drossel hoped the jurors would appreciate the source. If this hard-as-nails lady of the night who had seen it all over a ten-year period had been so unnerved by the tone of Kibbe's voice, then it must truly have been ominous.

She told of managing to get the door open, and falling and being half pushed out the door, then the police car pulling up and taking off after the fleeing white car.

When it was time for cross-examination, defense attorney Phil Kohn stepped forward, his yellow notepad in hand. He had long anticipated cross-examining this witness, believing her vulnerable, but when it came time to do so he would just as soon have publicly questioned the true intentions of Quasimodo.

Guffie had admitted at a pretrial hearing that she had testified at the assault trial under the influence of heroin. She had looked terrible at the preliminary hearing on the murder charge, even though the cops were trying to keep her clean. Kohn knew she hated Kibbe and her anger was close to the surface, and he was fully prepared to rake her over the coals as a bitter and prejudicial witness. But then he'd run into her in the hallway that morning before she testified. She no longer had spiky hair; she was pregnant and showing and dressed in a maternity smock; she was wearing an "I Love Jesus" button. After engaging her in casual conversation, Kohn realized that Guffie had also mellowed considerably—no doubt part of her newfound religion. Kohn knew she would come off sympathetically, and that he'd have to handle her carefully in front of the jury.

When his cross began, Kohn asked Guffie if she had been an "angry person back in 1987."

"Not really, sir. Confused. Afraid."

"Mr. Kibbe originally asked you to pose for pictures and you indicated that had he given you any money for that purpose, you were going to rip him off."

"Yes."

"So, you were going to take the money he was going to give you and not pose for the pictures."

"Yes."

Kohn raced through pages of questions, asking one or two on each page. There wasn't much he could do with her, other than bring out that she had been arrested the night of the assault on an outstanding warrant. He just wanted her gone.

When he went back to the defense table, Kohn took his seat beside Kibbe, who showed no emotion. Although Kohn had found Kibbe to be bright and friendly in their discussions, he was not participating very much in his own defense. For weeks leading up to trial, Kibbe had been on a suicide watch, with jailers passing by his cell every thirty minutes, night and day. The head of El Dorado County's jails, Lt. Jerry Tackett, was a friend of Steve Kibbe's, and Tackett watched out for his celebrity inmate. With the eating habits of a ten year old, Kibbe ate nothing but peanut butter sandwiches, bananas, chocolate bars, and Coke. Just before trial, jailers brought him a pizza, which he loved. In his cell, he watched TV—talk shows and soap operas; he hated sports—and played Game Boy. The attitude of his jailers was to indulge him; whatever it took to keep him amused and not suicidal. As for his crimes, Roger had acknowledged to Kohn having impulses he couldn't control, as close to an admission of guilt as he came. Kohn had decided, already, that he would not put Kibbe on the witness stand.

Next, the police officers who investigated the Guffie assault testified to arresting Kibbe and finding his crime kit. They itemized its contents, including the two pieces of white cordage. Then, the Sacramento police fingerprint expert who testified at the Guffie trial told of finding Kibbe's right-ring-finger print on the handcuffs.

Drossel was pleased with the Guffie testimony. Guffie herself, obviously upset and at times crying, had been an effective witness. She had held up well.

With the physical evidence of murder still to come, he considered Guffie icing on the cake. But she was a human connection for the jury, allowing him to argue later that Debra Guffie had been an intended murder victim, one who had gotten away from Roger Kibbe.

Something none of the other women had been able to do.

CRIMINALIST Faye Springer took the stand on the afternoon of the third day.

After going over her education and experience, the prosecutor asked her to define trace evidence.

"Trace evidence refers to a category of physical evidence that's usually small in size," Springer explained, "and it normally would include fiber, hair, paint, and polymer evidence. Also, particle identifications such as pollens or wood or plant material. Usually it's small items that require a microscope for characterization."

Bob Drossel asked about fiber evidence.

"Fibers are the basic beginning component that goes into making up a fabric," said Springer, clearly in her element. "Individual fibers are the single units that are used to make up a thread, then the threads are woven into some kind of fabric."

"Why is fiber evidence significant?"

"It's significant in that it's easily transferred between two objects, particularly if those two objects are made of some kind of fabric."

"Are fibers delicate?"

"Fibers are fairly tenacious, not like blood or semen evidence that will break down at a fairly predictable rate depending on how they're stored. Manmade fibers can last years and years."

Springer described the procedure she followed for removing fibers from tape lifts—"I will just sit there at the microscope for sometimes hours pulling off individual fibers"—and mounting them for microscopic examination.

Getting down to specifics of the Darcie Frackenpohl case, Drossel asked about two fibers used as exemplars.

They came from the carpet mat of Roger Kibbe's white Hyundai, Springer explained. "I ended up sending them to McCrone Associates in Chicago."

"Why did you send the fibers there?" asked Drossel.

"I had some additional work I wanted them to do."

Springer had known just who to send the fibers to when she had been stymied by the tiny particles on the fibers. McCrone had the expertise and equipment, she knew, to handle such minute trace evidence.

The first in a series of large color photographs, blown up and mounted on posterboard so jurors could see the microscopic evidence with their own eyes, was placed into evidence.

With pointer in hand, Springer stood in front of the photographs, pinpointing the dark particles.

Then, two other exhibits were introduced: blowups of the two fibers Springer had removed from Frackenpohl's dress. She pointed out where one of the fibers had the dark particles and a speck of what she thought was paint, and showed that the other one did not.

"I wanted McCrone to characterize the dark particles and the speck and tell me what they were," she explained.

What Springer did not say was that she had been afraid to let the fibers out of her sight, so she had personally taken them to Chicago—in her beat-up briefcase that went everywhere with her—and stayed around to help out with the examinations.

Drossel asked what she'd done in her own lab.

Springer said she used equipment such as a Fourier transform infrared spectrophotometer and gas chromatograph mass spectrometer to analyze the fibers from the dress and the sample fibers from the Hyundai. They were the same color, shape, size, and made out of the same polymer. "I compared the dyes used in the fibers, too, and found them to be the same."

"Your conclusions?"

"All four fibers are the same kind of fiber that was used for car mats in the make and model Hyundai that Mr. Kibbe drove," Springer said.

Drossel paused to allow it to sink in for the jury.

They then moved on to the hair evidence.

Regarding the human hair found on Darcie's dress, Springer said it was similar in all respects to several hairs that had been removed from Kibbe's inner thigh area under the authority of a search warrant after his arrest for murder.

As for the animal hair found on Darcie's dress, investigators, including Springer, had managed to get samples from the Kibbes' two cats when they served the search warrant on the Placerville cabin. "One cat was very cooperative," she added, "and one was not."

"First, how do you tell the difference between dog and cat hair?" Drossel asked.

"Under a microscope, cat hairs look almost as if they don't have a root. A dog hair has a spade-like root that's very obvious. Other animal hairs have similar distinctions."

"Did you compare the hairs from the cats with the animal hairs off the dress?" Drossel asked.

"Yes. One cat was brown and the other was white. There were hairs off the dress that looked similar to both. So, I compared a brown hair off the dress with hair from the brown cat, and the same for the white cat. Although you can't classify cat hair as unique to an individual—any more than you can human hair—I can say that brown and white cat hairs were on the victim's dress, and that they looked similar to the hairs off the two cats."

Then it was time for the cordage.

Springer testified as to her analysis of the seven pieces of cordage from the three locations—the three pieces recovered at the Frackenpohl crime scene, the cord used to make the garrote and the extra 6-foot-long cord from the crime kit, and the two pieces found in storage space 427 at Tupelo.

"What was the purpose of your examination?"

"I could see that the cordage was similar, but I was looking for some uniqueness. That's when I noticed certain particles that seemed to be reoccurring on the various pieces of cordage."

Photos of the cordage shot with a 35mm camera through a microscope at 400 magnification were displayed. Springer pointed out the specks of red paint and also what she called "black, rubber-like particles."

"As to the black particles, were you able to ascertain what that substance was?" Drossel asked.

"No. But I was able to determine that they all had the same physical appearance and elemental makeup."

"Did you analyze the red paint?"

"Yes. The red paint on all seven pieces of cordage was similar in everything I was able to analyze. Color and appearance, but also in organic and elemental composition."

Springer explained that the amount of red paint on each piece of cord varied, from "only a few red particles" on the crime-kit cord strung between the two dowels to "large smears of red particles" on a piece of cordage from Tupelo.

"Do you have an opinion as to how the red paint got on the cordage?" Drossel asked.

"It got there while the paint was wet, and it was applied in some manner that made very small particles, such as spraying."

"Are you indicating that the different pieces of cordage were in the same environment at one point?"

"Everything I was able to see indicates that there is a common source for the paint," Springer said. "I believe you can make a strong association that these seven pieces of cordage at some time were exposed to a similar environment."

Drossel was finished with his direct examination of Springer, and his timing couldn't have been better. At the end of the day, he would be sending the jurors home for the night with a very clear picture of the same red paint on all the cordage.

"I have no further questions at this time."

The next morning, Springer was back on the stand.

Defense attorney Tom Kolpacoff stepped forward.

"Miss Springer, what does 'tunnel vision' mean?"

"In terms of crime scenes, it has to do with overfocusing in a case on a theory you may have early on."

"Did you keep an open mind in this case?"

"Yes," said Springer.

She told of having authored a published scientific article, "Crime Scene: Avoiding Tunnel Vision."

The defense attorney's question had been rather like asking Billy Graham if he was a true believer.

"Does the fact that you have been an employee since 1972 of the Department of Justice, the state's top law enforcement agency, affect your ability to make a judgment that may be beneficial to a defendant?"

"No, I don't think so. I have made judgments that have been beneficial to defendants."

"Regarding your testimony as to the car mat fibers all being from a 1986 Hyundai, did you do any checking with the manufacturer as to the number of vehicles they produced that year with a blue interior?"

"I tried. I called Hyundai, the distributor out of Los Angeles, and he wasn't able to tell me how many. He gave me the names of the manufacturers of the carpeting, which was made in Korea, so I wrote a letter but never got a reply."

"You don't know how many cars they made in 1986?"

"No."

"Do you know whether they used the same type of carpeting in a 1985 Hyundai or 1987 Hyundai?"

"That I can't tell you."

"Would it be fair to say, then, from the investigation you conducted, you were not able to determine the number of car manufacturers that used the same carpeting that was in the Hyundai?"

"In this particular case I did not. However, if you take a blue carpet from a Hyundai versus a blue carpet from a Ford, I would be very surprised if I could not tell them apart, even though they might look physically similar."

Under questioning, Springer stated that she never did find the source of the red paint on the cordage as a result of police searches of Tupelo and other residences of Kibbe's, although nine miscellaneous items painted red had been brought to her for a comparison. She also said that the red paint spill on the car mat did not match the paint from the cordage, which was some kind of acrylic. "I have run a lot of acrylic-based paints and not found the right one," she said. "It may be some kind of blend of acrylic."

Asked why she thought her colleague, Jim Streeter, hadn't been able to see the red paint on the cordage before she found it, Springer shrugged. "He told me that he had examined them for their general features like construction, length, how many pieces of yarn went into weaving. But other than that, you'll have to ask him."

"In this case," Kolpacoff said, "we have very few fibers on the Frackenpohl dress. Five in all?"

"Right. I found five—two matched the fibers from the car mat. In my experience, I would say that I would be very happy with recovering five fibers in all of my cases."

Drossel withheld a smile. His key scientific witness was doing just fine.

The defense attorney tried to dispense with the hair evidence in a few choice questions.

"Would you agree," Kolpacoff said, "that human hair evidence is an extremely less valuable form of identification than fingerprints?"

"Yes. We don't identify individuals by hair. It is most useful for the exclusion of individuals."

"Is there a term that is sometimes used regarding hair evidence?"

"Well, we tend to call it corroborative evidence."

"When a body has been outside for a period of time, it's not uncommon to find animal hairs, is that correct?"

"That's true, yes."

"Did you compare the animal hairs you removed from the Frackenpohl dress with coyote hair?"

"No."

"Raccoon?"

"No."

"Squirrel?"

"No, but I've looked at those animals before."

"Miss Springer, you cannot identify the animal hairs obtained on the Frackenpohl dress as being identical to the white or brown cat from the Kibbe residence, can you?"

"No, I cannot say that."

Kolpacoff was nearing the end.

"Miss Springer, you submitted the fibers with the football-like properties on them to McCrone Associates."

"Yes."

"And you received a report back from them dated May 4, 1990."

"That sounds about right," said Springer, remembering that was about when she had learned that the dark particles were some kind of fungal spores.

"Since that time, have you done any investigation to determine whether or not fungus is common to floors of automobiles?"

"Well, only that it's common to the floor in my personal GMC that has french fries growing out of it with lots of fungus at this moment."

The jurors and courtroom spectators laughed.

So did Kolpacoff. "That's a good test. No further questions."

Before Springer had left the courtroom, Judge Finney, who was given to moving trials along at near breakneck speed, said, "Next witness."

Knowing Finney, Drossel tried to keep a line of witnesses in the hallway. Woe to any attorney in this court who didn't have someone ready to climb onto the stand.

"Skip Palenik," Drossel announced.

Once sworn in, the tall, round-shouldered Palenik, who defined his profession as "analytical microscopist," said he had been interested in microscopes since he was eight years of age. It wasn't difficult imagining him as a youth tinkering with his chemistry set while other boys were out playing ball. He recited his educational background (B.A., chemistry, University of Illinois) and work experience.

"In layman's terms, what do you do?"

The prosecutor understood the importance of making sure all these scientific terms and pieces of evidence being bandied around were understandable. Jurors hopelessly confused by the prosecution's experts, he knew, were inclined to acquit.

"We use microscopes of various types and microchemical methods to solve problems involving either small amounts of material or small particles. We have skills in manipulating these very small particles and being able to do an analysis of them. These can be anything from pigments in paintings whose authenticity are questioned to identifying particles floating in a pharmaceutical solution. We work for fiber companies, doing patent infringement work. In short, we try to correlate what something is or where it could have come from by its identity and characteristics."

"You work for McCrone Associates, a private lab?"

"Yes. We're an independent analytical laboratory specializing in microscopy for government, industry, whoever will hire us. We've worked for both the prosecution and the defense in criminal and civil cases in this country and abroad."

Palenik explained that he had become involved in the I-5 investigation when Faye Springer called him and asked if he could look at some fibers.

"She described them as having 'little footballs' on them, and she didn't know what they were," he said. "Also, on one fiber she had seen some red paint she wanted analyzed."

"What procedure did you use?"

"Just looked at them under a microscope. At first, I didn't see the football-shaped particles. I saw the red paint, and I thought that's what she was talking about. But then I saw them. Right away, I could tell, just on the basis of their morphology—shape, in other words—that they were fungal spores. And they were present on both samples."

Palenik went on to describe his much more complicated analysis of the paint present on the one carpet fiber from Darcie's dress and on the fibers from Kibbe's Hyundai floor mat, where paint had been spilled.

"I used a technique called electron microprobe analysis, which permitted the elemental analysis so we could look at the inorganic composition of this material."

Drossel was ready to press rewind and do that one again, but Palenik, who had testified more than a hundred times, caught on.

"It's just a big tube, basically," he said. "You place your particle on an aluminum plate and it tells you the elements inside the material."

"What was your conclusion?"

"The red paint particle from the fiber in question was qualitatively the same as the red paint particles on the floor mat. There were ten elements present that I could identify. It doesn't mean they came from the same can of paint, necessarily, although they might have. What it does mean is that they had exactly the same elemental composition. I cannot say that they absolutely, lay-my-life-down-on-it have to be from the same source, but everything that I could do to distinguish them from different sources failed. All the paint particles were essentially identical, this in a world where there are jillions—good scientific word—of different types of red paints to choose from."

Before Drossel could ask another question, Palenik continued thoughtfully: "In my opinion, it would be very unlikely that you would be able to go out somewhere and find paint of identical elemental composition on fibers that were also identical in all measure respects and have them not be from a common origin."

Drossel looked down at his notes. There were a few more questions to ask, more ways Palenik could say the same thing. But how many times did the microscopist have to hit the nail on the head? The spike driven in by Springer had been finished off by the heavy hitter from Chicago.

"I have no further questions."

Tom Kolpacoff's cross-examination was short, although, it turned out, not short enough.

"The ten elements you found in the paints," he said, "would you consider them common elements?"

"They are common in paint, not necessarily all at one time," Palenik answered. "But I think every one of them I have seen at one time or another in paint."

"But it's not unusual for paint to have all ten elements, is that correct?"

"I can't say I've seen a sample with those particular ten elements before, no. For example, sodium and chlorine, two of them, are outside contaminants."

"Outside contaminants in what respect?"

At the defense table, Phil Kohn had a bad feeling. It was after four o'clock on a day that had not gone well for the defense. *Just sit down, Tom. Let's get out of here.*

"Sodium and chlorine have no particular use in paint," Palenik said. "And they are the common ingredients of salt. Anyone who painted in any area where there was salt spray could be expected to put some salt in the paint can."

The red paint had just gotten more unique.

"As for the football shapes," said Kolpacoff, trying to recover by changing the subject, "you cannot tell the type of fungi from these spores?"

"That is correct."

"Therefore, you can't tell how common the fungus is?"

"That's correct, yes."

"I have no further questions."

Kohn had never been big on fiber evidence; he just didn't think it looked as good in real life as on paper. But Faye Springer hadn't been caught shading it to favor the prosecution; she had been very straightforward about her findings and the jury had listened. As for her cordage testimony, had they been playing chess, Kohn would have happily offered and/or accepted a draw here and now. If there had only been cordage from Guffie and Frackenpohl, he could have argued, however weakly, that maybe the two prostitutes knew each other, maybe the Frackenpohl rope came from Guffie, maybe prostitutes carried rope for some reason. But the cordage from Tupelo was the third side of a triangle that boxed Kibbe in, which was why Kohn had fought hard in a pretrial motion to have the search of Tupelo (and everything found there) thrown out as "overly broad." He had lost, and now was stuck with cordage from all three locations having the same red paint.

As for Skip Palenik, Kohn considered him a tremendous witness for the prosecution. He had corroborated Springer, and in addition, found identical paint on the fiber from the dress and in fibers from the carpet of the Hyundai.

"Next witness," said Judge Finney.

"Jim Streeter," Drossel responded.

After raising his right hand and swearing to tell the truth, Streeter related how he became involved in the I-5 murder investigation when he was called out to several murder scenes to examine the physical evidence.

He told of receiving Darcie's pink dress from Detective Jim Watson, and processing it for trace evidence by taking tape lifts. He said he noted cutting on the dress.

"Are you familiar with the terms 'functional' versus 'nonfunctional' cutting?" asked Drossel.

"Yes."

"Could you define those terms?"

"A functional cut serves some purpose. That is, to expose a certain area of the body or remove the garment. Nonfunctional cuts, such as up the sides or in the shoulders or along the bottom seams, don't go anywhere. They serve no obvious purpose."

Drossel took Streeter through the extensive clothes cutting in the garments of all four murder victims.

"Is it possible for you to tell as a criminalist what caused those cuts?" Drossel asked.

"My opinion is a sharp instrument was used to make these cuts, but I cannot tell you whether or not it's a knife or scissors or some other type of instrument."

"In your career as a criminalist—how many years has that been?"

"Eighteen years."

"Have you ever seen these types of nonfunctional cuts on clothing at any crime scene?"

"No."

Streeter also told of his effort to determine if the pieces of cordage were the same type, and produced by the same manufacturer. He admitted, however, that the cordage was too common to narrow down very much.

On cross-examination, Tom Kolpacoff asked if Streeter had ever performed the same fiber comparisons on the Frackenpohl dress that Faye Springer had.

"I actually looked at the tape lifts with the microscope and could not see the same things she saw," Streeter admitted.

"You did not observe any red paint on the cordage, is that correct?"

"Correct, I did not observe that."

"If you saw it you wouldn't ignore it?"

"Given my background and training, I might not be able to recognize its significance."

"But if you saw the paint on the cordage from three locations, wouldn't you, as a criminalist, think that was potentially significant?"

"While my eyes may see it, my mind may not interpret it."

Kolpacoff sat down and Streeter was dismissed.

After the jury was sent home for the weekend and his client escorted away to jail, Kohn slowly packed up his briefcase. In evaluating the day's scientific testimony, he knew that nonfunctional cutting, as espoused by Streeter, would not have carried the day. Nor would the similar-cordage business. For Christ's sake, Streeter hadn't even seen the red paint on the cordage. It was Faye Springer's work, backed up by Skip Palenik, that defined the government's case.

Kohn knew Springer's story; he also knew if she and her hubby hadn't moved to Sacramento when they did, his client, Roger Kibbe, would not be sitting in this courtroom.

CHAPTER TWENTY-THREE

The fifth day of testimony began with Lora Heedick's boyfriend, James Driggers, stepping into the witness box. A big man, he was dressed in the orange jumpsuit of a state prison inmate—an outfit about two sizes too small for him, and his muscular arms and shoulders threatened to burst free of the straining fabric.

"You're serving time for some offense?" prosecutor Bob Drossel asked.

"Yes, sir. Receiving stolen property."

"And what is your sentence?"

"Three years. State prison."

Driggers explained he'd been in a year, which meant he'd serve at least another year before he could be paroled.

Drossel showed his witness a picture.

"Do you recognize this person as Lora Heedick?"

"Yes."

"What type of relationship did you have with her?"

"She was my girlfriend."

"Did you have another relationship besides?"

"Yeah. We did drugs together and did things to make money to get drugs. She was into some prostitution."

"Did you assist in that capacity?"

"Yes, I did."

"I would like to draw your attention to April 20, 1986, and specifically the last time that you saw Lora Heedick alive. Do you have that time frame in mind?"

Drossel couldn't believe it, but the hard-ass convict who no doubt pumped iron daily behind bars had gone blubbery and was grabbing for the Kleenex. This was better than he could have hoped for, although the prosecutor still feared he'd get eaten up by the defense on this witness.

"Yes, I remember," Driggers said, blowing his nose.

Drossel took him through events that night: his walking down South 9th Street looking for Lora, and her pulling up in an older white car. Driggers said he got into the car, Lora introduced him to the man, and they shook hands.

"Did you notice anything about his hand?"

"Yeah. I noticed he had rough features to his hand. It was not real clean, like a workingman's hand, you know."

"What about the size?"

"Fair-sized. I didn't swallow his hand with mine."

"Did he seem excited? Nervous? Quiet?"

"He seemed real quiet and what I would call withdrawn. He didn't say much."

Driggers told of the man volunteering that he could get some drugs at his shop nearby, and Lora suggesting that Driggers get out of the car and wait for their return.

"I waited—all night."

The con went back to the tissues.

Driggers identified a picture of Kibbe's white Maverick as the type of car his girlfriend rode off in that night.

Drossel asked Driggers if he remembered attending a physical lineup at Sacramento County Jail on September 1, 1988.

"Yes, I do."

"You were asked as a witness to view five individuals for identification purposes?"

"Yes."

Drossel showed him snapshots taken that night of the five men in the lineup; they were all middle-aged, and about the same height and build.

"And the person you picked out as the man who drove off with Lora was?"

"Number two in the lineup."

"And who is number two?" Drossel asked.

"The defendant."

Well and good, but unfortunately the prosecutor now had to bring out the fact that Detective Kay Maulsby, on orders she didn't particularly agree with, had shown Driggers a picture of Kibbe six months before the lineup.

"I told her that it looked very much like the guy that was in the car that night," Driggers said.

Had seeing that picture subsequently influenced his pick in the lineup? No, Driggers said.

The defense would surely disagree.

On cross-examination, Phil Kohn started off with a line of questioning to show that Driggers himself had been a suspect for months in the murder of his girlfriend.

"Did you ever beat up your ex-wife, Debbie Richardson?" Kohn asked from somewhere out in left field.

Drossel jumped up. "Objection as to relevancy."

"Mr. Kohn?" the judge asked.

"I'm going to ask Mr. Driggers about his relationship with his ex-wife."

"Objection," Drossel said forcefully.

The judge directed the jury and witness to leave the room so he could hear the lawyers out.

When the door shut behind the last juror, Kohn said, "I have police reports, Your Honor. This guy, according to his ex-wife, had her have intercourse with other men in front of him, and he would masturbate while they were doing it. He'd have sex with the men when they were done."

"What does this have to do with this case?" asked Judge Finney.

"The sexual aspect of the case," Kohn persisted. "The police have released Mr. Driggers as a suspect. The defense hasn't. I think there is a reason why he would make the identifications that he did. And the reason is that he wants to take the pressure off himself."

"This kinky sexual conduct is hearsay and it's not relevant," Drossel countered. "I can see where we're heading: toward improper impeachment of the witness."

The judge allowed Kohn to resume his line of questioning of Driggers to see where it went; however, he did so out of the presence of the jury.

Kohn again asked if he ever beat up his ex-wife, Debbie Richardson.
"Yeah. She beat me up, too."
"Did you ever threaten to kill her?"
"No."
"Did you ever threaten to pour acid on her face?"
"No."
"Did you ever force her to have sex with other men in your presence?"
"No."
Kohn was stymied. "All right, nothing further."
Judge Finney wanted to be clear before he brought the jury back.
"These questions will not be put to this witness without Mr. Kohn making
a bona fide offer of proof. Bring the jury in."
Kohn hammered away at Driggers's late-in-the-game identification
of Kibbe, pointing out his earlier failures to do so, including that he was
shown a photo lineup that included the defendant as early as January
1987—eighteen months before he finally ID'ed Roger Kibbe.
On redirect, Drossel asked simply: "Is there any question in your
mind that the person you identified at the physical lineup is the person
Lora Heedick was with the last time you saw her?"
"No, sir. I wouldn't be up here right now if I had any doubt."
"No further questions."
Not bad, Drossel thought. He saw Driggers coming across as credible,
even with his sordid past. And the defense had not gotten into him as
badly as Drossel thought they might.
Detective Kay Maulsby came next.
She told the jury how Roger Kibbe first became a suspect in the I-5
series, for her, when she saw the crime kit from the Debra Guffie assault
case in the property room of the Sacramento Police Department.
She testified to having found the pieces of cordage during the search
of Tupelo, thereby providing a key link in the "chain of evidence"—the
chain that led directly to the DOJ lab where Faye Springer had gone to
work on the cordage.
On cross-examination, Phil Kohn stayed on James Driggers's case by
pulling out negative information that Maulsby had learned about Driggers
during her investigation of him as a possible murder suspect.

"Who is Debbie Richardson?" asked Kohn, who knew there was more than one way to skin a cat in a court of law.

"James Driggers's ex-wife," Maulsby said.

"Did you have a telephone interview with her on July 31, 1987?"

"I did."

"Did she indicate she had been beaten up by Mr. Driggers?"

"Yes."

"Did she indicate to you she had been grabbed by the throat by Mr. Driggers."

'Yes.'

"Without going into detail, did she indicate to you that he had some very bizarre sexual preferences?"

"Yes."

"Which included having her have sex with other men while he watched?"

"Yes."

Kohn was not finished putting forth damaging information about the defense's very own murder suspect. He asked Maulsby about her interview of a cousin of Lora Heedick's. The detective confirmed that the female cousin had seen bruises on Lora that Driggers had reportedly inflicted.

"Did she tell you that Lora advised her that Mr. Driggers had threatened to burn her eyes out with a cigarette?"

"Yes."

"Did all of these statements lead you to believe that Mr. Driggers was a suspect in Lora Heedick's murder?"

"I still considered him a suspect at that point."

Maulsby also was asked to explain in further detail how she had shown the lone picture of Kibbe to Driggers, thereby arguably polluting his later identification of Kibbe—instead of giving up Lt. Ray Biondi as the real culprit in the scheme, she took the heat herself. She was, however, able to qualify her actions when Kohn generously left her an opening.

"I did not put the picture in front of him and say, 'Is this the man you saw with Lora?'" Maulsby explained. "What I said was, 'Is this person familiar to you? Have you seen this person in the stroll area?'"

Kohn elicited from Maulsby that she had taken would-be eyewitness Carmen Anselmi to a number of public rental facilities, including Tupelo, where Roger Kibbe was manning the desk, and that Charmaine's mother failed to recognize him as the man who drove off with her daughter.

Vito Bertocchini's name was called by the prosecutor on the sixth day of testimony.

He told of responding to the murder scene off Correia Road and Highway 12 on July 15, 1986, and finding Stephanie Brown's body floating facedown in 3 feet of water. He described the debris under her rear bra strap and how the waistband of her shorts were turned in, as if someone had re-dressed her.

"Were you able to ascertain if there was any evidence of tire tracks from a vehicle pulling in there?"

"When we arrived, paramedics and firemen were already on the scene. Any type of tracks that would have been there had been driven over."

Bertocchini told of subsequently recovering Brown's tank top from the water, and later, the pair of scissors.

Drossel then turned to the Sabrah investigation.

The detective testified to Carmen Anselmi's working with a police artist to come up with the composite of the suspect her daughter had ridden off with, and how he had circulated the composite to various police departments.

"Did at some point the name Roger Kibbe come into play as a suspect in this series?" Drossel asked.

"His name did come up, yes."

"Under what circumstances."

Bertocchini explained how the patrol deputy in his department had made the stop on Kibbe, and passed along word that he looked a lot like the composite.

"Do you remember a point in time, as far as you were concerned, when you considered him a suspect?"

"That would have been after my first interview with him on December 15, 1986."

"Could you point him out?"

"He's seated at the end of that counsel table wearing a white-and-green striped shirt."

It was a psychological ploy: Drossel wanted as many witnesses as possible to point a finger at the defendant.

When it was his turn, Phil Kohn asked what had caused Bertocchini to see Kibbe as a suspect after that first interview.

"This may sound ridiculous," the big cop admitted, "but I just had a gut feeling. Part of it was that he knew the locations. He traveled Highway 12, where Stephanie Brown was found. He traveled on I-5, where she and Charmaine Sabrah had been abducted. He knew the Ione area, where Sabrah's body was found. He admitted to contacting prostitutes."

"Anything else?"

Bertocchini nodded. "He had a two-seater sports car and looked like the composite."

Kohn asked whether or not Kibbe had been read his Miranda rights prior to the interview.

"No, not that day," Bertocchini said.

"How did you conclude the interview?"

"We took photos and fingerprints. I asked if he would be willing to take a polygraph exam and he said he had to contact his brother. He made a phone call to his brother. He came out and said he would get back to us. He and his wife left."

It was the first time anyone had come close to mentioning Steve Kibbe at the trial, and Drossel knew it would probably be the last. He had thought long and hard about whether to call the cop brother to the stand, but decided doing so would break a trial attorney's cardinal rule: don't ask a question you don't know the answer to. For Steve Kibbe had refused to talk to authorities any more about his brother.

Kohn tried to show that Roger hadn't been free to leave during the interview, thereby impugning the legality of Bertocchini's first contact with Kibbe, but it was thin gruel.

Next, the pathologist who had performed the autopsy on Stephanie Brown testified that she had died six to eight hours before he had examined the body next to the irrigation ditch at 9:00 A.M. on the morning she was discovered.

"What opinion did you form as to cause of death?" Drossel asked.

"She died from asphyxia due to ligature strangulation and being submerged in the water. I feel she was probably alive when she went into the water."

Drossel looked at his notes. He didn't recall anything about drowning in the coroner's report.

"There was abundant frothy white fluid in her air passages," the pathologist continued without being asked. "This can occur with strangulation alone. Usually, when there is this amount of frothy material, it means that the victim has inhaled water, which is mixed with air and produces the froth."

The pathologist, with whom Vito Bertocchini had to fight so hard to get a rape-kit examination done had not mentioned to detectives the day of the autopsy that Stephanie was probably still breathing when she hit the water.

Jo-Allyn Brown came to the stand to testify about the last time she saw Stephanie.

After identifying a picture of her smiling daughter, Jo-Allyn told of Stephanie's visit earlier in the evening of her disappearance. "She came home to do her laundry and visit."

"What time was that?" Drossel asked.

"From about six thirty to around nine o'clock that evening."

The prosecutor went over what Stephanie was wearing—the same clothes she had on when her body was found—and her mother said Stephanie's hair had been in a ponytail.

Jo-Allyn forced herself to look at Kibbe. He was looking down at the table, and rocking slowly in his chair.

"Was that the last time you saw your daughter?"

"Other than at the mortuary," Jo-Allyn said.

"I'm sorry," Drossel said, "I meant alive."

"Yes," Jo-Allyn said sadly.

On her way out of the courtroom, Jo-Allyn Brown stared down at the man they said had killed her daughter.

Roger Kibbe had a *People* magazine at the table.

Stephanie Brown's roommate, Patty Burrier, testified to Stephanie's having arrived to pick her and her boyfriend up around midnight on July 15, 1986, when they had car trouble.

Next, Patty's former boyfriend, Jim Frazier, the radio disc jockey, came to the stand.

"After Stephanie gave us a lift to my place, I wanted to make sure she knew her way home," he said. "At first I suggested that she wait for us because I was going to be proceeding to work, which was in the same direction and on the way back to her and Patty's place. But she didn't want to do that."

"What happened then?" Drossel asked.

"I wrote directions"—Frazier was struggling with his emotions—"for her on a piece of paper."

Having talked to him previously, the prosecutor knew that the young man carried enormous guilt. Had he written the right directions? Had he done everything he could to ensure that she would return home safely? Frazier still agonized over what happened that night five years ago.

Frazier said he explained the directions to Stephanie and went over them with her several times because she seemed to be unclear. "I thought I made it very clear she needed to go northbound on I-5 to get home. I told her southbound would take her out in the middle of nowhere."

"And you saw her drive off?"

"Yes, I did."

"Did you ever see her again?"

Frazier shook his head. "Never."

Drossel directed Frazier's attention to a large map displayed before the jury.

"Do you see the arrow, 'Brown's car abandoned'?"

"Yes, I do."

"In terms of where Stephanie was intending to go that night, what direction is that from Sacramento?"

"South," Frazier said, his voice barely audible. "The wrong direction."

"I have no further questions."

"Mr. Kohn?" Judge Finney said.

"No questions," said Phil Kohn.

Moving on to the next victim, Drossel called an Amador County detective regarding the discovery of Charmaine Sabrah's body on November

9, 1986. "There was some black material around her neck knotted very tightly," he said.

Drossel then called the decidedly Old World pathologist who had autopsied the remains in the bed of his pickup. "It was referred to as a tailgate autopsy," the pathologist said a bit defensively when given the chance, "but I just didn't see any reason to go anywhere with the body."

The pathologist said he found the cause of death to be "asphyxia due to strangulation by ligature."

When the next witness, Carmen Anselmi, was summoned, she entered the courtroom, took one look at Kibbe sitting at the defense table, and yelled: "Hey, that's the guy! That's him!"

"That's enough," Judge Finney barked.

Drossel hurried over to his witness. "Please, we'll get to that later."

The shrill accusation had broken the practiced calm and formality of the courtroom, unsettling the judge, the three trial lawyers, and the jury—although the defendant hadn't even turned around—and causing the assembled news reporters covering the trial to scribble furiously into their notepads. If the outburst had been poor courtroom etiquette, it had made for good courtroom drama.

Judge Finney gave the proper admonishments to the jury to disregard the matter, and when Carmen Anselmi took the stand there was a brave effort on everyone's part to pretend it had never happened.

After Charmaine's mother had taken the oath, Drossel led her through a series of questions designed to detail her last night with her daughter. The night of dancing, their late snack, then heading for home and their fateful car trouble.

"And when the car broke down," Drossel said, "what did you and Charmaine do?"

"She wanted to walk to a light we could see far away, but I said 'No, let's stay here.' And she was crying at first like—I don't know, like she knew something was going to happen. I said, 'Let's stay here; nothing will happen.'"

She related how after they'd waited for two hours a man in a dark sports car pulled up behind them and asked if they needed help.

"Of course he knew we needed help," she said derisively, looking right at Roger Kibbe, who sat with his chin cradled in one hand.

After she and her daughter decided they should make a phone call, Anselmi said she had been the one to get into the man's car because "I didn't want to take a chance with Charmaine, you know, so I went."

"Where did he take you?"

"To a place nearby that had a phone."

"What did you do?"

"I called the club we had just left, but everyone had gone home. I had him take me back to my daughter."

"Then what happened?"

Anselmi was beginning to show the strain.

"I told my daughter—I said he was okay. She was worried about the baby because she was breast-feeding—I suggested she should go. He had offered to give her a ride home but couldn't take us both in his car."

"Did you see your daughter get in the car?"

"Yes, I did. And I never saw her again."

At that moment, Anselmi came unglued, breaking down and sobbing as if she had just gotten the news of her daughter's death.

"Would you like a recess?" the judge asked.

She shook her head. "No, no. I want to get it over with."

"All right," the judge said understandingly. "Would you care for a glass of water?"

"Maybe."

The bailiff came forward and poured her a glass.

When she had recovered a bit, Drossel took her through her efforts with a police artist to come up with the composite picture of the suspect. He then brought out that she had also attended the September 1, 1988, physical lineup, although she did so separately of James Driggers.

"Were you able to identify anyone?"

"No, I just wasn't sure." Waving her hand at Kibbe, she said, "He'd gained weight. He had a full beard. He had on a baggy sweatshirt. How could I recognize him that way?"

"You are pointing to the defendant?"

"Yes, that's him."

On cross, Phil Kohn brought out that prior to the physical lineup Anselmi had been shown by Detective Vito Bertocchini on December 19, 1986—four days after Bertocchini's first interview with Roger Kibbe—a photo lineup with six photos, one of which was Kibbe.

"You did not identify anybody, did you?"

"No."

"I have no other questions," said Kohn, who wanted nothing more to do with the heartsick mother and grandmother who had somehow managed to squeeze into her directtestimony that she had adopted Charmaine's son and was raising him.

The defense attorney knew that Carmen Anselmi's most dramatic moment came not from the witness stand but from the doorway of the courtroom. It was not part of the record, but could it ever be erased from the minds of the jurors?

CRIMINALIST Faye Springer was recalled to the stand to testify to fiber evidence in the uncharged murders.

AfterpreviouslyexaminingallthetapeliftsfromCharmaineSabrah'sclothing that had been taken much earlier by Jim Streeter and finding nothing, Springer, a week after RogerKibbe's arrest for murder, had asked to see the garments herself. When she had gotten to the pantyhose, she'd made an interesting discovery: they were still inside out.

"What was the significance of this?" asked Drossel.

"Well, I'm not sure men would appreciate this," Springer said, showing a thin smile, "but when you remove pantyhose, they always end up inside out. In fact, I'm not sure you can take off pantyhose and not have that happen. The surface I was interested in as far as fiber transfers was the outside surface, of course, not the inside."

"What did you do then?"

"I turned the pantyhose inside out and did a dozen or so tape lifts on the surface that had been on the outside when she was wearing them."

Drossel had Springer move to a row of photographic blowups. "And what did you find?" he asked.

"Carpet fibers," she said, pointing to one picture.

"How many fibers did you find?"

"Looks like I characterized four."

"What color were those four?"

"Blue, all of them were blue."

Springer explained she compared the fibers with sample blue fibers— she had pictures of them, too—from the seats of Kibbe's Datsun 280Z.

"As you can see, they look very similar," she said. "The dye is the same, and they're a nylon, trilobular material from a velour fabric."

Drossel moved Springer along to Lora Heedick.

"I had exemplar fibers from the Maverick seats," she explained, pointing to other oversize pictures that looked nothing like the Datsun fibers. "They're a multicomponent material, composed of rayon fibers which were breaking apart or decomposing, probably due to age."

Drossel was letting Springer tell her story.

"I compared these to fibers I found on Heedick's socks." The pointer flew to another color picture.

Springer had called up the clothing from that case, too, and gone all over it again.

"These are also decomposing rayon fibers. As you can see, the rayon is actually separating from the adhesive, as in the exemplars."

Not as strong a scientific indictment as the more unique fiber and cordage evidence in the Darcie Frackenpohl case, but nonetheless, Faye Springer had found convincing trace evidence in two other cases that tied Charmaine Sabrah and Lora Heedick to cars driven by Roger Kibbe.

THE PROSECUTION'S last witness was called for the purpose of tying all the evidence together, and along the way, to tell the story of a diabolic serial killer.

Lt. Ray Biondi outlined his twenty-nine years of police work, including the last fifteen years as head of the Sacramento County Sheriff's Department Homicide Bureau. He estimated he had investigated between 400 and 500 homicides in that time; nine were serial murder cases.

After a voir dire examination, the court found, over Phil Kohn's half-hearted objection, Biondi qualified to be an expert in serial murder investigations, thereby opening the door for him to state his opinions regarding the I-5 cases and serial killings in general.

"What are some of the common denominators a homicide detective looks for in a suspected serial killing case?" Drossel asked.

"It is usually a matter of asking yourself several questions: Who are the victims? Is there some common thread between the victims? How were they obtained by the suspect? Are there common threads in the manner of killing and in the activity that occurred with the victims?"

"In the I-5 investigation, did you come to the conclusion that one person was responsible for each crime?"

"Yes."

Drossel introduced a large chart that listed the four murder victims and Debra Guffie, along with several columns of information on each case. The first column was *Activity Last Seen*, and the prosecutor asked Biondi to explain the significance of this category for each victim.

"Starting with the first known victim, Lora Heedick," Biondi said, "she was known as at least a part-time prostitute. She was engaged in prostitution activity, which put her in the category of a very easy target and vulnerable to being picked up by a stranger.

"Stephanie Brown was lost on Interstate 5 going the wrong direction from where she was headed that particular night. Because of those circumstances, she was a person who was vulnerable to an abduction. She was a high-risk victim.

"Charmaine Sabrah was stranded on Interstate 5 with her mother in a broken-down car. She was vulnerable and in a high-risk situation, too.

"Darcie Frackenpohl was working as a prostitute. This fact and her willingness to get in a car with a stranger made her a high-risk victim.

"Debra Guffie was also working as a prostitute. Again, she was an easy target."

The next category was *Body Crime Scene.*

"There are several common threads that occurred in these cases when you look at where the body was found and the crime scene. In each case there was some nudity. My interpretation is that there was probably some sexual assault suffered by these victims, all young women found either partially or totally nude. There was some kind of control involved in the form of restraints. In Heedick, her wrists were bound behind her. In Brown, there was evidence that she had been bound, although no bindings were found at the scene. In Sabrah, she was bound with pieces of her own clothing cut to make bindings. In Frackenpohl, there was evidence of cordage at the scene that could have been used for bindings. Although it was never determined if Darcie was bound, she was gagged, which is a form of control. In Guffie, my interpretation of the crime kit is that it contained the implements that would have facilitated all the things that were done in the murders."

"Miles Transported," read Drossel.

"This category has to do with the considerable mileage from where the victims were last seen or abducted to where the body was found," Biondi explained. "Heedick was last seen in Modesto and her body was found in the lower part of Sacramento County deposited in heavy underbrush off a steep riverbank. The distance was approximately 50 miles. Brown was presumably abducted where her car was found, and her body was discovered in an irrigation ditch 20 miles away. Sabrah was found in a lightly wooded area 44 miles from her disabled car. Frackenpohl was last seen working the stroll area in West Sacramento. She was found 100 miles away."

"Now, why is the miles transported, anywhere from 20 to 100 miles, significant to you?" Drossel asked.

"It's significant in that I think it's a reasonable interpretation that this is a ritual that this one killer is doing," Biondi said. "I came to this conclusion because in all the cases it's unnecessary to drive so far. If it was simply to hide the body, there were desolate areas much closer to each of the places where the victims were last seen. I think the transportation of the victim is something that allows the person committing the murder more time to be with the victim to carry out whatever activity he is doing."

"Does the transportation aspect have any significance to you in respect to hindering the police investigators' trying to solve a murder?"

"Yes, that's another factor," said Biondi. "Any time you involve more than one jurisdiction, the case becomes extremely complex. In all these cases, the victim is last seen in one jurisdiction, and the body found in another. In some of the cases they're the subject of a missing persons report in one jurisdiction, but the murder case is being investigated by another. One interpretation would be it's a deliberate attempt by the same person to diminish the chances that he'll be caught. It also delays the identification of the victims—none of them had personal identification on them—which hinders and delays the murder investigation."

Biondi went down the list:

- Heedick was last seen in Stanislaus County and her body was found in Sacramento County;
- Brown's car was found in Sacramento County and her body was found in San Joaquin County;
- Sabrah was abducted in San Joaquin County and her body was found in Amador County;
- Frackenpohl was last seen in Yolo County and her body was found in El Dorado County.

"There seems to me to be a deliberate attempt to cross jurisdictional lines," Biondi said, "and complicate the investigation."

Drossel moved his expert witness on to the next column on the chart: *Nonfunctional Cutting.*

"This is not done for the purpose of removing a garment or cutting it up to facilitate some type of binding," Biondi explained. "It's an activity that only has meaning to the killer. Perhaps some psychological meaning."

"In your experience investigating four hundred to five hundred homicides," Drossel said, "have you seen nonfunctional cutting before?"

"This is the first time I have seen this."

"Do you consider that a unique factor?"

"I consider it very unique."

Cause of Death.

"Ligature strangulation was the cause of death in all these cases," Biondi said. "When it came to Frackenpohl, there was an improvement in the method. In at least two of these cases the ligature was made from the victim's own clothing. With Darcie, there was an extra control device, a garrote, which is a more efficient way to use a ligature."

In Guffie, Biondi said, there was an improved, custom-made garrote found in the crime kit—"still another progression."

Sex Motive.

"Because the victims were all young females and there was either partial nudity or total nudity, a sexual motive was probably present. In a lot of serial murder cases, it's been my experience that usually the killer's true motivation is power and control over another person. It's a sexual assault, certainly, but it's also a way to dominate a person. And I can see that in these cases, particularly in Frackenpohl, where there were more control devices, a need the killer had to express dominance over his victim."

Drossel took Biondi over the contents of the crime kit. "The handcuffs are a control device," said the detective. "In Frackenpohl, a murder committed about three weeks before theGuffie assault, no determination could be made as to whether she had been bound. But the presence of the handcuffs in the Guffie crime kit is a possible explanation; handcuffs could have been used to control Frackenpohl and were removed and taken from the scene."

As to the cordage fashioned into a garrote, Biondi described it as a "dramatic improvement" over the tourniquet device used on Frackenpohl. "It has to do with inside experience. The killer knew what had worked well, and what didn't work well. He wanted to improve his efficiency. The longer he killed, the better he got at it. He was coming to the crimes prepared, and had some things preplanned."

The piece of 6-foot cord from the crime kit could have been used as a "control device in the car during transportation or perhaps as a leash to lead the victim to the crime scene, such as when he took Frackenpohl down the roadway to the place where she was killed."

The vibrator, Biondi said, was "associated with some type of sexual activity."

Drossel asked what the significance might be of the scissors found in the crime kit.

"An instrument to be used to make the nonfunctional clothes cutting we see in the murder cases," Biondi said.

"Are you aware of scissors being found at a murder scene?" Drossel asked.

"Yes," Biondi said. "At the Brown scene, scissors were found in the ditch where her body was recovered."

The two rubber hair bands could have been used to keep the victims' hair from "entwining or entangling in the ligature," Biondi said. "Early on there was one very distinguishing dissimilarity between the cases: Stephanie Brown's hair was cut. We did not see the hair cutting in the other murders. We later speculated that possibly because no ligature was found with the victim, that the hair was cut to remove the ligature, which was then taken from the scene."

Drossel was nearing the end.

"The term 'Green River' has been brought up at this trial," he said. "Are you familiar with it?"

"Yes, I am."

In cross-examining one of the detectives earlier, Phil Kohn, promoting the defense's theory that investigators had suffered "tunnel vision" in building their case against Roger Kibbe, had tried to hint that the I-5 killings may have been committed by the same person responsible for the unsolved Seattle-area killings.

"How are you familiar with that term?" Drossel asked.

"I know some of the investigators who have worked on the case for years. Also, I traveled to Seattle and talked to the Green River investigators on this case."

"What type of killings were involved in the Green River incidents?" the prosecutor asked.

"Primarily prostitutes who were picked up near the Seattle Airport, an area known for prostitution, and their bodies found in rural areas—body dumps—and by the time they were found usually badly decomposed and with a lot of animal activity."

"Was the cause of death determined on those bodies?"

"In many of the cases they have no cause of death because of the decomposition and animal damage," Biondi said. "In at least one case they presumed ligature strangulation because of the presence of a piece of clothing around the victim's neck."

"Does the Green River Killer in your mind relate to the I-5 series of victims?"

"I spent an entire day talking to the investigators there, going over all the details of our cases and comparing cases with them," Biondi said thoughtfully. "I left unable to establish any viable links."

Phil Kohn began his cross-examination of Biondi by asking if during the search of any of Kibbe's residences or storage spaces, any items that could be connected to any of the victims were found.

"No."

Biondi still thought that Kibbe might have stashed some of it—purses, ID cards, jewelry—to keep as trophies, like an antelope head on a hunter's wall.

"In the Green River killings you spoke about," Kohn said, "where the cause of death was ligature strangulation, what was the implement used?"

"The victim's clothing," Biondi said.

"Is it not unusual in a homicide to find that strangulation was the cause of death and that the victim's clothes was used as an implement?"

"It's a fairly common manner of strangulation."

Still, there *were* those apparent similarities, exactly what had caused Biondi to spend a day in Seattle. But rather than provide Kibbe with a scapegoat, Biondi would have turned the tables on the defense's strategy. Since he knew Kibbe was the "I-5 Killer," if those killings were done by the person who was responsible for the Green River slayings, ergo, Roger Kibbe had killed forty-one women in the Seattle area between 1982 and 1983 and was himself the long-sought "Green River Killer."

"In these cases up in Washington"—Kohn wasn't giving up—"you indicated that the bodies were dumped in a remote area, is that correct?"

"Yes."

"In rural areas?"

"Well, more remote than rural. A lot of the bodies were along the Green River off the highway."

"But certainly not in an area where the body would be easily located?"

"Correct, heavy underbrush."

"Not unlike the cases you described on the chart?"

"Yes."

"In these cases up in Washington, are you familiar with whether the killer would have crossed jurisdictional lines as you indicated the 'I-5 Killer' did?"

"I believe there was crossing of jurisdictional lines; city and county boundaries in that series."

"When you talk of jurisdictional lines in the I-5 cases, what are you talking about?"

"County boundaries."

"It is your opinion that the reason it was done in these cases is to avoid detection because two agencies would be involved, is that correct?"

"That's one of the reasons," Biondi said. "As I said, I also feel it was ritualistic in that it allowed some time for the suspect to be with the victim."

"Did the Green River investigators, if you know, attempt at some point to link their cases to some murders down in San Diego?" Kohn asked.

"Yes."

Kohn asked about what type of cases San Diego had, and Biondi summarized what he knew.

Curiously, when the Green River killings stopped in 1985, the San Diego series began—and there *were* similarities. Due to Roger Kibbe's familial connections to the San Diego area, Biondi had also talked to San Diego detectives during the I-5 investigation. San Diego had ended up with forty-one victims—ironically, the same number credited to the "Green River Killer"—mostly prostitutes picked up in downtown San Diego. Their bodies were found 35 to 45 miles away in the rural Pine Lake area. There had been no evidence of clothescutting. Unlike I-5 but similar to Green River, the body-dumping sites had been clustered; bodies repeatedly dumped in the same area, some within yards of where another body had been previously found. San Diego had a city/county task force that predictably became embroiled in politics and infighting, and disbanded. Eventually, a suspect was arrested and convicted of two of the murders; however, San Diego detectives became convinced they had more than one series overlapping and that there were at least two killers, maybe more. Yet, by 1989 the killings had stopped.

Moving on, Kohn speculated aloud that if a killer was looking for women to abduct, control, and kill, "as you've indicated these cases are about," he could easily find a prostitute to get in his car, without looking for stranded motorists. "There would be no guarantee," he went on, "that Brown and Sabrah would end up stranded on the road."

"No guarantees. In their cases, it was happenstance."

"Doesn't that distinguish Sabrah and Brown from Heedick, Frackenpohl, and Guffie?" Kohn asked.

"They were all victims of opportunity."

"They were," Kohn agreed. "But Brown and Sabrah were victims of an opportunity that was happenstance."

"By design," Biondi countered, "if the killer also cruised the highway looking for just such opportunities."

"But you don't know that?"

Biondi looked hard at the defense attorney. "That's *exactly* what occurred in Brown and Sabrah," he said.

Interestingly, it was Kohn who brought up the name Karen Finch. "There was a woman named Karen Finch who was stabbed to death?"

"Yes."

"Were there cuts on her clothes?"

"Yes."

Biondi understood why the prosecutor had excluded Finch from the list of I-5 victims, but he had not liked it. The fact that they had a serial killer known to use a sharp instrument as part of his ritual didn't make it so surprising that one victim ended up stabbed. And in every other way, Finch had fit the victim mold.

"She is not part of the group of deaths you have identified here, is that correct?" Kohn continued.

"That's correct."

"The Finch case has never been solved, is that correct?"

"There's been no one charged in that case," said Biondi, who certainly did believe the Finch case had been solved.

On redirect, Drossel asked if Biondi had taken into consideration in his analysis that the killer had come across different circumstances from one victim to another, thereby leading to slight variations in each case.

"Sure, because we're dealing with human behavior here," Biondi said. "One victim may be a fighter, another one may be very passive. One victim may require more control. In the case of Darcie Frackenpohl, perhaps she was a screaming, struggling type, which might account for why she was gagged. That's not unusual in other serial murder cases I have seen. Some victims require more control than others."

"Would a person known to cruise highways and visit prostitution areas fit the type of killer you believe is responsible for these cases?" the prosecutor asked.

"Yes. At least two of the cases occurred on Interstate 5. That would require the suspect to traverse that highway until he came across an opportunity. When more came to light about Roger Kibbe, we factored in that he had a number of vehicles with unexplained high mileage, and a reputation for driving great distances."

Drossel had a last question.

"How do you interpret the common threads in these four murders and the assault case?" the prosecutor asked.

"In my opinion, with the categories we have up there and the analysis that has been done, there is a signature of one killer in these cases."

It wasn't quite enough.

"And again, the categories you've used to determine this 'signature'?"

"The nonfunctional clothes cutting and the miles transported are the two primary categories. But the cause of death, the body crime scene, the sex motive, just across the board it is a very unique criminal signature."

"No further questions."

"All right," said Judge Finney. "The witness is excused. People rest?"

Drossel had remained standing. "People rest."

THE DEFENSE of Roger Kibbe was notably brief.

In his opening statement, defense attorney Phil Kohn told the jury: "Mr. Kibbe has met with his counsel and he's decided not to testify. Nothing is worse in a case than for everyone to sit in the courtroom and wait anxiously for someone to testify, and then the defense rests its case. We are not going to do that. Mr. Kibbe is prepared to rely on the state of the evidence as put forth by the prosecution and by the four witnesses that the defense will present today."

Robert Shomer, a licensed psychologist, former Harvard professor, and expert on eyewitness identification, took the stand in the defense's effort to debunk the prosecution's witnesses who had pointed the finger at Roger Kibbe—Carmen Anselmi, James Driggers, Carol Stockton.

"What are the major ways in which eyewitness identification has been studied?" Kohn asked.

"It's involved people seeing things, remembering what they had seen, and being tested to see if they can identify something. 'Identification' is a fairly simple word but it has a very complex meaning."

It came out that Shomer's own testing of eyewitnesses had involved mostly his own college students, and was theoretical in nature. In fact, he had not met or talked to any of the I-5 eyewitnesses.

"In terms of how good people are at remembering faces and identifying them later on," Shomer said, "on average we get about 80 percent accuracy under ideal conditions. So, people are still not acting like a camera."

Shomer said physical lineups and photo lineups were "fine as long as you don't contaminate that memory by information you present to that person beforehand."

In a series of three "hypotheticals" presented by Kohn with no names used—in fact, they were the exact circumstances of the prosecution's three eyewitnesses—Shomer reacted to the information provided, concluding that both time and suggestibility had played major roles in their eventual identification.

"I would have grave suspicions about validity," he concluded. "From a psychological standpoint, they wouldn't be called identifications at all. They would be called statements of someone who really believes what they're saying. They are not necessarily lying. But from a psychological standing they are not valid identifications."

On cross-examination, Drossel asked Shomer if he had a reputation as a defense witness.

"I have no idea," he said.

"You tell us you have testified two hundred fifty to three hundred times. Hasn't it always been for the defense?"

"So far."

"And do you believe you continually testify for the defense because you hold some positions on eyewitness identification that are contrary to the views of your peers?"

"Absolutely not," Shomer huffed.

"This area of eyewitness identification is actually a portion of the studies in psychology, isn't that correct?"

"I suppose."

"It's not a science like medicine, correct?"

"That's absolutely incorrect. It is more of a science than medicine is."

A few questions later, Judge Finney sent both the jury and the witness from the room.

From the bench, the judge looked down scoldingly at Kohn. "I don't think this gentleman is helping your cause in maintaining that what he has done is a scientific endeavor. He is a professional witness. He runs with the answers. There is not one shred of evidence at this point that witness methodology, for lack of a better word, debunking witness identification, is scientific or accepted within the scientific community. I have had over the years several eyewitness experts testify. I have had hundreds of psychiatrists and psychologists testify, and I have never heard anybody try and put the patina on it that this gentleman is trying to do."

Once the judge had cooled off, Shomer came back for Drossel to finish his cross.

The next witness, Raymond Farrell, was a master parachute rigger who owned his own parachute company.

Farrell identified the cordage in the case as Mil C5040 Type 3, "commonly known as 550 cord because it has a break strength of 550 pounds."

"Is this cord common in your industry?" Kohn asked.

"It's real common."

In addition to use in parachute rigging, Farrell said he had sold the cord to dog trainers for training purposes, for clotheslines, and even to a group of musicians once for stringing bongos and African drums.

"It's commonly available in places other than a parachute shop?"

"Yeah."

"Have you ever seen any colored marks, in particular, any red marks, on any 550 cord when it comes from the factory?" Kohn asked.

"It doesn't come from the factory marked, but it's common to find the marks on the cordage. It's done at the factory when they're manufacturing canopies."

"What's the purpose of the markings?"

"They usually string this type of cordage out on a line table and they'll put out hundreds of yards of cordage at once. And they have a marking grid they use for cutting and sewing canopies. At a couple of parachute factories where I have worked, they used colored-coded markings to indicate where to cut and sew."

"It doesn't have to be red?"

"Right. Any color. It's common to use a bright color, like red or green or blue."

"And what is that paint applied with?" he asked.

"Usually felt-tip markers are the easier thing to use," Farrell said.

Kohn seemed to have gone one question too far, but he recovered. "Can it be spray-painted on?" he asked.

"It can be sprayed on if you're trying to cover a wider area, such as on a four-line release system—you mark a larger portion of line to indicate which line to pull."

Farrell held his fingers about 4 inches apart to show how wide an area of line would be sprayed.

On cross, Drossel went for the heart.

"You mentioned that there can be some red substance put on those cords during manufacturing, is that correct?"

"Yes. To know where you are going to cut the line."

"You mentioned felt-tip marker could be used."

"Yes, it is pretty common."

"That is more common than some other types of substance, such as paint?" Drossel asked.

"In my experience, felt markers were the most common used at the factory that I worked in."

"I have no further questions."

John Thorton, a professor of forensic science at the University of California, Berkeley, was called next.

He testified to having reviewed the reports of Faye Springer and Skip Palenik and to reading their testimony.

"Would you tell us the approximate size of the red paint particles on this exhibit?" asked Tom Kolpacoff, pointing to the piece of cordage from the crime kit.

"It's six microns," Thorton said. "That would be six-millionths of a meter, a meter being a little greater than a yard."

"To use a real scientific term, it's an itsy-bitsy particle?"

"It's a very, very small particle. I would consider this to be at about the lower possible range of size for any forensic examination. If it was any smaller, I don't think it would have been of any value for forensic purposes."

Thorton described the ten elements found in the red paint by Skip Palenik to be "expected components of paint," although he said the sodium and chlorine might well be contaminants as suggested by the prosecution's expert.

Thorton also agreed that the dark football-shaped particles were fungal spores.

"Are fungal spores unusual to see?"

"No."

"Does dirt contain fungal spores?"

"Yes."

As for the hair evidence, Thorton said, "In an elimination sense, hair evidence is very useful. If the issue is whether or not a particular hair came from an individual, then it's my opinion that hair is a miserable form of evidence."

However, Thorton did state that he believed it possible to compare animal hairs for purposes of identifying the type of animal it came from. He agreed that the animal hairs found on Darcie Frackenpohl's dress were cat hairs.

When it came to the nonfunctional cutting of the victims' clothing as testified to by Jim Streeter, Thorton said he believed some of the cuts were tears in the fabric. But whatever advantage that had bought the defense in terms of putting some distance between the scissors found in Kibbe's crime kit and the clothes cutting was lost on Kolpacoff's next exchange with the defense's own criminalist.

"In your professional opinion, is there any way of telling what type of instrument made those cuts?"

"I think they're scissor cuts."

Drossel began his cross-examination by asking Thorton if he had any problems with the methodology used by Faye Springer in her work on the I-5 cases.

"No, I don't."

"Do you know Skip Palenik's reputation in his particular area of microscopy?"

"Yes. Mr. Palenik enjoys immense stature with the forensic science community for his abilities as a forensic microscopist."

"You never physically examined fibers or cordage or hair or clothing except the pink dress we have in this courtroom?" Drossel asked.

"That's correct."

"And the pink dress was first examined by you in court with a magnifying glass just a couple of days ago. Is that correct?"

"Yes."

"Is it correct that you are suspect of some of Jim Streeter's analysis?"

"That would be a fair characterization."

"And you're testifying without having actually physically looked at the rest of the clothes evidence?"

"Not to be argumentative, but I think I can tell a good egg from a bad one without laying one," said Thorton.

Drossel went over Thorton's tears-versus-cuts testimony, highlighting the sizable number of cuts that Thorton confirmed. His testimony had the effect of corroborating most of the cuts found by Streeter, with the added bonus of identifying scissors as the cutting instrument, something Streeter had not done.

"You're familiar with the terms 'functional' and 'nonfunctional' cuts?" Drossel asked.

"Yes. I have no quarrel with that concept."

"Then Mr. Streeter's definition of 'nonfunctional' cutting makes sense to you?"

"Yes, it does."

Drossel, who decided to quit while ahead, thought Thorton had turned into a pretty fair prosecution witness.

The last defense witness was Cliffe Harriman, a private investigator and retired FBI agent.

Harriman had been called to critique the physical lineup of September 1, 1988, at which James Driggers had picked out Roger Kibbe. Shown a picture of the lineup, Harriman said, "There is one individual designated as number two whose attire is sufficiently distinguishable from the other four that it tends to automatically direct your attention to that one individual to the exclusion of the others."

Of course, number two was Roger Kibbe.

Harriman's reasoning: All five men were wearing gray sweatshirts, but Kibbe's looked the darkest.

On cross, Drossel asked if Harriman had been at the lineup.

"No, sir, I was not."

"Have you seen the videotape of the lineup?"

"No, sir, I have not."

"You are basing your opinion on a photograph of the lineup?"

"That's correct."

"Do you know if these shades of coloring are true or whether they may have to do with the film or lighting?"

"No, sir."

When Harriman stepped down, Judge Finney asked if there would be any further witnesses.

"No further witnesses," said Kolpacoff.

"Defense rests."

"GOOD morning, ladies and gentlemen," Assistant D.A. Bob Drossel said to the jurors. "I thank you for your patience and attention during the course of this trial.

"In my closing argument, I want to take a look at the law, particularly on murder, and then fit the facts of this case, the evidence, into the law to show you how defendant RogerKibbe is guilty of first-degree murder."

Drossel began a detailed examination of the physical and circumstantial evidence in the Darcie Frackenpohl murder case, instructing jurors that one type of evidence had no greater weight than another.

He reminded the jurors it had been proven through fiber evidence that Frackenpohl had been in Kibbe's car. He reminded them that the cordage found at the scene had been judged by microscopic examination to be identical in every measurable way to cordage found in Kibbe's possession.

"Imagine the scale of justice," he said. "The People have put evidence of guilt on one side of that scale, and it has come down pretty far beyond a reasonable doubt that Roger Kibbe unlawfully, willfully, deliberately, and with premeditation took Darcie Frackenpohl's life.

"We have the testimony of Faye Springer, who did the comparison work on the trace evidence. The defense's own criminalist didn't have any problems with her methodology or procedures. No problems. Her findings? That the two fibers taken off that pink dress"—he pointed to Darcie's dress, visible atop the exhibits—"were matched to the floor mat of Kibbe's Hyundai.

"Then we had Skip Palenik. Again, the defense criminalist agreed that he was tops in his field. Skip's separate findings were actually confirmation of Faye, and then he went a step further with the fibers. He found them to be unique. They had the same fungal spores. And one of the fibers recovered from Darcie's dress had the red paint from the spill on the rear floor mat. I ask you: How did her dress pick up that fiber if she wasn't in Roger Kibbe's car?"

Drossel reviewed the cordage evidence, too.

"It was proven that the cordage from all three locations had been in a similar environment at one time. Springer gave her opinion that the red paint could have gotten on the cordage when someone was spray-painting."

As for the master parachute rigger's testimony regarding cordage being marked at the factory when parachute canopies were being cut and sewn, Drossel said, "Does it really matter how those seven pieces of cordage from three locations got contaminated? The fact is that they did. Whether by some manufacturing process or by some overspraying at some other point in time. The fact is it's still there."

The prosecutor reminded the jurors of evidence of Kibbe's black eye around the time of Frackenpohl's disappearance, and the testimony he'd elicited from one of the pathologists that a black eye can show up minutes to hours after a blow, and last several days to two weeks or more.

"Kibbe gave at least two stories as to how he got that black eye," Drossel said. "Why? We don't know. Could the true version be that Darcie Frackenpohl was able to get a blow in? Maybe she was a feisty gal who wasn't going to be submissive. Maybe she got a blow in with her fist, her elbow, her knee, or her foot. Maybe she wasn't going to go willingly. The time period is right, and the circumstances are right."

Drossel looked up from his notes, and moved a step or two closer to the jury.

"What about premeditation? This murder was considered and planned beforehand, based on the evidence. Doesn't the crime scene say it all?

"Let's make some reasonable interpretations here. Darcie's nude body. Obviously, based on the evidence, there is some sexual motive. If you want to discount that evidence, it's clear that he had hatred toward women. You can see in those exhibits. Darcie was gagged with her own pantyhose. What's the significance of that gagging, and the control and manipulation he had over her? Was he saying, 'Don't scream. Don't scream. I won't hurt you, cunt, bitch'? Was he playing with her? Was he taking the garrote, tightening it as he was walking down the road with her? Tightening it just a little more, 'I won't hurt you'? Was he playing with her? Did he receive some sexual arousal? Or did he just want to watch her die? Control and manipulation. Time to be with her. Play with her. Watch her. Tightening it all the time. 'Be good and I won't hurt you.' Loosening it if she's good, tightening it when she struggles. Aren't these reasonable interpretations?

"We know she died at the scene because there was fecal material on her buttocks, none on her clothing. Jim Streeter told us her clothes must have been taken off before she died, but we don't really need to know that. We also don't need to know whether the clothes cutting occurred before death or after. We just need to know that it happened."

There was more to say, about the trace evidence, about the uncharged crimes that helped to show motive in the Frackenpohl murder, about the items found in the crime kit, about the eyewitnesses, about the defense witnesses, about Kibbe's automobiles. Drossel said it, then told the jury: "We've come full circle from the opening statement through the evidence to closing argument. We started this trial with a bus tour. Traveling those roads of the San Joaquin and Sacramento areas, the Sierra foothills, the Tahoe basin. We did travel that roadway. The worst human behavior possible. The most repugnant behavior possible of a human being. Compelling evidence to show Roger Kibbe did it. Compelling evidence.

"Ladies and gentlemen, based on the totality of the circumstances, there's one logical conclusion to be drawn and that is the defendant is guilty. Roger Kibbe is guilty of first-degree murder; the willful, intentional, deliberate, premeditated murder of Darcie Frackenpohl.

"The People ask you to return a verdict of guilty of murder in the first degree."

"IT'S NOT my intent to go through all of the evidence that counsel has just gone through," said Phil Kohn as he began the defense's closing argument.

"The prosecutor this afternoon gave one of the finest charges to the jury I have ever seen or heard. It was also probably the most emotional charge to a jury that I have ever seen. We make no contest of the fact that these were terrible crimes. These were brutal crimes. It was murder. It was murder in the first degree.

"But the fact is that this is a circumstantial evidence case. The law says when you are using circumstantial evidence it is necessary for an inference to be proved beyond a reasonable doubt. So if you take those facts from other cases and you use them to try to convict my client of Darcie Frackenpohl's murder, which is the only issue you are to decide, you must believe each one of these facts beyond a reasonable doubt, to a moral certainty. That doesn't mean similar, doesn't mean close, it means certainty."

Kohn referred to Carmen Anselmi as "probably the saddest part of this trial." He shook his head. "The pain she is going through must be incredible. We all know that. But the facts are she couldn't identify my client in a photo lineup or a physical lineup. When she was taken on a tour of storage facilities and was as close to my client as I am to you she didn't identify him. Then she comes to this courtroom under the pressure she's under and makes an identification.

"Mr. Driggers is a little different. His testimony changes. When he first talked to police he'd only seen the man for a minute, and only a side view of his face. When he comes to court he'd been in the car for five minutes and gets a full-face view. Why? Because he wants to solve it and put it behind him, too. I'm not going to maintain he's a liar. I am maintaining everything about his identification grows in his mind as time goes on.

"Roger was a suspect very early on in this case, and they focused on it. That's important because it explains the identifications, it's important because it explains the procedures used in the laboratory.

"Mr. Drossel wants us to believe that Faye Springer is a scientist who just simply looks at a microscope and where the fibers fall, they fall. No bias. No interest. Just a scientist. Until she testified that she cannot do work for the defense, cannot give opinions for the defense, because she works for the California Department of Justice.

"When we look at the fiber evidence, Ms. Springer says it was probably a primary transfer because of the number of fibers she found. In other words, that pink dress had to have been in Mr. Kibbe's Hyundai. That doesn't mean that someone else could not have been in that car and picked up those fibers. Kim Quackenbush testified that she and Darcie occasionally wore clothes belonging to each other. Did she wear Darcie's dress and was she in that car and did she pick up the fibers? It's entirely possible that Darcie was never in that car. There is no way of saying when that dress was in that car, if it was in fact in that car. If it was not the night she disappeared, then a week before or three weeks before? There is no evidence to that.

"Another problem I have: How many fibers did they have to look at until finally finding something of Mr. Kibbe's that was consistent? That's my problem. And the hairs—okay, Mr. Kibbe cannot be eliminated. Does that mean he did it?"

As for the cordage evidence, Kohn said, "The reason the defense brought Mr. Farrell forward was to indicate to you that that cord is commonly sold in military surplus stores and marine supply stores and in many other stores. The prosecution says this is unique evidence because of the red paint. Mr. Farrell explained how red paint can get on there during the cutting and sewing of canopies."

Kohn was winding down.

"Our burden is not to prove Roger Kibbe is innocent. That's not the burden placed on the defense. The prosecution has the entire burden. I have highlighted certain areas of evidence which the defense thinks raise a reasonable doubt. You have to search all the evidence, review the law, and I implore you to make a decision based on the law and on the evidence and not on emotion."

THE JURORS began deliberating at 9:05 A.M. on March 18, 1991. At 11:45 A.M., they took a noon recess.

After their return from lunch, compliments of El Dorado County, jury foreman John Zucconi, an employee of the South Lake Tahoe Long's Drugs, sent a note to the judge.

When court reconvened at 1:54 P.M., the lawyers and defendant were back at their respective tables.

"The Court has received a note indicating the jury has reached a verdict," Judge Finney said.

"Yes, we have," said the foreman.

"Please hand the verdict to the bailiff."

When the judge received the verdict form, he glanced at it but kept a poker face. "All right. I'll read the verdict.

"We, the jury, find the Defendant, Roger Reece Kibbe, guilty of the crime of murder in the first degree, in violation of Section 187 of the California Penal Code."

May 10, 1991

"*People* versus *Kibbe*," said Judge Terrence Finney. "The matter is set for judgment and sentence. Mr. Kohn?"

It had been fifty-three days since the jury's verdict.

Phil Kohn stood. "Your Honor, I have advised my client not to talk to Probation due to the fact that there are other cases that are out there. Based on that, we have decided to put forth no evidence."

"Mr. Drossel?" said Finney.

Taking his place before the bench, Bob Drossel said, "There is no question in the People's mind that the statutory term of twenty-five years to life is appropriate."

"What other choice is there?" the judge asked.

"There may be a quirk in the law as to probation."

Indeed, Kohn had submitted on his client's behalf an application for probation.

"When you consider the factors against probation," Drossel went on, "certainly there should not be much choice in the judge's mind. There was a showing of intent to plan and execute this crime. We have the violent conduct portrayed, which certainly shows a danger to society. As expressed in the probation report, the victim's mother, Judy Frackenpohl, who will not be here today, is clear about what she thinks should happen to the defendant: death. But that's not an option of this court."

In retrospect and after all the work that had gone into the case and the swift verdict by the jury, Drossel would very much like to have been seeking the death penalty. He believed in it, and considered Roger Kibbe an especially good candidate for that particular brand of justice.

"Based on these and other factors," Drossel continued, "the People urge the Court to follow the statutory term of twenty-five years to life."

Judge Finney cleared his throat.

"Mr. Kibbe, if you will please stand."

Kibbe rose; at his side, Kohn did, too.

"The defendant's application for probation is denied. The Court finds the factors against probation outweigh those in favor of probation. The only sentence under the law I can impose is the twenty-five years to life. Therefore, the defendant is sentenced to twenty-five years to life.

"In addition to this sentence, a period of parole pursuant to Penal Code Section 3000 commences upon the defendant's release from state prison. The period of parole shall not exceed life."

The judge informed Kibbe of his rights of appeal.

"Do you have any questions about your rights?"

"No," Kibbe responded.

"Do you understand you have sixty days to appeal?"

"Yes," Kibbe said.

"All right."

With that, court was adjourned.

El Dorado County Sheriff's Deputy Robert Dougherty escorted Kibbe from the courtroom into the secured hallway on their way back to the jail in an adjacent building. The convicted killer would wait there, his home for the past three years, until transported to state prison.

"What's new, Bob?" Kibbe asked casually.

"I'm probably doing better than you are, Roger."

"I'm not surprised about the time," Kibbe said nonchalantly. "I've been waiting for this for three years."

"I bet you're kinda relieved," Dougherty said. "Now you can sweep all this under the carpet and just start doing your time. Where do you think they're going to send you?"

"Kohn thinks Pelican Bay."

They were now waiting for the service elevator to take them to the ground floor, where they would exit through a back door and walk 100 yards down a fenced path to the jail.

"You're probably better off going there. You'll be locked down in your own cell and not have to worry about the general population," the deputy said about California's new maximum security prison reserved for the most dangerous of the dangerous.

"Yeah, I've had my own cell for the last three years so it's nothing new. For sure I don't want to go to the prison where that big guy who testified against me is doing his time. He wants a piece of me."

Having sat through the entire trial and listened to all the testimony, Dougherty had no doubt that Kibbe was referring to James Driggers.

The elevator arrived and they climbed in for the short ride down from the second floor.

"I'm sure a lot of people want a piece of you, Roger," Dougherty said as the door closed and the elevator started its descent with a groan. "But why do you think that guy wants you so bad?"

"Because I killed his girlfriend."

Dougherty looked at his charge curiously. "Roger, you're finally admitting that you killed someone?"

"Yeah," Roger Kibbe said, throwing up his arms in exasperation. "I've killed a few women. What's the big deal?"

DRAMATIS PERSONAE

Kay Maulsby still works in the Homicide Bureau of the Sacramento County Sheriff's Department. "She's not only an excellent homicide investigator," says her mentor, Ray Biondi, "but she's one of the best interviewers and interrogators I've ever seen." A year after Roger Kibbe's arrest for murder, Maulsby encountered another serial killer: James David Majors, who murdered ten people in seven months in California and Arizona. The case was solved by Maulsby and her partner, Bob Bell. Majors now resides on California's Death Row.

Faye Springer continued to review evidence in the I-5 investigation, and in July 1992 made another match of seat fibers to Roger Kibbe's Datsun 280Z in the death of KarenQuinones, a twenty-five-year-old prostitute who disappeared from downtown Sacramento in November 1986. Her body was found the following month in Napa County, 40 miles away. Cause of death was ligature strangulation; cordage connected to wooden dowels was still in place around her neck, although the cordage was not the same type that helped convict Kibbe. Springer left the California Department of Justice lab in 1996 to work at Sacramento County's new state-of-the-art crime lab, where she practices her trace evidence specialty and operates the lab's new $250,000 electron scanning microscope. In the same year that Roger Kibbe was convicted of murder, Springer's analysis of fibers, paint chips, andhair helped convict Warren James Bland, a fifty-one-year-old career sex offender, in the torture death of a seven-year-old girl. Bland is on Death Row awaiting execution by lethal injection.

Vito Bertocchini tired of the slow pace of detective work and returned to street action in the San Joaquin County Sheriff's Department Patrol Division. He worked as a canine officer with his German shepherd partner for six years. He is presently assigned to Vice. "I have never forgotten Stephanie or Charmaine," Bertocchini says of his two I-5 murder cases. He continues to search for new evidence, and hopes one day to see Roger Kibbe stand trial for their murders. Bertocchini is working with state legislators and victims' rights groups in pushing for a new state law that will allow for the single prosecution of a serial killer for crimes committed in various jurisdictions, thereby streamlining a system that still today works to the benefit of killers like Roger Kibbe. Bertocchini's partner, **Pete Rosenquist**, left the sheriff's department in 1995 for a job in the San Joaquin County District Attorney's Office as a criminal investigator. "I'm doing the same thing," says Rosenquist, "without all the politics." **Larry Ferrari**, the third San Joaquin detective assigned to the I-5 task force, is also working as a criminal investigator in the D.A.'s office, alongside Rosenquist.

Ray Biondi, a year after Roger Kibbe's arrest, declined to accept a departmental Distinguished Service Award from his supervisor. His job had been made "twice as hard as it should have been" by having to continually butt heads with a "mostly indifferent administration," he told his boss. After I-5, Biondi led two more successful serial murder investigations before retiring in 1993. He consults occasionally on homicide investigations, and still pesters the Sacramento County District Attorney's Office about filing murder charges against Kibbe. "It's a low priority for the D.A. because Kibbe has been convicted of murder and is in prison," Biondi says. "Seeing him convicted of the other murders is not a low priority for those victims' families."

Stan Reed continues to work Homicide with uncommon tenacity. In 1991, he identified and arrested Eric Royce Leonard, aka "The Thrill Killer," who was subsequently convicted of six murders and sentenced to die. In 1996, after seven years of investigative work, Reed arrested Joseph Consorti for the vicious 1989 killing of a five-year-old girl. And in 1997, he arrested Duane Hackney for the decade-old sexual assault and murder of eleven-year-old Vickie Skanks.

Jim Streeter left DOJ in 1993 for a position as a forensic scientist with the State of Montana crime lab in Missoula, where his specialty is DNA analysis. He says the effectiveness of DNA technology has increased by "quantum leaps" in the decade since Roger Kibbe's arrest—"We're able to do a lot more with a lot less." Streeter believes that the single foreign hair and few sperm cells recovered from Stephanie Brown, and the sperm cells from Karen Finch, could today be successfully analyzed to see if there is a match of genetic markers with Kibbe.

Carmen Anselmi is raising Charmaine's son, Sabri, now twelve years old, in Sacramento. Being an older single parent living on her late husband's survivor benefits has not been easy for Carmen, now sixty-three. She adopted Sabri when he was a year old and he calls his grandmother "Mom," although he knows of his mother's fate. "I told him when he started asking questions," Carmen says. "He's very angry. It has affected him in school and everything. I think we'll both feel better when we have a trial for his mother's murder and her killer is convicted."

Judy Frackenpohl has advanced in her career with a food service company and still lives in Seattle, where she raised her son, Larry, now twenty-five, an expert skier who works at ski resorts. She says Roger Kibbe's conviction for killing her daughter, Darcie, gave her "no personal satisfaction because he's still alive," although she was pleased to see him "off the streets." Judy thinks about her daughter every day. "Darcie made her choices. Maybe they weren't the right choices, but she didn't choose to die."

Jo-Allyn Brown, and her husband, Tom, still reside in the rural ranch-style home where Stephanie was raised. Their surviving three daughters live close by. Stephanie's youngest sister, Michaela, twenty-eight, now the mother of two, says, "We aren't the same people. There's a deadness to us all." Jo-Allyn has always wanted to know what happened at the end. "The man who was the last to see Stephanie alive will probably never tell."

Jo-Allyn says she and Tom were glad Kibbe was convicted of one killing, "but he's still eating three meals a day and our daughter is dead. Is that fair?"

Debra Guffie, the one who got away and first pointed the finger at Roger Kibbe, has disappeared.

James Driggers, Lora Heedick's boyfriend, was discharged from parole in April 1994. His present whereabouts are unknown.

Robert Drossel transferred from the El Dorado County District Attorney's South Lake Tahoe office to the main office in Placerville, were he supervised the attorney staff and handled major prosecutions until his retirement in 1997. "Roger Kibbe did a lot of cruising in his cars looking for victims," Drossel says. "The song 'On the Road Again' kept running through my mind during the trial. I don't think we'll ever know for sure just how many he's good for." The man who successfully prosecuted Roger Kibbe for murder lives quietly with his family on California's north coast.

Phil Kohn, Roger Kibbe's lead defense lawyer, works for the Clark County Public Defender's Office in Las Vegas, handling death penalty cases. "I think the prosecutors erred in not filing special circumstances in the Darcie Frackenpohl murder and making it a death penalty case," Kohn says. "How hard would it have been to prove kidnapping? The evidence showed he walked the victim down that road to do damage to her. That's a kidnap, according to the statutes."

Harriet Kibbe still lives in northern California. So angry at detectives for coming to her place of work and trying to intimidate her, she has to this day not spoken to authorities about her husband or the murder case against him. Not long after Roger's conviction, she began visiting him at Folsom State Prison. The visits continued nonstop for four years. "I still needed to make it better," Harriet says. "I was consumed with wanting to make up for whatever part I had played in ruining his life. Then one day he called to say they were transferring him down south. I went to see him, knowing it would be the last time but not telling him. I said, 'You know, I still love you, but there are all these dead bodies.' Roger said, 'Well, they're all gone.' " Among the murders Harriet says Roger confessed to her: the Napa County victim (Karen Quinones). "Not a day goes by when I don't think of Roger and his victims," she says. "The one picture I keep seeing in my head is Stephanie Brown's. Why hers and not the others', I don't know." Harriet, who last visited Roger in early 1996, received a twenty-first wedding anniversary card from him on April 25 of that year. She sells insurance door-to-door with her common-law husband, Robert Hunter. She has never divorced Roger Kibbe.

Steve Kibbe never visited his brother Roger after his arrest for murder. "Roger has not sought contact with me or anyone else in the family," says Steve, who felt ostracized by fellow law enforcement officers as a result of his brother's crimes. "I bent over backwards to cooperate with the investigators, even talking to Roger over the phone and allowing them to record it. I told the detectives I was *not* my brother's keeper, but I still got slam-dunked by them." He is also angry that he and the rest of his family were hounded by the news media. "There were more victims than those named in court," he says. "I spent thirty-two years in law enforcement. I want to go out now and leave this behind me." Steve Kibbe retired from the Douglas County, Nevada, Sheriff's Department in early 1998.

Jack Kibbe, now in his eighties, lives quietly in suburban San Diego, some fifteen miles from Roger's childhood home in Chula Vista. He remembers, years ago, being pestered by Roger to come out and watch him skydive. Seeing his son jump out of an airplane wasn't something Jack was crazy about doing, but finally he relented. That day, Roger's main chute didn't deploy and he had trouble getting his reserve to open. "If it had been another few seconds he wouldn't have made it," Jack recalls. "I often think it's just too bad Roger got his reserve chute open. It's a terrible thing for a father to think, I know. But all those women would still be alive today."

Roger Kibbe is inmate #E99227 at Pleasant Valley State Prison in Coalinga, California. He declined to be interviewed for this book. His longtime cell mate at both Folsom and Pleasant Valley, Dale Sanders, reports that Roger doesn't have many friends behind bars and lives in "constant fear" of running into a relative of one of his victims in the prison yard. For that reason Kibbe also avoids the shower room, going days without bathing. He loves chess and watches a lot of television; his favorite shows are "Married with Children" ("Roger is crazy about Kelly Bundy," says Sanders), "America's Most Wanted," and "Cops." He is assigned to a job in the yard crew, and is given a trash bag every morning to pick up the prison yard. Sanders says that when alone in their cell at night, Kibbe tells him stories about his crimes, often while sitting on his bunk drinking a Pepsi and eating a Hershey bar. "He hates his mother for the way she treated him as a child," Sanders says, "and has never visited her grave." Among the murders Sanders says Kibbe has told of committing: Karen Finch. All his victims had long hair for a reason: "Once you get your hands in a woman's hair, you can do anything with them," Roger tells Sanders. "Just pull back and there's nothing they can do." The way he would get women to pull over, Kibbe explains, was to find one that "looked good," speed ahead, pull over, open his hood, and fake car trouble. He claims Stephanie Brown and Karen Finch both fell for this tactic, although he adds that Stephanie "asked me a question as if she was lost. I looked both ways for traffic and grabbed her."

EPILOGUE

Through the years following Roger Kibbe's conviction in the murder of Darcie Frackenpohl, and long after he left the sheriff's department and joined the San Joaquin County District Attorney's Office as a criminal investigator, Vito Bertocchini never forgot Stephanie Brown, Charmaine Sabrah, and the other women whom he believed Roger Kibbe had also murdered.

With the advance of DNA in criminal investigations, Bertocchini obtained a search warrant in 2000 to collect a sample of Kibbe's blood. He drove to Pleasant Valley State Prison, and served Kibbe with the warrant requiring him to provide blood for scientific analysis. The inmate said he would probably faint during the procedure. As he rolled up a shirt sleeve for the prison nurse, Kibbe added, "I hate the sight of blood."

After that came the laborious process of working the cold cases from the files and storage archives of the various jurisdictions involved as Bertocchini searched for viable evidence that could be compared to Kibbe's DNA.

Three years later, after Kibbe was linked through his DNA to additional murders, Bertocchini returned to the prison, along with his former partner, Pete Rosenquist, then retired. Bertocchini told Kibbe the DNA results.

"Do you want to talk about these cases?" Bertocchini asked.

"I don't know," Kibbe said.

"Here's what's going to happen, Roger. We've got you made on these other cases. The D.A. will probably file special circumstances, which could mean the death penalty. If you want to avoid that, you need to start talking."

It wasn't as if Bertocchini cared a whit about sparing Kibbe's life. Rather, he wanted to provide some closure for the families of Kibbe's victims. With the exception of Darcie Frackenpohl's family, none had seen anyone convicted of killing their loved one. With Kibbe now close to 70 years of age, and given that appeals in a California death penalty case could take up to 20 years to be exhausted, chances were good that even if he was sentenced to be executed Kibbe would die of natural causes in prison.

Kibbe seemed to be studying his hands, which were folded in his lap. "Okay," he said softly. "I can tell you about four of them."

As Bertocchini would later explain, that was the "start of the process." Eventually, Kibbe confessed to kidnapping, raping and murdering a total of seven women: Darcie Frackenpohl, whom he had already been convicted of killing, Stephanie Brown, Charmaine Sabrah, Lora Heedick, Karen Quinones, Barbara Ann Scott, whose body was found in 1986 on a golf course next to an airport Kibbe went to for skydiving flights, and Lou Ellen Burleigh, a missing person in 1977 whose remains had never been found.

Bertocchini believes Kibbe also murdered Karen Finch. There was no DNA evidence that fingered Kibbe, however, and Kibbe denied killing her. "In talks with me," Bertocchini said, "Roger claimed that strangulation is not a violent way to die. When he strangled a woman, he says she just went to sleep. With Finch, there was a violent struggle, during which she was stabbed in the chest and her throat slashed. I think he viewed slugging it out with a woman and stabbing her to death a failure, and one he was not willing to admit to."

Information given by Kibbe as to where he had dumped Burleigh's body aided authorities in locating her remains in 2011. During an eight-hour, video-taped session with Bertocchini, Kibbe described all seven abductions, rapes and murders in excruciating detail. The man across from him, Bertocchini now saw with his own eyes, was a heartless serial-killing machine. Kibbe spoke softly, with neither the tone nor volume of his voice changing for hours on end. He appeared devoid of any remorse or emotion.

On September 29, 2009, as part of a plea deal to avoid the death penalty, Kibbe, his hair white and sporting a long, scraggly beard to match, entered guilty pleas in a San Joaquin County courtroom to the six additional murders. Five weeks later, he was sentenced to six life terms without the possibility of parole.

Convicted serial killer Roger Kibbe is still incarcerated at Pleasant Valley State Prison in Coalinga, Fresno County. Since his additional convictions and receiving life without parole, he is classified at Level 4, a designation given the most dangerous inmates in the state prison system.

Before Bertocchini retired in 2012, he visited Kibbe. The detective found Kibbe clean-shaven with a buzz cut and more weight on his frame, all of which made him look 20 years younger than he had in court three years earlier.

Kibbe told the detective that he stayed in his cell most of the time because there were "lots of violent inmates" in Level 4 and he didn't want to be around them. As a result of his new classification, he no longer had all the privileges he once had, and he said he especially missed making arts and crafts.

"He knows there's always a possibility that he may run into an inmate who was related to one of his victims," Bertocchini reports. "He knows he could be killed by someone out for revenge or just wanting to make a name for himself in prison. Kibbe lives in fear of that happening."

In spite of Kibbe's confessions and life sentence that guarantees he will die in prison, Bertocchini does not feel his own strong sense of closure in the case he worked on and off for 24 years. "We linked Kibbe to six murders committed between 1986 and 1987, and one in 1977. I don't believe this guy killed once then stopped for ten years before deciding to become a serial killer. What was he doing for those ten years? And for that matter, before 1977? That thought is scary. Really scary."

ABOUT THE AUTHOR

Bruce Henderson is the author or coauthor of more than twenty nonfic-
tions books, including #1 *New York Times* bestseller *And the Sea Will Tell*,
a true story of murder on a South Seas island, and *Fatal North: Murder
and Survival on the First North Pole Expedition*, winner of a national book
award from the American Society of Journalists and Authors. He lives in
Menlo Park, California. Find Bruce on the web at: www.brucehenderson-
books.com.

Stephanie Brown, nineteen, a suntanned girl-next-door type, disappeared on California's Interstate 5 after venturing into the night to give her roommate a lift.

Charmaine Sabrah, twenty-six, was enjoying a night out with her mother when her car broke down on I-5 and she accepted a ride from a stranger in a sports car.

Lora Heedick, twenty, and her boyfriend were in search of money for street
drugs on the night she got into a car with a middle-aged man
and was never seen alive again.

Karen Finch, twenty-five, a single mother, disappeared on the way home after
spending the weekend with her young daughter.

Debra Guffie, a twenty-nine-year-old heroin junkie who would have been the next I-5 victim, escaped and pointed the finger at Roger Kibbe.

Darcie Frackenpohl, seventeen, a Seattle high school student turned teenage runaway, disappeared while working as a prostitute in Sacramento.

Roger Reece Kibbe, forty-eight, on the night he was arrested
for assaulting Debra Guffie.

Roger Kibbe skydiving, late 1970s.

Roger Kibbe, with daughter, Carolyn, then fourteen, 1976.

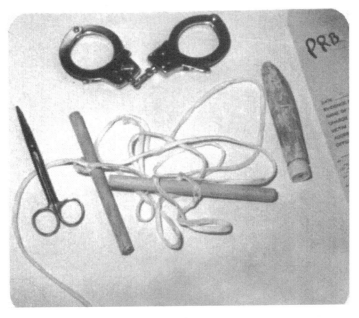

"The Crime Kit" Roger Kibbe had with him when he assaulted Debra Guffie contained white cordage, wooden dowels, handcuffs, a vibrator, and scissors.

Pair of scissors fished from the ditch where Stephanie Brown's body was found. Detectives were puzzled by the cut clothing of the victims.

Homicide detective Steve Kibbe, right, being honored as Officer of the Year for the Douglas County (Nevada) Sheriff's Office the same week that his brother, Roger, became the prime suspect in the I-5 murders. (Credit:*Record-Courier.*)

Former Chula Vista Police juvenile officer Leo Kelly is still haunted by what he found in 1954 in a fifteen-year-old boy's closet.

Roger Kibbe's childhood home at 545 Casselman, Chula Vista, a placid San Diego suburb six miles north of the United States–Mexico border.

Criminalist Jim Streeter, who first identified the "nonfunctional" cutting of many of the victims' clothing.

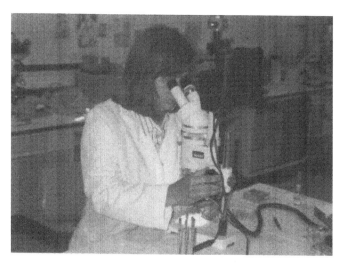

Criminalist Faye Springer, the legendary "trace evidence" expert who broke the case open with her microscopic findings.

Detective Kay Maulsby, the rookie homicide detective who helped to unmask a killer, receiving an award and congratulations from Sacramento sheriff Glen Craig for her work on the I-5 murder case.

Homicide lieutenant Ray Biondi, experienced at finding serial killers, fought administrative battles that threatened to derail the I-5 investigation. (Credit: Dick Schmidt, *Sacramento Bee.*)

Harriet Kibbe visiting Roger at Folsom Prison, 1994.

David "Vito" Bertocchini of the San Joaquin County Sheriff's Department with his canine partner, Barry, 1994. The burly ex-street cop, new to Homicide, took personally the killing of the first beautiful young woman.

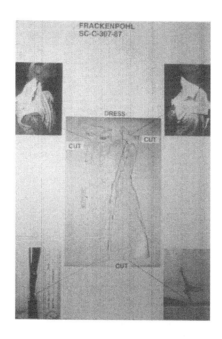

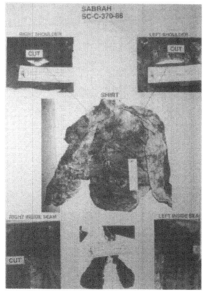

Evidence of cut clothing presented at trial.

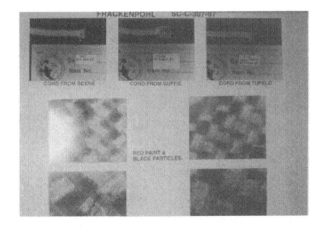

The three pieces of white cordage that tied Roger Kibbe to murder.

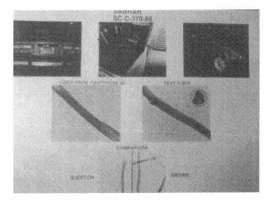

Seat fiber trace evidence presented at trial.

Made in the USA
Middletown, DE
18 September 2018